ENDORSEMENTS

The absence of Jewish perspectives in New Testament interpretation has been a tragedy for the church, amplified by an infusion of theological anti-Judaism in conservative Reformed readings. Messianic Jewish scholarship restores what's been lost, through a fresh, distinctly Jewish hermeneutic that resonates with the text. Russ Resnik's captivating new commentary on Mark as a Jewish account, told by a Jew, in Jewish terms, is a first-rate example deserving of a wide readership.

—Stephen Burnhope (PhD, King's College London), former Vineyard senior pastor and author of the *New Perspective: the God of Israel, Covenant, and the Cross.*

Scripture was guided by the Holy Spirit, who worked through the unique personalities of each author. Rabbi Russ Resnik gives us deep insight into the background and personality of a Jewish man, not named John Mark—yet he was both John (to the Jewish world) and Mark (to the Roman world). That tiny little nugget gives you a picture of some of the insights you will gain as you devour this book. Resnik is a scholar who writes to non-scholars. Anyone who is passionate about understanding the background of the sacred texts will enjoy this enlightening offering.

—Ron Cantor, D. Min, MPT, President of *Shelanu* TV, Tel Aviv

Like Mark before him, Resnik introduces us to a very Jewish Jesus, stripping from him the Roman robes in which history has clothed him, dressing him again in his own garments, so we see him as he is, Yeshua ben Yosef, a Jew among Jews, and incomparably more. Don't miss this informed, accessible, warm, and literary look at the ultimate Jewish life.

—Rabbi Stuart Dauermann, PhD, Director, Interfaithfulness

I loved it! Really well-written and thoroughly enjoyable. It will be my "go-to" source for Mark! Russ is an experienced Messianic leader— communicator, counselor, congregational leader and for many years General Director of the Union of Messianic Congregations. This new commentary reflects Russ's character and commitments to the best of both Jewish and Christian scholarship and heartfelt devotion to the Messiah Yeshua.

Russ is reintroducing the person of Yeshua to many as both a perfect Jewish man, God in the flesh, and the very embodiment of the Besorah – "the Good News." I also appreciate Russ not being anachronistic by making the mistake of reading more contemporary Jewish thinking and resources into second Temple literature. For this, I applaud Russ's effort as he helps us mine the treasures of the Gospel of Mark without reading the future into the past.

—Dr. Mitch Glaser, President, Chosen People Ministries

I am enjoying this commentary immensely. It is well-informed on top recent scholarship and, of course, on Yeshua's early Jewish context! Resnik explains Mark in readable language that also translates the common Gentile renderings back into their native Judean and Galilean settings.

—Craig S. Keener, F. M. and Ada Thompson, Professor of Biblical Studies, Asbury Theological Seminary

Russ Resnik and I have theological disagreements that will not be sorted until the Messiah comes (or, as he would say, "comes back"), but I find much value in this commentary: solid contextualization of Jesus in Jewish practice and belief, attention to the nuances of Mark's language and style, consideration of up-to-date scholarship, all presented in a format both accessible and engaging. Mark: Witness to the Ultimate Jewish Life not only corrects many antisemitic readings still prevalent in New Testament studies, but it also shows the Gospel's ongoing challenge to any who confess Jesus as Lord.

—Amy-Jill Levine, University Professor of New Testament and Jewish Studies Emerita, Vanderbilt. Co-editor of *The Jewish Annotated New Testament* and author of *The Gospel of Mark: A Beginner's Guide to the Good News.*

What a wonderful resource Resnik has provided us with. This commentary is both accessible and academic, engaging with top-notch historical and contemporary scholarship on Mark. Resnik helps us to read Mark in a way that honors the thoroughgoing Jewishness of the New Testament and rightfully challenges the history that has all too often taught us otherwise. Highly recommended!

—Jennifer M. Rosner, author of *Finding Messiah: A Journey into the Jewishness of the Gospel,* Affiliate Associate Professor of Systematic Theology, Fuller Theological Seminary.

Mark: A Witness to the Ultimate Jewish Life is an invaluable Messianic Jewish contribution to the study of Mark's Gospel. It is filled with key insights curated by a senior Messianic rabbi. I highly recommend this commentary for personal enrichment and group Bible study!

—David Rudolph, PhD; Professor of New Testament and Jewish Studies, The King's University

The publication of this serious commentary is a landmark event. Here is New Testament scholarship caringly applied by a Jew who affirms the Jesus of the Gospels as Israel's Messiah. Resnik restores Yeshua to his true original setting, making rich use of Old Testament textual parallels and pulling back the curtain on 1st century Israel. Russ has a gift of clear analysis without losing the essential, devotional quality of Mark's Gospel. I enthusiastically recommend this well-crafted volume.

—Eitan Shishkoff, Haifa Bay, Israel; Founder: Tents of Mercy & Fields of Wheat

MARK
WITNESS
TO THE
ULTIMATE JEWISH LIFE

Books in the Messianic Commentary Series

Matthew
Presents Yeshua, King Messiah

Mark
Witness to the Ultimate Jewish Life

Acts
of the Emissaries
The Early History of the Yeshua Movement

Sha'ul / Paul
God's Shaliach (Apostle) Corresponds with the
Corinthians

Rabbi Paul Enlightens the
Ephesians
on Walking with Messiah Yeshua

Paul Presents to the
Philippians
Unity in the Messianic Community

Paul's Letter to
Titus
His Emissary to Crete, About Congregational Life

James the Just
Presents Applications of Torah

John's Three Letters
on Hope, Love and Covenant Fidelity

Jude
on Faith and the Destructive Influence of Heresy

Yochanan (John)
Presents the Revelation of Yeshua the Messiah

A MESSIANIC COMMENTARY

Mark
Witness to the Ultimate Jewish Life

Russell L. Resnik

Lederer Books
An imprint of
Messianic Jewish Publishers
Clarksville, MD 21029

Copyright © 2025 by Russell L. Resnik

All rights reserved. No part of this publication may be reproduced, stored in a retrieval system, or transmitted in any form or by any means without the prior permission of the publisher, except for brief reviews in magazines, journals, etc. or as quotations in another work when full attribution is given.

The use of short selections or occasional page copying for personal or group study is permitted and encouraged, within reason. However, we ask that you respect the intellectual property rights of the author.

Unless otherwise noted, all quotations from Scripture are from the Complete Jewish Bible, copyright © 1998, 2016 by David H. Stern. All rights reserved. Used by permission of Messianic Jewish Publishers, 6120 Day Long Lane, Clarksville, MD 21029.

Printed in the United States of America
Graphic Design by Yvonne Vermillion,
MagicGraphix.com

ISBN: 978-1-951833-46-6

2025 1

Published by
Lederer Books
A division of
Messianic Jewish Publishers
6120 Day Long Lane
Clarksville, Maryland 21029

Distributed by
Messianic Jewish Resources Int'l.
www.MessianicJewish.net
Individual and Trade Order Line: 800-410-7647

Email: lederer@messianicjewish.net

Acknowledgements

I am grateful for all the friends, colleagues, and study partners through the years who contributed whether directly or indirectly to this volume. My chavurah in Albuquerque studied the Besorah of Mark together through 2019 and the early months of 2020, and their insights and probing questions fueled my later work on this commentary. I am grateful for this contribution along with their tremendous prayer support through the years until today. Both the chavurah and the commentary used the *Complete Jewish Bible,* and I gladly acknowledge the pioneering translation work of my friend David Stern of blessed memory. My lifelong brother Eitan Shishkoff provided detailed and incisive feedback on the manuscript itself, which led to numerous improvements. My wife, Jane, always reminds me of the need to speak in real-life language and answer the (usually) unspoken reader's question, "Why are you telling me this?" Her influence shines throughout the commentary. I also thank Rabbi Barry Rubin and his team at Messianic Jewish Publishers for their vision of a Messianic Jewish commentary series covering the entire New Testament or B'rit Hadashah. I am proud to contribute to this ongoing project.

CONTENTS

Endorsements .... i-ii
Acknowledgements vii
General Editor's Preface xi
Introduction xiii
Season 1: *Galilee: Revelation Amidst Resistance* 1
   Prologue in the Desert 5
   Season 1, Episode 1: Proclamation in the Galil 23
   Season 1, Episode 2: Opposition in the Galil 41
   Season 1, Episode 3: The Call of the Twelve 59
   Season 1, Episode 4: Yeshua's Stories Conceal and Reveal 73
   Season 1, Episode 5: Spiritual Encounter among the Gentiles 85
   Season 1, Episode 6: Two Remarkable Healings and a Mixed Reception 97
   Season 1, Episode 7: Equipping the Twelve 107
   Season 1, Episode 8: A Halakhic Interlude 123
   Season 1, Episode 9: A Gentile Foray and Continuing Incomprehension 137
Season 2: *On the Way to Jerusalem* 153
   Season 2, Episode 1 (10): Turning-point— The First Warning 155
   Season 2, Episode 2 (11): A Mountain-top and a Crowd 171
   Season 2, Episode 3 (12): A Second Warning is Misunderstood 183
   Season 2, Episode 4 (13): Further Instructions along the Way 197
   Season 2, Episode 5 (14): The Third Warning 211

Season 3: *Jerusalem: Welcome, Rejection, and Resurrection* 227

    Season 3, Episode 1 (15): Yeshua Enters Jerusalem 231

    Season 3, Episode 2 (16): Inquest in Jerusalem 247

    Season 3, Episode 3 (17): A View of Things to Come 265

    Season 3, Episode 4 (18): The Last Passover 283

    Season 3, Episode 5 (19): Betrayal, Desertion, Arrest, and Trial 301

    Season 3, Episode 6 (20): Death and Resurrection 319

Bibliography 339

Glossary 343

Index 349

General Editor's Preface

Nearly all Bible commentators emphasize the importance of understanding the historical, cultural and grammatical aspects of any text of Scripture. As has been said, "A text without a context is a pretext." In other words, to assume one can understand what God has revealed through those who present his Word—prophets, poets, visionaries, apostles—without knowing the context is presumption. To really understand God's Word, it's essential to know something about who wrote it and to whom, what was actually said and what it originally meant, and when, where, and why it was written.

By now, everyone knows the New Testament is a thoroughly Jewish book, written almost entirely by Jews, taking place in and around Israel. The people written about—Paul, Peter, James, John, etc—were all Jews who never abandoned their identities or people. The topics covered—sin, salvation, resurrection, Torah, Sabbath, how to "walk with God," the Millennium, etc—were all Jewish topics that came from the Hebrew Scripture. The expressions were Jewish idioms of that day. So to fully understand the New Testament, it must be viewed through "Jewish eyes," meaning the Jewish historical, cultural, grammatical must be examined.

There are commentaries for women, men, teens, even children. There are commentaries that focus on financial issues in the Bible. Others provide archaeological material. Some commentaries are topical. Others are the works of eminent men and women of God. But until now, no commentary series has closely looked at the Jewish context of each of the New Testament books.

Some of the world's top Messianic Jewish theologians contributed their knowledge and understanding. Each has written on a book(s) of the New Testament they've specialized in, making sure to present the Jewish aspects—the original context—of each book. These works are not meant to be a verse-by-verse exegetical commentary. There are already many excellent ones available. But these commentaries supplement what others lack by focusing on the Jewish aspects along with explaining the book itself.

Several different authors wrote these commentaries, each in his own style. Just as the Gospels were written by four different men, each with his own perspective and style, these volumes too have variations. We didn't want the writers to have to conform too much to any particular style guide, other than our basic one.

You may see some Hebrew expressions or transliterations of Hebrew names in the New Testament. Thus, one writer might refer to the Apostle to the Gentiles as Paul. Another might write *Sha'ul*, Paul's Hebrew name. Still another might write *Saul*, an Anglicized version of *Sha'ul*. And some might write *Saul/Paul* to reflect, not reject, the different ways this servant of Messiah was known.

Another variation is the amount of reference material. Some have ample footnotes or endnotes, while others incorporate references within the text. Some don't have an enormous number of notes.

We have plans for a Messianic Jewish commentary series on the entire Bible. Though much has been written on the books of the Hebrew Scriptures, some by Messianic Jews, there hasn't been a full commentary series on the Tanakh, the "Older" Testament. But we hope to publish such a series in the future.

So, I invite you to put on your Jewish glasses (if you're not Jewish) and take a look at the New Testament in a way that will open up new understanding for you, as you get to know the God of Israel and his Messiah better.

Rabbi Barry Rubin
General Editor and Publisher

Introduction

From my earliest years as a follower of Messiah, my first love, after Yeshua himself, has always been the Scriptures. The first morning after I had acknowledged Yeshua as my new master and teacher, I opened a pocket New Testament that I'd picked up along the way, and it seemed as if light were flooding from its pages. Ever since, I've loved the Scriptures as not just words on a page (or later a screen), but as a living and life-giving revelation. And I've embraced what I believe is a God-given assignment to read it regularly and deeply, to ponder its message, and to seek to live it out and convey it to others around me.

Before too long in my early days, I rediscovered the traditional weekly Jewish readings through the Torah, the Five Books of Moses. In the synagogue, we read through the Torah in its entirety every year, week by week, and portion by portion; the same portion in every synagogue around the world and throughout history. Later, after this rediscovery, I found myself drawn to the synoptic Gospels—Matthew, Mark, and Luke—which, like the Torah, rewarded deep and repeated reading with fresh and real-life insights. Also, like the books of Torah, these texts are largely narrative, stories that unfold with a richness and complexity that I—along with countless others—find profoundly uplifting and spiritually nourishing. For me, the Gospel texts also are Torah, "instruction" in the literal Hebrew, and I've found the Psalmist's portrayal of the man or woman who feeds on this expanded Torah to be spot on:

> His or her delight
> is in the Torah of the LORD,
> and on his Torah he meditates
> day and night.

> He shall be like a tree planted by streams of water
> that bears its fruit in its season;
> its leaves shall not wither,
> and whatever he does shall prosper. Psa. 1:2–3, my translation

For me, this has been a sort of theme verse for years. The "meditation" it refers to implies speaking the words of Scripture to one's own inner person or soul, taking the time to savor, chew on, and digest these words—and to act on them as well. For me, part of the action arising from this process has been teaching and applying Scripture in a wide range of settings, from a household of hippies studying by the light of a kerosene lamp in the mountains of New Mexico to gatherings all over the USA, and in Brazil, South Africa, Russia, and of course, Israel. This has all been rooted in this deep meditative reading the psalmist describes, and all the texts of the Bible lend themselves to this practice. But the sweeping narratives of the Torah and the Gospels (along with the Book of Acts) have been the most fruitful for me, especially, of late, the Gospel of Mark.

Why Mark in particular?

Recently my wife, Jane, alerted me to a fascinating podcast with David Brooks, the high-profile author and *New York Times* columnist, talking about how he, as a Jew, came to believe, first in God, and then in Jesus.

> In my community, sort of highly educated coastal, when you come to faith, you come to faith through Oxford. And so it's C. S. Lewis, it's J. R. R. Tolkien, it's Sheldon Vanauken, who wrote *A Severe Mercy,* and so you have a very classy kind of God and a sort of appropriately Britishly restrained kind of Jesus, and I sometimes wrestle against that. Jesus was a Jewish guy from the Middle East and when you actually see him through the Jewish lens, living in Jerusalem in a land of vicious conflict, with a series of highly organized power structures, which he upsets all at once, you realize Jesus is a total badass. He's not like a guy in a tweed jacket,

and so I came to defend a much more aggressive Jesus that shocks, and I came to believe in that.[1]

When I heard these words, I thought, "He must be reading Mark!" Brooks is describing the Jesus whom Mark portrays in great detail and with a vigorous literary style. Mark pictures a Jesus we need today, as Brooks intimates, amidst the "highly organized power structures" of our own time. This Jesus was a "Jewish guy from the Middle East," who led an incomparable Jewish life, and Mark provides a testimony to this life based on eye-witness accounts.

Furthermore, Mark's account is the earliest record we have of the life and teachings of Jesus, so it's foundational to the entire body of apostolic writings commonly called the New Testament. These writings, along with the rest of the Bible, continue to be widely read, cited, and argued over, even within our skeptical, materialistic, twenty-first century world. The Bible remains an essential document in our day of information overload. But it's also a book, or better, a collection of books, that can be confusing and overwhelming to an honest reader. To understand the Bible well, we have to recognize the architectural design and structure of the whole collection. For the Jewish world, the Torah, or Five Books of Moses, is foundational to the entire Tanakh, or Old Testament as it's called in the Christian world.[2] The texts of the entire Tanakh—an acronym for Torah, *Nevi'im* (Prophets) and *Ketuvim* (Holy Writings)—build upon the foundation laid down in its first section, the Torah, and are best understood as resting on that foundation.

---

1. "David Brooks on his conversion, vulnerability and the challenges of talking about morality," *The Sacred* podcast with Elizabeth Oldfield, 12/8/2021. Transcript available at https://www.theosthinktank.co.uk/comment/2021/12/08/david-brooks-on-his-conversion-vulnerability-and-the-challenges-of-talking-about-morality
2. The word "Torah" will appear many times throughout this commentary, and it's difficult to translate with one English term. In some cases, like this sentence, it refers to the Five Books of Moses, Genesis through Deuteronomy. It can also be used to refer to Scripture in general, as well as to Jewish commentary on Scripture. In other contexts it is understood, and translated, as "Law," but this term can be misleading because the word Torah itself means "teaching" or "instruction," and includes narrative as well as legal content.

In the same way, we can view the Five Books of Gospels plus Acts as foundational to the rest of the New Testament. Some of the other New Testament texts may have been put into writing before the earliest Gospel, as we'll discuss below, but the Gospel-Acts narrative provides the perspective for properly understanding the rest of the New Testament writings. Bible scholars and students might consider reading and interpreting Paul's writings, for example, through the lens of the Gospels, rather than vice-versa, as is usually the case. This approach is especially relevant to a Messianic Jewish perspective, since the Gospels all take place within a Jewish cultural setting, whereas much of the rest of the New Testament is concerned with the mission to the Gentiles. But for all readers, Jewish and Gentile, prioritizing the Five Books of Gospels-Acts means recognizing the Jewish background and setting of the New Testament, which reflects the major shift in biblical interpretation in recent decades that has shed abundant new light on the Bible. This commentary builds on that shift in interpretation to help us see Jesus, Yeshua, "through the Jewish lens" that David Brooks mentions.

Who Wrote This Foundational Account?

Mark is recognized by a wide spectrum of scholars as the first of the Gospels to be written down: "It is generally recognized that Mark represents the earliest attempt to reduce the apostolic tradition to a written form."[3] Many scholars believe that Matthew and Luke draw upon Mark. The author of Mark passed on "the apostolic tradition," but was not an apostle himself. He's traditionally thought to be the John Mark who traveled with the apostolic band and appears in Acts 12:12, 13:13, and 15:37, and is mentioned by name in some letters of the New Testament (Col. 4:10; 2 Tim. 4:11;

---

3. William L. Lane. *The Gospel according to Mark* (Grand Rapids: Eerdmans, 1974), 1. Another commentator mentions, "the general modern view that it was the earliest gospel to be written." R. T. France, *The Gospel of Mark: A Commentary on the Greek Text* (Grand Rapids/Cambridge: Eerdmans, 2002), 16.

Philem. 24; 1 Pet. 5:13). Like the other Gospels and Acts, Mark doesn't include the name of its author in its text but, "Most extant manuscripts have the title 'According to Mark' or '(The) Gospel according to Mark' at the beginning of the text, at the end of the text or in a side margin."[4] Mark was a very common Roman name, but not so common among the Jewish population, and only one Mark appears among the early followers of Yeshua, the John Mark just mentioned. It was common among Jews to have two names, one Hebrew (like John/Yochanan) and one Latin or Greek (like Mark); "Simon Peter" would be another example of this practice. If the Gospel had been originally anonymous, it's not at all clear why the name Mark would be added later, since Mark was not an apostle. Moreover, John Mark has a mixed record in Acts, where he abandons the apostolic team (13:13), which leads to Paul and Barnabas parting company over this issue (15:36–38). If an author or a community wanted to assign an author to an anonymous work, they could have found a better choice than Mark.

In addition, Papias, a second-century bishop in Asia Minor, saw Mark as representing the apostle Peter and his perspective (cited in Eusebius, *Historia Ecclesiae*, III. xxxix. 15).[5] Mark was accepted from the earliest times as one of the four canonical Gospels, along with Matthew, Luke, and John, based in part on its connection with Peter. Mark underlines this connection by introducing Shim'on (later called Peter) as the first follower of Yeshua (1:16) at the beginning of his account, and as the only disciple named at the end (16:7). This naming forms an *inclusio*, a literary technique that Mark often employs, of marking off a section with bookends of similar wording at its beginning and conclusion, thereby highlighting the theme of the whole section. By spotlighting Shim'on Peter at the beginning and end of his Gospel, Mark is indicating Peter's special role within it, consistent with the

---

4. Eckhard J. Schnabel, *Mark: An Introduction and Commentary*, Tyndale New Testament Commentaries, vol. 2. (London: Inter-Varsity, 2017), 8.
5. See Michael Pakaluk, *The Memoirs of St. Peter: A New Translation of the Gospel According to Mark* (Washington, DC: Regnery Gateway, 2019), xvi–xxii.

claim that this Gospel reflects Peter's first-hand testimony. Also, the names Shim'on and Peter appear with much greater frequency in Mark than in the other two Synoptic Gospels, Matthew and Luke.[6] And, finally, Mark's Gospel has the benchmarks of an eye-witness account, with its clear picture of the actions of Yeshua, including his private instructions to his disciples, and its concrete portrayal of life in the land of Israel and among the Jewish people.

Mark's account, therefore, is best understood as a testimony, in the sense defined by scholar Richard Bauckham: "the category of testimony is the one that does most justice to the Gospels both as history and as theology. As a form of historiography testimony offers a unique access to historical reality that cannot be had without an element of trust in the credibility of the witness and what he or she has to report."[7] The sense of eyewitness testimony is reflected in our title, *Mark: Witness to the Ultimate Jewish Life.*

As the testimony of Peter, or at least based on Peter's first-hand account, Mark can be dated quite early, possibly before the fall of Jerusalem in 70 CE. Mark, then, is essential to my proposed New Testament foundation, and therefore uniquely worthy of study. It is the earliest account we have of the life and ministry of Yeshua, and it's very early. But despite its unique position, Mark tends to be overlooked and under-appreciated in relation to Matthew, Luke, and John. This tendency goes back to the days of Papias, who linked Mark to Peter, as we've seen, but also considered him less reliable than Matthew, who was an actual apostle, appointed by Yeshua himself.[8] Papias also considered Mark to be inferior to Matthew in terms of his writing style—an inferiority that would apply in relation to Luke and John as well.

---

6. Richard Bauckham, *Jesus and the Eyewitnesses: The Gospels as Eyewitness Testimony,* 2nd Edition (Grand Rapids, Eerdmans, 2017), 125–26.
7. Bauckham, 505.
8. Lawrence M. Wills, "The Gospel According to Mark," *The Jewish Annotated New Testament,* Second Edition (henceforth JANT), eds. Amy-Jill Levine and Marc Zvi Brettler (New York: Oxford University Press, 2017), 67.

But while it may be true that Mark isn't as polished as the other Gospels, that doesn't diminish Mark's skill as a storyteller, or the power of the unified narrative he creates. Mark uses his unique narrative gift to convey profound truths about the human condition and about the character of the God of Israel and his response to human needs. This sometimes-neglected Gospel deserves a wide audience today. In Mark, Yeshua *demonstrates* who he is and what he stands for and he patiently draws us into understanding and following him. This action-oriented approach is particularly relevant amidst the current information overload that has sparked a return to oral culture in a twenty-first century version, and a longing for narrative and story over abstract propositions. In other words, Mark is a storyteller, not a theologian or dogmatist, and a highly skilled storyteller, as we will see. This is another reason for Mark's special relevance in our postmodern world, which values human stories over theories and abstractions.

In addition to being the earliest of the four Gospels, Mark is also the shortest, characterized by a simple and direct style that has sometimes been mistaken for a lack of depth. Instead, Mark reflects the foundational books of Genesis and Exodus in conveying profound theological truth through a richly constructed but largely unembellished narrative that rewards repeated, patient, and deep reading (or listening). Ironically, one of the main themes of this underappreciated Gospel is the underappreciated Messiah and the struggles of his half-formed followers. It's this very quality that makes Mark timelessly real and relevant, especially in our skeptical, post-religious age.

Purpose and Perspective

Scholars often interpret Mark's emphasis on Messiah's humility, suffering, and steadfastness as evidence that the Gospel is directed toward a community of (mostly Gentile) Yeshua-followers that was suffering persecution itself. A setting in Rome during the period of persecution under Nero (64 CE) is commonly (although by no means universally) given as the context for Mark's account, which is seen as primarily addressing the Gentile world. In addition, Mark's simple style and content seem to render his account less distinctly Jewish than the other Gospels. For example, Matthew and Luke both open with a genealogy that ties Yeshua's story into the narrative of the Tanakh. Mark, in contrast, dives right into the action, introducing the ministry of John the Baptist, or Yochanan the Immerser, after a brief, one-sentence introduction.

Despite such factors, however, Mark is also relevant to the Jewish world, and is more rooted in that world than is generally accepted. The John Mark of Acts, often considered to be a likely author of this Gospel, is clearly a Jew, whose mother has a large house in Jerusalem itself (Acts 12:12; also 12:25, 15:37). Jewish Yeshua-believers in the land of Israel, like their Gentile brothers and sisters in Rome, experienced opposition in the mid-first century, which would culminate in the uprising against Rome and the destruction of the holy temple in 70 CE, so that Mark's portrayal of a suffering Messiah—who suffered at the hands of the Roman authorities—would be relevant to Jews in first-century Israel. The lack of an introductory genealogy might mean that Mark was originally addressed to a Gentile audience, or it may simply reflect the eye-witness nature of the entire account. Mark didn't have access to firsthand testimony of the birth and early life of Yeshua, so he opened with a scene that his firsthand sources, probably including Shim'on Peter, did witness directly, the very public ministry of Yochanan (John) on the banks of the Jordan. Mark's audience most likely comprised both Jewish and Gentile followers of Yeshua, so that Mark sometimes must explain Jewish customs to the Gentiles, even though Jews are present as well.

Furthermore, Mark presents the good news of Messiah in distinctly Jewish ways. This is fitting if Mark is indeed based on the testimony of Peter, since Peter is the apostle to the Jews (Gal. 2:7–8). Like the foundational Jewish text, the Torah, Mark's account conveys its message primarily through narrative, rather than through a more theoretical or systematic presentation of doctrine. Mark often employs the sort of imaginative reading of the Hebrew Bible or Tanakh that appears later in the rabbinic discussions known as midrash. For example, as we'll see in our first chapter, Mark opens, "The beginning of the Good News" (1:1), echoing *B'reisheet,* "in the beginning," the opening word of the entire Torah. And Mark goes on to echo the language of *B'reisheet* or Genesis repeatedly in his first few verses, for example at Yeshua's immersion:

> Immediately upon coming up out of the water, he saw heaven torn open and the Spirit descending upon him like a dove; then a voice came from heaven, "You are my Son, whom I love; I am well pleased with you." (Mark 1:10–11)

The word translated as "torn open" here is a vivid term that appears only in Mark's account, hinting at the transcendent moment in Genesis when the heavens and the earth were created by the word of God, echoed in Mark in the voice from heaven. The image of the Spirit descending like a dove as Yeshua emerges from the water evokes the Spirit of God hovering over the surface of the water in Genesis 1:2. The three-fold word to Yeshua, "You are my son, whom I love; I am well pleased with you," (Mark 1:11) echoes ADONAI's three-fold command to Avraham later in Genesis, "Take your son, your only son, whom you love, Isaac" (Gen. 22:2; see the similar language addressed to the servant in Isa. 42:1).[9] Such imaginative reflection of the text of the Tanakh abounds throughout Mark and suggests a deep Jewish connection.

Another example of Jewish connection in Mark is a discussion about the greatest commandment or *mitzvah* (12:28–34). Mark cites the opening words of the Shema (Deut. 6:4), "Hear O Israel," rather than beginning with the next verse, "Love the LORD your God with all your heart . . ." as do Matthew (22:34–40) and Luke (10:25–28)

---

9. Concerning my use of ADONAI and LORD in small caps, see the comments at the end of this Introduction.

in a similar discussion. Mark seems more concerned than they are for the full context of the Shema, which has been a central Jewish text from time immemorial. Furthermore, in Mark, Yeshua's discussion with the "Torah-teacher" is friendly and collegial, in contrast with the incidents in Matthew and Luke that seem more adversarial. Indeed, throughout his account, Mark tends to put less emphasis on Jewish opposition than the other two synoptic Gospels. Furthermore, this incident illustrates Yeshua's role as teacher, which Mark highlights, even within his action-oriented approach. The title *Didaskalos*, "Teacher" in Greek, appears twelve times in Mark; "Rabbi," based on the Hebrew term, three times, and "Rabboni" once. "These accumulative figures are higher than the corresponding ones in Matthew (12 total) and Luke (13 total), although these Gospels are much longer than Mark's and devote extensive sections to Jesus' teaching."[10] The title of "Teacher" or "Rabbi" reflects the Jewish cultural setting of Mark.

Ultimately, we don't know who Mark's original audience was, and many theories abound to this day, but whether he is writing primarily to Gentiles or Jews, or both, and whether he's directly recording the testimony of Peter or not, he writes as a loyal Jew himself, proclaiming Yeshua to be Teacher, Messiah Son of David, the Son of Man as in Daniel 7, and the Son of God. And the internal evidence suggests that he's writing to a marginalized community facing severe opposition, possibly in the years leading up to and following the failed Jewish uprising against Rome, 67–73.

This proclamation of Yeshua as Messiah along with these other related titles is shaped by a distinctive and mysterious element, often termed the messianic secret, which underlies the whole book. In Mark, Yeshua "appears more intent on hiding his messianic identity

---

10. M. Robert Mansfield, *Spirit and Gospel in Mark* (Peabody, MA: Hendrickson, 1987), 47. The term "Rabboni" (Mark 10:51) appears only one other time in the NT, John 20:16, where the definition is added: "She cried out to him in Hebrew, '*Rabboni*!' (that is, 'Teacher!')."

than on revealing it," as I write in my book *Divine Reversal*.[11] Yeshua silences demons who recognize him as Son of God and are about to say so (1:24, 3:11, 5:7); he tells those he heals not to make him known (1:44, 3:12, 5:43, 7:36, 8:26), refuses the Pharisees' request for a sign (8:11–12), and even warns his disciples "not to tell anyone about him" (8:30). Yeshua's goal is not to deny his Messiahship, or to hide it indefinitely, but to reveal it in his own time and with its full implications made clear, especially the role of suffering. Mark's prologue, covered in our next chapter, sets his account firmly within the framework of Isaiah chapters 40 through 66 and Yeshua's hidden quality may be a reflection of Isaiah's portrayal of the servant:

> He will not cry or shout;
> no one will hear his voice in the streets.
> He will not snap off a broken reed
> or snuff out a smoldering wick.
> He will bring forth justice according to truth;
> he will not weaken or be crushed
> until he has established justice on the earth,
> and the coastlands wait for his Torah. (Isa. 42:2–4)

Further, the messianic secret motif may hint at Yeshua's identification with the "God who hides himself" (Isa. 45:15). It also resonates with Isaiah 53, the famous chapter of the suffering servant, which opens, "Who believes our report? / To whom is the arm of ADONAI revealed?" (Isa. 53:1). Isaiah's servant remains hidden and undervalued among those to whom he is sent:

> He was not well-formed or especially handsome;
> we saw him, but his appearance did not attract us.
> People despised and avoided him,
> a man of pains, well acquainted with illness.
> Like someone from whom people turn their faces,
> he was despised; we did not value him.

---

11. Russell Resnik, *Divine Reversal: The Transforming Ethics of Jesus* (Clarksville, MD: Lederer, 2010), 137.

Yeshua's resistance to public acclaim and recognition brings him into alignment with Isaiah's portrayal of the outsider-servant. Accordingly, Darrell Bock notes:

> Mark highlights Jesus as the suffering Son of Man and Servant proportionately more than any other Gospel. . . . Although Isaiah 53 is not cited, the descriptions of Jesus clearly parallel the portrait of the suffering servant, especially in the claim that his mission was to give his life as "a ransom for many" (10:45). The importance of understanding the suffering role probably explains Mark's record of the commands to silence given to those, including demons, who confessed Jesus as Messiah (1:44; 5:43; 9:9). Without an appreciation of his suffering, Jesus' messianic calling is misunderstood.[12]

This gradual revelation means that Yeshua doesn't bring his followers into his service fully formed, but through a teaching process involving action as well as words, a process that continues through the whole book. The emphasis on discipleship is rooted in the Jewish world of Yeshua's day. *Pirke Avot*, a seminal Jewish text from a century or so later, opens with a saying of the men of the Great Assembly: "Be careful in judgment; raise up many disciples; and make a fence for the Torah."[13] In Mark, Yeshua sometimes gets into debates over where "a fence for the Torah" should be placed, as with Shabbat regulations (2:23–3:6), but he's totally on board with raising up many disciples, starting in the opening scene in Galilee

---

12. David Turner and Darrell L. Bock, *Matthew and Mark,* Cornerstone Biblical Commentary, Vol 11 (Carol Stream, IL: Tyndale, 2005), 398.
13. *Pirke Avot* is literally "Chapters of the Fathers," but more commonly called "Ethics of the Fathers," or something similar. This text is part of the Mishnah, put into writing around 200 CE, but containing older oral material, so that it sheds light on the setting of Mark and the other Gospels. Pirke Avot remains one of the most influential texts in Judaism to this day. The "Great Assembly" mentioned in this saying was believed to have been convened by Ezra at the beginning of the Second Temple era (*The Koren Siddur* with Introduction, Translation, and Commentary by Rabbi Sir Jonathan Sacks [Jerusalem: Koren, 2009], 640).

when he calls Shim'on and Andrew, Ya'akov and Yochanan (1:16–20). The gathering and formation of disciples, especially the distinct group of the Twelve,[14] joins with the revelation of who Yeshua is to define the two major themes of Mark.

> Mark is writing in the context of, and for the guidance of, those who are now the successors to that early group of followers of Jesus, through whom the mission of the kingdom of God must now be carried forward as it has first been by those original disciples. So Mark sets those first disciples before his readers as a guide to their own following of Jesus.[15]

The two-fold theme of Yeshua's incremental self-revelation, and the formative process of disciple-making that grows out of this revelation, underlies the entire structure of Mark's Gospel. Mark enables a gradual discovery of Yeshua's true identity through the series of events and teachings that comprise his Gospel. And this discovery is meant to yield another: what it means to follow him.

The Three-part Geography of Mark's Account

Another key to the structure of Mark is its geography. The whole narrative is framed in a simplified three-part geographical setting, plus a prologue in the wilderness region of the Jordan River. I say "simplified" because we know from the other Gospels that Yeshua was born in Bethlehem before being brought back to Galilee by his family, that he visited Jerusalem multiple times, and even spent some time in Egypt (as an infant). Mark leaves all this out to provide a condensed three-part narrative that takes us from the banks of Lake Kinneret in Galilee to an empty tomb just outside the holy city,

---

14. Richard V. Peace, *Conversion in the New Testament: Paul and the Twelve* (Grand Rapids: Eerdmans, 1999), 109.
15. France, 28.

Jerusalem. As Yeshua gathers followers and leads them through this terrain, he first conceals and then gradually reveals the full truth of who he is and what he has come to accomplish . . . and what it means to follow him.

The outline for this commentary will follow Mark's geography, through which Yeshua journeys to reveal himself to his followers, to Israel, and to the world.

Following commentator R. T. France, who speaks of Mark's Gospel as a "Drama in Three Acts,"[16] I organize my commentary into three "Seasons." Stage drama may remain well-respected these days, but not too many people actually view it. Mark is written for a popular audience and an onscreen biopic might be a more fitting parallel today than a stage presentation.[17] I build on this parallel with division into numerous "Episodes" that take us through Mark's dramatic treatment of his subject matter. An episode may shift in location or emphasis, but each one works as a coherent unit within the dramatic whole, much like an episode of a series on Netflix or Amazon Prime. My division into episodes recognizes the traditional chapter divisions, but doesn't always follow them. Chapter and verse divisions for the whole Bible were developed in the late Middle Ages, and the Jewish and Christian versions differ slightly (and the Jewish versions, of course, don't include Mark and the rest of the New Testament), so I take some liberty with these divisions in this commentary.

Mark's three-part geography yields a three-season biopic portraying the life and message of Yeshua the Messiah.

---

16. France, 11–15.
17. My use of "biopic" reflects the widespread view among scholars that the genre of the gospels "best fits ancient biography, a genre normally expected to deal with historical facts insofar as possible (albeit told from the writer's perspective." Craig S. Keener *The Historical Jesus of the Gospels* (Grand Rapids: Eerdmans, 2009), 123.

INTRODUCTION

Mark: Witness to the Ultimate Jewish Life
A Biopic in Three Seasons

Season 1: *Galilee: Revelation amidst resistance* **1:14–8:21**

    Prologue in the wilderness, **1:1–13**

    Episode 1: Proclamation in the Galil, **1:14–45**

    Episode 2: Opposition in the Galil, **2:1–3:6**

    Episode 3: Yeshua and the Twelve, **3:7–35**

    Episode 4: Parables of the Kingdom, **4:1–34**

    Episode 5: Spiritual Encounter in the Gentile Realm, **4:35–5:20**

    Episode 6: Return to the Galil and Two Remarkable Healings, **5:21–6:6**

    Episode 7: Equipping the Twelve, **6:7–56**

    Episode 8: A Halakhic Interlude, **7:1–23**

    Episode 9: A Gentile Foray and Continuing Incomprehension, **7:24–8:21**

Season 2: *On the way to Jerusalem* **8:22–10:52**

    Episode 1 (10):[18] Turning-point: The First Warning, **8:22–9:1**

    Episode 2 (11): A Mountain-top and a Crowd, **9:2–29**

    Episode 3 (12): A Second Warning Misunderstood, **9:30–50**

    Episode 4 (13): Further Instructions along the Way, **10:1–31**

    Episode 5 (14): The Third Warning, **10:32–52**

Season 3: *Jerusalem: Welcome, Rejection, and Resurrection* **11:1–16:8**

    Episode 1 (15): Yeshua Enters Jerusalem, **11:1–33**

    Episode 2 (16): Inquest in Jerusalem, **12:1–44**

    Episode 3 (17): A View of Times to Come, **13:1–37**

    Episode 4 (18): The Last Passover, **14:1–42**

    Episode 5 (19): Betrayal, Desertion, Arrest, and Trial, **14:43–15:20**

    Episode 6 (20): Death and Resurrection, **15:21–16:8**

---

18. The number in parentheses in this list of episodes is cumulative. In other words, Episode 1 of Season 2 is the tenth episode of our whole series.

Each episode within these three seasons comprises a chapter of the commentary, and each chapter follows a three-part structure.

- **Overview:** Summary of the narrative flow of the episode and its place within the whole drama of Mark's account.

- **Peshat:** This Hebrew term is employed in Jewish biblical interpretation and refers to the "plain sense" of the text. This section includes verse-by-verse exposition that engages with issues of language and grammar, historical background, other commentaries, and so on.

- **Derash:** Another Hebrew term employed in Jewish biblical interpretation, *derash* means reflection on the text and its implications for our lives. This section may entail reflection on similar passages throughout the Bible, as well as real-life application, in accord with Mark's emphasis on discipleship, and in line with rabbinic teaching, which emphasizes behavior as well as belief.[19]

Throughout all three seasons, Mark explores the question of who Yeshua really is. He introduces Yeshua as Messiah and Son of God—but what do these terms mean? And do the people of Yeshua's day, including his own disciples, know that this is who he is? Mark recounts the first-hand, eye-witness process of discovery of Yeshua as Son of God and Messiah, and this is what makes his account so relevant to those of us who are drawn to the figure of Yeshua. As we pay attention to Messiah's words and deeds, we grow in the knowledge of him, which in turn changes the way we live.

The literature on the Gospel of Mark, like that of most of the books of Scripture, is vast. It's not unreasonable to question the need

---

19. "Derash" is from the same Hebrew root as "midrash," mentioned above. Both entail a creative exploration of the text at hand and, usually, application of the text to real-life issues. A recent monograph applies these two categories, plus "Remez" (hint) and "Sod" (secret or mystery) to its study of Mark: John DelHousaye "A Pardes Reading of Mark," https://www.academia.edu/7066021/A_Pardes_Reading_of_The_Gospel_According_to_Mark?email_work_card=title.

for any addition to this body of literature, especially a(nother) commentary on the whole book of Mark. In response to that question, I'll argue that Mark, which is a Jewish account of an incomparable Jewish life, deserves to be read and interpreted in distinctly Jewish ways, which I set out to do. Here are four emphases of our commentary that result from such a reading:

1. It is written from a Jewish perspective. Discussions of the original authorship, audience, and purposes of the Good News of Mark remain ongoing,[20] but the Jewish background of Mark is well attested. In the interview cited early in this Introduction, David Brooks says, "When I found faith I felt more Jewish than ever, but also more Christian than ever, and my Jewish friends said, 'Yeah, well that's not really allowed. If you accept Jesus then you're not on the team anymore,' and so that's a fair point." But this commentary will argue that that's *not* a fair point—Mark's Jesus is still on the Jewish team and his followers should be too. I appreciate Brooks' respect for Jewish communal boundaries, but Jesus was not one to let the religious gatekeepers have the last word—and certainly not one to agree that faith in him bumped one off the Jewish team.

2. It avoids the supersessionist or replacement-theology interpretations of Mark that dominated for centuries and are still commonplace today. Instead, we recognize that Mark's Gospel is a Jewish story told by a Jew. Therefore, this commentary doesn't follow the common practice of portraying the Jewish people and religion as a foil for Jesus. It doesn't seek to discredit the Jewish customs and perspectives that provide context for many scenes in Mark or to present Mark's Yeshua as replacing the Jewish people and their Torah. Rather, we'll see Yeshua as living out his message among the Jewish people and within the broad parameters of Torah. This approach will yield fresh insights for all readers and has special relevance for Jewish readers.

---

20. To follow these discussions, the reader is directed to the sources listed in the Bibliography section.

3. It involves what I call "deep reading," paying close attention to the narrative itself, its rich details, and all its compelling literary qualities. This approach reflects the way the great Jewish commentators of long ago read the texts of the Tanakh, listening deeply to their actual wording and savoring the richness of the details. Analysis and critical thinking have their place, but never overshadow the authority and plain sense (*p'shat*) of the text. This commentary seeks to reflect Mark's narrative style by following the storyline itself and respecting its dramatic pacing. The commentary (I hope) doesn't get bogged down in technical analyses of text and context, but draws on such discussions to help us hear and learn from Mark's account itself. As mentioned in footnote 20, the Bibliography provides an entry to the body of scholarly and more technical literature underlying this commentary.

4. It responds to Yeshua's call to follow him and to shape our lives in response to his message of the Kingdom of God, reflecting a Jewish emphasis on living out our faith, not just believing it in our heads or hearts. Accordingly, my Derash section is designed to be a resource for spiritual formation and discipleship, a resource that can be used both in individual and group study settings. My hope is that individuals and groups will use this commentary as a guide to their study of Mark over the course of several months, for example by reading and discussing one episode each week. Others may choose to binge, going through all three seasons in quick succession.

My text throughout, unless otherwise noted, is *Complete Jewish Bible* (CJB), occasionally modified to make it more accessible to the typical reader. For example, "Yesha'yahu" becomes "Isaiah"; "Yerushalayim" is "Jerusalem." In contrast, I will sometimes replace the familiar term "Good News" in CJB with the Hebrew term "Besorah," as introduced in chapter 1. Italicization of names and familiar words like "Yeshua," "Torah," "ADONAI," and "Shabbat" is removed in my citations of CJB. In line with common usage, I employ "Lord" to translate the Hebrew name YHVH, which is considered in Jewish tradition to be too holy to pronounce, at least in the present age. More often I use Adonai, meaning "Lord" or "my Lord" in Hebrew, in the same way. In both cases the use of small caps indicates that the word is a substitute for the ineffable divine name, and should be understood as a proper name.

Portions of this Introduction first appeared in *The Complete Jewish Study Bible*, ed. Barry A. Rubin (Hendrickson/Messianic Jewish Publishers and Resources, 2016).

SEASON 1

GALILEE: REVELATION AMIDST RESISTANCE

1:14–8:21

Our season opens after a prologue in Y'hudah or Judea, where Yohanan proclaims an immersion of repentance and forgiveness in preparation for one coming after him, one who will immerse not in water but in the Holy Spirit. When Yeshua arrives from the Galil and receives Yohanan's immersion, the Spirit descends on him and a heavenly voice announces that he is the chosen Son. The Spirit drives him into the wilderness where he is tempted for forty days.

After his forty-day trial, Yeshua returns to the Galil and begins to proclaim the good news that the Kingdom of God is near. He calls his first *talmidim,* or disciples, fishermen working on Lake Kinneret. On Shabbat, Yeshua and his new talmidim join those gathered in the local synagogue, where he teaches with unparalleled authority. He also encounters and overcomes demonic opposition, and word about him begins to spread. From the synagogue, Yeshua enters the home of his disciple, Shim'on, and heals his mother-in-law, along with many who come to the house after Shabbat seeking healing. Finally, he heals a man afflicted with the mysterious skin disease, *tzara'at.* These three acts of power in our first episode demonstrate the presence of God's Kingdom, and typify the deeds of Yeshua throughout Mark.

Our next episode reveals that human opposition, as well as demonic resistance, will be part of the story, with three encounters with the religious experts, paralleling the three examples of Yeshua's miraculous power in Episode 1. Episode 2 concludes as the religious experts join forces with the political establishment in seeking a way to do away with Yeshua. But he continues his ministry of healing and deliverance, and sends out twelve of his followers to proclaim the kingdom with similar authority. The opposition also advances with a new accusation against Yeshua, the claim that he is casting out demons by the power of the "prince of demons." Yeshua warns that such a claim constitutes blasphemy against the true source of his power, the Holy Spirit. Episode 3 closes with Yeshua's own family joining the opposition as they seek to interrupt his ministry. Yeshua declares that his true family are those around him who seek to do God's will.

Despite the opposition, Yeshua continues to attract large crowds and in Episode 4 he teaches them in parables about the Kingdom of God that he has been proclaiming all along. Ironically, the parables only provide revelation among those with ears to hear, while many remain deaf. Accordingly, our episode ends with the note that Yeshua explained everything in private to his own disciples.

Yeshua has been teaching from a boat just offshore on Lake Kinneret, and now, in Episode 5, he crosses the lake with his talmidim to the mostly-Gentile territory of the Gerasenes. On the way, they encounter an intense storm that threatens to swamp their boat until Yeshua calms the storm with a word, leaving his disciples awe-struck. He shows similar authority when they land and are immediately confronted by a man possessed by a legion of demons, which Yeshua casts out with a command. The locals are terrified by Yeshua's power and beg him to leave their territory, but the once-demonized man stays behind to proclaim throughout the region what Yeshua has done for him.

Yeshua and his band cross Lake Kinneret back to Jewish territory, where they are greeted by a large crowd, as well as by a synagogue leader asking Yeshua to come to his house and heal his daughter. On the way, a woman suffering from chronic bleeding slips through the crowd to touch Yeshua's robe and is immediately healed. But as Yeshua is speaking with her, some people arrive telling the synagogue ruler that his daughter has died. Yeshua insists on continuing to his house, where he takes the daughter's lifeless hand and raises her back to life. In three amazing acts of power in these two episodes, starting with the Gerasene demoniac, Yeshua has displayed his powers over the forces of death and impurity, but when he visits his nearby hometown, he can do very little because of their lack of faith. Episode 6 ends as Yeshua moves on to serve in other towns and villages of the Galil.

In Episode 7, he sends out the twelve talmidim chosen back in Episode 3, equipping them with authority over unclean spirits and instructions for expanding his Kingdom-of-God ministry. Before recounting their return, Mark tells the story of Herod's brutal execution of Yochanan the Immerser. Then he turns back to his account of the Twelve, who rejoin Yeshua and report on their successful mission. Before they can take a break, they're spotted by the crowds, who join them in a remote spot where Yeshua miraculously multiplies five loaves and two fish to feed 5,000 people. Afterwards, Yeshua sends his followers back to the other side of Lake Kinneret by boat. They're caught in a storm and Yeshua walks upon the surface of the water to join them. He steps into the boat, calms the storm, and his talmidim are amazed but still uncomprehending. When they land, they're again recognized by the crowds and Yeshua resumes his ministry of healing the sick.

Our next episode covers a widely misunderstood debate with some religious experts from Jerusalem concerning ritual purity. Yeshua resists their expanded version of the purity laws in favor of a more straightforward reading of Leviticus, declaring that it's what "comes out of a person that makes a person unclean!" Episode 8 closes as Yeshua lists the sort of thoughts and deeds that arise from within and cause defilement. From there, Yeshua travels into the largely Gentile territory of Tyre and Sidon, where his reputation precedes him. A Gentile woman approaches Yeshua and asks him to drive a demon out of her daughter. He initially refuses, but then responds to the woman's unusual level of faith and sets her daughter free. Continuing in Gentile territory Yeshua performs two more miracles, healing a deaf man and feeding a crowd of 4000 with a few loaves and fish. Finally, he returns to the Galil, where some of his opponents among the Pharisees challenge him to produce "a sign from Heaven." Yeshua refuses and departs by boat again, warning his followers about the "leaven" of the Pharisees and Herodians, but they misunderstand. The Kingdom of God, announced in Episode 1 has been on full display here in Episode 9 and throughout Season 1, mostly in the Galil. But the season draws to a close with Yeshua's ironic words: "And you still don't understand?"

PROLOGUE IN THE DESERT

1:1–13

Overview

"The beginning of the Good News of Yeshua the Messiah, the Son of God." The Good News according to Mark begins with a three-part title for the One the Good News is all about: (1) Yeshua (2) the Messiah (3) the Son of God.

This title introduces themes that will be developed throughout Mark's account. It belongs to a Jewish man with a common Jewish name who is declared to be the Jewish Messiah. This term, meaning the "anointed one," appears in the Tanakh to describe priests, prophets, and kings, most often King David, God's anointed one (1 Sam. 16:6–13; etc.) and also in a few places an anointed one of the line of David still to come (Psa. 2:2, 132:17–18). By the time of second-temple Judaism, the title "Messiah" carried with it the abundant promises of an heir of David who would restore David's dynasty as the universal kingdom of the Age to Come. The "Son of God" terminology is also deeply rooted in the Hebrew Scriptures, where it carries a variety of meanings, but perhaps the one most likely to stand out in this context is Son of God as the promised Davidic king, of whom God says, "I will be a father for him, and he will be a son for me" (2 Sam. 7:14).

Before Mark brings Yeshua onto the scene, however, he introduces Yochanan, who appears in the region of the Jordan River, which flows through this otherwise arid and stark landscape. By highlighting the location, the Jordan, Mark connects this scene to Israel's original entry into the land under Joshua. He also envisions a re-entry into the land after a time of exile. Yochanan is a "voice in the wilderness" fulfilling the words of the prophet Isaiah that picture ADONAI returning from exile in Babylon along with the remnant of Israel. Now, to prepare the people for God's return, Yochanan calls on people to be immersed in the river as a sign of *teshuvah*—their return to God. In this remote desert location far from the centers of political and religious power, the glory of ADONAI is about to be revealed, suggesting the theme of Divine Reversal that will run throughout Mark's account.[1] Divine Reversal refers to God's activity within human affairs to overturn, counteract, and reverse the ways of this world, revealing the ways of the World to Come. It's a theme that runs throughout Scripture, and is especially prominent in the life and teachings of Yeshua.[2]

In addition to the reversal of God's glory in a remote desert location, we see another reversal. Yochanan announces the coming of One whom he is unworthy to even serve, who "will immerse you in the *Ruach HaKodesh*—the Holy Spirit" (1:8).[3] In the next verse this exalted One presents himself to Yochanan and the crowds around him, not as a kingly figure, but as a humble Jew, with the common name Yeshua from the very ordinary town of Natzeret,[4] ready to receive the immersion of teshuvah from Yochanan. But as Yeshua emerges from the waters of immersion, a voice from heaven declares, "You are my Son, whom I love; I am well pleased with you" (1:11). God's glory is revealed in what appears lowly and ordinary to man, and it's evident that "Son of God" in the opening title may mean even more than Davidic King. Nevertheless, this

---

[1]. See Russell Resnik, *Divine Reversal: The Transforming Ethics of Jesus* (Clarksville, MD: Lederer, 2010).
[2]. Keener refers to the theme as "eschatological inversion—the exaltation of the lowly and the humbling of the proud." Craig S. Keener, *The Historical Jesus of the Gospels* (Grand Rapids: Eerdmans, 2009), 292ff.
[3]. Technically "Ruach HaKodesh" doesn't need an article, as in "*the* Ruach HaKodesh," because it already has one in the Hebrew syntax, but we'll follow the usage of CJB, which uses the definite article throughout.
[4]. Bauckham, *Jesus and the Eyewitnesses*, 85, lists "Jesus" as the sixth "most popular male name among Palestinian Jews, 330 BCE–200 CE."

exalted figure isn't going to receive any more accolades for a while; instead he's immediately driven away from the river valley and into the desert to be tempted by the Adversary. Divine Reversal frames the entire testimony of Yeshua as Mark will present it.

Peshat

1:1

> The beginning of the Good News of Yeshua the Messiah, the Son of God.

Mark opens with the same terminology that opens the Torah: The beginning (*Arche, B'reisheet*), suggesting that the appearance of "Yeshua the Messiah, the Son of God" is a sort of new creation. As we'll see shortly, the language of 1:9–13 strengthens this linkage with the opening chapters of Genesis.

Some of the earliest manuscripts lack the final phrase, *Son of God*, so that the question of Yeshua's full identity which runs as a thread throughout this Gospel is reflected in questions about the very text itself. It is beyond the scope of this episode to explore this issue in depth, but we'll follow Lane, France, and Bock[5] and most contemporary translations (NIV, NASB, ESV, NRSV 1989 ed., TLV), including our default CJB, in retaining "the Son of God" in Mark 1:1.

We've already seen that applying the title "Son of God" to a specific man would not necessarily sound outrageous to second-temple Jewish ears. It can be employed as a royal title, not a divine title, as in God's word to David in 2 Samuel 7:

> [12] When your days come to an end and you sleep with your ancestors, I will establish one of your descendants to succeed you,

---

5. R. T. France, *The Gospel of Mark: A Commentary on the Greek Text* (Grand Rapids/Cambridge: Eerdmans, 2002), 49. William L. Lane, *The Gospel according to Mark*. (Grand Rapids: Eerdmans, 1974), 41, fn. 7. David Turner and Darrell L. Bock, *Cornerstone Biblical Commentary*, Vol 11: Matthew and Mark (Carol Stream, IL: Tyndale House, 2005), 404.

one of your own flesh and blood; and I will set up his rulership. ¹³ He will build a house for my name, and I will establish his royal throne forever. ¹⁴ I will be a father for him, and he will be a son for me.

Psalm 2 reflects this language. It's a royal psalm about God appointing a king over Zion, who declares:

> "I will proclaim the decree:
> ADONAI said to me,
> 'You are my son;
> today I became your father.'" (vs. 7)

Psalm 89 speaks specifically about God's covenant with David and his dynasty:

> ²⁷ "He [the Davidic king] will call to me, 'You are my father,
> my God, the Rock of my salvation.'
> ²⁸ I will give him the position of firstborn,
> the highest of the kings of the earth."

The Davidic king is a son of God, "firstborn" in terms of status and position, not chronology. Back in Psalm 2, the king is introduced as the Lord's "anointed," or Mashiach/messiah in Hebrew. Mark uses this combination of words to introduce "Yeshua the Messiah, Son of God," initially signifying that he is the promised king descended from David. This terminology is presented simply, without elaboration, to be defined and explored in depth as Mark's account continues on. This narrative approach seems to contrast with a desire for doctrinal clarity and precision. But as we continue to read and hear Mark's account we'll recognize the advantages of this simple approach, which calls on the reader/hearer to listen well, to watch for what's going on beneath the surface, and to ponder the meaning of the various titles bestowed on Yeshua to discover who he really is.

1:2–8 [6]

² It is written in the prophet Isaiah,

"**See, I am sending my messenger ahead of you;
he will prepare the way before you.**" [Malachi 3:1]
³ "**The voice of one crying out:
'In the desert prepare the way for ADONAI!
Make straight paths for him!'**" [Isaiah 40:3] [7]

⁴ So it was that Yochanan the Immerser appeared in the desert, proclaiming an immersion of *teshuvah* for the forgiveness of sins. ⁵ People went out to him from all over Y'hudah, as did all the inhabitants of Jerusalem. Confessing their sins, they were immersed by him in the Jordan River. ⁶ Yochanan wore clothes of camel's hair, with a leather belt around his waist; he ate locusts and wild honey. ⁷ He proclaimed: "After me is coming someone who is more powerful than I—I'm not worthy even to bend down and untie his sandals. ⁸ I have immersed you in water, but he will immerse you in the *Ruach HaKodesh*."

The beginning of the good news for Mark is a "voice of someone crying out." This voice crying out, which belongs to a man named Yochanan, isn't itself the good news, but it rises up at the beginning to prepare the way for the good news. After citing the introductory words of the prophet Malachi, Mark goes on to frame his wilderness scene in words from Isaiah 40. For Jewish readers and hearers of the word in those days and long since, a single line can evoke the whole passage. One vibrant image can paint the whole picture in the mind of the hearer. So "the voice of one crying out" describes Yochanan and also paints the backdrop for the whole drama being enacted before us. Mark cites just one verse from Isaiah 40, but this citation is meant to bring the whole passage to mind:

---

6. This section draws upon Mark S. Kinzer, Russell L. Resnik, *Besorah: The Resurrection of Jerusalem and the Healing of a Fractured Gospel* (Eugene, OR: Cascade, 2021), 14–18.
7. CJB bolds direct citations of the Tanakh throughout its text.

> A voice of one crying in the wilderness:
> "Prepare the way of the LORD,
> make his paths straight."
>
> Every valley shall be lifted up,
> and every mountain and hill be made low;
> the uneven ground shall become level,
> and the rough places a plain.
> And the glory of the LORD shall be revealed,
> and all flesh shall see it together,
> for the mouth of the LORD has spoken. (Isa. 40:3–5 ESV)

Mark's citation of Isaiah 40:3 points ahead to the final phrase of the stanza: "And the glory of the LORD shall be revealed, / and all flesh shall see it together." Moreover, Isaiah 40 introduces the entire final section of Isaiah, chapters 40 through 66, and its appearance at the beginning of Mark's narrative alerts us to the Isaiah 40–66 framework of the entire account.

> One of the organizing principles of this Markan composition seems to be the demonstration that the beginning of the good news happened "as it has been written in Isaiah the prophet" (1:2). This is not just a reference to the citation of Isa. 40:3 in Mark 1:3; rather, echoes of Isaiah ... permeate the entire Markan prologue.[8]

Returning to Mark's reference to the "voice of one crying out," the sense is clear—Yochanan has come to summon Israel to "prepare the way for ADONAI," YHWH in the Hebrew of Isaiah 40. But the one who actually appears is Yeshua, who "came from Natzeret in the Galil and was immersed in the Yarden by Yochanan." When Yeshua emerges from the water after his immersion, as if to confirm that he

---

8. Joel Marcus, *Mark 1–8: A New Translation with Introduction and Commentary*, vol. 27, Anchor Yale Bible (New Haven; London: Yale University Press, 2008), 139. Marcus goes on to trace themes in Mark that reflect themes in "Deutero-Isaiah," as he terms this section, for example, forgiveness of sins; the wilderness; and how "the tearing of the heavens, the descent of the Spirit, and the content of the heavenly voice (Mark 1:10–11) recall Isa 63:11–64:1; 11:1–2, and 42:1 ... and Jesus' initial announcement of the good news of the nearness of the dominion of God (Mark 1:14–15) echoes Deutero-Isaiah's proclamation of the good news of the advent of [ADONAI's] royal rule in Isa 40:9–10; 52:7; 61:1–11."

is the one foretold by "the voice crying out in the desert," another voice, this time from heaven, cries out, "You are my Son, whom I love; I am well pleased with you."

This scene echoes the opening of Parashat Vayera ("And he appeared"):[9] "ADONAI appeared to Avraham by the oaks of Mamre as he sat at the entrance to the tent during the heat of the day. He raised his eyes and looked, and there in front of him stood three men" (Gen. 18:1–2). The Torah introduces the scene with the words "ADONAI appeared to Avraham," and what actually appears is a group of three men that Avraham sees standing outside his tent. As the narrative progresses, starting in Genesis 18:10, one of the men begins to speak in the first person as ADONAI, and continues to do so through the rest of the chapter. So, the chapter is introduced with the words "ADONAI appeared to Avraham," and he does so in the shape of a man who is revealed to be ADONAI as the chapter progresses. Likewise in Mark 1, the introductory words speak of preparing for a visitation of the LORD (*Kyrios* in Greek, translating *YHWH* in the Hebrew original of Isaiah 40) . . . and Yeshua is the one who appears. "It says a lot for the underlying Christology of Mark's gospel that he can allow the Baptist's words, which in themselves point directly to the coming of God, to be read as referring to the human Jesus."[10]

As in Genesis 18, the divine nature of the one who appears is made clear as the story unfolds. Yochanan says of him, "I have immersed you in water, but he will immerse you in the *Ruach HaKodesh*" (Mark 1:8). In the Tanakh it is ADONAI alone who immerses in or pours out the Ruach, the Spirit, as he will do in the last days (Isa. 32:15, 44:3; Ezek. 36:26–27, 39:29; Joel 3:1–2 [2:28–29 in Christian Bibles]). This immersion in the Spirit completes the work

---

9. *Parasha* refers to the section of the Torah read in the synagogue each week, so that all synagogues in the world are reading the same portion each week. When *parasha* is combined with the name of the specific portion it becomes *parashat*, as in this case Parashat Vayera.
10. France, 70. "Christology" refers to the theological study of the nature and character of the Messiah.

of teshuvah/repentance initiated in Yochanan's immersion in water. And as the Prophets reveal, this immersion is an essential part of the return of God's presence to Israel, and ultimately to all humankind. Indeed, after Yochanan is coming someone who is far more powerful than he!

Mark's citation of Isaiah 40:3 also reminds us of another verse in Isaiah that comes soon after:

> Go on up to a high mountain,
>   O herald of good news to Zion;
> lift up your voice with strength,
>   O herald of good news to Jerusalem;
>   lift it up, fear not;
> say to the cities of Judah,
>   "Behold your God!" (Isa. 40:9, ESV marginal reading)

"Herald of good news" in this passage is a single word in Hebrew, *mevasseret*, originally a military term for a messenger. His message is a related term, *besorah*, a report from the battlefield. These terms play a part in the accounts of the deaths of Saul (2 Sam. 4:10) and Absalom (2 Sam. 18:19–27), where they don't necessarily mean *good* news. Isaiah, however, definitely has good news in mind as he uses these terms to picture the herald watching out over the highway leading up to Jerusalem (Zion is a synonym for Jerusalem in this passage), eager to announce the approach of a significant someone. Since the entire block of Isaiah's prophecy beginning in chapter 40 is about Israel's return from captivity in Babylon, we understand that Isaiah's herald is watching the highway that comes from Babylon back to the land of Israel, back to Jerusalem.

Isaiah employs the besorah terminology again in 41:27, 52:7, and 61:1.This whole section of Isaiah provides foundational texts for Mark's entire narrative. By using the word "besorah" instead of "good news" or "gospel" we acknowledge the essential role of Israel, the Jewish people, in this story. The Messiah announced in this besorah is the heir of Israel's King David, who will come first to the people Israel, and restore David's dynastic rule over them from the Jewish capital, Jerusalem.

What is most striking in Isaiah 40 is that the herald isn't watching only for the return of the *Israelites* to Jerusalem, but also—and above all—for the return of *their God*. God's presence has gone into exile with Israel and his presence will return, leading them back to the land of their inheritance. Then the herald will cry out with the besorah to Jerusalem, "Behold your God!" He calls on the people to prepare the way for God's return, using images of highway building: "make his paths straight," and "the uneven ground shall become level, and the rough places a plain." Centuries later, when Mark quotes Isaiah, he applies these phrases as metaphors for repentance, for returning to God. After citing Isaiah's call to prepare the way of ADONAI, Mark tells us, "So it was that Yochanan the Immerser appeared in the desert, proclaiming an immersion involving turning to God from sin in order to be forgiven" (Mark 1:4). Immersion in water as a ritual enactment of purification and (re)dedication to God is based on passages like Ezekiel 36:26 and Zechariah 13:1, as well as priestly rituals of washing and purification, particularly in Leviticus. The *mikveh*, or ritual bath for purification, was already in use within the Jewish world of Yochanan's day, especially by the community at Qumran, not far from where Yochanan was preaching on the banks of the Jordan. So, when Yochanan issues his call to prepare the way for ADONAI, he doesn't invent a new ritual for that preparation, but he "repurposes the ritual" of the mikveh.[11]

The "good news" in Mark's opening verses is the besorah that the God of Israel is returning to his people *and* that the people need to return to their God.

---

11. Amy-Jill Levine, *The Gospel of Mark: A Beginner's Guide to the Good News* (Nashville: Abingdon, 2023), 5.

1:9–11

⁹ Shortly thereafter, Yeshua came from Natzeret in the Galil and was immersed in the Yarden by Yochanan. ¹⁰ Immediately upon coming up out of the water, he saw heaven torn open and the Spirit descending upon him like a dove; ¹¹ then a voice came from heaven, "You are my Son, whom I love; I am well pleased with you."

Yochanan calls on the people of Israel to prepare for the coming of the LORD, and says that one more powerful than himself will appear, one who will immerse the people not in water but in the *Ruach HaKodesh*. And then Yeshua appears, a man from a small and insignificant town in the Galil, and humbly receives Yochanan's immersion. Mark records events that happen "immediately" as Yeshua comes out of the water, introducing a word, *euthus* in the Greek, which will appear about forty times throughout his Besorah, far more often in Mark than in the other Gospels. It shapes his portrayal of Yeshua as a man of action, a man on the move toward his prophetic destiny. There's no reason, however, to imagine that those gathered at the Jordan recognize Yeshua in such terms, or as the one that Yochanan is referring to. But as he comes up from the water, his identity is made clear, at least to him and those reading this account: "You are my Son, whom I love; I am well pleased with you."

Before the voice speaks, though, Mark tells us that heaven is "torn open"—translating a Greek word based on the root *schizo*, rare terminology that appears only once more in Mark: "And the *parokhet* in the Temple was *torn* in two from top to bottom" (15:38, emphasis added). The appearance of the word only twice, in two crucial scenes, one near the beginning and one near the end, suggests that it forms an *inclusio*, alerting the reader to something essential happening here.[12] In Mark 1 the heavens are torn open to reveal God's presence and signal the descent of his Spirit upon Yeshua, who will immerse his followers in the same Spirit. In Mark

---

12. See the definition of inclusio in the Introduction (page xvii) and Glossary.

15, as we'll discuss later, the veil of the temple is likewise torn open to signify new access to God's presence, and a new era to come with Messiah's resurrection.

The "torn open" terminology also reflects the opening of heaven to the prophet Ezekiel: "In the thirtieth year, on the fifth day of the fourth month, while I was among the exiles by the K'var River, the heavens were opened, and I saw visions of God" (Ezek. 1:1). Even more significantly, "torn open" echoes the words of Isaiah:

> Where is he who brought them up from the sea
> with the shepherds of his flock?
> Where is he who put his Holy Spirit
> right there among them? . . .
>
> We wish you would *tear open* heaven and come down, so the mountains would shake at your presence! (Isa. 63:11, 19 [64:1], emphasis added)

Like Mark 1:10 this passage describes a chosen one coming up from the water, the descent of the Spirit, and heaven torn open. The Septuagint, or LXX, the widely used Greek translation of the Tanakh, which Mark often draws upon, employs the same "*schizo*" terminology here as in Mark 1:10.

> In Mark, then, God has ripped the heavens irrevocably apart at Jesus' baptism, never to shut them again. Through this gracious gash in the universe, he has poured forth his Spirit into the earthly realm. Like the tearing of the heavens, this advent of the Spirit is an eschatological event.[13]

"Eschatological" here refers to the conclusion of this age and the inbreaking of the age to come. Mark's immersion scene hints at the final drama of human history, and also at the opening drama of creation: "in the beginning God created the heavens and the earth." The Spirit descending like a dove upon Yeshua as he emerges from the water is parallel to the Spirit of God *hovering* (bird-like) over the

---

13. Marcus, *Mark 1–8*, 165.

surface of the waters in Genesis 1:2. And a voice coming from heaven echoes "And God said" in Genesis 1 (vss. 3, 6, 9, 11, 14, 20, 24, 26).

The heavenly voice resembles what is called a *bat qol*, or "daughter of a voice," in rabbinic literature, "a voice that sounds forth from heaven to express God's will and may quote scripture and/or declare a favorable evaluation of a person."[14] But the voice here in Mark differs from a typical *bat qol* in being a personal, rather than public, communication. The voice confirms and amplifies what Yochanan has already declared about the one coming after him. But in Mark's account this confirmation comes only to Yeshua himself—and to us as we hear the story—not to the crowds gathered to hear Yochanan. Later in the narrative, when Yeshua returns to Galilee and continues his ministry there and then in Jerusalem, he will not be recognized as an apocalyptic figure, let alone as the Son of God. Mark's entire account traces the gradual and often painful revelation of who Yeshua is. At his immersion, apparently only Yeshua hears the heavenly voice, as suggested in the actual wording, "*he* saw heaven torn open and the Spirit descending upon him like a dove; then a voice came from heaven, '*You* are my Son'" (Mark 1:10–11, emphasis added). The wording suggests that only Yeshua saw heaven torn open and the Spirit descending, and it may also be that only Yeshua heard the voice from heaven. Note the wording, "You are my Son," addressed to him directly, rather than "This is my Son," as in Matthew 3:17.

As Mark's account continues, it's clear that the heavenly revelation of this opening scene has little or no impact on Yeshua's reputation in his own community. But as we hear the account, we remember its opening words, "the Besorah of Yeshua the Messiah the Son of God." The heavenly voice not only confirms that title; it reveals a deeper meaning. As noted above, "Son of God" is a title of the Davidic king, and linked to "Messiah" or anointed one, it points to the promised king descended from David. But the heavenly voice

---

14. Marcus, *Mark 1–8*, 160. See also Levine, *Mark*, 9.

reveals a unique divine Sonship. "You are my Son, whom I love; I am well pleased with you." This description of Yeshua reflects the words of ADONAI in Isaiah 42:

> Here is my servant, whom I support,
> my chosen one, in whom I take pleasure.
> I have put my Spirit on him.

This is another sign of the Isaiah 40–66 framework of Mark. The heavenly voice also echoes ADONAI's three-part description of Isaac as he commands Abraham to offer him up: "Take your son, your only son, whom you love" (Gen. 22:2). As with a human father and son, God and Yeshua share the same nature and are bound together in deep and abiding love. And of course the linkage to the *Akedah*, the binding of Isaac, suggests that Yeshua too will be offered up as a sacrifice to God.

To confirm the unique status of Yeshua, the Spirit descends on him like a dove (cf. Isa. 42:1). This is the second of three mentions of the Spirit of God in the prologue. First, Yeshua is the one who "will immerse you in the *Ruach HaKodesh*" (1:8); second, he is the one on whom the *Ruach* or Spirit descends like a dove (1:10); and third, he is driven out to the wilderness by the *Ruach* or Spirit (1:12). Mark's three-fold mention of the Spirit within a few verses of the Prologue highlights the essential role of the Holy Spirit in his whole portrayal of the words and deeds of Yeshua.

1:12–13

> [12] Immediately the Spirit drove him out into the wilderness, [13] and he was in the wilderness forty days being tempted by the Adversary. He was with the wild animals, and the angels took care of him.

Mark will explore the meaning of "Son of God" throughout his whole account, but early on he reveals that this title does not shield Yeshua from difficulty and trials.

This is the second appearance of "immediately" (after 1:10), a word that helps Mark maintain the vitality and quick-paced action of his account. It's especially notable here, when Yeshua might be tempted to kick back and rest in the divine love and favor he receives at his immersion. Instead, he's driven out to be tempted by the Adversary. Testing comes immediately after immersion, but God's favor is still evident as "the angels took care of him."

This sequence of immersion and then (immediate) testing reflects the Israelites' escape from Egypt, when they crossed Yam Suf, the "Red Sea," and immediately were tested.

> Moshe led Israel onward from the Sea of Suf. They went out into the Shur Desert; but after traveling three days in the desert, they had found no water. They arrived at Marah but couldn't drink the water there, because it was bitter. . . . There ADONAI made laws and rules of life for them, and there he tested them. (Exod. 15:22–25)

Exodus is also the backdrop for Isaiah 40, which Mark draws upon in the first verses of his Besorah. Isaiah portrays the return from exile as a new exodus for Israel, a new deliverance from the bondage of a Gentile world power and into the service of ADONAI. By undergoing the immersion-temptation sequence, Yeshua signals his identification with his people Israel and also signals that he will accomplish for them a new exodus as prophesied by Isaiah. This identification is strengthened by Mark's mention of the detail that Yeshua was "in the wilderness forty days," reflecting the forty years that Israel spent in the wilderness. The citation of forty days also links Yeshua to Moses, who also fasted for forty days in the wilderness, specifically upon Mount Sinai, as he ascended to receive the Torah (Exod. 24:18; 34:28). As we'll see shortly, in Episode 3, Mark provides another hint of a new Moses when Yeshua goes up a mountain to summon the Twelve and send them out (Mark 3:13).

Yeshua's temptation enacts another, much earlier, scene in the Torah, reflected in the language of 1:12. The Spirit *drives* Yeshua out into the wilderness. This portrayal contrasts with Matthew and

Luke, in which Yeshua is *led by the Spirit* into the wilderness. Rather, Mark describes this scene in a way that brings us back again to the beginning of Genesis, specifically to Adam's expulsion from the garden. Adam and Eve were tested in the garden, and failed, and will again be tested outside the garden by the harsh circumstances that the LORD God decreed in Genesis 3:16–19.

Likewise, Yeshua is driven out into the wilderness to be tested. The Greek word *ekballei* appears in Mark in various forms to describe the driving out of demons, and it also appears in the Septuagint in Genesis 3:24: "and he *drove out* the man." Mark is echoing Genesis in his account of Yeshua's temptation to reveal that Yeshua joins with humankind in the wilderness of life that all human beings share. The Spirit drives Yeshua out of the Edenic conditions of 1:10–11, but Yeshua is tempted *after* his departure, not *before* as were Adam and Eve.

Yeshua is tempted by the Adversary ("Satan" in Greek, reflecting the Hebrew of Job 1–2, Zech. 3), but he is in the wilderness under the impetus of the Ruach. He is with the wild animals—perhaps reflecting Adam with the animals in Genesis 2—not in Eden, however, but in the non-garden conditions of human life. There "the angels took care of him," in a reversal of the closing scene of Gen. 3 in which the cherubim block the way back to the tree of life. The opposing forces of Satan and Spirit/angels highlight the dimension of spiritual conflict in this episode, setting the stage for Mark's entire Besorah, in which the Spirit-empowered Yeshua (1:10)[15] is continually confronting and driving out the forces of spiritual opposition.

In this temptation scene, Mark doesn't record a decisive victory over the Adversary as do Matthew and Luke. Rather he emphasizes Yeshua's presence within the post-Edenic world, sharing in its struggles, but returning in power to his homeland to announce the

---

15. It's good to remember in this context that the very title "Messiah" means "Anointed One"—anointed by the Spirit of God.

kingdom to his own people (1:14–15). His victory is muted, but nonetheless, as Yeshua takes on the conditions of human life that all share, he prevails on behalf of the descendants of Adam.

The reference to wild animals here may also reflect the opening of the heavens in 1:10. "Wild animals" is *chayot* in Hebrew, a term Ezekiel uses repeatedly to describe his vision of heaven opened up, referred to above.[16] He introduces the *chayot* in 1:5 "there appeared to be four living creatures that looked like human beings," and mentions them repeatedly in describing his vision (1:13, 14, 15, 19, 20, 21, 22). In the Hebrew Bible, the Adversary or Satan appears as a participant in the heavenly court (Job 1–2, Zech. 3, as noted above). Now, he is afoot upon the earth, tempting the Son of God, and opposed by other forces from the heavenly realm, the wild animals and the angels. Mark doesn't tell us the outcome of this encounter, but the next episode will open with Yeshua boldly announcing the Kingdom of God. The stage is set for the intense spiritual conflict that will rage throughout Mark's Besorah.

Derash

- Why does Mark open with "The *beginning* of the Besorah . . ."? Don't we know that the first line of any book is its beginning? Perhaps (along with establishing the connection to Bereisheet, "In the beginning") he's saying this is the beginning of the Besorah for *you*, dear reader; a fresh encounter, whether for the first time or after many times, an encounter with the authority and immediacy of the message of Yeshua the Messiah the Son of God. We use the term "life-changing" too readily in today's culture, but this encounter with the one Mark announces in verse 1 really can be life-changing.

---

16. The classic translation of the Gospels by the German Hebrew scholar Franz Delitzsch uses "chayot" in Mark 1:13, and defines the term as "wild animal; a type of angel" in the margin; *The Delitzsch Hebrew Gospels: A Hebrew/English Translation* (Marshfield, MO: Vine of David, 2011), 124.

One of the morning prayers of the Siddur highlights the daily renewal of creation, signaled by the return of light each morning:

> In compassion He gives light to the earth and its inhabitants, and in His goodness daily, continually, renews the work of creation.[17]

As we continue through the Besorah of Mark, can we read it as a source of daily renewal empowered by the words and deeds of Messiah Yeshua?

- The section of Isaiah, chapters 40–66, which frames Mark's whole account, is also the source of the seven "Haftarot of Comfort" in synagogue tradition. These passages are read in the synagogue each week between Tisha B'Av (anniversary of the destruction of Jerusalem, first by Babylon in 586 BCE and then by Rome in 70 CE) and Rosh Hashanah. "Comfort" references the opening words of Isaiah 40, "Comfort, comfort my people, says your God," and the following chapters picture the hope of redemption for Israel, a hope that Yeshua the Messiah will embody in Mark's Besorah. You can watch for signs of this hope as we continue through the account.

- In contrast with Mark, Matthew (3:13–15) and John (1:29–34) record Yochanan's explicit recognition of who Yeshua is at his immersion. Luke adds the background information that Yochanan is part of the same extended family as Yeshua, and that Yeshua's mother, Miriam, visits Yochanan's mother before his birth (Luke 1:36–56). Mark leaves out this information, perhaps to highlight Yeshua's lack of reputation and social status as he first appears on the scene. (I will occasionally cite the other Gospels, to highlight a point about Mark's Gospel, without attempting to explain or resolve the apparent differences between them. I'm not trying to create a

---

17. Koren Siddur, 90.

Harmony of the Gospels because such an effort can miss the distinct perspectives of each Gospel writer.)

Despite his apocalyptic and heaven-splitting introduction, Yeshua, as we soon learn, is unrecognized by those closest to him, and Mark will spend his whole Besorah revealing who Yeshua is, with mixed results. What does this tell us about the presence of God in the world today? In our own lives? How do we live in a way that is less likely to miss God's presence and more likely to perceive him when he appears in our world?

- Baptism followed by testing as in Mark contrasts with the popular idea among believers in Yeshua that baptism leads to a new life that is, or should be, trouble-free; that immersion marks a new birth into a life of victory and overcoming. How does Yeshua's example provide a corrective to such views?

Season 1, Episode 1

Proclamation in the Galil

1:14–45

Overview

After his immersion and testing in the wilderness of Y'hudah (Judea), Yeshua returns to the Galil, the region north of Judea and Samaria, which includes the Kinneret or Sea of Galilee, with its surrounding towns and villages. There he proclaims his core message, expanding on the message Yochanan had proclaimed: the Kingdom of God has drawn near; return to God and believe in the Good News.

In the verses that follow, Yeshua enacts the presence of the Kingdom he has announced, even though forces of darkness still abound. He summons his first four disciples—Shim'on (later named Peter) and his brother Andrew, and Ya'akov and Yochanan, sons of Zavdai—to abandon their ordinary lives, follow him, and become "fishers for men." With these four, Yeshua enters the synagogue in the town of K'far-Nachum on Shabbat and begins to teach. His authoritative teaching in the synagogue is *amazing* to the congregants and *triggering* to an unclean spirit present within one of them. It cries out, "What do you want with us, Yeshua from Natzeret? Have you come to destroy us? I know who you are — the Holy One of God!" The congregants are further amazed when Yeshua simply commands the unclean spirit to depart and it obeys him. Yeshua's fame begins to spread throughout the surrounding region of the Galil.

Yeshua and his four followers leave the synagogue and go to the home of one of them, Shim'on, there in K'far-Nachum, where

Yeshua heals Shim'on's mother-in-law, who is ill. When Shabbat ends, the whole town gathers around Shim'on's door bringing sick and demonized people for Yeshua to heal and set free. Like the unclean spirit in the synagogue, these demons know who Yeshua is, but this time he does not permit them to speak.

Early in the morning, before dawn, Yeshua goes off by himself to pray, but Shim'on and some others find him, telling him, "Everyone is looking for you." But Yeshua tells them that they need to go to the neighboring towns and proclaim the message there, which they do, proclaiming the message in synagogues throughout the Galil and expelling demons. In the process, Yeshua is approached by a man suffering from *tzara'at*, a mysterious skin disease. Yeshua cleanses him of the disease at his request and tells the man to present himself to a priest to confirm the cleansing, as mandated in the Torah. Instead, the man spreads the word of what Yeshua has done, swelling the numbers of people coming to Yeshua for help. He can no longer enter any town, but stays out in the country, where people come to him from all around.

In this episode Yeshua performs three specific acts of Kingdom intervention, in addition to his widespread acts of healing and deliverance: casting out an unclean spirit in the synagogue of K'far-Nachum; healing Shim'on's mother-in-law; and cleansing a man afflicted with *tzara'at*. Amazing deeds like these will characterize Yeshua's ministry throughout Mark's account, as Yeshua demonstrates the presence of God's Kingdom through his encounter with the Forces of Death.[1]

---

1. I borrow this terminology from Matthew Thiessen, *Jesus and the Forces of Death: The Gospels' Portrayal of Ritual Impurity within First-Century Judaism* (Grand Rapids: Baker, 2021), who uses it to describe the three "forces" of *tzara'at* or "scale disease" (as in Mark 1:40), genital discharges (5:25), and corpse defilement (5:35, 41), as well as "demonic impurity" in chapter 6. Mark's frequent use of the term "unclean spirit" (1:23–27; 3:11, 30; 5:2–12; 6:7; 7:25; 9:25) ties right into Thiessen's notion of demonic impurity.

Peshat

1:14–15

> [14] After Yochanan had been arrested, Yeshua came into the Galil proclaiming the Good News from God:
>
> [15] "The time has come,
> God's Kingdom is near!
> Turn to God from your sins
> and believe the Good News!"

When Yochanan is taken from the scene (and Mark will tell us how this happens in chapter 6), Yeshua launches his own ministry, not in the southern region of the Jordan where Yochanan preached, but in his home territory of the Galil, the largely rural area in the north of the land of Israel and west of the Kinneret or Sea of Galilee. Yeshua's opening proclamation there is a bit puzzling. He proclaims the Good News and part of his proclamation is to believe the Good News! We can understand this phrasing by remembering that in the context of the Tanakh and the Jewish world of Yeshua's day, "believe" means more than intellectual agreement or abstract faith. The word implies active trust in the message, faithfulness toward it, which, as we'll see, goes hand-in-hand with repentance, or *teshuvah*, "turning/return" in Hebrew—a whole-hearted, behavioral response to this message about the Kingdom of God. Teshuvah is not an addendum to the Good News, but inherent to it. The proclamation doesn't just let us know that "God's Kingdom is near," it also calls us to turn from our own ways and align ourselves with that kingdom. And by calling this message "the Good News of *Yeshua the Messiah*," Mark implies that it is in and through Yeshua that the Kingdom of God has drawn near.

David Gushee helps us grasp the significance of the "Kingdom of God" theme in the Jewish world of Yeshua's day.

> The idea of God's rightful reign over all the earth was sharpened and made plaintive by the experience of the Jewish people's suffering at the hands of foreign tyrants. Brokenhearted Israel

asserted, while in the direst straits—*the God of Israel is king of all the earth!* Such a proclamation by Jews while in foreign lands, or in their own land under foreign domination—as in first-century CE Roman-occupied Judea—was intrinsically subversive and could be perceived as revolutionary.[2]

This subversive and revolutionary proclamation is also "Good News," especially when it declares that "God's Kingdom is near." In CJB, "Good News" translates the Greek term *euangelion* in Mark 1:14–15, as well as the underlying Hebrew term *besorah*, as we saw in the Prologue (pages 12-13). This terminology appears several times in Isaiah, beginning with chapter 40, where it's the glad tidings of a herald announcing the return of the king. Before the king appears, the herald goes forth and proclaims his glory so the people can prepare for his coming. So believing the Good News in Mark 1:15 means believing that the King is approaching and his reign is about to begin—so get ready! We shouldn't miss the sense of urgency in Yeshua's proclamation. It's in line with Jewish apocalyptic writings of this period, writings that speak of profound changes that are coming, or are already in play, to bring the current age to its end and prepare for the Age to Come foretold by the Hebrew prophets. God's Kingdom is near!

Yeshua's urgent apocalyptic message is good news specifically for Israel, the Jewish people. It's the fulfillment of all that the people have been hoping for, especially the visions of Isaiah as Mark reveals in his accounts of Yeshua's immersion in the Yarden. To underline this allusion to Isaiah I employ the term for "good news" reflecting his own language: *Besorah.*[3]

This besorah, however, is rooted not only in Isaiah, but also in the Torah and all the Prophets, and now its "time has come." Now Yeshua enters Israel's story as the One who will activate and accomplish the besorah in his own life. All humankind will benefit

---

2. David P. Gushee, *The Moral Teachings of Jesus: Radical Instruction in the Will of God* (Eugene, OR: Cascade, 2024), 5–6.
3. "Besorah" is capitalized when it appears as the title of Mark's account, or the account of the other Gospel writers, and left uncapped when it refers to an announcement or proclamation of good news.

from the besorah of Yeshua the Messiah, but its fulfillment is linked in an essential way with Israel, the Jewish people, and with the land of Israel, their inheritance—including the region of the Galil where Yeshua launches his ministry.

1:16–20

> ¹⁶ As he walked beside Lake Kinneret, he saw Shim'on and Andrew, Shim'on's brother, casting a net into the lake; for they were fishermen. ¹⁷ Yeshua said to them, "Come, follow me, and I will make you into fishers for men!" ¹⁸ At once they left their nets and followed him.
>
> ¹⁹ Going on a little farther, he saw Ya'akov Ben-Zavdai and Yochanan, his brother, in their boat, repairing their nets. ²⁰ Immediately he called them, and they left their father Zavdai in the boat with the hired men and went after Yeshua.

Yeshua's announcement in 1:14–15 doesn't allow for a passive or theoretical response, but requires following him. Yeshua launches his ministry as he's walking along the shore of Lake Kinneret, the Sea of Galilee, and calls two local fishermen, Shim'on and Andrew, to follow him. They respond immediately and Yeshua summons two more local fishermen, Ya'akov son of Zavdai and Yochanan, his brother. All four men leave everything behind, including in the case of Zavdai's sons, their father and what seems to be a thriving family business employing hired men. Yeshua isn't looking for admirers or even advocates, but for those willing to abandon everything to follow him and become "fishers for men."

This opening scene features Shim'on. He's introduced first of the four initial followers of Yeshua, and his name is repeated in the introduction: "Shim'on and Andrew, Shim'on's brother" instead of the simpler "Shim'on and Andrew, his brother," as in the next pair, "Ya'akov Ben-Zavdai and Yochanan, his brother." Later, after visiting the synagogue in K'far-Nachum (1:21–28), Yeshua will enter the home of Shim'on and Andrew and heal Shim'on's mother-in-law. The next morning, when Yeshua goes alone to a remote spot to pray, it's "Shim'on and those with him" who go out to find him.

In our Episode One, then, Shim'on's name appears five times, and twice more in later episodes (3:16; 14:37)—significantly enough, for a total of seven appearances. But early on Shim'on is renamed Peter (3:16), and this name shows up 19 times in Mark, considerably more often, relative to the length of the text, than in Matthew or Luke.

The final appearance of the name Peter comes at the very end of Mark's Besorah—"But go, tell his disciples and Peter that he is going before you to Galilee" (16:7 ESV)—bookending with the first appearance of Shim'on at the beginning of the account. In this case, the two references of Shim'on/Peter "form an *inclusio* around the whole story, suggesting Peter is the witness whose testimony includes the whole. This is striking confirmation of the much disputed testimony of Papias [cited in our Introduction] to the effect that Peter was the source of the Gospel traditions in Mark's Gospel."[4]

1:21–28

> [21] They entered K'far-Nachum, and on Shabbat Yeshua went into the synagogue and began teaching. [22] They were amazed at the way he taught, for he did not instruct them like the Torah-teachers but as one who had authority himself.
>
> [23] In their synagogue just then was a man with an unclean spirit in him, who shouted, [24] "What do you want with us, Yeshua from Natzeret? Have you come to destroy us? I know who you are — the Holy One of God!" [25] But Yeshua rebuked the unclean spirit, "Be quiet and come out of him!" [26] Throwing the man into a convulsion, it gave a loud shriek and came out of him. [27] They were all so astounded that they began asking each other, "What is this? A new teaching, one with authority behind it! He gives orders even to the unclean spirits, and they obey him!" [28] And the news about him spread quickly through the whole region of the Galil.

K'far-Nachum, more commonly known as Capernaum, was a town on the northwest shore of Lake Kinneret, significant enough to have a customs post—where Yeshua calls Levi (2:1, 13–14)—as well as a Roman officer, and most likely his troops, in residence (Matt. 8:5–6).

---

4. Bauckham, *Eyewitnesses*, 125.

K'far-Nachum, as we'll soon discover, is also the hometown of Shim'on and Andrew. It may have served as a home base for Yeshua's ministry in the Galil, as he returns there "after a while" (2:1), and again after extensive ministry journeys (9:33–10:1a), bookending (or forming an *inclusio* with) 1:21 to conclude Yeshua's ministry in the Galil and shift our attention to the regions of Y'hudah on the way to Jerusalem.

For this episode, though, K'far-Nachum's most important feature is its synagogue, where Yeshua enters with his original four-man band of followers on Shabbat. Mark notes this fact without elaboration, suggesting that it's normal behavior for Yeshua, which it would be for any Jewish man of his time and place (3:1; 6:2). He begins to teach, which again isn't exceptional for a participant in the synagogue service, although we imagine Yeshua may have been invited to do so, as he was in Natzeret (Luke 4:16–18), or as Paul was in Pisidian Antioch (Acts 13:14–16). Teaching in the synagogue is familiar and expected, but the teaching itself amazes the other synagogue attendees with its evident authority, in contrast with the words of their Torah-teachers. We won't have long to speculate about what is so authoritative in Yeshua's teaching. One commentator notes, "The *authority* (*exousia*) that the audience recognizes probably consisted in the fact that Jesus did not explain Scripture with reference to other rabbis: he expounded the will of God with resolute immediacy."[5] This may be true, but the unfolding scene itself reveals another—and perhaps primary—cause of amazement. A man with an unclean spirit confronts Yeshua.

> The terror of the scene is increased by the description of the demoniac as "a man in an unclean spirit." This phrase is usually interpreted as a Semitic idiom meaning "a man *with* an unclean spirit." But a literal interpretation has a great deal to commend it: the man's personality has been so usurped by the demon that the demon has, as it were, swallowed him up.[6]

---

5. Eckhard J. Schnabel, *Mark: An Introduction and Commentary*, Tyndale New Testament Commentaries, vol. 2 (London: Inter-Varsity, 2017), 57.
6. Marcus, *Mark 1–8*, 192.

When this man rails at Yeshua, he calmly orders the spirit invading him, "Be quiet and come out of him," and the man is set free. Here is what the other worshipers find so amazing and authoritative about this new teaching: "He gives orders even to the unclean spirits, and they obey him!"

Just as Yeshua's calling of his first four followers provides sandals-on-the-ground reality to his opening proclamation of God's Kingdom (1:15), so does this initial public contact with the demonic realm. Because Yeshua is present in the synagogue, "God's Kingdom is near," and this presence flushes out unclean spirits that had been lurking unseen. The clash of spiritual forces introduced in Yeshua's encounter with the Adversary (1:12–13) continues throughout Mark's Besorah, especially in Season One, Galilee (1:32–34; 3:11–12; 5:15–18; 6:7, 13; 7:25–26). This dynamic helps explain why demons and unclean spirits are so much more prevalent in the Gospels than in the rest of the Bible—the incursion of the Kingdom draws out the opposing forces that had previously been content to operate behind the scenes.

The unclean spirit declares to Yeshua, "I know who you are — the Holy One of God!" This moment is filled with irony: A spirit that is unclean announces the presence of holiness, its opposite quality; this unholy voice confirms the holy words, "You are my Son, whom I love" (1:11); and it says "I know who you are," when the synagogue worshipers are left wondering, "What is this?" (1:27). Yeshua tells the unclean spirit to be quiet, a command he repeats a little later (1:34), and in numerous different contexts throughout his journeys, as noted in the Introduction. Yeshua, of course, doesn't need or want validation from the unholy forces that oppose him, but he also doesn't need or want a haphazard reveal of who he is and what he's about. He has a strategy of revelation that unfolds throughout Mark's Besorah, a strategy that ironically is often advanced through Yeshua's encounters with the forces of darkness.

1:29–39

[29] They left the synagogue and went with Ya'akov and Yochanan to the home of Shim'on and Andrew. [30] Shim'on's mother-in-law

was lying sick with a fever, and they told Yeshua about her. ³¹ He came, took her by the hand and lifted her onto her feet. The fever left her, and she began helping them.

³² That evening after sundown, they brought to Yeshua all who were ill or held in the power of demons, ³³ and the whole town came crowding around the door. ³⁴ He healed many who were ill with various diseases and expelled many demons, but he did not allow the demons to speak, because they knew who he was.

³⁵ Very early in the morning, while it was still dark, Yeshua got up, left, went away to a lonely spot and stayed there praying. ³⁶ But Shim'on and those with him went after him; ³⁷ and when they found him, they said, "Everybody is looking for you." ³⁸ He answered, "Let's go somewhere else — to the other villages around here. I have to proclaim the message there too — in fact this is why I came out." ³⁹ So he traveled all through the Galil, preaching in their synagogues and expelling demons.

Yeshua leaves the synagogue, still accompanied by his first four followers, so that as we hear the details of Mark's account, we see it all from the perspective of this little band. They have abandoned their fishing business to follow Yeshua, but one of them, Shim'on, still maintains a home in K'far-Nachum where he watches out for his mother-in-law. It's also the home of his brother Andrew, and Shim'on may be the head of the household, since his parents and father-in-law—and even his wife—aren't mentioned at all. Apparently once the priority of following Yeshua is established, familial relations and responsibilities continue on, however modified they might need to be. Shim'on will continue to travel with Yeshua throughout Mark's account, but the home base in the Galil mentioned several times (2:1; 3:20; 7:17; 9:28, 33), is most likely Shim'on's house.

Yeshua heals Shim'on's mother-in-law with a simple touch, in notable contrast with the dramatic scene of deliverance earlier in the synagogue. Yeshua raises her from the sick bed—the same verb in Greek for raising a dead girl (5:41–42) and for raising the dead in the general resurrection (12:26). She resumes her usual place within the household, probably serving a Shabbat meal to conclude the holy day. We sometimes joke that Shim'on wanted his mother-in-law healed so that she could get back to her woman's work and feed everyone, but "serving" is an exalted term in Mark's Besorah (see 1:13, in reference to the angels; 10:45) and a fitting outcome to a healing that foreshadows the resurrection to come.

After Shabbat ends, the townspeople bring the sick and oppressed to Shim'on's door to be healed. In a private home Yeshua heals on Shabbat itself, and he expels an unclean spirit in the midst of a Shabbat service in the synagogue, but public and large-scale healing and deliverance are postponed until the conclusion of Shabbat.[7] Mark pictures the simple piety of the Jewish townspeople, who wait patiently until Shabbat ends to bring their afflicted loved ones to Yeshua. In this early episode, Mark recognizes the norms of Shabbat observance, which Yeshua will later expand in ways that bring conflict. When Yeshua expelled demons that evening, "he did not allow the demons to speak, because they knew who he was." He thereby avoided a repetition of the scene in the synagogue that morning when the unclean spirit shouted, "I know who you are — the Holy One of God!" Yeshua will control his own message and reveal himself in the way and timing of his choice, and he has no desire for validation from unclean spirits. Here Mark is highlighting the messianic secret theme outlined in the Introduction. We might ask why Yeshua so publicly heals the sick and drives out demons if he wants to keep his ministry quiet. The demons often initiate the confrontation with Yeshua, so that he must act to expel them, but what about the healings? Why does Yeshua seem to invite folks to be healed, when he doesn't want news of his healings to spread? Yeshua has declared that God's Kingdom is near (1:15), and healing and the restoration of human well-being is inherent to that kingdom. Yeshua doesn't heal and drive out demons primarily to prove who he is; rather he heals and drives out demons *because of who he is*, and

---

7. Later Jewish law or *halakha* will permit certain activities on Shabbat within a home that are not permitted in general, such as carrying domestic items needed for the enjoyment of the holy day. Even in Yeshua's time, healing within a home on Shabbat may have had a different halakhic status than public healing.

as indispensable expressions of his kingdom, which is already but not yet here.[8]

After what must have been a late night ministering to many who were ill and afflicted with demons, Yeshua gets up before sunrise and goes out to a "lonely spot" to pray. Shim'on takes the lead in tracking him down, reflecting his emerging role among the disciples, but Yeshua declines to return to K'far-Nachum. Instead, he is focused on a wider mission. He must continue to proclaim the message of the Kingdom in the villages of the Galil by preaching in their synagogues (note again the Judaism- positive picture here) and expelling demons. The spiritual conflict first portrayed in Yeshua's wilderness encounter with the Adversary continues to characterize Yeshua's entire mission as proclamation of the besorah is linked with casting out evil spirits.

When Yeshua tells Shim'on and the rest, "this is why I came out" (1:38), we might wonder where he came out from. He did come out from K'far-Nachum to this lonely spot, but there's a hint of something more here, as in the key texts of 2:17—"I didn't *come* to call the 'righteous' but sinners!"—and 10:45—"the Son of Man did not *come* to be served, but to serve." In Mark, unlike the Besorah of Yochanan (John), we're never told explicitly where Yeshua came from to announce the Kingdom, call sinners, and serve, but we are confronted with that mystery and left to ponder it.

1:40–45

> [40] A man afflicted with *tzara'at* came to Yeshua and begged him on his knees, "If you are willing, you can make me clean." [41] Moved with pity, Yeshua reached out his hand, touched him and said to him, "I am willing! Be cleansed!" [42] Instantly the *tzara'at* left him, and he was cleansed. [43] Yeshua sent him away with this stern warning: [44] "See to it that you tell no one; instead, as a testimony to the people, go and let the *cohen* examine you, and offer for your cleansing what Moshe commanded." [45] But he went out and began spreading the news, talking freely about it;

---

8. We'll explore the notion of the already-but-not-yet kingdom in our next episode.

so that Yeshua could no longer enter a town openly but stayed out in the country, where people continued coming to him from all around.

Amidst Yeshua's travels through the Galil, a man suffering from *tzara'at* approaches him seeking help. *Tzara'at* is a Hebrew term used extensively in Leviticus 13 and 14. It's often translated as "leprosy," but the symptoms described in Leviticus don't match those of what's known as leprosy today. Furthermore, *tzara'at*, unlike leprosy, can affect not only human bodies, but also garments (Lev. 13:47–59) and houses (Lev. 14:33–53). Its effect is not just physical, but ritual—the one with *tzara'at* is not just sick, but impure or unclean, and he or she can render others unclean: "Everyone who has *tzara'at* sores is to wear torn clothes and unbound hair, cover his upper lip and cry, 'Unclean! Unclean!' As long as he has sores, he will be unclean; since he is unclean, he must live in isolation; he must live outside the camp" (Lev. 13:45–46). When Moshe's sister Miriam is afflicted with *tzara'at* after she and Aharon slandered him, Aharon pleads with Moshe, "Oh, my lord, do not punish us because we have done foolishly and have sinned. Let her not be as one dead . . ." (Num. 12:11–12 ESV). Commentator Jacob Milgrom says the bearer of *tzara'at* "is treated like a corpse" and can "contaminate not only by direct contact but, unlike all other impurity bearers, also by . . . being under the same roof," and therefore, like a corpse, must be isolated.[9] For this reason, the Talmud (b.Sanhedrin 47a) likens healing *tzara'at* to raising the dead.[10]

But this particular man suffering from *tzara'at* ignores the restrictions and approaches Yeshua, confident that he can cleanse him, "If you are willing." Early manuscripts of Mark record two different versions of Yeshua's response. In both versions he says, "I am willing! Be cleansed!" But some manuscripts have Yeshua

---

9. Jacob Milgrom, *Leviticus 1–16: A New Translation with Introduction and Commentary*, vol. 3, Anchor Yale Bible (New Haven; London: Yale University Press, 2008), 819.
10. The prefixed "b." before the name of the specific talmudic reference indicates it's from the Babylonian Talmud, compiled in the Mesopotamian Jewish community that was dominant in late antiquity. Another version, compiled slightly earlier in the region of Tiberias by the Sea of Galilee, is called the Jerusalem or Palestinian Talmud, prefixed either with "j." or "p.".

moved by anger, not by pity as in CJB.[11] The "anger" interpretation is supported by verse 43, where Mark describes Yeshua "sending out" the man with the same term he just used for casting out demons in 1:34 and 39. And when Yeshua sternly warns the man to keep silent in 1:43, Mark uses a word related to "snorts with anger." Finally, if the early manuscripts that portray Yeshua responding with anger here reflect the original, it's not hard to imagine a scribe or copyist changing this rather shocking word with the more familiar "moved with pity," as in many other early manuscripts.

If Yeshua responds to the request for cleansing with anger, then, what is he angry about? Some commentators imagine he's angry with the purity laws of the Torah and the whole system that regulates and enforces them. This makes little sense, however, in context of this story, since Yeshua sends the man to the priest to validate his cleansing as Moses commanded, indicating Yeshua's respect for the whole system. The popular NIV version translates 1:41 as "Jesus was indignant," suggesting that he may have been indignant at the man questioning whether he'd be willing to cleanse him of *tzara'at*, which would be consistent with Yeshua speaking harshly to him in 1:43 when he "casts him out" to show himself to the *cohen*. But it's more in line with the drama of Episode 1, and all of Mark, to imagine Yeshua as being indignant or angry with the evil forces behind the condition of *tzara'at*. Episode 1 unfolds after Yeshua's encounter with the Adversary in the wilderness (1:13), and shows how the encounter with evil continues in the Galil, with three specific examples: casting out the unclean spirit in the synagogue of K'far-Nachum; healing Shim'on's mother-in-law in his nearby home; and cleansing *tzara'at* here. These are distinct conditions described with specific terminology: Yeshua "casts out" unclean spirits, but he doesn't "cast out" illness, he "heals" it; he "cleanses" the one with *tzara'at*, but not the sick or demonized, who are always described as distinct categories in Mark. But however different these

---

11. For a discussion of the technical issues behind this difference in manuscripts see commentators Marcus, *Mark 1-8*, 209; France, 115; both favor "anger" over "pity" as the original reading, as do a few modern translations. See also Thiessen, 55–60, for an extended treatment of the "anger" issue.

conditions may be, they all reflect the incursion of evil into Israel (and into all nations of humankind), and the authority of the King to turn back this incursion.

One final issue in 1:41 needs to be cleared up before we leave this episode—"Yeshua reached out his hand, *touched him* and said to him, 'I am willing! Be cleansed!'" Touch has a vital role in Yeshua's healing ministry throughout Mark (3:10; 5:27–31; 6:56; 7:33; 8:22–23) . . . but one afflicted with *tzara'at* is unclean and will render unclean anyone who touches him. Readers who imagine that Yeshua is angry at the purity code of Torah see him defying that code by touching a "leper," but the code doesn't specifically forbid touching such a person. It's not a sin (or rejection of Torah) to become unclean; rather it means one has to stay away from holy objects and places (especially the temple) because it would be a sin to pollute them. This brings us to one of the most radical elements in this whole story. Yeshua's holiness isn't corrupted by contact with the unclean as would normally happen; rather it "uncorrupts" the unclean and makes it pure. Touching a leper normally makes one unclean; when Yeshua touches the "leper" he becomes clean. Yeshua displays a holiness that is "contagious,"[12] a "prophetic, invasive holiness that needs no protection, but reaches out to sanctify the profane." [13] This invasive holiness reflects the presence of God's Kingdom pushing back against the forces of death that have broken into the created order, including this little corner of the Galil.

Significantly, Yeshua sends the man to the priest for confirmation of his cleansing, in accord with the Torah. The priest cannot cleanse *tzara'at*—that is the work of ADONAI himself—but he has the authority to certify the cleansing, and Yeshua endorses that authority and its place in providing "a testimony to the people" (1:44). He repeats the familiar command to the cleansed man to tell no one about what's happened, but the man goes out and freely spreads the news (and we don't know whether he ever makes it to

---

12. Thiessen, 20.
13. Mark Kinzer, "Beginning with the End," in *Israel's Messiah and the People of God: A Vision for Messianic Jewish Covenant Fidelity*, ed. Jennifer M. Rosner (Eugene, OR: Cascade, 2011), 107.

the priest), so that Yeshua "could no longer enter a town openly but stayed out in the country" (1:45), ironically reflecting the conditions of someone with *tzara'at*, who has to stay away from towns and dwell apart (Lev. 13:46). A further irony appears in Mark's Greek text, which has Yeshua staying out in "desert places," employing the same Greek term for wilderness as in Yeshua's temptation (1:12–13) and his early-morning retreat to a "lonely spot" (1:35). Yeshua may be dwelling apart, but he's dwelling with ADONAI. And the people still find a way to get to Yeshua and continue "coming to him from all around," setting the stage for our next episode, in which Yeshua will face opposition, not from the spiritual forces of death as in Episode 1, but from human forces and institutions.

Derash

- This episode opens with Yochanan—the one preparing the way of the LORD—locked up in custody. The "voice crying out" is silenced and God's prophetic agenda seems to have suffered a setback. But in the same breath Mark tells us that Yeshua has returned to the Galil proclaiming the heart of God's prophetic agenda, the Kingdom of God. The human stage is filled with conflict, setback, apparent defeat, but amidst all this, Yeshua announces the irrepressible Kingdom message. What lessons for our own lives might we draw from this scene?

- In the Prologue, I defined "gospel" or "good news" in Mark as "besorah," the announcement that "the God of Israel is returning to his people *and* that the people need to return to their God." In this episode, Mark adds that this announcement is about the Kingdom of God. Yeshua has appeared as the promised heir of David, to restore his dynasty, so that all the promises of the Hebrew Prophets can finally be fulfilled (c.f. Acts 3:21). This besorah summons hearers to acknowledge the King and submit their lives to him. How does this besorah of the Kingdom compare to versions of the gospel we most often hear today? To versions you might have already assumed in your understanding of the gospel?

- "Follow me" is Yeshua's foundational command in Mark—not "Believe/trust in me," as emphasized in John and much current religious discourse. This is not to minimize the importance of faith, but simply to point out that real faith is measured in footsteps, steps taken to follow Yeshua and his example of active compassion and service. Mary Oliver captures the impact of Yeshua's call in her poem, "Six recognitions of the Lord":

  > Oh, feed me this day, Holy Spirit, with
  > the fragrance of the fields and the
  > freshness of the oceans which you have
  > made, and help me to hear and to hold
  > in all dearness those exacting and wonderful
  > words of our Lord Christ Jesus, saying:
  > *Follow me.*[14]

  It's a worthy prayer for any disciple, a prayer for daily spiritual empowerment to respond in depth to Yeshua's "exacting and wonderful" call to follow him.

- Mark clearly highlights Shim'on (Peter) in Episode 1, validating the idea that Mark bases his account on Peter's eyewitness testimony. This focus also provides a specific model of following Yeshua, so that discipleship is portrayed not in abstract, but in personal and concrete terms. Shim'on's name is common—perhaps the most popular Jewish man's name of the era[15] — encouraging us to think of him as an Everyman figure, a person like us in many regards, even as we recognize his distinctive values and perspectives as a first-century Galilean Jew. Yeshua calls Shim'on and his brother Andrew to follow him, and immediately adds, "and I will

---

14. Mary Oliver, *Devotions: The Selected Poems of Mary Oliver* (New York: Penguin, 2017), 127.
15. Bauckham, *Eyewitnesses*, 85.

make you into fishers for men!" It seems like fishing for souls is inherent to following Yeshua. How can we incorporate this calling into our own lives? We might be put off (and put others off as well) by standing on a street corner, or a blog site, handing out tracts, so in what other ways can we translate our allegiance to Yeshua from a private and personal matter into a way of life that engages and challenges others? That's how Yeshua lived and he's calling us to follow him.

- For his early-morning prayer Yeshua withdraws to a "lonely spot," or *eremon topos* in the original Greek (1:35). The same word, *eremon*, is translated "wilderness" in the temptation scene of Mark 1:12–13. As in the Torah itself, wilderness is the place of both testing and revelation, of both trial and deep encounter with God. In both aspects, it's a place of separation from the ordinary, domesticated scenes of everyday life. Consider how Yeshua's withdrawal to the wilderness in both its aspects prepares him for the Kingdom mission—and how such withdrawal might work in your life as well.

- Preparation for the Age to Come entails *teshuvah*, "turning" or repentance, including at times turning from the religious status quo. So, we shouldn't be surprised that Yeshua's apocalyptic besorah conflicts with the religious systems that seek to provide guidance and support for this age. In a Jewish context, I term this religious system "halakhic" in contrast with the "apocalyptic" religion that Yeshua embodies. The term halakha is based on the Hebrew word for "walk" or "go." It provides guidance for walking in the ways of Torah amidst the everyday realities of life, in contrast with the apocalyptic emphasis on the life to come. The clash between apocalyptic and halakhic religion will unfold throughout Mark's account, and we'll discover that Yeshua at times integrates both.

Messiah Yeshua walks, and we are called to walk with him, in the midst of a pre-apocalyptic world that awaits full redemption. He proclaims a Kingdom that is near, at hand, accessible, but also not-yet. In the words and deeds of Yeshua the powers of the Kingdom-yet-to-come are already moving in this world despite its unbelief and opposition. In this already-not-yet context he called his first followers, and calls us today to follow as well.

Season 1, Episode 2

Opposition in the Galil

2:1 – 3:6

Overview

Episode 1 closes with Yeshua staying out in the country because his mighty works have drawn such great crowds that he can no longer go into town. After a while, he does return to his home base in K'far-Nachum—and immediately attracts an unmanageable crowd. The crowds include not only multitudes of admirers but also those who oppose him, joining on a human level with the spiritual opposition portrayed in Episode 1. Indeed, Episode 2 includes three specific examples of human opposition, just as Episode 1 included three specific examples of Yeshua's miraculous power.

The first example comes when Yeshua pronounces forgiveness over a paralyzed man brought to him for healing. The surging crowd includes some Torah-teachers who, without saying anything out loud, question Yeshua's right to forgive sins, thinking it's blasphemous to claim a power that belongs only to God.

The second example is set in motion when Yeshua calls the tax collector Levi Ben-Halfai to follow him, and soon after sits down to dine in Levi's house, joining him and many tax collectors and other certifiable sinners. The religious experts somehow notice this assembly and question why Yeshua as a renowned religious teacher would break bread with such people. Yeshua tells them that it's just this sort of person that he is calling. A little later he defuses potential opposition to his practice, or non-practice, of fasting with three pithy metaphors indicating that his presence has brought a new approach to religious practice that can't be confined to the old customs.

Finally, Yeshua encounters opposition over his practice of Shabbat. Contrary to the view of many commentators, he doesn't set aside Shabbat, but he does engage in the sort of interpretation of its rules and restrictions that will characterize discussions among the rabbis in the coming centuries. Yeshua consistently favors more lenient interpretations that permit his hungry disciples to eat as they're traveling with him through a grain field, and allow for healing as a life-giving act reflecting the very meaning of Shabbat.

The culmination of the institutional opposition Yeshua encounters in these episodes is that Pharisees join forces with members of Herod's party—their natural foes—in plotting to do away with Yeshua. Our episode closes with a summary of Yeshua's ministry, showing how its influence is spreading far beyond its home base in the Galil. This summary echoes Mark's summary statements at the end of Episode 1, bookending the account of opposition from the authorities with scenes of Yeshua's overwhelming reception among the people.

Peshat

2:1–12

> After a while, Yeshua returned to K'far-Nachum. The word spread that he was back, ² and so many people gathered around the house that there was no longer any room, not even in front of the door. While he was preaching the message to them, ³ four men came to him carrying a paralyzed man. ⁴ They could not get near Yeshua because of the crowd, so they stripped the roof over the place where he was, made an opening, and lowered the stretcher with the paralytic lying on it. ⁵ Seeing their trust, Yeshua said to the paralyzed man, "Son, your sins are forgiven." ⁶ Some Torah-teachers sitting there thought to themselves, ⁷ "How can this fellow say such a thing? He is blaspheming! Who can forgive sins except God?" ⁸ But immediately Yeshua, perceiving in his spirit what they were thinking, said to them, "Why are you thinking these things? ⁹ Which is easier to say to the paralyzed man? 'Your sins

are forgiven'? or 'Get up, pick up your stretcher and walk'? [10] But look! I will prove to you that the Son of Man has authority on earth to forgive sins." He then said to the paralytic, [11] "I say to you: get up, pick up your stretcher and go home!" [12] In front of everyone the man got up, picked up his stretcher at once and left. They were all utterly amazed and praised God, saying, "We have never seen anything like this!"

Our last episode closed with Yeshua "no longer [able to] enter a town openly" because "people continued coming to him from all around" (1:45). Apparently enough time has passed to allow Yeshua to return to K'far-Nachum. Or it's possible that Yeshua didn't return openly, but in secret, perhaps at night. Either way, the wording of 2:1 suggests that K'far-Nachum is home base for Yeshua, as we discussed in the last episode. The house is soon thronged by crowds seeking to hear and see, and be touched by, the word of authority and power that Yeshua brings with him.

It's no wonder that four men carrying a pallet bearing a fifth man, their paralyzed friend, can't get through this crowd to get close to Yeshua. But they don't give up. A house like this would normally have a ladder or staircase to access its flat roof, where the owners might sleep on a warm night or do some tasks that required more space than the small indoor space allowed. Somehow the four comrades got their paralyzed friend up to the roof. They put the stretcher down and began digging through the layers of reeds and clay and thicker branches that rested on the log roof beams. It's a testimony to the noise level and intensity of the scene in the house that no one paid attention to what was going on overhead until the friends broke through and lowered the stretcher down to Yeshua's feet. Mark says that Yeshua saw their "trust," more commonly translated "faith," here in 2:5. In Mark's account, trust or faith is not an abstract quality, not something that happens just in the heart or the head, but something that is, or inevitably becomes, visible. It's also more active than "faith" as we commonly use the word, and better captured by the "trust/trusting" terminology of CJB. The friends trusted that Yeshua could heal, and so they did whatever it took to access his healing power—and that's the trust that Yeshua saw.

Yeshua's response to this trust was even more striking than the roof demolition and lowering of the stretcher: "Son, your sins are forgiven." Before we consider the radical implications of these words, we should note that linking healing and forgiveness doesn't mean that disease is always caused by sin. In this particular case, though, there is a linkage between sickness and sin, either in fact or in the mind of the paralytic. It may be cases like this that the talmudic sage Rav Hiyya has in mind when he says: "A sick man does not recover from his sickness until all his sins are forgiven him" (b.Nedarim 41a).[1] In the New Testament, Ya'akov (James) instructs a sick person to ask for prayer and anointing by the elders, and the "prayer offered with trust will heal the one who is ill — the Lord will restore his health; and if he has committed sins, he will be forgiven" (James 5:15). The implication here is that the sins will be forgiven by the same Lord who restores health. But when Yeshua tells the paralytic, "Your sins are forgiven," the Torah-teachers who are sitting there taking it all in assume—correctly as it turns out—that Yeshua is pronouncing forgiveness on his own authority, and they object, "Who can forgive sins except God?" (2:7).

> Since it is God who forgives, [the Torah-teachers] view his statement as *blasphemy,* but Jesus' followers claimed the power of forgiveness (cf. Mt. 16.19; 18.18; Jn 20.22–23). . . . In the Hebrew Bible, humans may intercede with God to forgive, but they—even Moses—never forgive directly (e.g. Num. 14.19; Am. 7.2).[2]

The power to forgive "claimed" by Jesus' followers in this note derives from a relationship with Messiah. They/we forgive on the basis of our union with the forgiving Messiah. It's not simply a human virtue (although it is also that), but a reflection of our priestly

---

[1]. Rav Hiyya goes on to cite Psalm 103:3, "He forgives all your offenses, / he heals all your diseases."
[2]. Wills, "Mark," JANT, 74.

status in Messiah, particularly in the very verses cited here, Matthew 16:19; 18:18; and John 20.22–23.

In the little house in K'far-Nachum, Yeshua seems to be forgiving sin on his own authority, removing with his own word any obstacles to healing the paralytic. In other words, he doesn't contradict the Torah-teachers' objection that only God can forgive. Instead, he tells them he'll prove that he has unique, God-given authority by healing the man right before their eyes. Yeshua introduces the title "Son of Man" here, which becomes the title he uses for himself most frequently in Mark (2:10, 28; 8:31, 38; 9:9, 12, 31; 10:33, 45; 13:26; 14:21 [twice], 41, 62), This phrase could simply mean a human being, as it does in its many appearances throughout Ezekiel (starting with 2:1) but that's not how Yeshua is using it here. Yeshua is not saying that humans in general, all "sons of man," have authority to forgive sin, because he validates that authority by miraculously healing a complete paralytic, which humans in general cannot do. Indeed, the people crowding around him are amazed, saying, "We have never seen anything like this!" (2:12).

> The authority given to the Son of Man is proved by a miracle performed not by people in general but by this one Son of Man in particular, in such a way as to set him apart from the rest of humanity, who recognise a unique power at work, and ascribe glory to God (v. 12).[3]

What does this "Son of Man" title mean on the lips of Yeshua? Daniel Boyarin, a preeminent scholar of early Jewish literature and himself an observant Jew, traces the impact of Daniel's "Son of Man" imagery within the Jewish world of Yeshua's day.

> The reasons that many Jews came to believe that Jesus was divine was because they were already expecting that the Messiah/Christ would be a god-man. *This expectation was part and parcel of*

---

3. France, 128.

Jewish tradition. The Jews had learned this by a careful reading of the Book of Daniel. . . .[4]

This "careful reading" of Daniel would include 7:13–14, which is a key to many crucial passages in Mark:

> I kept watching the night visions,
> when I saw, coming with the clouds of heaven,
> someone like a son of man.
> He approached the Ancient One
> and was led into his presence.
> To him was given rulership,
> glory and a kingdom,
> so that all peoples, nations and languages
> should serve him.
> His rulership is an eternal rulership
> that will not pass away;
> and his kingdom is one
> that will never be destroyed.

When Yeshua claims that "the Son of Man has authority on earth to forgive sins" (Mark 2:10), he is invoking the "rulership" over all peoples, nations and languages declared in Daniel 7:14. As Boyarin notes,

> Throughout the Gospel, whenever Jesus claims [authority or "rulership"] to perform that which appears to be the prerogative of divinity, it is the very [authority] of the Son of Man that is being claimed, which is to say a scriptural authority based on a very close reading of Daniel 7.[5]

As we'll see, this understanding of the Son of Man terminology in Mark is an essential key to interpreting his entire Besorah, including another incident of controversy later in Episode 2.

---

4. Daniel Boyarin, *The Jewish Gospels: The Story of the Jewish Christ* (New York: New Press, 2012), 57, emphasis original.
5. Boyarin, 58.

2:13–22

¹³ Yeshua went out again by the lake. All the crowd came to him, and he began teaching them. ¹⁴ As he passed on from there, he saw Levi Ben-Halfai sitting in his tax-collection booth and said to him, "Follow me!" And he got up and followed him.

¹⁵ As Yeshua was in Levi's house eating, many tax-collectors and sinners were sitting with Yeshua and his *talmidim*, for there were many of them among his followers. ¹⁶ When the Torah-teachers and the *P'rushim* saw that he was eating with sinners and tax-collectors, they said to his *talmidim*, "Why does he eat with tax-collectors and sinners?" ¹⁷ But, hearing the question, Yeshua answered them, "The ones who need a doctor aren't the healthy but the sick. I didn't come to call the 'righteous' but sinners!"

¹⁸ Also Yochanan's *talmidim* and the *P'rushim* were fasting; and they came and asked Yeshua, "Why is it that Yochanan's *talmidim* and the *talmidim* of the *P'rushim* fast, but your *talmidim* don't fast?" ¹⁹ Yeshua answered them, "Can wedding guests fast while the bridegroom is still with them? As long as they have the bridegroom with them, fasting is out of the question. ²⁰ But the time will come when the bridegroom is taken away from them; and when that day comes, they will fast. ²¹ No one sews a piece of unshrunk cloth on an old coat; if he does, the new patch tears away from the old cloth and leaves a worse hole. ²² And no one puts new wine in old wineskins; if he does, the wine will burst the skins, and both the wine and the skins will be ruined. Rather, new wine is for freshly prepared wineskins."

It's not hard to picture Yeshua leaving the little house in K'far-Nachum, perhaps the next morning, and taking a short walk to the peaceful shore of Lake Kinneret. But now the shore isn't so peaceful—the crowd shows up there, too. Yeshua resumes teaching them, as he "came out" to do (1:38). As he's passing on from the shore, he encounters Levi Ben-Halfai sitting in his toll-booth, where he'd have access to travelers on the lakeside road as well as on the lake itself. K'far-Nachum was a border town between the territories of the rulers Antipas and Philip, and thus an appropriate place to collect taxes or fees.[6] Like Shim'on and Andrew, Yaakov and Yochanan, Levi hears Yeshua's call and immediately gets up and starts following him. But unlike the first four followers, Levi is a disreputable character, a tax-collector serving Rome or one of its client governments.

As when he forgave the paralyzed man, Yeshua's choice of Levi is provocative, bound to stir up controversy. And he stirs up more controversy by joining Levi at his home for dinner, along with many other tax-collectors and sinners. Tax-collectors are "sinners" simply because of their profession—which was usually made more despicable by the addition of corrupt practices—but not all sinners are tax-collectors; that label applies to people practicing obvious sins in general. This is not the sort of crowd that any religious leader should break bread with. Somehow a few Torah-teachers and *P'rushim* see this scene (had they also been invited to the dinner?) and question what Yeshua was doing. He responds with a saying that goes beyond explaining the dinner arrangements to characterize his entire ministry: "I didn't come to call the 'righteous' but sinners!" Not only does Yeshua remind us of his target audience, but he raises the question, as in 1:38, of where he came from when he came to call sinners. Is he referring to his arrival in the Galil after the arrest of Yochanan (1:14), or to a mysterious emergence from the presence of his Father hinted at in 1:11 and later at the transfiguration (9:7)?

Some of Yeshua's critics are Torah-teachers, commonly translated "scribes" (from the Greek *grammateus* [sing.]), and first mentioned in 1:22, where their teaching is contrasted with Yeshua's teaching "with authority." As the original Greek implies, the Torah-teachers are experts in the text and in the details of its interpretation, and in Mark they often find fault with Yeshua, regardless of his evident authority, because he operates outside of their interpretive grid. Other critics are *P'rushim*, or Pharisees. It's possible for one

---

6. France, 131.

person to be both "scribe" and "Pharisee," but the terms are not synonymous. Torah-teachers focus on technical expertise with the text; P'rushim are more intent on how to live out the text. They comprised one of four Jewish "schools" in the second-temple era described by Josephus, along with Sadducees, Essenes, and a "Fourth Philosophy." The term P'rushim is related to Hebrew terminology for separation, and they did separate into *chavurot* or "voluntary eating fellowships" that combined ritually pure dining with in-depth discussion of the Torah.[7] It's easy to imagine how they'd be scandalized by Yeshua, a self-professed teacher in Israel, dining with such recognizably "sick" folk (2:17).

In the same context, Yeshua draws flak because he and his talmidim don't join in a fast being observed not only by the Torah-teachers and P'rushim, but also by the followers of Yochanan. We're not told the occasion of this fast, but it's clearly not the one day of fasting ordained by the Torah, Yom Kippur, because Yeshua isn't accused of violating Torah here. Instead the issue, as with the dinner at Levi's house, involves traditions and interpretations that are one step removed from the actual text of Scripture. These traditions, Yeshua claims, must be flexible, especially in the presence of the "bridegroom," the one who will appear at the eschatological feast of the Age to Come, as in Isaiah 62:45, where ADONAI himself is the bridegroom (compare Isa. 61:10–11; Hos. 2:16–20; Rev. 19:7–9). But even in citing this joyous analogy, Yeshua hints at dark times coming first, when the bridegroom is "taken away from them" (2:20)—doubtless referring to his arrest and crucifixion already looming on the horizon, the first hint of what will become a dominant theme in Mark: the sufferings of the Son of Man. Then Yeshua changes metaphors, comparing his presence to new, unshrunk cloth that can't be used to patch an old garment, and—even more memorably—to new wine that can't be contained in an old, inflexible wineskin. The old garment and wineskin shouldn't be

---

7. Marcus, *Mark 1–8*, 519.

understood as the Torah, in contrast with the new era of the Spirit that Yeshua introduces. Rather they represent the religious status quo, which is often incompatible with the Kingdom of God that has now drawn near. In the following section Yeshua demonstrates the sort of Torah flexibility that his presence calls for.

The juxtaposition of these two metaphors—wedding/bridegroom and new wine/new patch—yields a further insight. The bridegroom is present, but will be taken away; the new wine is here to stay. By his very act of appearing among his people, Yeshua has inaugurated the Kingdom, but for the Kingdom to be fully established, he must be taken away for a time. This picture reflects the already-but-not-yet theme often referred to by commentators and theologians: the Kingdom of God is *already* here (or at hand as in Mark 1:15), *but not yet* here in fullness. The already-but-not-yet theme sheds light on many passages in the New Testament and will run throughout Mark's account.

2:23–3:6

> [23] One Shabbat Yeshua was passing through some wheat fields; and as they went along, his *talmidim* began picking heads of grain. [24] The *P'rushim* said to him, "Look! Why are they violating Shabbat?" [25] He said to them, "Haven't you ever read what David did when he and those with him were hungry and needed food? [26] He entered the House of God when Abiathar was *cohen gadol* and ate the Bread of the Presence," — which is forbidden for anyone to eat but the *cohanim* — "and even gave some to his companions." [27] Then he said to them, "Shabbat was made for mankind, not mankind for Shabbat; [28] so the Son of Man is Lord even of Shabbat."
>
> 3 Yeshua went again into a synagogue, and a man with a shriveled hand was there. [2] Looking for a reason to accuse him of something, people watched him carefully to see if he would heal him on Shabbat. [3] He said to the man with the shriveled hand, "Come up where we can see you!" [4] Then to them he said, "What is permitted on Shabbat? Doing good or doing evil? Saving life or

killing?" But they said nothing. ⁵ Then, looking them over and feeling both anger with them and sympathy for them at the stoniness of their hearts, he said to the man, "Hold out your hand." As he held it out, it became restored. ⁶ The *P'rushim* went out and immediately began plotting with some members of Herod's party how to do away with him.

The P'rushim accuse Yeshua's followers of violating Shabbat by picking and eating heads of grain as they walk through the field. Yeshua doesn't defend his men by saying that Shabbat is an old wineskin ready to be replaced. Rather, he argues from the Tanakh for the sort of flexible wineskin of Torah that is suitable for the kingdom that has drawn near. Notably, as the Son of David (10:47–49; 11:10) Yeshua invokes an example of Torah flexibility from the life of David (1 Sam. 21:1–6). When David and his men were hungry and in need of food, the normal limitations of temple (or tabernacle) practice could be temporarily set aside. Yeshua mentions this incident taking place "when Abiathar was *cohen gadol* [high priest]," but 1 Samuel portrays David interacting with the priest Ahimelech, father of the better-known Abiathar (1 Sam. 22:21–22; 23:6, 9; 30:7). Commentators deal with this apparent contradiction at length, with various solutions, including the idea that Yeshua is referring to the whole section of 1 Samuel where Abiathar is found, so that "when Abiathar was *cohen gadol*" might better be translated, "in the days of Abiathar," or "in the passage about Abiathar."[8] AJ Levine provides an intriguing alternative: "I think Mark has Jesus deliberately misquote the story in 1 Samuel 21 to show the lack of knowledge on the part of the Pharisees. And so Mark 2 raises the question of how well we know the texts we consider to be sacred."[9]

David, of course, is the founder of the dynasty that will build the temple under Solomon and sustain it for centuries, so it's all the more fitting that tabernacle/temple practice be adapted to serve

---

8. See David Turner and Darrell L. Bock, *Cornerstone Biblical Commentary, Vol 11: Matthew and Mark* (Carol Stream, IL: Tyndale House, 2005), 423–424.
9. Levine, *Mark* 19.

David's life and well-being. Shabbat is to be honored, of course, but so is human life and, as JANT comments, "David could supersede the law to meet human needs"—especially because of who David is. Far from invalidating the teachings of the Hebrew Scriptures, then, Yeshua is engaging in the sort of discussion of Jewish law or halakha that will become a hallmark of rabbinic literature in the centuries ahead. What is new and unique in Yeshua's halakha is its apocalyptic element, the nearness of the Davidic Kingdom of God because of the presence of the heir of David, Messiah Yeshua himself. His halakha is radical, but it is true to form in seeking to uphold and fulfill the teachings of Torah within the changing circumstances of real life, including the approach of the Kingdom.

As Yeshua develops his halakhic argument, however, he doesn't call himself Son of David, but Son of Man, as he did back in 2:10. But first, he cites a principle that will appear in similar form in later rabbinic discussions: "Shabbat was made for mankind, not mankind for Shabbat." In the Talmud, many years later, some rabbis are discussing exceptions to the rules of Shabbat, such as circumcision on the eighth day, even if it's a Shabbat, or taking action to save a life. Rabbi Yonatan ben Yosef (who lived in the second century CE) cites Exodus 31:14, "For it [Shabbat] is holy *to you*," to argue, "it is committed to your hands, not you to its hands" (b.Yoma 85b). Numerous rabbis are involved in this discussion, citing details in the text of Torah along with logical arguments to reach a level of consensus, if not total agreement. Yeshua also cites Scripture, but invokes his own authority as Son of Man, who is seen in Daniel 7:14 as God's agent upon the earth, sharing in divine authority. Hence he has authority to regulate Shabbat observance, and does so here in accord with the same principle invoked centuries later in a different context in the Talmudic reference above.

To be fair, Yeshua and his disciples aren't facing the sort of threat to life or health that the rabbis would see as overriding the Shabbat regulations, but that may be the very point here, as Boyarin notes: "not only does the Torah authorize healing of the deathly sick on the Sabbath, but the Messiah himself, the Son of Man, is given sovereignty to decide how to further extend and interpret the Sabbath law."[10] Therefore, "here in Mark we find a Jesus who is fulfilling the Torah, not abrogating it."[11] Hence the title "Son of Man" is not just introduced in Episode 2, but is defined and illustrated on the way to addressing the question that underlies Mark's whole account, "Who is Yeshua?"

But of course Yeshua's response to his critics doesn't settle the issue of proper Shabbat observance. Indeed, as a halakhic issue, it's going to generate abundant discussion down through the centuries. So, in our next Shabbat event, healing a man with a shriveled hand (3:1–6), Yeshua again isn't questioning the validity of Shabbat itself, but arguing over how Shabbat is best observed. He asks, "What is permitted on Shabbat? Doing good or doing evil? Saving life or killing?" "Saving life" is the idea behind the later formulation of *pikuach nefesh*, literally "watching over a life (or soul)," namely that saving a human life overrides all religious regulations, including the Shabbat restrictions. Yeshua's interlocutors should agree with the priority of life, but they remain silent. As in 1:41–43, Mark notes Yeshua's emotions here, "feeling both anger with [his critics] and sympathy for them at the stoniness of their hearts" (3:5). As Mark reveals who Yeshua is throughout his narrative, he includes a portrayal of his very human emotional state; Yeshua, the exalted Son of Man, faces the full range of feelings experienced by all the sons of man.

As if to underline how fitting it is for Yeshua to heal on Shabbat, Mark describes this healing in passive terms: Yeshua doesn't touch the man or even tell him to be healed; he only says, "Hold out your hand"—which is perfectly acceptable to say on Shabbat—and it becomes restored (3:5; compare the passive description of forgiveness in 2:5). In a sense it's God healing on Shabbat, so it must be okay for Yeshua to do so as well.

---

10. Boyarin, 67.
11. Boyarin, 65.

But how is healing a shriveled hand by whatever means equivalent to saving a life? In the kingdom ushered in by Yeshua, all illness and infirmity is seen as an incursion of death into life, and pushing back such incursion is always urgent—hence Mark repeatedly uses the Greek term *eutheos*, "immediately" (40 times in Mark out of 80 times in the whole New Testament), especially in reference to Yeshua's acts of healing and deliverance. In *Jesus and the Forces of Death*, Matthew Thiessen argues that ancient Jewish thinking associates illness with death, and continues: "If sickness is closely associated with death, then the healing of illnesses, of whatever sort, is an effort to move someone across the barrier that separates life from death and illness."[12] The "forces of death," whether sickness or demonic oppression, have no place within the kingdom that Yeshua has inaugurated, especially on the holy day of Shabbat. So Yeshua heals the man with the shriveled hand, not to challenge Shabbat restrictions, but to honor the spirit of Shabbat.

Ironically, Yeshua's religious opponents among the Pharisees could well be accused of violating the same spirit of Shabbat when they "immediately" (there's that *eutheos* word again) begin plotting with some Herodians to do away with Yeshua.[13] Making plans for the sort of violent deed implied in "doing away with" someone has no place on Shabbat as the day of peace, when it's forbidden to make concrete plans for any sort of work, let alone violence. The original Greek term for "doing away with" is the same one the unclean spirit used back 1:24—"What do you want with us, Yeshua from Natzeret? Have you come to *destroy* us?" Perhaps Mark is hinting at the underlying source of the Pharisees' opposition, just as Yeshua was hinting at the same issue when he asked whether "doing evil" or "killing" were permitted on Shabbat (3:4). The Pharisees, in their

---

12. Thiessen, 167.
13. The term "Herodians" is left undefined in Mark and appears only here and in 12:13, and its parallel, Matt. 22:16. It likely refers to Jewish supporters of the rather controversial Herodian dynasty of the time.

pious zeal, are ignoring the very Torah they seek to defend and channeling demonic energies.

Episode 2 closes with the P'rushim and Herodians plotting Yeshua's end:

> The powers that will drive Jesus to death are beginning to materialize; near the beginning of his ministry, the end is already in sight. But this very fact seems to give a new urgency to his mission. The next passage [our Episode 3] will highlight the eschatological gathering of "all Israel" to Jesus and his renewed success in the battle against the demons.[14]

Episode 2, "Opposition in the Galil," opened with Yeshua's healing of a paralyzed man, and it closes with his healing of a "shriveled" and thereby paralyzed hand. Our episode closes, but opposition to Yeshua will continue throughout his ministry, as will his power to heal and restore those who are immobilized by the forces arrayed against God and his kingdom. In the episodes to come, the confrontation will only intensify.

Derash

- Given the pervasiveness of both sin and of sickness, the linkage between sin and sickness may also be pervasive, but we must avoid attributing particularly grave illness to particularly grave sin (see John 9:1–3). So, in ministering to the sick, we must never blame them for their condition, but at the same time we can be ready to offer the help actually needed, which may include teshuvah and forgiveness. Teshuvah plays no explicit role in the healing of the paralytic (Mark 2:1–12), but the act of digging through the roof to get to Yeshua might be interpreted as an act of teshuvah. What does it suggest about the relationship between teshuvah and faith/trust, and healing itself?

---

14. Marcus, *Mark 1–8*, 254.

- Yeshua says, "The ones who need a doctor aren't the healthy but the sick. I didn't come to call the 'righteous' but sinners!" (Mark 2:17). In contemporary America, those who profess faith in Yeshua are often dismissed as self-righteous, as focusing on the "healthy" middle class and obsessed with celebrity and worldly success. Such criticisms cannot be simply dismissed as the words of the unbelievers. Instead, if we desire to genuinely follow Yeshua, we might find it worthwhile to remind ourselves of these words of the Master and assess how well we're enacting them in real life.

  One commentator's note on 2:21–22 is particularly relevant to this sort of assessment:

  > The question posed by the image of the wedding feast and the two atom-like parables is not whether disciples will, like sewing a new patch on an old garment or refilling an old container, make room for Jesus in their already full agendas and lives. The question is whether they will forsake business as usual and join the wedding celebration; whether they will become entirely new receptacles for the expanding fermentation of Jesus and the gospel in their lives.[15]

  Surely these are questions worthy of our consideration.

- Yeshua's disputes with the religious leaders reflect the tension between the apocalyptic and the halakhic approach to religious life, as we've noted. But even as he contends with the halakhic leaders, he argues in halakhic terms, as in 2:25–28 and 3:4. Even as he pushes for a more flexible, apocalyptic application of Torah, he honors Torah as the word of God—thus providing a model for his followers. We'll see this dynamic tension between the halakhic and the apocalyptic dimensions as we continue on through Mark.

---

15. James R. Edwards, *The Gospel according to Mark*, The Pillar New Testament Commentary (Grand Rapids, MI; Leicester, England: Eerdmans; Apollos, 2002), 92.

- In Jewish practice we honor Shabbat as a gift from God, which he commands us to "remember" (Exod. 20:8). Rabbi Lord Jonathan Sacks wrote concerning *Havdala*, the conclusion of Shabbat:

  > Havdala is to the end of Shabbat what Kiddush [the blessing over wine] is to the beginning: the marking of a transition from secular to holy time and vice versa. It is our way of fulfilling the commandment to 'Remember the Sabbath day,' understood by the Sages to mean: 'Remember it at the beginning and at the end' (*Pesahim* 106a).[16]

  The command to remember means that Israel, the Jewish people, are responsible for ushering in Shabbat with our blessings and for providing the transition from Shabbat to the ordinary weekdays with the ritual of Havdala. In this sense, Shabbat is made or given for humankind. The unique, new-wine element that Yeshua brings to remembering Shabbat is that the Kingdom of God, the profound Shalom of the Age to Come, which Shabbat observance has always hoped for and anticipated, is now present in Messiah.

---

16. Koren Siddur, 724–25. The unique relationship of Israel, the Jewish people, with Shabbat is noted in Exodus 31:16–17.

SEASON 1, EPISODE 3

THE CALL OF THE TWELVE

3:7–35

Overview

Episode 2 ends with the ominous collusion of Pharisees and Herodians in "the synagogue,"[1] probably the synagogue in K'far-Nachum that Yeshua visited back in 1:21. The forces that oppose Yeshua and will eventually bring about his death are already gathering, early in his ministry. Here in the familiar terrain of the Galil, the stage is beginning to be set for the final scenes of Yeshua's ministry in Jerusalem.

As Episode 3 opens, then, we are still in the region of K'far-Nachum, and Yeshua walks out of town with his talmidim to nearby Lake Kinneret. Crowds follow him there, not just from the Galil, as in Episode 1, but from Judah and Jerusalem, and from beyond the Jordan. Yeshua continues healing many and driving out unclean spirits, and he also continues with his own plan for revealing himself, again forbidding the unclean spirits to make him known. Yeshua's ministry of power and compassion is expanding, as is opposition to it, and this moves Yeshua to take another step in accomplishing his mission.

From the shores of the Kinneret, he departs to higher ground, where he will enlist twelve men from among his followers to be with him and to be sent out to preach the kingdom with authority. Immediately after this strategic advance, as if in response, the

---

1. CJB has "a synagogue," but numerous translations have "the synagogue," reflecting various ancient manuscripts. The definite article suggests that it's the synagogue in K'far-Nachum, which would align with the geographical flow of the drama.

59

strategy of opposition advances with a new accusation against Yeshua, the claim that he is casting out demons by the power of the "prince of demons," Satan himself. Yeshua warns that such a claim constitutes a grave insult, blasphemy, against the true source of his power, the Holy Spirit.

Our episode closes with Yeshua's own family joining, perhaps unwittingly, the demonic and institutional forces that oppose him. They're concerned that he's not in his right mind and they seek to interrupt his ministry. Yeshua declares that his true family are those around him who do what God wants.

Peshat

3:7–12

> [7] Yeshua went off with his *talmidim* to the lake, and great numbers followed him from the Galil. [8] When they heard what he was doing, great numbers also followed him from Y'hudah, Yerushalayim, Idumea, the territory beyond the Yarden, and the Tzor-Tzidon area. [9] He told his *talmidim* to have a boat ready for him, so that he could escape the crush of the crowd if necessary, [10] for he had healed many people, and all the sick kept pressing forward to touch him. [11] Whenever the unclean spirits saw him, they would fall down in front of him and scream, "You are the Son of God!" [12] But he warned them strictly not to make him known.

Mark 3:7–12 serves as a bridge between Episode 2 and Episode 3, providing a summary of Yeshua's ministry that sets the stage for his enlistment of the Twelve in the following verses. Furthermore, 3:7–12 seems to form an inclusio with 1:45, the close of Episode 1, bookending the account of opposition in the Galil in Episode 2 with portrayals of Yeshua's overwhelming reception among the people before and after. The places named in 3:7–12 all have substantial Jewish populations, but they extend beyond the Galil and include Gentile areas such as the region of Tyre and Sidon (Tzor-Tzidon in CJB), hinting at the authority of the Son of Man among "all peoples, nations and languages" (Dan. 7:14). The geographical detail here also alerts us to how far people were willing to travel, that is, to walk, in many cases for days, to see and hear Yeshua in person. This passage anticipates a Gentile mission to come, but Yeshua doesn't inaugurate it at this point. He simply continues healing and driving out demons, some of which make the clearest declaration of Yeshua's identity, screaming "You are the Son of God!"

As in 1:25 and 34, Yeshua silences the demons, because this announcement of his true identity is premature and he wouldn't want it to come from unclean spirits in any event. Commentator William Lane brings out another possible reason for Yeshua's silencing of the demons.

> The demons addressed Jesus as the divine Son of God in a futile attempt to render him harmless. These cries of recognition were designed to control him and strip him of his power, in accordance with the conception that knowledge of the precise name or quality of a person confers mastery over him.[2]

In the face of opposition both natural and supernatural, however, Yeshua retains control and sets the pace of initiating his Kingdom. In the next episode, Yeshua inaugurates the next phase in his strategy of revelation by appointing twelve of his followers to be with him, to proclaim the Kingdom, and to have authority to expel demons (3:13–15).

3:13–19

> [13] Then he went up into the hill country and summoned to himself those he wanted, and they came to him. [14] He appointed twelve to be with him, to be sent out to preach [15] and to have authority to expel demons:
>
> [16] Shim'on, to whom he gave another name, "Kefa";

---

2. Lane, 130. See also Schnabel, 84.

[17] Ya'akov Ben-Zavdai and Yochanan, Ya'akov's brother — to them he gave the name "B'nei-Regesh" (that is, "Thunderers");

[18] Andrew, Philip, Bar-Talmai, Mattityahu, T'oma, Ya'akov Ben-Halfai, Taddai, Shim'on the Zealot,

[19] and Y'hudah from K'riot, the one who betrayed him.

Still in the Galil, Yeshua leaves the shores of Lake Kinneret for the higher ground surrounding it. "Hill country" in CJB is usually translated as "the mountain" (ESV, NRSV, TLV, Marcus), so that Yeshua's going up hints at the repeated scenes of Moses ascending Mount Sinai. Two scenes in particular stand out. In Exodus 19, Moses goes up to God (v. 3) and the LORD reveals his intention to make Israel "my own treasure," or *segulah* in Hebrew, meaning a "treasured possession" (v. 5). This terminology is echoed in Mark's description of the Twelve as "those he wanted" and those appointed to be with him (Mark 3:13–14). In another ascent of Mount Sinai, this time accompanied for most of the way by the seventy elders, Moses erects twelve pillars representing the twelve tribes of Israel before he goes up (Exod. 24:1–4). Thus, both Mark and Exodus link ascending the mountain with choosing the people of God and with the number twelve, hinting that Yeshua is a new Moses, or a prophet like Moses, as promised in the Torah (Deut. 18:15–18).

A look at Messiah's call itself reveals seven components: He

1) summoned to himself

2) those he wanted, and

3) they came to him.

4) He appointed twelve to

5) be with him,

6) to be sent out to preach and

7) to have authority to expel demons.

The Twelve are called from among the larger body of followers into an especially close relationship with Yeshua. Before they are sent out, they are appointed to "be with him." The emphasis here is on a deepening of master-disciple relationship rather than on the creation of a new ecclesial office of "Apostle," a term attached to the Twelve in other contexts, but which does not appear in this passage in many of the early manuscripts.[3] The Greek verb form *apostello* does lie behind "sent out" in 3:14, but what's emphasized here is the closeness of relationship and the reality of learning from Yeshua before being sent out on a mission for Yeshua.

Mark names each one of the Twelve, even though seven of them, listed in 3:18 from Philip through Shim'on the Zealot, don't appear anywhere else in his account. Richard Bauckham describes the Twelve as a sort of "collegium" or panel of eyewitnesses to Yeshua's ministry, a team that remained in place after the resurrection with which Mark concludes.[4] The same team appears by name also in Acts 1:13, and Peter explains that Y'hudah, Judas Iscariot, one of the Twelve, must be replaced.

> Therefore, one of the men who have been with us continuously throughout the time the Lord Yeshua traveled around among us, from the time Yochanan was immersing people until the day Yeshua was taken up from us — one of these must become a witness with us to his resurrection. (Acts 1:21–22)

Throughout Acts the Apostles are key figures, ensuring the continuity of Messiah Yeshua's message in the new and expansive conditions of the post-resurrection world. It's evidence of the early, eyewitness nature of Mark's account that he doesn't treat apostleship as the foundational office recognized in Acts and other, later,

---

[3]. Many manuscripts and translations add a parenthetical note to verse 14, as in ESV: "And he appointed twelve (whom he also named apostles)." Amid numerous references to the Twelve and to disciples in general, the word "apostle" appears only one other time in Mark, at 6:30.

[4]. Bauckham, 94. Bauckham addresses the discrepancies between two of the names in the list of Twelve—Levi vs Matthew as the tax collector, and Thaddeus in Mark vs Judas son of James in Luke and Acts. See Bauckham's Table of the Names of the Twelve on p. 113.

writings of the New Testament.[5] Still, Mark's list of all twelve names establishes the continuity between his account and the eyewitness testimony accepted by the Jerusalem Yeshua-community of Acts after Messiah's resurrection.

But why the number twelve, specifically? Twelve, of course, echoes the Twelve Tribes of Israel, as we've noted, and some scholars have taken its appearance here as a *replacement* of the Twelve Tribes, the core of a "new Israel." But the Twelve are better understood as an *affirmation* of the original Twelve Tribes of Israel, which are symbolically represented by the twelve disciples chosen by the Messiah of Israel. Bauckham is particularly helpful here.

> Israel in its beginning in the wilderness was taken as prototypical for the restored Israel of the messianic age. Jesus' appointment of the Twelve symbolized the claim that in his own ministry this messianic restoration of Israel had already begun in nucleus. The appointment of the Twelve constituted, as several scholars have argued, a prophetic sign of what God was doing in Jesus' ministry.[6]

And what God was "doing in Jesus' ministry" included the fulfillment of all his promises to Israel. In addition to representing the Twelve Tribes of Israel and their future restoration, the Twelve are being sent out to the Twelve Tribes of their day to preach and expel demons—that is, to inaugurate the Davidic kingdom as a step toward the restoration to come. There's no indication that their mission takes them beyond the Jewish towns and villages of the Galil. But it is in accord with (and not replacing) Israel's calling that the Twelve sent to all Israel will eventually have an impact far beyond Israel.

---

5. See for example the frequent use of the term "apostles" in Luke's Gospel—six times compared to once or twice in Mark—or Paul's repeated use of Apostle as an authoritative title. (At least some of Paul's letters are earlier than Mark's Gospel, but Mark's eyewitness sources are earlier still.)

6. Bauckham, 95. The idea of the Twelve as a prophetic sign is borne out in Matt. 19:28//Luke 22:30; Rev. 7, 21.

3:19b–35

Then he entered a house; [20] and once more, such a crowd came together that they couldn't even eat. [21] When his family heard about this, they set out to take charge of him; for they said, "He's out of his mind!"

[22] The Torah-teachers who came down from Jerusalem said, "He has Ba'al-Zibbul in him," and "It is by the ruler of the demons that he expels the demons." [23] But he called them and spoke to them in parables: "How can Satan expel Satan? [24] If a kingdom is divided against itself, that kingdom can't survive; [25] and if a household is divided against itself, that household can't survive. [26] So if Satan has rebelled against himself and is divided, he can't survive either; and that's the end of him. [27] Furthermore, no one can break into a strong man's house and make off with his possessions unless he first ties up the strong man. After that, he can ransack his house. [28] Yes! I tell you that people will be forgiven all sins and whatever blasphemies they utter; [29] however, someone who blasphemes against the *Ruach HaKodesh* never has forgiveness but is guilty of an eternal sin." [30] For they had been saying, "He has an unclean spirit in him."

[31] Then his mother and brothers arrived. Standing outside, they sent a message asking for him. [32] A crowd was sitting around him; and they said to him, "Your mother and your brothers are outside, asking for you." [33] He replied, "Who are my mother and my brothers?" [34] Looking at those seated in a circle around him, he said, "See! Here are my mother and my brothers! [35] Whoever does what God wants is my brother, sister and mother!"

This section involves an intercalation or sandwich structure: the scene of Yeshua's conflict with the religious authorities is placed between two slices of conflict involving Yeshua and his own family. As Yeshua's mission intensifies through sending the Twelve, so does the opposition, both on the familial/communal level and on the institutional level, which is unwittingly reinforcing the spiritual-level opposition.

In the middle scene, scribes come down from Jerusalem, the religious-political center, to the Galil, where Yeshua is ministering, which entails a journey of three to seven days.[7] Apparently, as Yeshua's fame spreads beyond the Galil, so does the institutional anxiety. The Jerusalem authorities show up with some new talking points: "He is possessed by Beelzebul" and "by the prince of demons he casts out the demons." Yeshua's supernatural healing power and his evident authority over the demonic realm reveal his anointing by the Spirit (1:10) and validate his self-identity as the Son of Man (2:10, 28). These scribes have come up with a way to invalidate Yeshua's works of power, and thereby his entire ministry. Yeshua's response to their accusation reveals much about the spiritual conflict raging around him: First, this conflict is not random but led and presumably coordinated by the "prince of demons," whom Yeshua's critics call Beelzebub, and whom Yeshua identifies as Satan, the same being he encountered in his initial temptation scene (1:12–13).

This hint of a coordinated effort is reinforced when Yeshua refers to the forces of evil as a "kingdom," which is by definition unified under its king. If the kingdom were divided, or if its own king were to attack it, it would quickly fall. But, Yeshua notes, it is self-evident that this kingdom is still standing and operating, which leads to another revelation about the nature of the spiritual opposition.

Satan remains in charge of his kingdom, but Yeshua renders Satan unable to resist his incursions into this kingdom. Yeshua can drive out demons not because he is cooperating with their chief, as the scribes claim, but because he has overpowered their chief. It will become clear as Mark's account continues, however, that this overpowering is not yet conclusive. Evil spirits will continue to be driven out, as in 5:1–13, 6:13, 7:26–30, and 9:14–28. The binding of the strong man allows Yeshua (and his disciples as in 6:13) to

---

7. Jeffrey P. Garcia, "Jesus and His Pilgrimage Practices," (https://library.biblicalarchaeology.org/department/jesus-and-his-pilgrimage-practices/).

dismantle his kingdom piece by piece, but the kingdom, however impaired, remains standing for now.

Yeshua defines the accusation that he is operating by the power of an "unclean spirit" (3:30) as a blaspheming of the Holy Spirit—a most serious counter-charge, reflecting Exodus 22:27 [28] and Leviticus 24:10–16. Later in Mark, when Yeshua is falsely accused of blasphemy by the high priest, he's condemned by the council of chief priests, elders, and scribes as worthy of death (14:53–64). Ironically, in the current scene, it is Yeshua's accusers who are guilty of blasphemy, specifically blasphemy against the Holy Spirit, and by implication worthy of death, since this is an unforgivable sin. In Mark's laconic style, he hasn't mentioned the Holy Spirit since the opening episode, in which the Spirit descends like a dove upon Yeshua and soon after drives him into the wilderness to be tempted by Satan. Now it is revealed that these two forces, Satan and the Spirit, have been contending ever since, at least in Yeshua's repeated acts of driving out demons, which display Yeshua's evident empowerment by the Spirit. Those who seek to deny his authority by attributing this power to an evil spirit are not insulting Yeshua, but the Holy Spirit who is working through him.

Yeshua issues a stern warning to those who would resort to such defamation in opposing him. But why is blaspheming the Holy Spirit a uniquely unforgivable sin? Commentator William Lane explains:

> Blasphemy is an expression of defiant hostility toward God. The scribes were thoroughly familiar with this concept under the rubric "profanation of the Name," which generally denoted speech which defies God's power and majesty. The scribal tradition considered blasphemy no less seriously than did Jesus.[8]

Lane joins many scholars in assuming that "the scribal tradition," which is recorded in later rabbinic writings, may be rooted in the time of Yeshua and earlier. Accordingly, he goes on to cite a comment from the third-century Sifre on Deuteronomy: "The Holy

---

8. Lane, 145.

One, blessed be he, pardons everything else, but on profanation of the Name he takes vengeance immediately." Lane continues,

> This is the danger to which the scribes exposed themselves when they attributed to the agency of Satan the redemption brought by Jesus. The expulsion of the demons was a sign of the intrusion of the Kingdom of God. Yet the scribal accusations against Jesus amount to a denial of the power and greatness of the Spirit of God.[9]

Spiritual confrontation in Mark reveals the power of the Holy Spirit over all evil and impure forces, and validates Yeshua's mission of purifying and giving life. In Mark, confrontation with the satanic forces reveals the Holy Spirit as palpably real and actively engaged in this world through the deeds of Yeshua, and his followers as well (3:15, 6:13), regardless of the mounting opposition of the gatekeepers.

Mark sandwiches this disturbing picture of confrontation between Yeshua and the religious experts within two slices of conflict between Yeshua and his family.

In the first slice (3:20–21), Yeshua's relatives show that they're a good Jewish family by worrying that he's not getting enough to eat . . . but they go beyond this friendly concern by trying to take charge of him, saying "He's out of his mind!" They may have reached this conclusion after seeing their son, whom they thought they knew well, surrounded by swarms of people, unable to live a normal life, or even to enter a town without creating massive drama, and openly contradicting the religious authorities. Yeshua's family is concerned for him and perhaps for the family reputation as well.

In the second slice (3:31–35), Yeshua appears to reject or renounce his "earthly family," which can be seen as a radical, apocalyptic application of Torah passages like Exodus 32:25–29 and Deuteronomy 33:8–9. The Fifth Commandment still stands—"Honor your father and mother, so that you may live long in the land which ADONAI your God is giving you" (Exod. 20:12). But the

---

9. Lane, 145.

urgency of the times, with the Kingdom of God drawn near, demands an even greater loyalty. Yeshua will reiterate this demand, and its reward, in Mark 10:29–30. The Fifth Commandment promises the reward of living long "in the land ADONAI your God is giving you," but the incursion of the Kingdom preempts that promise, at least in the immediate context of Yeshua's earthly ministry. In this context, Yeshua envisions a new family, brought together not by birth and ties of kinship, but by doing "what God wants"—a quality that can be ascribed to the Twelve whom Yeshua called to be with him, to learn from him, and to take on his mission.

Derash

- Throughout this whole episode we see the supernatural encounter between the Kingdom of God and the kingdom of Satan, which Yeshua indicates in his parable is still intact, even if its strong man can be bound (3:23–26). Accordingly, when Yeshua commissioned the Twelve, he sent them out to proclaim (perhaps a better translation than "to preach") "and to have authority to expel demons" (3:14–15). Do we see this two-part commission as a *relic* of the past or as *relevant* for today? For some, the idea of demons or evil spirits sounds hopelessly primitive and irrelevant in our 21st century world, but their prominent appearance in the Gospels—and Yeshua's empowerment of his followers to overcome them—should warn us not to write them off. What part are we playing, or should we be playing, in the supernatural clash of the two kingdoms?

- The calling of the Twelve doesn't look so much like the creation of a new religious office—Apostle—as the deepening of master-follower relationship, the sort of relationship recognized and prized within the Jewish world, as noted in *Pirke Avot*:

> Yose ben Yo'ezer of Zereda used to say: Let your house be a meeting place for Sages; sit in the dust at their feet, and with thirst drink their words.
>
> Yehoshua ben Perahya used to say: Get yourself a teacher, acquire a companion, and give everyone the benefit of the doubt.[10]

Our episode in Mark adds the truth that nearness to the Sage Yeshua issues forth in effective proclamation and works of power, as the Twelve will report later (6:7–13). Being "with" Yeshua in 3:14 is the way the talmidim will learn from him and begin to emulate his ways. The Master teaches not only with words, but by his example and his very presence. Being with him is not only about relational intimacy, as precious as that is, but also about taking on his ways. Matthew captures a saying of Yeshua that expands upon this truth:

> Come to me, all of you who are struggling and burdened, and I will give you rest. Take my yoke upon you and learn from me, because I am gentle and humble in heart, and you will find rest for your souls. For my yoke is easy, and my burden is light. (Matt. 11:28–30)

The yoke is an instrument of labor and service; we are joined to Yeshua to share in his redemptive work in the world and mysteriously this participation produces rest for our souls.

- Yeshua's warning against blaspheming the Holy Spirit (Mark 3:28–30) can be terrifying, and those of us who are spiritual leaders sometimes need to help individuals who believe they've committed the unforgivable sin. But, as R. T. France notes,

  > . . . it may be safely be asserted that the vast majority of pastoral cases involving those who fear they have committed or might commit 'the unforgiveable sin' have little or nothing to do with what this saying is talking about. It is a

---

10. Avot 1:4, 6. Koren Siddur, 642.

warning to those who adopt a position of deliberate rejection and antagonism, not an attempt to frighten those of tender conscience.[11]

In other words, the counsel I've sometimes given, and heard others recommend, is sound: If you're troubled about committing the unforgivable sin you probably haven't committed it. It's unforgivable because it involves a hardening of the heart that precludes being convicted of the sin at all.

- Our episode ends with Yeshua resisting his own family members, including his mother (3:31–35). Later, when Yeshua is on his way to Jerusalem, a man approaches him and asks what he must do to obtain eternal life. Yeshua says, "You know the *mitzvot* — '**Don't murder, don't commit adultery, don't steal, don't give false testimony**, don't defraud, **honor your father and mother**'" (10:19). The commandments are still in place, and are life-giving to those who follow them, but when the man asks for something more, Yeshua tells him to sell all he has, give the proceeds to the poor, and follow him (10:21).

This passage illustrates the relationship between halakhic and apocalyptic religion mentioned in Episode 1. The halakha still stands: Honor your father and mother. But the apocalyptic stands as well, in light of the nearness of the kingdom: Sell all you have and follow me. In real life today, how do we balance the command to honor father and mother with Yeshua's radical call to follow him? This radical call has special applicability to Jewish people, who risk alienating or even losing their family when they accept Yeshua. We can't deny his apocalyptic call, but we also believe we are called to stand with, and bear witness within, our extended Jewish family. In what specific ways can we reconcile the halakhic and the apocalyptic in a matter like this?

---

11. France, 177.

Season 1, Episode 4

Yeshua's Stories Conceal and Reveal

4:1–34

Overview

Yeshua's ministry in Galilee has drawn huge crowds and created popular acclaim, but has also stirred up mounting resistance among the religious gatekeepers. Equally troubling is the growing sense that the big crowds don't really understand Yeshua's message of the nearness of God's kingdom and the need to repent and believe. The crowds are attracted to Yeshua's evident power over disease and demonic infestation. They are amazed by it, but puzzled as well (1:27; 2:12), and we don't hear anything about their repentance. In the final frame of our last scene (3:31–34), even Yeshua's family, those who would seem closest to Yeshua, didn't respond at all to his call to repentance and belief.

This mixed response, however, doesn't move Yeshua to abandon his home territory. Rather, he remains in the region of Lake Kinneret, where he gathers another large crowd and begins to teach them in parables. Ironically, these parables might help explain the dynamics behind Yeshua's mixed reception, but they do so in veiled language that most of his hearers won't understand, at least at first. He includes metaphorical portrayals of the Kingdom of God that he has been proclaiming since the outset, which help to put the current resistance in perspective, at least for those with ears to hear. After the first of these stories, the famous parable of the sower, Yeshua takes his closest followers aside to make sure that they at least understand. He follows with three more parables, the last two explicitly about the Kingdom of God. Our scene concludes, "but privately to his own disciples he explained everything" (4:34).

Peshat

4:1–12

> Again Yeshua began to teach by the lake, but the crowd that gathered around him was so large that he got into a boat on the lake and sat there, while the crowd remained on shore at the water's edge. ² He taught them many things in parables. In the course of his teaching, he said to them: ³ "Listen! A farmer went out to sow his seed. ⁴ As he sowed, some seed fell alongside the path; and the birds came and ate it up. ⁵ Other seed fell on rocky patches where there was not much soil. It sprouted quickly because the soil was shallow; ⁶ but when the sun rose, the young plants were scorched; and since their roots were not deep, they dried up. ⁷ Other seed fell among thorns, which grew up and choked it; so that it yielded no grain. ⁸ But other seed fell into rich soil and produced grain; it sprouted, and grew, and yielded a crop — thirty, sixty, even a hundred times what was sown." ⁹ And he concluded, "Whoever has ears to hear with, let him hear!"
>
> ¹⁰ When Yeshua was alone, the people around him with the Twelve asked him about the parables. ¹¹ He answered them, "To you the secret of the Kingdom of God has been given; but to those outside, everything is in parables, ¹² so that
>
> they may be always looking but never seeing;
> always listening but never understanding.
> Otherwise, they might turn and be forgiven!"

In the first parable, a farmer sows his seed but it falls upon different kinds of soil, so that only a fraction of the seed bears fruit. When Yeshua's followers, including the Twelve, ask for the meaning of the parable (or parables in general), he says that "everything is in parables" to the outsiders so that they will not understand and turn—

a saying that has long puzzled readers of Mark. Yeshua appears to be saying that he speaks in parables to deliberately veil his message to "those outside" in order to prevent them from turning and being forgiven. But this interpretation would seem to contradict the simple imperative of Yeshua's message to repent and believe in the besorah, and his assurance that "all sins will be forgiven the children of man" (3:28). Furthermore, it's the normal function of a parable to reveal, not to conceal, as we saw in Yeshua's parable about Satan and his kingdom in 3:23–27. The parable of the lamp, which appears a few verses down (4:21–22) teaches that what is now hidden or secret must be brought to light.

To explain his use of parables, then, Yeshua cites the heavenly court scene of Isaiah 6. There Isaiah is told that judgment shall come, despite the efforts he must undertake to warn the people, but a remnant will remain after judgment, with the potential to respond. Such an interpretation is consistent with Yeshua's words about "the elect" to be preserved through the apocalyptic events that lie ahead, as we'll see in Mark 13:20–23, 27. More to the point, perhaps, is Yeshua's own conclusion to the parable, spoken before he takes his followers aside to explain it to them: "He who has ears to hear, let him hear" (4:9). Even in the climate of spiritual hardness—seeing but not perceiving, hearing but not understanding—some can see and hear, and Yeshua exhorts them to do so, as he goes on to explain the parable.

Yeshua is citing Isaiah 6 to explain the sort of hardness, compared to a roadside in the parable, that he encounters among his own people. The concluding words of the parable—"He who has ears to hear, let him hear"—provide hope that the outcome pictured in 4:11–12 is only temporary or partial, since some may hear and understand. The outcome Yeshua describes may be, as in Isaiah, a means of advancing the broader plan of God. This interpretation suggests that the outsiders "need not be permanently written off, that the division between insiders and outsiders is not a gulf without bridges."[1] These words are especially poignant when we remember that in this stage of Mark's account, the "outsiders" are all Jewish—including the "very large crowd" gathered around him by Lake Kinneret (4:1–2), and his own mother and brothers in the preceding scene (3:31–32). Satan's snatching-away of the word is not sufficient to frustrate God's whole plan of redemption, and Yeshua's revealing the secret of the Kingdom of God to "the twelve" (4:10), hints that the twelve tribes continue to have a place within that plan.

Reading Mark with such a hope is consistent with Isaiah's vision, in which the prophet sees the LORD sitting upon a throne and responds,

> Woe to me! I am doomed! —
> because I, a man with unclean lips,
> living among a people with unclean lips,
> have seen with my own eyes
> the King, *ADONAI-Tzva'ot*!" (Isa. 6:5)

An angel touches Isaiah's unclean mouth with a burning coal, saying "your iniquity is gone, your sin is atoned for," and Isaiah responds to God's call for someone to send to Israel, even though the people will not understand and be healed (6:9–10). Isaiah 6 ends with mention of a "tenth," a "trunk" that remains after judgment, and the concluding line: "the holy seed will be its trunk" (6:13). We can recognize literary bookends here, with Isaiah as a one-man remnant at the beginning of the chapter, and the tenth/trunk/holy seed at the end. So too, in Mark 4, we may discern hints of a remnant within Israel that responds to the word that is sown.

Nonetheless, God's purpose of hardening Yeshua's audience, or a good portion of it, at least for a time, remains, as does the irony that God uses the Adversary to advance that purpose, by "devouring" the word sown upon the hard and impenetrable path. As a further irony, the involvement of Satan in this process is mentioned only as if in passing, even though Satan was introduced in the

---

1. France, 201.

opening scene of Mark as a primal cosmic adversary. Here Mark recognizes Satan's role in resisting the proclamation of the Kingdom, employing the term "Kingdom of God" for the first time since Yeshua's opening declaration in 1:15. Satan's role is to oppose the Kingdom, but he's mentioned here only in passing, only in one part of a complex parable, as if to keep him in his place. And within the scene of hardening and the vulnerability of God's word, the possibility of repentance remains, so that outsiders in the end "might turn and be forgiven."

4:13–20

> [13] Then Yeshua said to them, "Don't you understand this parable? How will you be able to understand any parable? [14] The sower sows the message. [15] Those alongside the path where the message is sown are people who no sooner hear it than the Adversary comes and takes away the message sown in them. [16] Likewise, those receiving seed on rocky patches are people who hear the message and joyfully accept it at once; [17] but they have no root in themselves. So they hold out for a while, but as soon as some trouble or persecution arises on account of the message, they immediately fall away. [18] Others are those sown among thorns — they hear the message; [19] but the worries of the world, the deceitful glamor of wealth and all the other kinds of desires push in and choke the message; so that it produces nothing. [20] But those sown on rich soil hear the message, accept it and bear fruit — thirty, sixty or a hundredfold."

We can understand the institutional resistance to the message of the kingdom, but what is behind this failure to respond in depth even among those drawn to Yeshua? Yeshua's parable about Satan's kingdom in Mark 3 revealed that Satan is the organizing force behind the unclean spirits opposing Yeshua. The parable of the sower reveals that Satan's activity goes beyond the obvious level of spiritual conflict, that is, demonic manifestations, to have impact upon the whole mission of Yeshua. Satan is the one who steals the word from the hearts of those who are unprepared to receive it. The word isn't sown into a benign, or even neutral, setting, but into a setting actively patrolled by the adversary. The first major component of Yeshua's ministry, preaching the word of the Kingdom (1:14–15, 38–39; 3:14; 6:12) entails confrontation with spiritual evil as surely as does the component of casting out demons.

France notes that the different types of soil represent different types of people, different ways of hearing the word that is being sown (4:14). He terms the soil along the path "the worst type of soil," which the seed fails to penetrate at all, and continues:

> Such ineffective hearing is attributed to the activity of [Satan], who, as the focus of the opposition to the purpose of God and the ministry of Jesus, is naturally determined to prevent the knowledge of God's kingship from being grasped.[2]

Satan is revealed as "the focus of the opposition" to Yeshua's mission and his malignant spiritual forces resist the spread of the word, so that Messiah confronts cosmic evil not just in casting out unclean spirits, but throughout his whole ministry. This sense is heightened by Yeshua's remark to the twelve: "Do you not understand this parable? How then will you understand all the parables?" (4:13). Yeshua's question here "suggests that the parable of the four soils is the key to all other parables and thus the key to understanding the paradox of the presence of the kingdom of God in Jesus' ministry, which is accompanied by resistance and hostility."[3] Why is this parable the key to the rest? Because it explains the opposition and obstacles to the message, which Yeshua and his followers have already encountered, and which will grow more intense as they continue on. This parable also pictures the success of the message and the growth of the Kingdom. This mysterious

---

2. France, 205.
3. Eckhard J. Schnabel, *Mark: An Introduction and Commentary*, Tyndale New Testament Commentaries, vol. 2, ed. Eckhard J. Schnabel (London: Inter-Varsity, 2017), 104; France, "it is the key to all the rest," 204; Marcus, *Mark 1-8* "in explaining the Parable of the Sower, Jesus unlocked 'all the parables,'" 310.

already-but-not-yet quality of the Kingdom, which we've already noted, is essential to understanding it as well as the parables that picture it.

4:21–25

> [21] He said to them, "A lamp isn't brought in to be put under a bowl or under the bed, is it? Wouldn't you put it on a lampstand? [22] Indeed, nothing is hidden, except to be disclosed; and nothing is covered up, except to come out into the open. [23] Those who have ears to hear with, let them hear!"
>
> [24] He also said to them, "Pay attention to what you are hearing! The measure with which you measure out will be used to measure to you — and more besides! [25] For anyone who has something will be given more; but from anyone who has nothing, even what he does have will be taken away."

Mark's wording here indicates that Yeshua is still speaking to his close followers ("the people around him with the Twelve"), and he's still in the parable + explanation mode. The parable itself is 4:21–23; its meaning and impact are sketched in 4:24–25. Yeshua's words in 4:24—"Pay attention to what you are hearing!"—state in plain prose what 4:9 says poetically: "Whoever has ears to hear with, let him hear!"

This parable is linked to the parable of the sower in two additional ways that help us understand its impact. First, both parables speak of the word or message. The sower sows the word; this parable pictures light, a frequent metaphor in the Tanakh for the word, as in Psalm 119:105 (NJPS): "Your word is a lamp to my feet, / a light for my path." Second, the Greek word translated "in order that" in 4:12 is repeated four times in quick succession in 4:21–22. This word introduces the citation from Isaiah 6 that explains why the truth must be concealed from some, and it reappears four times in 4:21–22 to declare that the truth in the end must be revealed. Marcus links these two intertwined passages with the whole sweep of Mark's Besorah:

> This rejection of the word [in 4:11–12] leads inexorably to Jesus' death, a result that, from the divine perspective, is necessary (8:31; 9:31; 10:33–34); he is killed by those who cannot grasp his identity and who look and look but never see, hear and hear but never understand. . . . The obscurity of the word thus ultimately serves the purpose of its revelation by leading to Jesus' revelatory death; what was hidden was hidden only *in order that* it might come into the light.[4]

The obscurity of the parable of the sower is instrumental in creating the revelation to come, and "nothing is hidden, except to be disclosed."

4:26–34

> [26] And he said, "The Kingdom of God is like a man who scatters seed on the ground. [27] Nights he sleeps, days he's awake; and meanwhile the seeds sprout and grow — how, he doesn't know. [28] By itself the soil produces a crop — first the stalk, then the head, and finally the full grain in the head. [29] But as soon as the crop is ready, the man comes with his sickle, because it's harvest-time."
>
> [30] Yeshua also said, "With what can we compare the Kingdom of God? What illustration should we use to describe it? [31] It is like a mustard seed, which, when planted, is the smallest of all the seeds in the field; [32] but after it has been planted, it grows and becomes the largest of all the plants, with such big branches that the birds flying about can build nests in its shade."
>
> [33] With many parables like these he spoke the message to them, to the extent that they were capable of hearing it. [34] He did not say a thing to them without using a parable; when he was alone with his own *talmidim* he explained everything to them.

Two final parables are linked as similes of the Kingdom of God, returning explicitly to the theme mentioned in 4:11. Like that first parable, these two address the secret, hidden nature of the Kingdom,

---

4. Marcus, *Mark 1-8*, 319.

how it can be present in seed form in the words and deeds of Yeshua, and still not yet present.

In the first parable, the man who sows the seed is also the man with the sickle, who will harvest the seed in the end. This might be another hint addressing the issue that pervades Mark's Besorah, the identity of Yeshua, who is not only announcing the Kingdom and teaching its principles, but is also the agent of the judgment to come. Yeshua here is hinting at the authority inherent to his Son-of-Man self-designation, based on Daniel 7, and previewed in chapter 2 when he claimed authority to forgive sins and to shape the practice of Shabbat. This title will be developed extensively in our second and third seasons, beginning at Mark 8:31. Ironically, though, in this parable the man "doesn't know" (4:27) how the seeds sprout and grow, perhaps hinting at the humanity of the one who will ultimately come with his sickle. The real focus of the parable, however, is not the man who sows and reaps, but the seed itself, and ultimately the Kingdom of God. Its point is that this Kingdom has its own life and dynamic, and is not dependent on human effort or the strategies that human wisdom might concoct.

The parable calls for confidence in the nature of the seed and its potential for growth. In telling this tale, Yeshua is building on his audience's familiarity with the cycle of sowing and reaping, the reliability of seed in producing a crop in the end—which they have depended on for their entire lives in the largely agrarian setting of Galilee. He's also drawing on the first, defining parable, in which the sower sows the word (4:14). It's hard not to imagine that the seed here is also the word, and to thereby trust in its power to grow and increase. The Kingdom currently struggling to emerge amidst opposition and indifference will in the end be fully manifest. "Despite appearances to the contrary, it is growing, and the harvest will come. But it will come in God's time and in God's way, not by human effort or in accordance with human logic."[5]

Our second parable in this pair employs another agrarian simile: The Kingdom of God is like a mustard seed. And like the first, it

---

5. France, 215.

contrasts the inauspicious planting, in this case of a tiny seed, with a more impressive outcome. Still, the outcome in this parable, "the largest of all plants," seems more modest than the harvest pictured in the parable of the sower, "thirty, sixty or a hundredfold." But the point of this second parable is the contrast between the humble beginning—the mustard seed is proverbially tiny, as in Matthew 17:20, or multiple sayings in the Mishnah[6]—and the impressive outcome.

This impressiveness is heightened by a detail Mark provides: "the birds flying about can build nests in its shade." This wording reflects Ezekiel's vision of a return from Babylonian captivity:

> *ADONAI Elohim* says, "From the top of this tall cedar, from its highest branch, I will take a shoot and plant it myself on a high and prominent mountain. I will plant it on the highest mountain in Israel, where it will put out branches, bear fruit, and become a noble cedar. Under it will live all kinds of birds; winged creatures of every description will live there in the shadow of its branches." Ezek. 17:22–23[7]

In the context of Ezekiel 17, this shoot is a remnant of the people Israel, or perhaps a remnant of the Davidic dynasty, exiled in Babylon, restored to the land of Israel, and thriving there once again. In Ezekiel 17,

> God employs the allegory of *the cedar* to promise the restoration of the Davidic monarchy (Isa. 11:1–10; Jer. 23:5–6; 33:15). The cedar, the grandest of trees, will tower over all the other trees (nations), and all will see the power of God, who is responsible for the fall and rise of Judah.[8]

Rashi cites a *targum*, or early paraphrase of the scripture, which interprets "I will take a shoot" in Ezekiel 17:22 as, "And I will take the King Messiah and I will establish him." What appears to be a

---

6. E.g. Nid 5:2, Toh 8:8, Naz 1:5.
7. The image of a mighty tree providing a nesting place for birds also appears in Ezek. 31:6, referencing Assyria, and in Dan. 4:12, 21 referencing Nebuchadnezzar.
8. *The Jewish Study Bible*, eds. Adele Berlin, Marc Zvi Brettler, and Michael Fishbane (New York: Oxford University Press, 2004), 1072.

small detail in Yeshua's parable—birds nesting in the shade of the mustard bush—evokes a vision of restoration. The restored Davidic dynasty is already present, but still to come, in the seed-ministry of Yeshua. In a typically ironic twist, the symbol of this restoration is not a noble cedar, but a huge mustard plant. "Like many parables, this one is humorously satirical: the kingdom is like a scrubby, invasive bush!"[9] Nonetheless, the restoration is underway.

Derash

- Yeshua explains his use of parables by citing Isaiah 6 to suggest that the people's failure to understand his message is somehow part of God's overriding purpose. Yeshua had ended the parable of the sower with the words, "He who has ears to hear, let him hear" (4:9)—providing hope that the failure to hear and understand described in 4:11–12 is only temporary or partial. The resistance Yeshua describes may be, as in Isaiah, a means of advancing a broader prophetic agenda. This interpretation of Mark 4 seems to echo Paul's view of Israel's prophetic role in Romans 9–11, especially 11:25.[10] How might this view affect our understanding of historic Jewish resistance to Yeshua and his message?

- The four different soils of the parable of the sower reflect four different responses to the word that is sown, four different conditions of heart that affect how one receives the message of the Kingdom. The parable describes the way things are, rather than exhorting the hearers to prepare their hearts to receive the message. Still, we might be able to derive some lessons on cultivating a receptive heart and bearing fruit—thirty, sixty or a hundredfold. What actions to accomplish this are suggested by this parable?

---

9. Wills, "Mark," JANT, 79.
10. I provide a deeper comparison of Mark 4 and Romans 11 in my article, "Spiritual Confrontation in the Besorah of Mark" in *Kesher: A Journal of Messianic Judaism* Issue 43 (Summer/Fall 2023).

- Jewish New Testament scholar A.J. Levine draws three lessons from the parable of the mustard seed (4:30–32):

    First, some things need to be *left alone*. . . . Second, sometimes we need to *get out of the way*. . . . Finally . . . the kingdom of heaven is found in what today we might call "our own backyard" in the generosity of nature and in the daily working of men and women.[11]

    How do these lessons align (or misalign) with what we've heard Yeshua teaching in the Besorah of Mark so far?

- Levine goes on to describe Yeshua's parables in terms that help us understand why he used parables to speak to the multitudes, even though he had to explain everything afterwards to his followers (4:34–35). Her description of the parables forms a fitting conclusion for this chapter:

    They challenge, they provoke, they convict, and at the same time they amuse. At each reading, when I think I've got all the details explained, something remains left over, and I have to start again. The parables have provided me countless hours of inspiration, and conversation. They are pearls of Jewish wisdom. If we hear them in their original contexts, and if we avoid the anti-Jewish interpretation that frequently deforms them, they gleam with a shine that cannot be hidden.[12]

---

11. Amy-Jill Levine, *Short Stories by Jesus: The Enigmatic Parables of a Controversial Rabbi* (New York: HarperOne, 2015), 182.
12. Levine, *Short Stories*, 305.

Season 1, Episode 5

Spiritual Encounter Among the Gentiles

4:35–5:20

Overview

Episode 4 opened with Yeshua getting into a boat on the lake of Kinneret and sitting in it as he taught the crowds in parables. Now, Yeshua—perhaps still in the same boat—directs his talmidim to cross over to the other side of the lake, to the mostly-Gentile territory of the Gerasenes.[1] As they go, they're overtaken by a fierce windstorm that threatens to swamp the boat. The talmidim awaken Yeshua, who has been sleeping amidst the storm. He rises and quiets the storm with a word of command, leaving his followers amazed and wondering who their master can be to possess such powers.

As soon as they reach the shore, they are met by a man emerging from among some nearby burial caves to confront them, crying out, "What do you want with me, Yeshua, Son of God *Ha'Elyon*? I implore you in God's name! Don't torture me!" The man is possessed by a legion of demons and Yeshua casts them out into a nearby herd of pigs, who rush down into the sea and are drowned. When the locals see what has happened, including the sight of the

---

[1]. Many commentators note the difficulty that Gerasa, one of the ten cities of the Decapolis, is some distance from the Sea of Galilee. Some manuscripts of Mark refer to the Gadarenes, who lived much closer to the lake, but "[m]ost scholars regard 'Gerasenes' as the original reading. It is possible that Mark refers to Gerasa as a term designating the entire territory of the Decapolis" (Schnabel, *Mark*, 116). The Decapolis, or "Ten Towns" in our translation (5:20) is "a federation of ten predominantly Gentile cities east of the Sea of Galilee," Wills, "Mark," JANT, 80.

once-demonized man sitting there clothed and in his right mind, they're terrified and plead with Yeshua to leave their territory. As Yeshua sets out to depart, the man begs to go with him, but Yeshua tells him to stay and tell his friends what the Lord has done for him. Our episode ends as the once-demonized man proclaims in the Decapolis region what Yeshua has done for him so that everyone marvels.

Peshat

4:35–41

> [35] That day, when evening had come, Yeshua said to them, "Let's cross to the other side of the lake." [36] So, leaving the crowd behind, they took him just as he was, in the boat; and there were other boats with him. [37] A furious windstorm arose, and the waves broke over the boat, so that it was close to being swamped. [38] But he was in the stern on a cushion, asleep. They woke him and said to him, "Rabbi, doesn't it matter to you that we're about to be killed?" [39] He awoke, rebuked the wind and said to the waves, "Quiet! Be still!" The wind subsided, and there was a dead calm. [40] He said to them, "Why are you afraid? Have you no trust even now?" [41] But they were terrified and asked each other, "Who can this be, that even the wind and the waves obey him?"

Mark brings our attention back to the boat he mentioned at the beginning of Episode 4, where it provided a place for Yeshua to sit in the classic Jewish mode as a teacher and address the crowd. A similar craft was discovered in 1986, during a severe drought that lowered the water level of Lake Kinneret (more commonly called the Sea of Galilee). Two local fishermen with an interest in archaeology, Moshe and Yuval Lufan, came upon the hull of an ancient boat protruding from the mud. They notified the authorities and eventually the boat was recovered and placed on display at the nearby Kibbutz Ginosar, where countless people, including your author, have seen it over the years. It dates from the time of Yeshua and may well resemble the boats that play such a big role in Mark. The remains are 27 feet long and 7.5 feet wide, with a maximum preserved height of a little over four feet. It's a shallow boat that would allow for fishing close to the shore—and for seating a speaker close enough to be heard by those on the shore. The boat was made of ten different varieties of wood, suggesting either a wood shortage that required lots of improvising or repeated patching and rebuilding over the years, or both. Either way, it's a humble vessel that reflects the earthy, hard-working Galilean setting of the story of Yeshua.[2]

In that same everyday Jewish setting, the account of a windstorm threatening to sink the boat would not be unfamiliar. This particular account might well remind hearers of the story of the prophet Jonah, who was also asleep in a craft ready to sink amidst a windstorm. Like Yeshua, Jonah is awakened by terrified shipmates and becomes the means of calming the storm. But Jonah doesn't speak to the wind and the waves; rather he calms them by having the sailors cast him into the sea, because his guilt has caused the storm. Both stories end in Gentile territory: Jonah is swallowed by the famous sea creature, and thrown up on the shore three days later. From there he goes to the Gentile capital Nineveh to begrudgingly bring a message of repentance that saves the Ninevites from God's judgment. Yeshua, in contrast, goes willingly to Gentile territory and encourages the spread of God's message among them (Mark 5:19).

In Jonah's story, the sailors delivered from the storm "feared the LORD greatly; they offered a sacrifice to the LORD and they made vows" (Jonah 1:16 NJPS). In Mark, the disciples in the boat with Yeshua are also filled with fear even after the natural danger has passed, and ask each other, "Who can this be, that even the wind and the waves obey him?" Here, it's a contrast with Jonah that is most telling: Jonah stills the winds and waves by being thrown into the sea; he's passive and the calming is God's work. In Mark, Yeshua himself stills the windstorm actively and on his own authority. He

---

2. https://en.wikipedia.org/wiki/Sea_of_Galilee_Boat.

takes authority not only over the wind, but over the waves as well, the sea more generally, which appears frequently in the Tanakh as a symbol of chaos and opposition to God (for example, Isa. 51:9–10; Psa. 18:16 [15], 104:6–7; Job 26:11–12).

Likewise, in the narratives of Torah, especially the Exodus from Egypt, the God of Israel demonstrates his sovereign authority by controlling the forces of nature. In Mark, it is a very human Galilean who takes charge, but not on a human level. Paradoxically, he acts on a supernatural level, reminding us that "[t]he cosmic overtones in the Gospel account must not be missed."[3] In our previous episode, Yeshua pictured the Kingdom of God as hidden and becoming manifest in gradual and mysterious ways; here the focus shifts to the King, who appears rather ordinary, but is present in evident power and authority even over the forces of nature. This revelation leads to the talmidim's question, "Who can this be?" which both echoes and moves beyond the one raised in the K'far-Nachum synagogue in episode 1: "What is this?" (1:27). Now the focus isn't on the evident supernatural power, but on the one wielding that power. The persistent question of Yeshua's identity is gradually being answered, not as a theoretical issue, but one of urgent significance. This emphasis on Yeshua's kingship will build throughout the rest of Mark, as will the opposition to his kingship.

5:1–10

> [1] Yeshua and his *talmidim* arrived at the other side of the lake, in the Gerasenes' territory. [2] As soon as he disembarked, a man with an unclean spirit came out of the burial caves to meet him. [3] He lived in the burial caves; and no one could keep him tied up, not even with a chain. [4] He had often been chained hand and foot, but he would snap the chains and break the irons off his feet, and no one was strong enough to control him. [5] Night and day he

---

3. Lane, 177. See also Marcus, *Mark 1–8*, 340.

> wandered among the graves and through the hills, howling and gashing himself with stones.
>
> [6] Seeing Yeshua from a distance, he ran and fell on his knees in front of him [7] and screamed at the top of his voice, "What do you want with me, Yeshua, Son of God *Ha'Elyon*? I implore you in God's name! Don't torture me!" [8] For Yeshua had already begun saying to him, "Unclean spirit, come out of this man!" [9] Yeshua asked him, "What's your name?" "My name is Legion," he answered, "there are so many of us"; [10] and he kept begging Yeshua not to send them out of that region.

As soon as Yeshua and his party set foot on the shore, Yeshua is accosted by a man coming out from among the tombs, who had been bound with chains but had torn them apart. One commentator calls this encounter "the supreme exorcism in the Gospel of Mark," and a fulfillment of the parable of the other strong man in 3:27, who was also bound in chains, but didn't break free.

> By means of these allusions to 3.27, the subjugation of this unbindable strong man suggests another dimension to the readers: Jesus' riddle is finding an answer and *the* strong man is being subdued. As Jesus banishes the legion of *daimones* and delivers the man from the tombs, the "prince of the *daimones*" [3:22] suffers a major defeat.[4]

The answer to Yeshua's "riddle"—"How can Satan cast out Satan? (3:23)—is enacted in the most concrete fashion: this unchained strong man is subdued by a word of command, freed from the powers of the evil one, and left "clothed and in his right mind" (5:15), as an archetype of the deliverance that accompanies the Kingdom of God. In stark contrast with Yeshua's initial encounter with an unclean spirit in a synagogue on Shabbat (1:23), this encounter takes place in a scene of multiple impurities, among tombs

---

4. Peter Bolt, *Jesus' Defeat of Death: Persuading Mark's Early Readers*. Society for New Testament Studies Monograph Series 125 (Cambridge: Cambridge University Press, 2003), 146–147. Cited in Thiessen, 146.

in Gentile territory, with "a great herd of pigs feeding there on the hillside" (5:11). This change of scene reveals that Yeshua's confrontation with demonic forces is not a matter of a local holy man contending with localized spirit-beings, but a matter of cosmic proportions. The Kingdom of God is rooted in Israel but not limited to the land or people of Israel; its Messiah-king is the Son of Man, who is given "dominion and glory and a kingdom, that all peoples, nations, and languages should serve him" (Dan. 7:13–14). Thus, the encounter with the Gerasene demoniac hints at the coming ministry to the Gentiles (cf. 3:8; 7:24–30; 15:39) foretold by the Hebrew prophets.

As part of "the supreme exorcism" in Mark, the defiant words of the demonized man are revealing. In 5:7 we hear the final demonic declaration in this Besorah; there will be further encounters with demons, but this is the last time Mark lets them have a voice. This demon-possessed man cries out, "What do you want with me, Yeshua, Son of God *Ha'Elyon*?" The language here reflects that of the first demonic encounter, in 1:21–28, which ends with Yeshua's reputation spreading "everywhere throughout all the surrounding region of Galilee." Our current encounter will end with the liberated man going off to proclaim in the predominantly Gentile region of Decapolis. In this scene, "Already the foundation has been laid for the extension to the Gentiles of the ministry and mission of the Jewish Messiah (13:10; 14:9)."[5]

Mark enhances this preview of the outreach to the Gentiles by noting the title the demoniac uses for Yeshua, "Son of God *Ha'Elyon*." El Elyon, God Most High, is a name that first sounds in the Bible on the lips of the Gentile priest-king Malki-Tzedek and is then affirmed by Abraham (Gen. 14:18–24). The use of this title both strengthens the suggestion of a coming mission to the Gentiles and links that mission to the legacy of Abraham, in whom "all the

---

5. France, 233.

families of the earth shall be blessed" (Gen. 12:3). It also suggests a more militant theme, as Marcus notes:

> The "Most High God" in OT and Jewish texts is associated not only with Gentiles but also, more particularly, with the sovereignty of the God of Israel over the whole earth, even Gentile realms (Deut. 32:8; Dan. 4:17). This sovereignty was already established by a primordial triumph over anti-God powers (Isa. 14:12–15; cf. Deut. 32:7–8), but it was reasserted by subsequent divine defeats of those powers' human exponents, i.e. the armies of the Gentiles, in holy war (Gen. 14:10; Pss 9:3; 47:2; 83:18 . . .). Our passage may reflect this background: by casting out the legion of demons, the "Son of the Most High God" is subduing a hostile Gentile territory through a saving act of holy war.[6]

The sense of warfare is also evident as Yeshua commands the unclean spirit to name itself, which is often an aspect of driving out invasive spirits. The demon had declared Yeshua's name or title, but that didn't help him resist Yeshua's overwhelming power. Now Yeshua demands the demon's name, and it answers, "My name is Legion, there are so many of us." A legion is a Roman military unit, officially numbering 5000, but in actual deployment smaller, perhaps nearer to the number of pigs that are about to be infested with the demons. More significant than the number itself is the Roman military terminology, suggesting that this is a confrontation on a supernatural level between the Davidic king and the powers of this world symbolized in this case by Rome.

Yeshua's incursion into the Gentile territory of the Gerasenes was not a side-trip, but a preview of a wider invasion to come, an invasion whose outcome is already assured by the sovereign authority Yeshua bears, despite arriving on this scene in a humble fishing boat. His repeated encounters with the demonic realm reflect the present and future triumph of the Son of the Most High God in Israel and beyond.

---

6. Marcus, *Mark 1–8*, 344.

5:11–20

¹¹ Now there was a large herd of pigs feeding near the hill, ¹² and the unclean spirits begged him, "Send us to the pigs, so we can go into them." ¹³ Yeshua gave them permission. They came out and entered the pigs; and the herd, numbering around two thousand, rushed down the hillside into the lake and were drowned. ¹⁴ The swineherds fled and told it in the town and in the surrounding country, and the people went to see what had happened. ¹⁵ They came to Yeshua and saw the man who had had the legion of demons, sitting there, dressed and in his right mind; and they were frightened. ¹⁶ Those who had seen it told what had happened to the man controlled by demons and to the pigs; ¹⁷ and the people began begging Yeshua to leave their district.

¹⁸ As he was getting into the boat, the man who had been demonized begged him to be allowed to go with him. ¹⁹ But Yeshua would not permit it. Instead, he said to him, "Go home to your people, and tell them how much *ADONAI* in his mercy has done for you." ²⁰ He went off and began proclaiming in the Ten Towns how much Yeshua had done for him, and everyone was amazed.

As if to underscore that we're in Gentile territory, Mark mentions "a large herd of pigs feeding near the hill" where Yeshua is taking charge over the legion of unclean spirits. At their request, he allows the demons, who can no longer remain in the man, to relocate into the pigs, which immediately rush down the hillside into the lake and drown. This scene raises some questions that Mark doesn't really answer. First, why do the demons so strongly desire to remain in that region (5:10) and to inhabit a body, any body, even a pig's? In the parable Yeshua told to explain his power over demonic forces, he spoke of the strong man and his "house," which Yeshua symbolically "ransacks" by driving out demons (Mark 3:23–27). Matthew records another saying in which Yeshua uses the imagery of a house or home: "When an unclean spirit comes out of a person, it travels through dry country seeking rest and does not find it. Then it says to itself, 'I will return to the house I left.' When it arrives, it finds the house standing empty, swept clean and put in order" (12:43–44). With no body to inhabit, the unclean spirits seem to be restless and exposed, longing for another home—and undoubtedly dangerous because of that—but we are not told why that is.

A second unanswered question in this story is an ethical one. Yeshua allows the demons to inhabit a nearby herd of pigs, which ends up destroying this valuable asset of the local people. It's an undeniable destruction of property, whether intended or not (and whether the property is kosher or not), but the storyteller doesn't spend time trying to sort that out. Instead, he simply paints the dramatic scene, and sets it alongside the equally dramatic sight of the demonized man sitting in Yeshua's presence, "dressed and in his right mind" (5:15)—which terrifies the locals at least as much as does the report of the pigs going berserk.

The Gerasenes beg Yeshua to leave, and then the cleansed demoniac begs Yeshua to allow him to go with him, and Mark employs the same word, *parakaleo*, for both contrasting responses. The request of the Gerasenes is also paradoxical. The earlier miracles stirred up amazement and engagement with Yeshua among those who beheld them (Mark 1:27, 45; 2:12; 4:41); only here does a miracle lead to Yeshua being shown the exit door.

As Yeshua departs, he does not invoke the messianic secret and instruct the demoniac to tell no one what has happened. Instead he forbids him from following him (back to Galilee) and directs him, "Go home to your people, and *tell them* how much ADONAI in his mercy has done for you" (5:19, emphasis added). Perhaps the secret applies specifically within Israel and not to the prototypical Gentile mission, because the secret is necessary for the fulfillment of the vision of Isaiah 6, and the formation of a remnant within Israel, as suggested in Mark 4:11–12. Israel remains at the center of the plan of redemption, even if the fulfillment of that plan on Israel's behalf must be delayed. A more immediate—but partial—fulfillment is at hand for the Gentiles, and in Mark's unrelenting irony it advances here through the expulsion of unclean spirits in an unclean place into unclean creatures.

Even though the locals have begged Yeshua to depart, when the man who is delivered remains behind and reports how much Yeshua had done for him, "everyone was amazed," (5:20). Just as Yeshua's ministry in the Galil opened in the synagogue of K'far-Nachum with an amazing encounter with the demonic realm, so does his first ministry outside the land of Israel open with an amazing deliverance from a legion of unclean spirits.

Derash

- It's a longstanding Jewish custom to read the Book of Jonah on the afternoon of Yom Kippur. In his classic work, *Days of Awe*, the great Israeli author S. Y. Agnon provides some reasons for this custom:

  > The Book of Jonah is read from beginning to end, in order to teach us that no man can fly away from God, as David, peace be upon him, said (Ps. 139:7–10) "Whither shall I go from Thy spirit?' . . .

  > Another reason why we read the Book of Jonah is because it informs us that God pardons and forgives those who turn in Teshuvah, as we are told in the case of Nineveh. . . .

  > Another reason for reading the Book of Jonah is because the prophecy of Jonah purposes to teach us that the compassions of God extend over all that He has made, even idolators—then how much more do they extend over Israel![7]

  How do these themes of teshuvah (repentance) and God's mercy over all humankind play out in Mark's story of the stormy crossing?

---

7. S. Y. Agnon, *Days of Awe* (New York: Schocken, 1948), 262–63.

- The Jewish-Christian commentator Joel Marcus highlights equally profound lessons hidden in the story of the stormy crossing:

  > The human challenge to God, "Don't you care?," is met by the divine challenge to the human being, "Why are you cowardly?" These are both real questions because both reflect realities—on the one hand the desperate human situation, on the other hand the divine assurance that "all shall be well and / all manner of thing shall be well" (T. S. Eliot, "Little Gidding," 5). The ultimate issue at stake in any given circumstance is which of these two realities will turn out to be determinative.[8]

  Marcus sees Yeshua's rebuke of his talmidim as a call to teshuvah, to turn away from fearfulness and toward God, trusting in his caring presence, even despite circumstances that call his presence into doubt. It's an exhortation that all Yeshua's followers might take to heart in the age of anxiety in which we are living.

- The closing scene with the cleansed demoniac is striking in two ways. First, as noted above, Yeshua breaks with his usual approach and tells the demoniac to go home and talk about what happened to him. But before that, the demoniac had begged Yeshua to allow him to go with him—a poignant expression of gratitude and honor. Like Yeshua's instruction to tell everyone what happened, this interaction also contrasts with Yeshua's usual approach, in which he enlists people to follow him (1:17, 20; 2:14; 3:13). Here, without an invitation, the demoniac expresses his desire to be with Yeshua out of gratitude for his deliverance—which might serve as an example for us. Are we sustaining the memory of our deliverance with a desire to stay close to Messiah?

---

8. Marcus, *Mark 1–8*, 339–340.

- It's also striking that Yeshua tells the demoniac to tell his people how much *ADONAI* in his mercy had done for him, and the man goes off proclaiming how much *Yeshua* had done for him. He's an outsider in this story, but somehow he understands that what this Jew from Galilee is doing is God in action, which Mark records as another hint at the identity of Yeshua.

Season 1, Episode 6

Two Remarkable Healings and a Mixed Reception

5:21–6:6

Overview

Yeshua returns from his incursion into Gentile territory and is again greeted as soon as his boat reaches the shore. This time it's not a demonized man who meets Yeshua, but the opposite sort of character, a synagogue leader named Ya'ir, who asks him to come lay hands on his gravely ill daughter. Yeshua and his band set out for Ya'ir's house, followed by a large crowd pressing in on every side, which includes a woman suffering from chronic bleeding. Our episode, then, features two unnamed female characters in desperate need of healing; one the daughter of a community leader, the other seeking to remain unseen amidst a disorderly crowd; one afflicted for twelve years, the other twelve years old. Both the woman and the girl are in a state of ritual impurity and both are delivered by Yeshua's touch. Mark emphasizes the essential role of faith in both miraculous encounters.

As Yeshua is on his way to the house of Ya'ir, the woman suffering from chronic bleeding reaches out to touch his robe and is immediately healed. Yeshua turns to ask who touched him. The woman becomes frightened and falls before him to admit that it was she. Yeshua affirms her trust and validates her healing, the first of two great miracles in this episode, which will be added to the miraculous exorcism of our previous episode for a total of three.

Meanwhile, people come from Yair's house to tell him his daughter has died. Yeshua reassures Ya'ir and insists on continuing to his house, now accompanied only by his three closest talmidim, Kefa, Ya'akov, and Yochanan. Going into the daughter's room with the three as well as the girl's parents, he takes her lifeless hand in his own and restores her to life with a simple word of command. He instructs those with him to say nothing about this amazing event and then tells them to give her something to eat.

From there, Yeshua returns to nearby Natzeret, his hometown, where he goes to the synagogue on Shabbat and begins to teach. After these two miraculous healings, the response of Yeshua's neighbors seems mixed at best, and Yeshua speaks his famous words, "A prophet is not without honor, except in his own hometown." After healing a few sick people there, Yeshua, amazed at the lack of faith in Natzeret, moves on to teach in other towns and villages of the Galil.

Peshat

5:21–34

> [21] Yeshua crossed in the boat to the other side of the lake, and a great crowd gathered around him. [22] There came to him a synagogue official, Ya'ir by name, who fell at his feet [23] and pleaded desperately with him, "My little daughter is at the point of death. Please! Come and lay your hands on her, so that she will get well and live!"
>
> [24] He went with him; and a large crowd followed, pressing all around him. [25] Among them was a woman who had had a hemorrhage for twelve years [26] and had suffered a great deal under many physicians. She had spent her life savings; yet instead of improving, she had grown worse. [27] She had heard about Yeshua, so she came up behind him in the crowd and touched his robe; [28] for she said, "If I touch even his clothes, I will be healed." [29] Instantly the hemorrhaging stopped, and she felt in her body that she had been healed from the disease. [30] At the same time, Yeshua, aware that power had gone out from him, turned around in the crowd and asked, "Who touched my clothes?" [31] His *talmidim* responded, "You see the people pressing in on you; and still you

ask, 'Who touched me?'" [32] But he kept looking around to see who had done it. [33] The woman, frightened and trembling, because she knew what had happened to her, came and fell down in front of him and told him the whole truth. [34] "Daughter," he said to her, "your trust has healed you. Go in peace, and be healed of your disease."

Like our previous episode, this episode opens with Yeshua crossing Lake Kinneret and being greeted upon arrival, but there's a contrast: at the earlier crossing, Yeshua was greeted by a man with an unclean spirit coming out from among unclean tombs; now he's greeted by the most respectable sort of man, Ya'ir, a synagogue dignitary.[1] But even with Ya'ir there's a threat of contamination, because his daughter is on the verge of death, a source of ritual impurity. Nevertheless, he entreats Yeshua to come and lay hands on her and heal her before it's too late.

Yeshua sets out, followed by an eager crowd that presses in on him from all sides, a crowd that includes a woman with "a discharge of blood" (ESV)—yet another source of uncleanness. Mark describes her condition in terms that reflect the language of Leviticus 15:19–31, especially as that passage appears in the Septuagint.[2] The "hemorrhage" afflicting the woman is most likely related to the menstrual flow, which would normally place her in a state of *niddah*, according to the Hebrew of Leviticus 15:19. The Mishnah, put into writing around the year 200 CE, devotes an entire chapter to this condition. A woman is *niddah* through the time of her monthly flow and seven days afterwards, but if the flow does not cease, the woman is termed a *zavah* (Lev. 15:25), which has its own chapter in the Mishnah. This appears to be the condition of our unnamed woman. A married woman must refrain from marital intimacy when in a state of *niddah* or *zavah*.[3] The woman in our story, then, if she was

---

1. Numerous commentators agree that this scene most likely takes place in K'far-Nachum, Yeshua's base of operations in the Galil.
2. Thiessen, *Jesus and the Forces of Death*, 83–85. Thiessen also notes that Mark is dealing in these scenes with three sources of impurity: unclean spirits in Gerasa; death in the case of Ya'ir's daughter (at least temporarily); and the flow of blood from which the woman suffers (*Jesus and the Forces of Death*, chapters 4 and 5; cf. France, 235–36).
3. Wills, "Mark," JANT, 80.

married, would have been forbidden to be intimate with her husband for the whole twelve years of her affliction.

Furthermore, she would have transmitted impurity to anyone who came in contact with her. According to Leviticus, a person who is impure cannot participate in worship at the Tabernacle (or later the Temple), and anyone they touch becomes disqualified as well. Such impurity might not have been so important in a Galilean village far from the Temple, but it was still to be avoided, and those infected with it had to undergo a process of cleansing outlined in Leviticus 15. It's not a sin to be ritually impure, but it is humiliating and burdensome. An impure person would be expected to keep his or her distance and especially not to touch anyone, which explains why our unnamed woman tries to remain invisible in the crowd and why she approaches Yeshua from behind . . . and touches only his clothing, not him directly.

When the woman makes contact with Yeshua, however, her impurity doesn't infect him; rather, power goes out from him and heals the woman. He is aware of this "discharge" of power that heals the discharge of blood and asks who touched his clothing. The talmidim remind Yeshua that countless people must have touched him in this jostling crowd, and their words suggest that they might have been impatient with the delay, knowing that Ya'ir's daughter was at the point of death. But Yeshua has sensed a unique touch, one that released healing power, and he keeps looking around him to see who did it. After a moment of hesitation, the woman comes forward to confess that she's the one who touched Yeshua, but she comes "frightened and trembling" (5:33), perhaps from fear of rebuke for mixing in with this crowd at all and for making the teacher impure, as well as awe at what has happened to her. But Yeshua doesn't become impure; rather she becomes pure. Yeshua speaks kindly to her, calling her "daughter," praising her for her trust, and affirming her healing as an outcome of that trust.

We can witness Mark's great skill as a storyteller here. He refrains from explaining the woman's illness itself, but recounts her harrowing twelve years and her suffering under many physicians, which consumed all of her resources and brought no improvement, as she had only grown worse. Likewise, Mark refrains from describing the regulations surrounding this condition and focuses instead on the woman's fearful actions. He cites her own words to let us know what she is dealing with and how risky it feels to her to approach a recognized holy teacher in her condition. In the end, we can almost feel her relief and gratitude when Yeshua calls her "daughter" and pronounces her healed.

It's a glorious moment of release, but commentators have sometimes missed the point of the story, even our often-cited R. T. France, who notes Yeshua's "apparently cavalier attitude to the laws of purity" here, which "will become a central feature of the story in chapter 7," for which Mark "has deliberately prepared the way by this sequence of narratives."[4] It's not the laws of purity that are the problem here, however, but impurity itself, for "the kingdom of God is a time of liberation from impurity, not from impurity laws (Zech. 13:1–2; 14:20–21)."[5] Yeshua doesn't come to set aside or minimize the regulations founded in the Torah; he comes to vanquish impurity itself along with its sources—demonic infestation, unclean bodily disorders, and death, as we'll see shortly in the account of another afflicted daughter.

5:35–43

> [35] While he was still speaking, people from the synagogue official's house came, saying, "Your daughter has died. Why bother the rabbi any longer?" [36] Ignoring what they had said, Yeshua told the synagogue official, "Don't be afraid, just keep trusting." [37] He let no one follow him except Kefa, Ya'akov and Yochanan, Ya'akov's brother. [38] When they came to the synagogue official's house, he found a great commotion, with people weeping and wailing loudly. [39] On entering, he said to them, "Why all this commotion and weeping? The child isn't dead, she's just asleep!" [40] And they jeered at him. But he put them all outside, took the child's father and mother and those with him, and went in

---

4. France, 235.
5. Wills, "Mark," JANT, 80.

> where the child was. ⁴¹ Taking her by the hand, he said to her, "*Talita, kumi!*" (which means, "Little girl, I say to you, get up!"). ⁴² At once the girl got up and began walking around; she was twelve years old. Everybody was utterly amazed. ⁴³ He gave them strict orders to say nothing about this to anyone, and told them to give her something to eat.

As the story shifts back to the synagogue official and his daughter, it reminds us that the opposition Yeshua faces doesn't come from "the Jews" per se, or even from every prominent Jewish individual. We're still in the Galil, not the religious center of Jerusalem, and here at least we witness this prominent Jewish figure falling at Yeshua's feet and recognizing his power to heal (5:22–23). And then the man brings him into his home. Yeshua's opposition doesn't include all the Jews, but is primarily from among the religious gatekeepers, centered in Jerusalem and operating in collusion with the imperial authorities of Rome. Here in the Galil, he is often met with a measure of respect, as he is by this local Jewish leader.[6]

Before they arrive at the official's house, however, messengers come to tell him it's too late, because his daughter has died, adding "Why bother the rabbi any longer?" The words convey respect for Yeshua as teacher, but they also seem harsh and insensitive toward the father. Nonetheless, at least for the reader, they also carry hope. Yeshua is "the rabbi," whose teaching has been accompanied by astonishing power (1:22, 27, 39; 4:38–41)—but, still, what can a teacher do in the face of death? The messengers' words don't discourage Yeshua, however, and he continues on with his three closest talmidim and the father to the house where people are already in the throes of mourning. Yeshua declares that the girl isn't dead, but only sleeping, words met with scorn by the mourners. These may be professional mourners, in accord with the later instructions of Rabbi Judah: "Even the poorest man in Israel [let alone a prominent man like

---

6. The term "synagogue official" is *archisynagōgos*, literally a "synagogue ruler," in Greek. The exact meaning of this position in a Second Temple era synagogue is unclear, but in line with the informal organization of synagogues in Second-Temple Judaism, he is a trusted member responsible for maintaining order and organizing the study and teaching that characterize synagogue life.

Ya'ir] should not hire fewer than two flutes and one professional wailing woman."[7] Such would be "experts on death... [who] know full well that the girl is dead and that dead people don't come back to life!"[8] Yeshua doesn't just put all these noisy mourners outside, as in our translation, but *drives* them out. Mark uses the same verb here, *ekballei*, that he often employs to describe driving out demons (1:34, 39; 3:15, 22; 6:13; 7:26; 9:28), suggesting that Yeshua's encounter with death in this scene is part of his ongoing, wider confrontation with the spiritual forces of contamination and destruction.

Yeshua takes the girl by the hand, again not challenging the purity laws that would keep him from touching the dead, but challenging death itself. And then with a simple phrase in Aramaic— *"Talita, kumi!"*—Yeshua calls the girl out of death and back to life. Recording this phrase in its original Aramaic adds to the poignancy of the scene, and is also the sort of "vivid detail" that we'd expect in an eyewitness account.[9]

In the sequence of three great triumphs of the Kingdom of God in Episodes 5 and 6 this is undoubtedly the greatest, a triumph over death itself. And yet it is pictured in the humblest of terms, with the girl rising up, walking around, and then being given something to eat, as if she'd just come home from a walk or an errand—and Yeshua exhorting the witnesses to keep this amazing news to themselves.

6:1–6

> Then Yeshua left and went to his home town, and his talmidim followed him. [2] On Shabbat he started to teach in the synagogue, and many who heard him were astounded. They asked, "Where did this man get all this? What is this wisdom he has been given? What are these miracles worked through him? [3] Isn't he just the carpenter? the son of Miryam? the brother of Ya'akov and Yosi

---

7. Ketubot 4:4 in Jacob Neusner, *The Mishnah: A New Translation* (New Haven and London: Yale University Press, 1988). Cf. Matt. 9:23, 11:17.
8. Marcus, *Mark 1–8*, 371.
9. Bauckham, *Eyewitnesses*, 55. Bauckham notes that the eyewitness account "could be that of Peter, James, John, or the girl's mother," or Jairus/Ya'ir himself—in other words any of the five who accompanied Yeshua as he raised up the girl.

and Y'hudah and Shim'on? Aren't his sisters here with us?" And they took offense at him. ⁴ But Yeshua said to them. "The only place people don't respect a prophet is in his home town, among his own relatives, and in his own house." ⁵ So he could do no miracles there, other than lay his hands on a few sick people and heal them. ⁶ He was amazed at their lack of trust.

Then he went through the surrounding towns and villages, teaching.

The events we've just covered probably took place in K'far-Nachum, Yeshua's base of operations in the Galil. Now he departs for Natzeret, not mentioned by name here, but elsewhere noted as his hometown, especially in Mark's prologue (1:9) and conclusion (16:6), as well as at 1:24, 10:47, and 14:67. With this strong emphasis, Mark highlights Natzeret as the prototypical hometown, with some typical hometown attitudes. The people are "astounded" or amazed at his teaching at first, just as the members of synagogue in K'far-Nachum were (1:22), and as the people will be at his second visit to the Ten Towns (7:37), and finally in Jerusalem (11:18). The same Greek word, *ekplesso*—which can be captured in the contemporary phrase "blown away"—is employed in all four events, but only here does it dissipate into questioning Yeshua and taking offense. To employ contemporary English again, the people remember Yeshua as a local guy and respond to his amazing teaching with, "Where did he get all this?"

Perhaps the most striking part of this vignette, though, is the conclusion: Yeshua is unable to do much here, beyond a few simple healings, because of a lack of faith among the townsfolk. The one who just days before calmed a deadly windstorm, cast out a legion of demons, healed a twelve-year-long affliction, and raised up a dead girl is finally brought up short by the unbelief and distrust of his own hometown. Mark underlines the indispensable quality of faith, or "trust" in our translation, to the workings of the Kingdom of God. The King acts on his own power and according to his own purposes, and yet is somehow and mysteriously limited by the response of those over whom he rules. And now it is Yeshua's turn to be amazed—with a different Greek word, *thaumazo,* which also described the response of the Gadarenes to Yeshua's power over the demonic realm (5:20). But here the amazement isn't the positive sort that springs up in the presence of miraculous power, but the opposite, shock at the utter lack of response. Yeshua seems to comfort himself with the saying, "A prophet is not without honor, except in his own hometown." From here, Yeshua can only keep going to bring his teaching to the towns and villages of the Galil.

Derash

- In contemplating and discussing this episode, keep in mind the sequence of events starting with Yeshua's crossing of Lake Kinneret in Mark 4:35–41, when he calms the storm with simple words. The talmidim are awe-struck and left wondering, "Who can this be, that even the wind and the waves obey him?" Throughout the Tanakh it is ADONAI, the LORD, who has such power over nature, as we mentioned in the commentary on Episode 5. The power Yeshua displays in stilling the wind and the waves plays out in the three scenes that follow, in which Yeshua takes command of unclean demonic forces, of an unclean bodily disorder, and of death itself. Mark caps this whole sequence with the ironic scene in Yeshua's hometown where his true nature is unrecognized and spurned. What lessons might we derive from the whole trajectory of this part of the besorah narrative?

- Mark employs his "sandwich" technique here in Episode 6, placing the story of the unnamed woman between the two slices of the story of Ya'ir's daughter. This technique reflects the actual sequence of events—Yeshua's ministry to the girl was interrupted by the woman's entreaty—but it highlights something more significant. Yeshua allows his very public interaction with a high-status man to be interrupted by a no-status woman, whom he treats with kindness and respect, despite her humiliating condition. Indeed, it is during the delay created by Yeshua's kindness to the woman that Ya'ir's daughter dies. It works out for the good in the end, of course, but there still may be lessons here regarding our priorities, especially in regard to what we label "ministry" in today's religious world.

- Ya'ir's daughter was twelve years old when she was raised up from death, a number that might seem ordinary enough, especially within the homey picture that Mark provides, which includes the simple Aramaic command to rise up, and the detail of giving the girl something to eat. But, of course, twelve is a number of completion and power, as in the twelve years of affliction in the previous miracle, or the twelve Yeshua appoints to be with him and sends out to preach and have authority over demons (3:14–15), who will reappear in our next episode. Given the significance of the number twelve, what are we to make of the fact that this girl—the first person raised from the dead in Mark's account—was twelve years old at the time? How does the symbolism of the number twelve add to the story and its relevance for us?

- Faith/trust plays an essential role in both miracles. Indeed, Yeshua tells the woman healed of the hemorrhage, "your trust has healed you"—highlighting not the power that flowed from him nor God's healing presence in general—but her trust. Likewise, Yeshua admonishes Ya'ir, "Don't be afraid, just keep trusting." Finally, in Natzeret, the lack of trust among the townspeople limits Yeshua's power to work miracles. How do we align this portrayal of faith/trust as indispensable with the idea of God acting in accord with his own plans and purposes and needing no human assistance? To what extent and in what way might we say that God is dependent on our faith?

Season 1, Episode 7

Equipping the Twelve

6:7–56

Overview

Yeshua regains momentum after a disappointing response from his own townsfolk by sending out the Twelve. These are the men he chose back in Episode 3 "to be with him, to be sent out to preach" (3:14). Now, to expand his impact, Yeshua equips them with authority over unclean spirits and with detailed instructions for their journey. They set out and begin to replicate the Kingdom-of-God ministry that Yeshua himself launched in Episode 1.

As Yeshua's reputation spreads because of his powerful words and deeds and those of his followers, some people start saying that he is Yochanan the Immerser, who was executed by King Herod, but is now risen from the dead—a belief that Herod himself shares. Mark recounts that Herod had arrested Yochanan because he was openly criticizing Herod's marriage to Herodias, wife of his brother Philip. Herod kept Yochanan in his dungeon, but held him in awe and liked to listen to him speak. After some time, at a banquet for Herod's birthday, the daughter of Herodias danced to entertain the (male) guests, who were so pleased with her dancing that Herod promised to reward her with anything she asked for, up to half of his kingdom. At her mother's prompting, she requested the head of Yochanan the Immerser on a platter, and Herod reluctantly complied. When Yochanan's followers heard of his murder, they came for his body and laid it in a grave.

In his typical sandwich style, after this gruesome tale, Mark returns to the story of the Twelve, who rejoin Yeshua and report on the success of their mission. Yeshua takes them to a secluded place where they can rest, but they're spotted by the crowds, who get to the place ahead of Yeshua. He has compassion on them because they're like sheep without a shepherd and resumes teaching them, and then feeds them in a miraculous fashion, multiplying five loaves and two fish to become more than enough food for 5,000 people.

Afterwards, Yeshua directs his followers, who had just helped with the food distribution, to take their boat to the other side of Lake Kinneret while he sends off the crowd and spends some time by himself in prayer. But as the talmidim are heading across the lake, the wind arises and they are struggling at their oars. In the middle of the night they see Yeshua walking upon the surface of the water close by, and scream in terror, thinking he's a ghost. Yeshua rebukes the talmidim for their fears, and the wind ceases. He steps into the boat, and the talmidim remain amazed and don't understand the full implications of Yeshua's mighty deeds. After landing at Ginosar, they are recognized by the crowds and Yeshua resumes his ministry of healing the sick.

Peshat

6:7–13

> [7] Yeshua summoned the Twelve and started sending them out in pairs, giving them authority over the unclean spirits. [8] He instructed them, "Take nothing for your trip except a walking stick — no bread, no pack, no money in your belt. [9] Wear shoes but not an extra shirt. [10] Whenever you enter a house, stay there until you leave the place; [11] and if the people of some place will not welcome you, and they refuse to hear you, then, as you leave, shake the dust off your feet as a warning to them."
>
> [12] So they set out and preached that people should turn from sin to God, [13] they expelled many demons, and they anointed many sick people with oil and healed them.

Mention of the Twelve reminds us not just of the special status of these insider-talmidim, but also of their connection to the Twelve

Tribes of Israel. This connection is further highlighted by Yeshua's list of their travel supplies, because it reflects the minimal gear of the Israelites in the wilderness. As their forefathers depended on God's provision of manna, the Twelve will have to depend on divine provision for their food—in this case supplied through the welcome of the people in various places. In Deuteronomy, Moses reminds the Israelites about these conditions of their journey:

> He humbled you, allowing you to become hungry, and then fed you with manna, which neither you nor your ancestors had ever known, to make you understand that a person does not live on food alone but on everything that comes from the mouth of ADONAI. During these forty years the clothing you were wearing didn't grow old, and your feet didn't swell up. (Deut. 8:3–4)

> I led you forty years in the desert. Neither the clothes on your body nor the shoes on your feet wore out. You didn't eat bread, and you didn't drink wine or other intoxicating liquor; this was so that you would know that "I am ADONAI your God." (Deut. 29:4–5 [5–6])

It's noteworthy that amidst this minimal list of provisions for the journey, Yeshua does allow the Twelve to take a staff, just as their ancestors were instructed to have a staff in hand as they ate the Passover meal in preparation for their journey into the wilderness (Exod. 12:11). A staff is not a mere accessory, but essential equipment for a demanding journey, and may also be a reminder of the miracle-working staff of Moses, which is fitting because the mission of the Twelve also involves the miraculous. Like their master, they not only preach the message of return to God, but also expel demons and heal the sick (cf. 1:34, 39), evidence of the miracle-working presence of the Spirit. This parallel between sending the Twelve and Israel's time in the wilderness reflects Mark's Exodus imagery in his Prologue,[1] and also anticipates the miraculous, manna-like feeding of the 5000 later in this episode.

---

1. See pages 18-19 in this commentary.

Before providing these instructions, Yeshua had directed the Twelve to travel in pairs, which doesn't reflect the Exodus account, but may be based on the Torah's requirement of two witnesses to confirm evidence (Num. 35:30; Deut. 17:7, 19:15; cf. 2 Cor. 13:1; 1 Tim. 5:19). The Twelve are bearing evidence of the greatest import—the coming of the Kingdom of God—and travel in pairs to confirm that evidence. This practice became the norm in the Messianic community (e.g. Acts 8:14, 11:30, 13:1–2, 15:39–40). It's "a sensible policy, providing mutual support and companionship,"[2] and it also testifies to the gravity of the message that the Twelve are bearing as they preach "that people should turn from sin to God" (6:12). They also cast out demons and heal the sick, pursuing the same three-fold mission as Yeshua himself. Indeed, as the Twelve go forth, it's the reputation of Yeshua that is enhanced, as we see in the next section.

6:14–29

> [14] Meanwhile, King Herod heard about this, for Yeshua's reputation had spread. Some were saying, "Yochanan the Immerser has been raised from the dead; that is why these miraculous powers are at work in him." [15] Others said, "It is Eliyahu!" and still others, "He is a prophet, like one of the old prophets." [16] But when Herod heard about it, he said, "Yochanan, whom I had beheaded, has been raised."
>
> [17] For Herod had sent and had Yochanan arrested and chained in prison because of Herodias, the wife of his brother Philip. Herod had married her, [18] but Yochanan had told him, "It violates the *Torah* for you to marry your brother's wife." [19] So Herodias had a grudge against him and wanted him put to death. But this she could not accomplish, [20] because Herod stood in awe of Yochanan and protected him, for he knew that he was a *tzaddik*, a holy man. Whenever he heard him, he became deeply disturbed; yet he liked to listen to him.

---

2. France, 247.

²¹ Finally, the opportunity came. Herod gave a banquet on his birthday for his nobles and officers and the leading men of the Galil. ²² The daughter of Herodias came in and danced, and she pleased Herod and his guests. The king said to the girl, "Ask me for whatever you want; I will give it to you"; ²³ and he made a vow to her, "Whatever you ask me, I will give you, up to half my kingdom." ²⁴ So she went out and said to her mother, "What should I ask for?" She said, "The head of Yochanan the Immerser." ²⁵ At once the daughter hurried back to the king and announced her request: "I want you to give me right now on a platter the head of Yochanan the Immerser." ²⁶ Herod was appalled; but out of regard for the oaths he had sworn before his dinner guests, he did not want to break his word to her. ²⁷ So the king immediately sent a soldier from his personal guard with orders to bring Yochanan's head. The soldier went and beheaded Yochanan in the prison, ²⁸ brought his head on a platter, and gave it to the girl; and the girl gave it to her mother. ²⁹ When Yochanan's *talmidim* heard of it, they came and took the body and laid it in a grave.

We might expect Mark to record the results of the mission of the Twelve here but instead, in his characteristic style, he inserts another account between the sending of the Twelve and their return. Their empowered ministry and call to repentance have raised Yeshua's profile in the Galil . . . and raised again the question of who Yeshua might be. Some believe he is Elijah the prophet, who must appear "before the coming of the great and terrible Day of ADONAI" (Mal. 3:23 [4:5]), or some other prophet. Others provide a new explanation: he is Yochanan the Immerser raised from the dead. Herod, ruler of Galilee and Peraea, buys into this belief, perhaps from a guilty conscience for having Yochanan beheaded in his dungeon despite knowing he was a holy man and often listening to his words (6:20).

The gruesome account of Yochanan's death reveals the shallowness and depravity of Herod's "kingdom." When Mark uses the term "King Herod," he's following common practice,[3] but this is actually Herod Antipas, a lesser ruler, exercising power as a tetrarch under Roman authority. Mark's use of the "King" title may be characteristically ironic or even mocking. Herod is beguiled by his step-daughter's dancing, probably of an erotic nature, at his birthday party, doubtless fueled by abundant servings of wine. He makes a foolish promise to the girl to grant her any reward she requests. The girl runs off to consult her mother and comes back with a demand for Yochanan's head to be brought to her on a platter. Herod is willing to sacrifice the righteous man to save himself the embarrassment of publicly walking back his words, and sends a soldier from his personal guard to execute the deed. Herod's birthday feast becomes a macabre and demonic rite, as Yochanan's head is passed from the soldier to the daughter to the mother. Yochanan's followers show up to collect the mutilated body and lay it in a grave. Mark closes this account without comment, letting it speak for itself, and perhaps foreshadow what lies ahead for Yeshua. Then he turns our attention back to the Twelve.

6:30–44

> [30] Those who had been sent out rejoined Yeshua and reported to him all they had done and taught. [31] There were so many people coming and going that they couldn't even take time to eat, so he said to them, "Come with me by yourselves to a place where we can be alone, and you can get some rest." [32] They went off by themselves to an isolated spot; [33] but many people, seeing them leave and recognizing them, ran ahead on foot from all the towns and got there first. [34] When Yeshua came ashore, he saw a huge crowd. Filled with compassion for them, because they were like sheep without a shepherd, he began teaching them many things.
>
> [35] By this time, the hour was late. The talmidim came to him and said, "This is a remote place, and it's getting late. [36] Send the

---

3. France, 252; Marcus, *Mark 1–8*, 392.

people away, so that they can go and buy food for themselves in the farms and towns around here." [37] But he answered them, "Give them something to eat, yourselves!" They replied, "We are to go and spend thousands on bread, and give it to them to eat?" [38] He asked them, "How many loaves do you have? Go and check." When they had found out, they said, "Five. And two fish." [39] Then he ordered all the people to sit down in groups on the green grass. [40] They sat down in groups of fifty or a hundred. [41] Then he took the five loaves and the two fish, and, looking up toward heaven, made a *b'rakhah*. Next he broke up the loaves and began giving them to the talmidim to distribute. He also divided up the two fish among them all. [42] They all ate as much as they wanted, [43] and they took up twelve baskets full of the broken pieces and fish. [44] Those who ate the loaves numbered five thousand men.

The followers of Yochanan lay their master's body in the grave; the followers of Yeshua return to their master after a successful mission in his name. Indeed, the mission is so successful that the disciples' report of it is cut short by a crowd that wants more of what they did on the mission. The crowd, ever-present throughout Yeshua's Galilean ministry, now becomes so great that Yeshua and his followers can't even take a break to eat. By phrasing the urgency of the crowd in these terms, Mark picks up a thematic thread that runs through all of Episode 7: food and eating. When Yeshua sent out the Twelve, he instructed them not to bring food supplies, because they could depend on the hospitality of at least some of the folks of the Galil. Then the scene shifts to a banquet, a gathering around food, where Yochanan's head, in gruesome irony, will be displayed to the guests on a platter, an object normally used for serving food. Now, Yeshua and his talmidim must forgo food to attend to the crowd, and will finally feed them in miraculous fashion, as we'll see shortly.

This crowd is demanding, but Yeshua is not irritated by them. Rather, he views them with compassion, as sheep without a shepherd and he "feeds" them with his rich teaching. Sheep and shepherd terminology is familiar to anyone at home in the Hebrew Scriptures, perhaps most famously in the opening words of Psalm 23: "The LORD is my shepherd; I lack nothing." This imagery in turn is rooted in the

Torah, where Moses responds to ADONAI's notice that he will shortly die by asking him to "appoint a man to be over the community, to go out and come in ahead of them, to lead them out and bring them in, so that ADONAI's community will not be like sheep without a shepherd" (Num. 27:16–17). In response, ADONAI designates Joshua, or Yehoshua, the longer form of "Yeshua," a man in whom is the Spirit, like his namesake Yeshua (Num. 27:18; Mark 1:10), as Moses' successor. Mark's wording here points to Yeshua as bearing the mantle of Moses and, like him, a shepherd to his people. "Like Moses, Jesus is called out of his preferred isolation [Mark 6:31] by *compassion* for the people (e.g. Ex. 3–4) who will abandon him."[4]

Underlying such imagery in the Tanakh is the ancient Near Eastern notion of the sovereign as a shepherd to his people, a benign and wise figure who can lead them to provision and safety. When Yeshua steps into this role he hints at his identity as both the successor of Moses and the descendant of David promised by ADONAI: "I will raise up one shepherd to be in charge of them, and he will let them feed — my servant David. He will pasture them and be their shepherd" (Ezek. 34:23; cf. Jer. 23:1–4).

As Yeshua tends the crowd with his teaching, the hour grows late, a time best understood in this context as mid-afternoon, since the evening or afternoon meal was usually eaten around the ninth hour, or three o'clock in the afternoon. This would be an appropriate time to dismiss the crowd so that folks could get home before dark, as the talmidim suggest (6:36). Yeshua, however, is unwilling to send them away hungry, and instructs the talmidim to provide food for them, indicating that serving the people entails not only the "spiritual" supply of teaching, healing, and deliverance, but also concern for the people's physical well-being. The dualistic understanding of soul vs body, spirit vs flesh, is foreign to the Jewish outlook of the time, and Yeshua addresses all aspects of human life. The talmidim, however, respond to his instructions with apparent sarcasm: "We are to go and spend thousands on bread, and give it to them to eat?" (6:37). Even after their successful mission and their

---

4. Wills, "Mark," JANT, 83.

months (or more) of seeing Yeshua at work, their imaginations have not been set free to recognize the presence of God's Shepherd-King among them.

Yeshua ignores the sarcasm and enlists his men to help feed this crowd right where they are in this "isolated" (6:32) and "remote" (6:35) spot. The original Greek word underlying both these terms is *eremos*, commonly translated "desert" or "wilderness." Although not captured by CJB, it also appears in 6:31 and is then repeated for emphasis in 6:32. *Eremos* is employed for "desert" or "wilderness" throughout the Septuagint, the ancient Greek translation of the Tanakh. In some of these Tanakh references as well as in Mark, "desert" or "wilderness" is portrayed not only as a dry and difficult terrain, but also as a place of encounter with God and even an ideal place of intimacy with him (e.g. Jer. 2:1–3; Hos. 2:16–20). In the Torah itself, the desert is the place where God sustained Israel day by day with manna, and Mark's detailed description of the feeding of the 5000 highlights its connection to the story of Israel's feeding in the wilderness.

> The arrangement of the crowd into field-groups of hundreds and fifties recalls the order of the Mosaic camp in the wilderness (e.g. Ex. 18:21). This detail is particularly striking because the documents of Qumran use these subdivisions to describe true Israel assembled in the desert in the period of the last days. If this concept is presupposed in verse 40, the multitude who have been instructed concerning the Kingdom is characterized as the people of the new exodus who have been summoned to the wilderness to experience messianic grace.[5]

The food motif in Episode 7, then, culminates in the feeding of 5000 in a desert place at the hands of a new Moses, who is also the promised Shepherd-King who will lead his people into the promised Kingdom that has drawn near (Mark 1:15). Thus, it is a preview of the banquet to come, when Messiah will "drink new wine in the

---

5. Lane, 229–30.

Kingdom of God" (14:25). And Yeshua doesn't leave his self-revelation at that, but will take it one step further—quite literally.

6:45–56

> ⁴⁵ Immediately Yeshua had his talmidim get in the boat and go on ahead of him toward the other side of the lake, toward Beit-Tzaidah, while he sent the crowds away. ⁴⁶ After he had left them, he went into the hills to pray. ⁴⁷ When night came, the boat was out on the lake, and he was by himself on land. ⁴⁸ He saw that they were having difficulty rowing, because the wind was against them; so at around four o'clock in the morning he came toward them, walking on the lake! He meant to come alongside them; ⁴⁹ but when they saw him walking on the lake, they thought it was a ghost and let out a shriek; ⁵⁰ for they had all seen him and were terrified. However, he spoke to them. "Courage," he said, "it is I. Stop being afraid!" ⁵¹ He got into the boat with them, and the wind ceased. They were completely astounded, ⁵² for they did not understand about the loaves; on the contrary, their hearts had been made stone-like.
>
> ⁵³ After they had made the crossing, they landed at Ginosar and anchored. ⁵⁴ As soon as they got out of the boat, the people recognized him ⁵⁵ and began running around throughout that whole region and bringing sick people on their stretchers to any place where they heard he was. ⁵⁶ Wherever he went, in towns, cities or country, they laid the sick in the marketplaces. They begged him to let them touch even the *tzitzit* on his robe, and all who touched it were healed.

Facing a lack of understanding among his closest followers, Yeshua doesn't remind them about what he has already revealed, but instead raises the stakes. He purposefully stays behind when he sends his followers back across the lake by boat, then dismisses the crowd and goes off into the hills to pray. Finally, aware that his talmidim are having a hard time getting across the lake on a windy night, he walks across the water to meet up with them. But Yeshua's amazing feat is not just a convenient way to catch up with his men; rather it's the culmination of a series of self-revealing acts in this section of Mark. In an earlier crossing of Lake Kinneret, Yeshua calmed a storm with simple words of command. The talmidim were awe-struck and left wondering, "Who can this be, that even the wind and the waves obey him?" (4:35–41). This sense of awe and the question of who this can be continue through Yeshua's acts of power on behalf of the demonized Gadarene (5:1–20); the woman with a discharge of blood (5:25–34); the daughter of Ya'ir, who has died (5:35–43); and the 5000 fed in the wilderness (6:34–44).

Now, to conclude this whole section, Mark has brought us to another stormy crossing of Lake Kinneret. As in the first crossing, and many other biblical passages, the sea is a symbol of chaos, of the forces opposing God's Kingdom. Earlier Yeshua calmed the sea; now, in an even greater expression of his sovereignty, he walks upon it, figuratively trampling it underfoot. He is not just a Galilean healer and miracle-worker—although he is that—but one far greater. He has mastery not only over individual illnesses and impurities, and not only over human deprivations like hunger, but over the very source of opposition to God's life-giving purposes. He not only calms the waters; he walks upon them in complete mastery.

Mark's comment as Episode 7 draws to a close is a bit of a letdown: the talmidim "were completely astounded, for they did not understand about the loaves; on the contrary, their hearts had been made stone-like" (6:51–52). The talmidim witness everything, including the amazing feeding of 5000 just hours before, and still don't know the answer to "who is Yeshua?" But there's more going on here than ordinary denseness: the phrase "Their hearts had been made stone-like"—or simply "were hardened," as in most translations—reminds us of ADONAI's hardening of Pharaoh's heart in Exodus 7–11. As often noted, this hardening by God came after Pharaoh's own hardening of heart, and it served ADONAI's purpose of multiplying his miracles and revealing his sovereignty to Egypt as well as to Israel (e.g. Exod. 10:1–2; 14:4). Mark is perhaps alerting us that the hard-heartedness of the talmidim is part of the plan to reveal Yeshua's identity and mission most fully. Accordingly, our episode closes, not with the hardness of the talmidim, but with Yeshua, after his display of the most awesome power, continuing on his mission of mercy throughout the region of Lake Kinneret.

Our episode ends with a detail that might seem minor, but is critical to the following passage, and to understanding Yeshua's way of life in general: "They begged him to let them touch even the *tzitzit* on his robe, and all who touched it were healed" (6:56). *Tzitzit* first appears in the book of Numbers, denoting the "fringe" or "tassels" that Israelite men were to wear on the corners of their garments. In the original Greek, Mark uses the word *kraspedon* here, often translated simply as fringe, or the like, but it is the "word used in the plural in the Septuagint (Num. 15:38–39; Deut. 22:12) and the NT (Matt. 23:5) for the tassels (*ṣîṣîyôt*) worn by Jewish males at the four corners of their garments to remind them of God's commandments," signifying that "our passage portrays Jesus as an observant Jew even to the tassels of his garment."[6] In Yeshua's case the tzitzit is not only a marker of Torah-loyalty, but also a means of conveying his healing power to all who sought it.

Derash

- AJ Levine questions the theory that Yeshua sends the Twelve out in pairs (Mark 6:7–13) to fulfill the Torah's requirement of two witnesses to confirm evidence (Num. 35:30; Deut. 17:7). Instead, she sees the two-by-two strategy as a sort of buddy system: "When the system works, the two-by-two mission helps create trust, the incentive to go that extra mile, the ability to deal with those birds and those thorns" (which choke out the seed of God's word in Mark 4:3–7).[7] The two-by-two approach is also reflected in Pirke Avot 1:4–

---

6. Marcus, *Mark 1–8*, 437, 439. Wills, "Mark," JANT, 83, agrees, noting here that "Jesus observes Torah." Bock, 456, sees *kraspedon* as *tzitzit* as "probably" the best understanding. France, 275; Schnabel, 160; Lane, 239, see this as a reasonable, although not necessary interpretation.

7. Levine, *Mark*, 30.

12, which lists pairs of sages who received and passed on the tradition from Yose ben Yo'ezer and Yose ben Yohanan to the famous pair of Hillel and Shammai. To this day, Jewish learning often involves a *chevruta*, a pair (or small group) of students in dialogue rather than a collection of solitary students. This strategy helps reverse the radical individualism of our modern era, which has infected even the religious world. We often hear teachings, songs, and slogans that exalt the individual, private experience with God, which is indeed a vital component of the spiritual life, but only a component. The communal shared experience is equally vital, and less prone to the errors of subjectivism and relativity that characterize our age. We might ponder how the two-by-two strategy can be integrated into our practice of study and spiritual formation today.

- In Episode 7, Mark employs his sandwich structure again to great effect, recounting the sending of the Twelve, then telling the horrific tale of Yochanan's beheading, and finally coming back to the return of the Twelve. Mark's account of the mission of Twelve doesn't include "Kingdom" language, but it does reflect the message Yeshua established at the outset:

> The time has come,
> God's Kingdom is near!
> Turn to God from your sins
> and believe the Good News! (1:15; cf. 1:34, 39)

The sandwich structure, then, contrasts two kingdoms—one borne by humble men sent out with minimal provisions, and the other glorifying the self and its pleasures; one calling men and women back to God, the other celebrating lust and excess; one giving life and the other rendering death. Mark's irony is that the kingdom that has the genuine goods is out of power and marginalized, while the kingdom adorned with pomp and power is revealed to be foolish and empty.

- Commenting on Mark 6:42 ("They all ate as much as they wanted"), the 19th century Orthodox rabbi Elijah Zvi Soloveitchik argues that as a Torah-observant Jew, Yeshua would have doubtless led the crowd in reciting the grace after the meal, or *Birkat Hamazon*, mandated in Deuteronomy 8:10: "So you will eat and be satisfied [or eat as much as you want, as in Mark], and you will bless ADONAI your God for the good land he has given you."[8] Commentator Joel Marcus adds:

  > Parts of this *Birkat Hamazon* are suggestively similar to the themes of our story and those of the related feeding in 8:1–10, for they call God the shepherd of Israel, emphasize his compassion, and invoke his mercy on "the kingdom of the house of David your anointed." The grace after meals at Qumran (4Q434a), similarly, emphasizes eschatological consolation ("As a man consoles his mother, so will he [God] console Jerusa[lem]"). Graces, indeed, are a natural context for ideas about "tasting" the bliss of the age to come.[9]

  We might then view the feeding of the 5000 as a preview of the great banquet of the Age to Come, as in Isaiah 25:6–8 (see also Isaiah 55:1–5, Matt: 8:11, etc.), but in Mark it's a characteristically ironic picture, with simple food—bread and (probably dried and salted) fish—and a setting in the middle of nowhere. The crowd doesn't seem to be aware of what's going on, and the talmidim, Mark tells us, "did not understand about the loaves" (6:52). So if it's a foretaste of the eschatological feast, it's lodged very much in the middle of this present age—another instance of the "already-but-not-yet" motif in Mark. How does this understanding of the

---

8. *The Bible, the Talmud, and the New Testament: Elijah Zvi Soloveitchik's Commentary to the Gospels*. Edited, with an introduction and commentary, by Shaul Magid (Philadelphia: University of Pennsylvania Press, 2019), 319.
9. Marcus, *Mark 1–8,* 409.

feeding of the 5000 help guide our way in following Yeshua in the wilderness of the 21st century world?

- Mark's portrayal of the tzitzit as a vessel of charismatic power helps overcome the bifurcation between Torah ("law") and Spirit that often crops up in Christian teaching. This Torah-and-Spirit view is in line with the vision of Moses—"I wish all of ADONAI's people were prophets! I wish ADONAI would put his Spirit on all of them!" (Num. 11:29)—and the prophets.

> I will give you a new heart
> and put a new spirit inside you;
> I will take the stony heart out of your flesh
> and give you a heart of flesh.
> I will put my Spirit inside you
> and cause you to live by my laws,
> respect my rulings and obey them. (Ezek. 36:26–27)

> "For this is the covenant I will make with the house of Israel after those days," says ADONAI: "I will put my Torah within them and write it on their hearts; I will be their God, and they will be my people." (Jer. 31:32 [33])

Throughout the scriptures, Mark included, it's not so much Torah vs Spirit as Torah enhanced and empowered by the Spirit, Torah written upon the heart. This vision will be fulfilled "after those days," but is already present among the faithful.

Season 1, Episode 8

A Halakhic Interlude

7:1–23

Overview

Mark's focus shifts from the series of awesome deeds in our previous episodes to a halakhic or legal debate over ritual hand-washing. Yeshua's acts of power began to reveal the fullness of his identity, at least to those with eyes to see, and now, as so often in Mark, the more mundane event of a legal dispute also reveals deeper truths about Yeshua and his mission.

The debate arises because a gathering of Pharisees and Torah-teachers from Jerusalem observe some of Yeshua's talmidim eating without first performing the traditional ritual of washing their hands. When the religious experts challenge Yeshua for permitting his followers to violate this practice, based on the "Tradition of the Elders," he turns the tables on them, citing instances in which they elevate the Tradition of the Elders above the clear demands of Torah, and "nullify the Word of God."

Regarding ritual hand-washing, Yeshua explains to the crowd that it's not what goes into a person from outside that makes him or her unclean, but what comes out of them. Later, alone with his followers, he explains how the body processes food and any impurities that may have entered with it, thus declaring "all foods ritually clean," as Mark notes in a famous and controversial comment. Then, in line with the Torah's teachings about impurity, Yeshua tells his disciples that it's what "comes out of a person that makes a person unclean!" The episode closes as Yeshua lists the sort of wicked thoughts and deeds that arise from within a person and cause defilement.

Peshat

7:1–13

¹ The *P'rushim* and some of the Torah-teachers who had come from Jerusalem gathered together with Yeshua ² and saw that some of his *talmidim* ate with ritually unclean hands, that is, without doing *n'tilat-yadayim*. ³ (For the *P'rushim*, and indeed all the Judeans, holding fast to the Tradition of the Elders, do not eat unless they have given their hands a ceremonial washing. ⁴ Also, when they come from the marketplace they do not eat unless they have rinsed their hands up to the wrist; and they adhere to many other traditions, such as washing cups, pots and bronze vessels.)

⁵ The *P'rushim* and the *Torah*-teachers asked him, "Why don't your *talmidim* live in accordance with the Tradition of the Elders, but instead eat with ritually unclean hands?" ⁶ Yeshua answered them, "Isaiah was right when he prophesied about you hypocrites — as it is written,

'These people honor me with their lips,
but their hearts are far away from me.
⁷ Their worship of me is useless,
because they teach man-made rules as if they were doctrines.'

⁸ "You depart from God's command and hold onto human tradition. ⁹ Indeed," he said to them, "you have made a fine art of departing from God's command in order to keep your tradition! ¹⁰ For Moshe said, '**Honor your father and your mother,**' and '**Anyone who curses his father or mother must be put to death.**' ¹¹ But you say, 'If someone says to his father or mother, "I have promised as a *korban*"' (that is, as a gift to God) '"what I might have used to help you,"' ¹² then you no longer let him do anything for his father or mother. ¹³ Thus, with your tradition which you had handed down to you, you nullify the Word of God! And you do other things like this."

Mark notes that Yeshua's interlocutors here are Pharisees, who are perhaps local, and Torah-teachers from Jerusalem, alerting us that we're likely to witness a confrontation between the wonder-working Galilean preacher and the religious gatekeepers, just as Torah-teachers "who came down from Jerusalem" had led the attack on Yeshua in 3:22–30. This detail also foreshadows Yeshua's journey to Jerusalem soon to begin. Mark notes that the religious experts "gathered together" with Yeshua. Such gathering usually has a friendly connotation (2:2; 4:1; 5:21; 6:30), but the context suggests that they've gathered more *against* him than with him. They've drawn close enough to be able to observe Yeshua's followers as they prepare to sit down to a meal and they see that they're eating with unwashed hands. Mark pauses to explain to his readers—which include a good number of Gentiles—that the Pharisees, along with "all the Judeans," practice a ritual of handwashing before meals, as well as washing household objects when they come in from the marketplace. This ritual involves rinsing the hands "up to the wrist" (7:4), as in our translation, or more in line with the underlying Greek word, "with a fist," or "with a handful" of water.[1]

Talmudic scholar Daniel Boyarin notes,

> As anyone who has seen Jews actually performing the ritual of hand washing would guess immediately, Mark is referring to the process of forming a loose fist with one hand and pouring water over that fist with the other. . . . If Mark was such a close observer and manifests such intimate knowledge of pharisaic practice, then my assumption as I read the passage is that he knew of what he spoke all the way down. This suggests that his perspective (as well as that of his Jesus) is firmly from within the Jewish world—nearly the opposite of what has been usually said of Mark.[2]

---

1. Lane, 246, citing parallel terminology in the Mishnah (Yadaim 1:1,2) and Talmud (Shabbat 62b). See also Schnabel, 162; Marcus, *Mark 1-8*, (441) supplies "'with a cupped hand' (the position in which modern religious Jews hold their hands while they wash them."
2. Boyarin, 116–17.

Our translation of "all the Judeans" in this scene instead of the more common "all the Jews" also helps clear up misconceptions about Mark and his message. "All the Jews" is a plausible translation, but it would be an exaggeration, the sort of everyday generalization we employ when we say, "everyone" is doing something, or they do it "all the time." But our translation suggests that Mark is not treating himself and his audience as "us" in contrast with "all the Jews" as "them"—especially as his perspective is "firmly from within the Jewish world," as Boyarin puts it. Rather Mark is contrasting the practice of Judeans in general, who dwell in the region where Jerusalem sits, with the practice of the Galileans in general. Both sets of practice are Jewish but, then as now, Jewish practice varies with locality. With this reading, the tension in this scene is easy to grasp. Members of the religious elite have shown up to observe and criticize the ways of the less-enlightened locals, particularly those following the wildly popular local figure, Yeshua. But the elites blunder; they base their criticism on what they frankly call "tradition" rather than on Scripture itself; and Yeshua leverages their own wording against them.

To be fair, this disputed tradition is rooted in Scripture, which requires routine washing of those serving in the Temple (or Tabernacle; Exod. 30:18–21; 40:30–32). This may be a case where the Pharisees are seeking to extend the priestly requirement to all Jewish people, which is an approach throughout their halakhic discussions. In addition, washings are required after contact with something unclean, as in Leviticus 15, and the Pharisee's tradition may have mandated routine washing before meals "just in case." Either way, Yeshua is ironically in the position of defending the basics of Judaism against the elaborations of the Jerusalem establishment:

> Jesus' Judaism was a conservative reaction against some radical innovations in the Law stemming from the Pharisees and Scribes [Torah-teachers] of Jerusalem. . . . Jesus, in this view, was fighting not against Judaism but within it—an entirely different matter. Far from being a marginal Jew, Jesus was a leader of one type of

Judaism that was being marginalized by another group, the Pharisees, and he was fighting against them as dangerous innovators.[3]

In this fight, Yeshua mobilizes Isaiah 29:13 to bolster his case with an argument very much in line with later rabbinic discussions of halakha, or Jewish law. The tradition of the Pharisees allows them to set aside the clear commandment of Torah to honor father and mother (Exod. 20:12; Deut. 5:16). A person can declare that the resources he might use to honor his parents by supporting them financially in their old age are *"korban,"* a word appearing frequently in Leviticus (starting at 1:2) and in Numbers to denote an offering, which Mark explains simply as "a gift to God" (7:11). It's not altogether clear how designating one's resources as korban enabled one to sidestep the command to use those resources to honor father and mother, but debates in the Mishnah (put into writing around the year 200 CE) demonstrate that this could be done.

> R. Eliezer says, "They unloose a vow for a person by [reference to] the honor of his father or mother."
>
> And sages prohibit.[4]

In other words, Rabbi Eliezer says that a vow like "korban" can be overridden by the need to honor father or mother, but the sages disagree. Christian commentator R.T. France cites "the possible conflict between the obligation of a vow [*korban*] and the duty owed to father or mother under the fifth commandment." He goes on:

> In such a case the rabbis whose views are reflected in the Mishnah inclined to give priority to the commandment, and so to allow a man to be released from his vow (m. Ned. 9:1). Jesus was apparently aware of a more rigorous scribal view which refused any such remission.[5]

---

3. Boyarin, 104–05.
4. B.Nedarim 9:1–2 in Neusner, 423.
5. France, 287.

This more rigorous view would block someone from using his or her resources to help their parents if these resources had once been dedicated as korban—the vow was unbreakable. However this worked in actual practice, the point is that Yeshua's critics—the Pharisees and Torah-teachers from Jerusalem—found a way to sidestep a clear commandment of Scripture with a more complex and ambiguous tradition derived from Scripture. Yeshua, as in much rabbinic discussion in the succeeding centuries, privileged the simple reading of Scripture over the traditions derived from Scripture, and he accused his foes of doing the opposite. This sets the stage for Yeshua to return to the clear sense of the Torah to delve into the true meaning of the purity laws that his opponents had sought to invoke against him.

7:14–23

> [14] Then Yeshua called the people to him again and said, "Listen to me, all of you, and understand this! [15] There is nothing outside a person which, by going into him, can make him unclean. Rather, it is the things that come out of a person which make a person unclean!" [16]
>
> [17] When he had left the people and entered the house, his *talmidim* asked him about the parable. [18] He replied to them, "So you too are without understanding? Don't you see that nothing going into a person from outside can make him unclean? [19] For it doesn't go into his heart but into his stomach, and it passes out into the latrine." (Thus he declared all foods ritually clean.) [20] "It is what comes out of a person," he went on, "that makes him unclean. [21] For from within, out of a person's heart, come forth wicked thoughts, sexual immorality, theft, murder, adultery, [22] greed, malice, deceit, indecency, envy, slander, arrogance, foolishness. . . . [23] All these wicked things come from within, and they make a person unclean."

Yeshua turns the confrontation with his critics into a teachable moment for the people around him. He explains that people are made unclean not by what goes into them, but by what comes out of them. It's a brief and poignant saying, but mysterious enough to be termed a "parable" when the talmidim ask Yeshua what it means (7:17). Yeshua begins his explanation by reminding the talmidim that any food that is eaten is processed in the stomach and then eliminated; it has no enduring impact on the body. Ironically, this excreted matter doesn't cause defilement. On a natural level it's unclean, of course, and must be disposed of properly (Deut. 23:12–14), but it is not mentioned as something that causes ritual impurity.

In *Jesus and the Forces of Death*, Matthew Thiessen traces Yeshua's triumphant interaction with the three sources of ritual impurity outlined in Leviticus, namely "*lepra* [a category of skin diseases], genital discharges of blood and semen, and corpses."[6] In the Torah, laws of kashrut, the regulations concerning permitted and forbidden foods, constitute a different body of regulations than laws of ritual purity. "While in English they are sometimes confused, the system of purity and impurity laws and the system of dietary laws are two different systems within the Torah's rules for eating, and Mark and Jesus knew the difference."[7] Kosher food can become ritually impure through contact with one of the three sources of uncleanness, but the notion that eating such food transmits uncleanness is not stated in the Torah and is an "innovative ruling" according to Boyarin, who goes on to say, "if the Pharisees argue that [contaminated] food itself contaminates, that is a change in the law."[8] It's against such a change in Torah that Yeshua is arguing, and he uses the ruling about korban as an example of another objectionable change in Torah that the Pharisees and scribes are advocating.

All this brings us to Mark 7:19b—"Thus he declared all foods ritually clean"—which has often been misinterpreted to mean that Yeshua canceled the kosher laws of the Torah, one of the primary

---

6. Thiessen, 188.
7. Boyarin, 113.
8. Boyarin, 119.

markers of Jewish identity throughout the ages.[9] Marcus, one of our most astute commentators, holds such an interpretation, although he also notes the difficulty with it:

> The explicit revocation of the OT kosher laws ascribed to Jesus by Mark in 7:19b probably goes beyond what the historical Jesus actually did; it needs to be borne in mind that "declaring all foods clean" is *Mark's* interpretation of Jesus' statement in 7:15, not Jesus', and that Matthew seems to have a much less radical interpretation of the dominical saying.[10]

In other words, Marcus agrees that "the historical Jesus" would be highly unlikely to overturn the kosher laws of the Torah, but he sees Mark as later adding the comment that Yeshua did just that. But if we trust Mark as a faithful interpreter of the life and teachings of Yeshua, this explanation won't stand.

Another commentator, from a more conservative perspective, writes:

> Since Jesus accepts Moses' authority as conveying the word of God (1:44; 7:10; 10:3; 12:26; cf. Matt. 5:17–20), the pronouncement of Jesus points to his authority as the Messiah and Son of God (1:1) who proclaims the new reality of the kingdom of God in which food no longer defiles a person, taking his followers back to the time before Moses when all food was clean.[11]

In other words, this commentator sees Yeshua as accepting Moses' authority in 7:10 and then somehow in 7:15 going back to a time

---

9. The phrase is literally, "thus cleansing all foods," implying that the digestive process itself cleanses the food. This wording underlies the KJV translation, "Because it entereth not into his heart, but into the belly, and goeth out into the draught, purging all meats," which treats the phrase as the words of Yeshua. We've noted that excrement doesn't defile, and is clean in that sense, but most commentators and translators, based on the Greek grammar here, see this phrase as an editorial comment by Mark.
10. Marcus, *Mark 1–8*, 458.
11. Schnabel, 169. The notion that "all food was clean" in "the time before Moses" is questionable, since the Torah says that Noah took clean and unclean animals into the ark (Gen. 7:2).

before Moses to nullify the food laws that Moses conveyed. Another conservative commentator agrees:

> Put simply, whereas in vv. 1–13 Jesus berates the scribes for undermining the authority of the OT law, in vv. 14–23 he apparently undermines one of its key provisions himself. While in vv. 1–13 Jesus' attack is directly only against scribal tradition, in vv. 14–23 the scribes are no longer mentioned and Jesus' criticism is directed instead against a fundamental principle of the OT law itself.[12]

Such problematic interpretations (coming from generally reliable commentators) are based on supersessionist presuppositions. In this view, Jewish identity and practice are superseded by Christian identity and practice. Jews who come to faith in Messiah relinquish their Jewish identity, or at least the practices that support a Jewish identity. Therefore, those aspects of Torah that sustain a distinct Jewish identity are superseded by a new, universal body of practices that eliminate the distinction. As another commentator has it:

> Once the Christian movement came to include significant numbers of non-Jews, it was inevitable that the food laws would become a matter of existential importance, as their literal persistence would make table fellowship between Jewish and Gentile Christians impossible.[13]

Comments like these are built on the assumption that Torah and the Jewish identity formed and sustained by Torah are superseded by the kingdom of God that Yeshua inaugurates, in which Jewish identity is longer that important or relevant. It's beyond the scope of this commentary to provide a critique of Christian supersessionism, and much material on the subject is available.[14] For our purposes, it's

---

12. France, 277
13. France, 278.
14. Sources pointing beyond a supersessionist perspective include Stuart Dauermann, *Converging Destinies; Jews, Christians, and the Mission of God* (Eugene: Cascade, 2017); Barry E. Horner, *Future Israel: Why Christian Anti-Judaism Must Be Challenged* (Nashville: B&H Academic, 2007); Mark S. Kinzer, *Jerusalem Crucified, Jerusalem Risen:*

enough to note that the entire commentary you are reading rests on a non-supersessionist foundation that recognizes the teachings of Torah as still in effect, although differing for Jews and Gentiles as they differ for males and females, for priests and Israelites. Our foundation also embraces Yeshua as a loyal Jew, whose revolutionary views often entailed a radical return to Torah, as we see in this scene, rather than a departure from it; Yeshua as a wonder-working prophet who would be recognizable (if not always recognized) as the promised Messiah of the Jewish people.

At this juncture it's helpful to recall that in this scene Yeshua is explicitly contrasting God's commands and "the Word of God" with human traditions (7:8, 13). As if to underline Yeshua's loyalty to the Torah, Mark prefaced this whole scene with mention in 6:56 of Yeshua's *tzitzit*, the fringe or tassel he wore on his garment "to look at and thereby remember all of ADONAI's *mitzvot* and obey them" (Num. 15:39). Yeshua's whole argument against his critics is that they set aside the Torah to "nullify the Torah," which would be a nonsensical tactic if he's in the process of nullifying the Torah himself, which he signals he will not do by wearing a *tzitzit*!

> How likely is it that Mark would stress obeying God's commandments in a story in which Jesus rejects God's commandments as they pertain to the consumption of impure animals? How rhetorically convincing would this story be if it were advocating the rejection of laws that most, if not all, Jews in the first century CE thought were divinely ordained?[15]

Christian readers might miss this point if they see the food laws of Torah as somehow less significant or less binding than its deeper

---

The Resurrected Messiah, the Jewish People, and the Land of Promise (Eugene: Cascade, 2018); Mark S. Kinzer, Russell L. Resnik, *Besorah: The Resurrection of Jerusalem and the Healing of a Fractured Gospel* (Eugene: Cascade, 2021); Jennifer M. Rosner, *Healing the Schism: Karl Barth, Franz Rosenzweig, and the new Jewish-Christian Encounter* (Bellingham: Lexham Academic, 2021); Calvin L. Smith, ed. *The Jews, Modern Israel and the New Supersessionism* (Broadstairs, Kent, UK: King's Divinity, 2013); R. Kendall Soulen, *The God of Israel and Christian Theology* (Minneapolis: Fortress, 1996).
15. Thiessen, 189–90.

teachings, but from a Jewish perspective these laws, along with the Sabbath and circumcision itself, have been key sources of Jewish identity and continuity since time immemorial, a "'boundary marker' by which Jews both identified themselves and were identified by outsiders as being set apart from their neighbors."[16]

Yeshua explains the significance of the purity laws with a poignant summary: It's not what goes into a person from outside but what comes out of a person that makes him unclean. Notably, the laws of impurity in Leviticus 15 deal with discharges, what comes out of someone's body. Yeshua draws upon this text to declare that it's what comes out of a person that makes him unclean. He emphasizes the heart as the source of the defilement that comes forth from us (7:21), just as he noted that what goes into us doesn't defile because it doesn't reach the heart (7:19), but is eliminated.

Daniel Boyarin comments:

> The explanation that Jesus gives is to interpret the deep meaning of the Torah's rules, not to set them aside. And it is this deep interpretation of the Law that constitutes Jesus' great contribution—not an alleged rejection of the Law at all. Not an exhortation, then, to abandon the Torah, but a call to deepen our genuine commitment both to practicing it and to incorporating its meanings, Jesus' famous saying can be seen as entirely within a Jewish spiritual world.[17]

The point of this "famous saying" is one Yeshua makes repeatedly: God's instructions to his people, and God himself, are not as concerned with the externals (although they undoubtedly have a role to play) as they are with the heart—the whole person, from the inside out. Yeshua appears on the scene to restore this heart emphasis and raise it to a whole new level.

---

16. Marcus, *Mark 1-8*, 441.
17. Boyarin, 124.

Derash

- Yeshua's teaching that it's not what goes into a person but what comes out of him that defiles may reflect a deep reading of the purity laws in Leviticus 15—a reading that goes beyond the literal instructions to derive a profound and practical spiritual lesson. How does this lesson apply to your own life and practice? What other examples of Yeshua's deep Torah can we recognize in Mark?

- Even as the kosher laws remain in place, Yeshua opens the way for more interaction between Jews and Gentiles by rejecting man-made laws of ritual purity. He also pushes back against religious elitists who at times impose standards that serve to elevate them at the expense of the uninitiated. His respectful yet flexible approach to Torah can serve as a model for his followers today.

- In Acts 10, Peter has a vision of a sheet lowered from heaven containing all kinds of unclean animals, and he hears a voice saying, "Rise, Peter, kill and eat." He responds, "Lord, you know I've never eaten anything unclean." This vision takes place well after the events of Mark 7. If Yeshua making all foods clean meant the end of the kosher laws, it's hard to imagine why, years later, Peter would still refuse to eat anything unclean. But even though Yeshua taught against the over-the-top purity rules of the Pharisees and not against all food laws, as we've seen, Peter still needs a divine vision to realize it is okay to associate with Gentiles, whom he had regarded as unclean (10:28). When Peter's critics call him to account for eating with Gentiles (11:3), he defends himself, not by citing Yeshua's teaching in Mark 7, but by telling them how the Holy Spirit fell on these Gentiles as he was speaking to them.

  So, Peter still keeps kosher, and that's not the issue in Acts 10, but he doesn't seem to grasp the impact of Yeshua's lifting of food restrictions based on "the tradition of the Elders"

(Mark 7:3, 5). He might have heard Yeshua say that all foods are (ritually) clean, but he failed to see how that applied to eating with Gentiles. The same sort of blind spot seems to be in place years later in Antioch, where Peter eats with his Gentile brothers and sisters in Yeshua, and then stops doing so when the party from James arrives (Gal. 2:11–14). This party was probably holding to a standard of ritual purity that went beyond Torah and created an illegitimate barrier to table fellowship with Gentile Yeshua-followers (which is why Paul becomes so indignant here).

All of this comes after Yeshua made his statement in Mark 7, but even his close followers are still not getting its full implications. Peter still doesn't get it years later, until he realizes that the point of his vision in Joppa is not to call any *person* unclean, which allows him to enter the house of Cornelius (Acts 10:28). It's easier to imagine how Peter and other Yeshua-followers might forget Yeshua's ruling in Mark 7 if it's about specific applications of purity regulations rather than about negating the whole body of kosher laws. Nonetheless, this story provides a lesson about our own blind spots, about how we can hear biblical truths yet fail to see how they apply in our real-life settings.

SEASON 1, EPISODE 9

A GENTILE FORAY AND CONTINUING INCOMPREHENSION

7:24–8:21

Overview

Immediately after challenging some traditional purity rules to establish a simpler and more open practice, Yeshua illustrates this flexibility by traveling into the largely Gentile territory of Tyre and Sidon ("Tzor and Tzidon"). As usual, he seeks to remain hidden after he arrives, but cannot—his reputation has apparently gone before him. A Gentile woman, native to the area, approaches Yeshua, asking him to drive a demon out of her daughter. Paradoxically, Yeshua refuses, saying that he has come to serve the Jewish people, but the woman persuades Yeshua to let her have what's left over from his primary calling to Israel, and her daughter is set free.

Yeshua and his band leave that area and take a roundabout journey back to the region of the Ten Towns east of Lake Kinneret—another largely Gentile area. There he performs two more miracles, healing a deaf man with a speech impairment and feeding a large crowd of 4000 with seven loaves and a few fish.

From there, Yeshua returns to Jewish territory, the western shore of Lake Kinneret, where he encounters some of his Pharisaic opponents who challenge him to produce "a sign from Heaven." Yeshua refuses, and departs by boat yet again, this time to the northern side of the lake, or the region of Beit-Tzaidah (8:22). On the way, he warns his followers about the *hametz* or leaven of the

Pharisees and Herodians, but they misunderstand and think he's talking about literal bread. He admonishes his men, exhorting them to open their eyes and ears to what is really going on, reminding them of the miraculous supply of bread when he fed 5000 on one occasion and 4000 on another. Our episode—along with the entire first season of Mark's biopic—closes with Yeshua's ironic words: "And you still don't understand?"

Peshat

7:24–30

> [24] Next, Yeshua left that district and went off to the vicinity of Tyre and Sidon. There he found a house to stay in and wanted to remain unrecognized, but keeping hidden proved impossible. [25] Instead, a woman whose little daughter had an unclean spirit in her came to him and fell down at his feet. [26] The woman was a Greek, by birth a Syro-phoenician, and she begged him to drive the demon out of her daughter. [27] He said, "Let the children be fed first, for it is not right to take the children's food and toss it to their pet dogs." [28] She answered him, "That is true, sir; but even the dogs under the table eat the children's leftovers." [29] Then he said to her, "For such an answer you may go on home; the demon has left your daughter." [30] She went back home and found the child lying on the couch, the demon gone.

It's hard to miss the transition between Yeshua setting aside the rigorous (and extra-biblical) purity regulations of the scribes and Pharisees and his immediate departure for the "unclean" Gentile region surrounding the prominent port city of Tyre or Tzor. By mentioning Sidon or Tzidon as well (although it doesn't appear until 7:31 in many manuscripts), Mark may intend to echo the story of Elijah, who also performed a miracle for a Gentile woman in the region of Tyre and Sidon (1 Kgs 17:8–16). Yeshua's halakha allows him to follow Elijah's example of interaction with Gentiles, without removing the essential boundary markers of Jewish identity established in the Torah. The prohibition against eating with unwashed hands that Yeshua had opposed probably required not eating with Gentiles at all, and avoiding interaction with them in general. In light of Yeshua's teaching, the Jewish markers given in Torah remain in place, but they don't render Gentiles unclean or prohibit interaction with them.

Now the possibilities for interaction with Gentiles have expanded, but this episode reveals that they're still not so simple.[1] Yeshua is visiting a Gentile region, but he remains firmly rooted in the Jewish world. First, he's probably staying in a Jewish house.[2] Moreover, when a Gentile woman approaches him for help, he tells her that the (Jewish) children must be fed first, perhaps implying that he is feeding them on this visit. In other words, Yeshua has traveled into this Gentile area, but is serving the Jewish people there, at least as his first priority.

So, if Yeshua is launching the mission to the Gentiles in this episode, as is often asserted[3] and made evident by his following journey to the largely Gentile Ten Towns (7:31), the launch is still based on the Jewish mission, and must defer to its priorities. Yeshua presents this idea to the Gentile mother in graphic terms, comparing her and her daughter to household dogs who are not entitled to the children's food. The woman accepts Yeshua's limitation, and comes back with a humble, but astute, response: she'll settle for the crumbs from the children's table. Such an answer, Yeshua says, merits a

---

1. See the discussion of this issue in the final item under Derash in our previous scene.
2. It's notable that Yeshua doesn't enter the Syro-Phoenician woman's house—nor does she ask him to—but heals her daughter from a distance. In this context, France (297) notes the "inappropriateness of the Jewish Messiah entering a Gentile house," and lists "the only other examples of healing at a distance in the gospels (Mt. 8:5–13/Lk. 7:1–10; Jn. 4:46–54, [which] probably also involve a Gentile subject or subjects."
3. France, 295–95; Edwards, 217; Marcus, *Mark 1–8*, 466. We should remember, however, that this is not Yeshua's first interaction with a Gentile. He had already welcomed a crowd from the surrounding Gentile territories, which likely included Gentile members (3:7–12), and had delivered a man with a legion of demons in the Gentile region of the Ten Towns (5:1–20).

gracious response, and her daughter is delivered of the demon immediately.

Nevertheless, Yeshua's initial words to the woman remain troubling. Does he really intend to deny her request? Joel Marcus provides a helpful explanation:

> Elsewhere in Mark, Jesus often ascribes healing to people's persistent faith (2:5; 5:34; 10:52; cf. Matt. 15:28). Two chapters later, moreover, Jesus will heal a demon-possessed child whose parent has interceded for him (9:14–29). As in our passage, the parent's request for healing is not immediately fulfilled; Jesus instead makes an initial response that sounds like a refusal (9:19a) but that turns out to be a ploy designed to evoke a significant expression of faith on the part of the parent (9:24; cf. also Matt. 8:5–13//John 7:46–53). This is also probably the Markan meaning here.[4]

But even as a "ploy designed to evoke a significant expression of faith," Yeshua's language seems harsh and even offensive—worthy of David Brooks' "total badass" description (see the Introduction, p. xv). He not only refuses the request of a mother in desperate need, but he insults her in the process. If Gentiles are no longer to be considered unclean, why does Yeshua compare them to dogs in this scene—especially if it's the scene that is launching the outreach to the Gentiles? But this may be precisely the point: as Yeshua begins to expand his ministry into the Gentile world, he makes it clear that this outreach doesn't mean the end of a distinct place for the Jewish people. They are still the "children" in God's household in a unique way, and they are to be fed first—implying both their distinctive status and the promise of later feeding the Gentiles as well. "There is apparently, then, an exceptionally close, familial relationship between Jesus, who is secretly God's son, and the Jews, whom he acknowledges as God's children—even if *they* do not acknowledge *him*. But children do not cease to be children simply because they

---

4. Marcus, *Mark 1–8*, 468.

disobey their parents' wishes."[5] When the Gentiles begin to benefit from the resources of God's household, as they will, they are to continue to acknowledge the Jews' status as children. In light of the emergence of supersessionism, anti-Judaism, and eventually antisemitism in the history of the (Gentile) church, Yeshua's words may reflect his prophetic foresight, as well as his ongoing concern for his people. Yeshua as Mark pictures him can be blunt and ironic to the point of sarcasm or seeming insensitivity, but Mark's readers do well to heed the point that he is making.

7:31–37

> [31] Then he left the district of Tzor and went through Tzidon to Lake Kinneret and on to the region of the Ten Towns. [32] They brought him a man who was deaf and had a speech impediment and asked Yeshua to lay his hand on him. [33] Taking him off alone, away from the crowd, Yeshua put his fingers into the man's ears, spat, and touched his tongue; [34] then, looking up to heaven, he gave a deep groan and said to him, "*Hippatach!*" (that is, "Be opened!"). [35] His ears were opened, his tongue was freed, and he began speaking clearly. [36] Yeshua ordered the people to tell no one; but the more he insisted, the more zealously they spread the news. [37] People were overcome with amazement. "Everything he does, he does well!" they said. "He even makes the deaf hear and the dumb speak!"

The roundabout route of return to the Kinneret region via Sidon has often been noted, sometimes as evidence of Mark's supposed unfamiliarity with the geography of Israel and surrounding lands. But whatever the explanation for this route, it's clear that it remains within Gentile territory, and Mark may be deliberately highlighting this fact by mentioning Sidon, even though it's odd for Yeshua to go so far out of the way to include that town in his itinerary. This journey ends in the largely Gentile area of the Ten Towns, where Yeshua performs a second notable miracle benefiting a Gentile of

---

5. Marcus, *Mark 1–8*, 469.

the region (the first being the deliverance of the Gerasene demoniac in 5:1–20). Healing the deaf man is also the second of three miracles among the Gentiles here in Episode 9.

This miraculous healing seems more difficult, or at least more gradual, than Yeshua's typical healing by a simple word or touch. He takes the man away from the crowd to heal him, uses saliva as well as physical touch, groans deeply and finally pronounces a command in Aramaic, "*Ephphatha*—be opened!"[6] The detail of citing the original Aramaic in this scene, as in the healing of the daughter of Yair in 5:41, suggests that Mark is drawing upon an eyewitness account. The use of Aramaic here (although this isn't the case in Mark 5) also makes sense because we're in Gentile territory, where Aramaic would be the common language. At the same time, Mark's description also draws upon the Jewish Scriptures, specifically the prophetic vision of Isaiah 35:5–6a:

> Then the eyes of the blind will be opened,
> and the ears of the deaf will be unstopped;
> then the lame man will leap like a deer,
> and the mute person's tongue will sing.

With typical Markan irony, this eschatological sign takes place among the Gentiles, and it happens against the background of continuing "deafness" among the Jewish people, who have ears to hear, but aren't hearing—including Yeshua's own followers (Mark 4:9, 12–13; 6:51–52; 7:17–18; 8:17–18).

The miracle is followed by Yeshua's usual instructions to keep it secret, and by the usual failure of the crowd (who somehow had formed even after Yeshua took the deaf man off by himself) to follow the instructions, as they "zealously . . . spread the news." Their final words—*He has done all things well* (literal translation)—echo the final words of the Creation account in the Septuagint: "God saw everything that he had made, and indeed it was very good"

---

6. Our translation has *Hippatach* here, which is the Hebrew equivalent.

(Gen. 1:31).⁷ It's doubtful whether the Gentile, or mostly Gentile, crowd in the Ten Towns region would be aware of Isaiah's prophecy or the wording of the Creation account, even in its Greek version. Mark, however, perhaps again with his typical irony, links this event with Isaiah and the Torah itself. The emerging mission to the Gentiles is no accident, and is not at odds with God's election of the Jews; rather, it is rooted in the calling of Israel, the Jewish people, to bring salvation to all peoples. And it is rooted in the texts that they have honored and preserved through the centuries.

8:1–10

> ¹ It was during that time that another large crowd gathered, and they had nothing to eat. Yeshua called his *talmidim* to him and said to them, ² "I feel sorry for these people, because they have been with me three days, and now they have nothing to eat. ³ If I send them off to their homes hungry, they will collapse on the way; some of them have come a long distance." ⁴ His *talmidim* said to him, "How can anyone find enough bread to satisfy these people in a remote place like this?" ⁵ "How many loaves do you have?" he asked them. They answered, "Seven." ⁶ He then told the crowd to sit down on the ground, took the seven loaves, made a *b'rakhah*, broke the loaves and gave them to his *talmidim* to serve to the people. ⁷ They also had a few fish; making a *b'rakhah* over them he also ordered these to be served. ⁸ The people ate their fill; and the *talmidim* took up the leftover pieces, seven large basketsful. ⁹ About four thousand were there. ¹⁰ After sending them away, Yeshua got into the boat with his *talmidim* and went off to the district of Dalmanuta.

When Mark tells us, "It was during that time that another large crowd gathered" (8:1), he likely means that we're still in the Ten Towns region, especially as he recounts the departure of Yeshua and his band shortly afterwards. The crowd that gathers, then,

---

7. Marcus, *Mark 1–8*, 475; Edwards 227; Schnabel (178) comments: "It is unclear whether Mark wants his readers to note an echo of Genesis 1:31 . . . reinforcing the notion of the restoration of creation at the time of God's present coming."

would be largely or entirely made up of Gentiles. The astonished outcry of the people, "Everything he does, he does well!" (7:37), may have inspired many to follow Yeshua into this remote place (8:4), and stay there with him for three days . . . until they ran out of food. Whatever the make-up of this crowd, Yeshua shows the same compassion for them as he did for the undoubtedly Jewish crowd in 6:30–44. Indeed, several details of this miraculous feeding reflect those of the earlier one, but there are three significant, if subtle, differences, reflecting the likely Gentile setting of the second feeding miracle:

1. The three-fold use in the first feeding account of the Greek word *eremos*, meaning "desert," "isolated" (6:32), or "remote" (6:35) is not repeated in the second.[8] As noted earlier, *eremos* is employed for "desert" or "wilderness" throughout the Septuagint and describes the setting for Israel's feeding with manna. In Mark 8:4, Yeshua's talmidim do describe the scene as *eremia*, virtually the same word, but the three-fold emphasis is lacking, so that the term is downplayed in comparison with its use in Mark 6.

2. Yeshua says he feels sorry for the people in 8:2, but the "sheep without a shepherd" language of Mark 6:34 in the first feeding is lacking. The shepherd terminology is based on Moses' words when he asked ADONAI to appoint a new leader to take over after his death, "so that ADONAI's community will not be like sheep without a shepherd" (Num. 27:16–17). Mark echoes this language in the Jewish setting, but not in his account of the second feeding.

3. Finally, in Mark 8, Yeshua simply tells the people to sit on the ground, without the detailed instruction to sit down in "groups of fifty or a hundred" (6:39–40) given in the first feeding, which, as

---

8. *Eremos* also appears in the Greek of 6:31, although it's not reflected in CJB.

we saw, reflected the organization of the camp of Israel in the wilderness.

The feeding of the 4000, then, is similar to the feeding of the 5000 in Mark 6, but in a version fit for the surrounding peoples, not Israel in particular. Yeshua's opening of the Kingdom to the Syro-Phoenician woman, with the recognition that the Kingdom belongs in particular ways to the Jewish people, is reiterated in the feeding of the 4000—which is no less miraculous, of course. If we are witnessing the opening scenes of the Gentile mission, it's clear again that this mission in no way displaces Israel and the calling of the Jewish people. And it's clear that the goal of this mission is the Messianic banquet foreshadowed first in the feeding of the 5000, and now again, as a preview of the great banquet of the Age to Come, as the *Jewish Study Bible* notes at Isaiah 25:6–8:

> When the new cosmic order emerges, the illusions that befuddle the nations will disappear, and the survivors from all nations will enjoy access to true teachings, which emanate from the God of Zion. Cf. [Isaiah] 2:1–4; 19:18–25; 23:15–18.[9]

8:11–21

> [11] The *P'rushim* came and began arguing with him; they wanted him to give them a sign from Heaven, because they were out to trap him. [12] With a sigh that came straight from his heart, he said, "Why does this generation want a sign? Yes! I tell you, no sign will be given to this generation!" [13] With that, he left them, got into the boat again and went off to the other side of the lake.
>
> [14] Now the *talmidim* had forgotten to bring bread and had with them in the boat only one loaf. [15] So when Yeshua said to them, "Watch out! Guard yourselves from the *hametz* of the *P'rushim* and the *hametz* of Herod," [16] they thought he had said it because they had no bread. [17] But, aware of this, he said, "Why are you talking with each other about having no bread? Don't you

---

9. Jewish Study Bible, 832.

see or understand yet? Have your hearts been made like stone? [18] You have eyes — don't you see? You have ears — don't you hear? And don't you remember? [19] When I broke the five loaves for the five thousand, how many baskets full of broken pieces did you collect?" "Twelve," they answered him. [20] "And when I broke the seven loaves for the four thousand, how many baskets full of broken pieces did you collect?" "Seven," they answered. [21] He said to them, "And you still don't understand?"

Along with the differences between the two miraculous feeding accounts, they do share a similarity: they're both part of a thread of references to food and feasting in this section of Mark. Back in Episode 7 (Mark 6:7–56), Yeshua sent out the Twelve with instructions not to bring food supplies, but to rely on the hospitality of folks in the Galil. Then the scene shifted to a banquet, a gathering around food, which ended with the head of Yochanan the Immerser being displayed on a platter, an object normally used for serving food. Finally, Yeshua and his talmidim feed the crowd in miraculous fashion. Here in Episode 9, after Yeshua and his talmidim feed another crowd in miraculous fashion, the talmidim forget to bring bread with them when they leave for the other side of Lake Kinneret. Yeshua warns them against the *hametz* (leaven)—essential for baking bread—of their opponents, and reminds them of the two miraculous feedings, which should have enabled them to better understand Yeshua, his miracle-working power, and his role in hosting the messianic banquet to come.

But before we reach this final moment of Season One, some Pharisees arrive on the scene to challenge Yeshua, just as another group of Pharisees did right after the first miraculous feeding. They demand "a sign from Heaven" to validate Yeshua's ministry. It seems like an odd request, because Yeshua has been providing signs all along—including his recent feeding of thousands of people with a few loaves of bread, as well as healing the blind and lame, the deaf and mute, in prophetic fulfillment of Isaiah 35:5–6. Here a sign "from Heaven" might imply something greater even than these works of power, perhaps an apocalyptic display in the sky above.

From Mark's perspective, however, this wording may serve to tie the challenge of the Pharisees to the previous scene, the feeding of the 4000. We've noted that both miraculous feedings reflect the account of Israel's feeding on manna in the wilderness, introduced in Exodus 16:4: "ADONAI said to Moshe, 'Here, I will cause bread to rain down from heaven for you. The people are to go out and gather a day's ration every day. By this I will test whether they will observe my Torah or not.'" Manna is "bread from heaven," and the loaves miraculously multiplied to feed thousands may be understood by those with a heart to understand as bread from heaven. There's another important link to our story in Exodus 16:4, ADONAI's intention to *test* the people through the provision of bread. Our translation of Mark 8:11 reads, "they wanted him to give them a sign from Heaven, because they were out to trap him." More literally it would read, "they wanted him to give them a sign from Heaven, *testing* him." "Testing" translates the original Greek word that first appears in the account of Yeshua's 40-day testing in the wilderness by Satan (Mark 1:13)—suggesting that Yeshua's religious adversaries share something of the character of the prototypical adversary, *ha-satan* in Hebrew. Testing is also an element in God's provision of manna—will the people accept this humble food and use it according to the directions the LORD provides? (Exod. 16:4–7, 14–30; Deut. 8:2–3). Furthermore, in Exodus, as in Mark, the provision of bread from heaven is followed by a scene in which the Israelites *test* ADONAI (Exod. 17:1–7), at Massah and M'rivah.

> If only today you would listen to his voice:
> "Don't harden your hearts, as you did at M'rivah,
> as you did on that day at Massah in the desert,
> when your fathers put me to the test;
> they challenged me, even though they saw my work."
> (Psa. 95:7–9)

ADONAI's plea in Psalm 95 is echoed in Yeshua's words as he "sighs deeply in his spirit[10] . . . 'Why does this generation want a sign?'" (8:12). Yeshua sighs because this generation, particularly these influence-leaders among this generation, have ignored the import of his deeds of power and mercy, hardened their hearts, and put him to the test.[11] Furthermore, the sort of sign they're asking for—a public display of awesome supernatural power that no one could deny—would be counter to Yeshua's whole strategy of working largely in secret or mysterious fashion. His greatest public miracles, the two feedings of multitudes that immediately preceded this encounter with his critics, both took place in a remote area. And Yeshua knows that even a sign from Heaven such as his critics demand will not convince them. When Yeshua does produce the ultimate sign, it will be of an entirely different nature . . . as he is about to reveal to his talmidim in Season Two.

This brings us to the final interaction of Season One.

As noted above, when Yeshua goes off with his talmidim, he warns them against the leaven (*hametz*) of the Pharisees and of Herod. In the ancient world, leaven for baking bread was not the yeast sold in little packages that we see today. Rather, yeast spores were (and still are) present in the air. Flour was mixed with water to make dough and allowed to sit, and it became leavened simply through the "influence" of the surrounding air. Or, one might make bread by adding sourdough starter, dough already infused with leaven, to a fresh batch. Before Passover, when we clean out our homes to get rid of leaven, we're not just looking for items made with yeast; we clear out everything made of flour (from the five

---

10. Literal translation. CJB has "heart" here, but the underlying Greek word is *pneuma* or "spirit."
11. The repeated use of "generation" in 8:12 is another link to the Torah, which speaks of the evil or perverse generation of the wilderness in Deuteronomy 1:35 and 32:5, 20. Yeshua will use "generation" again in this sense in Mark 8:38, 9:19. The Mishnah at one point cites similar words of R. Akiva: "The generation of the wilderness has no portion in the world to come and will not stand in judgment, for it is written *In this wilderness they shall be consumed, and there they shall die* (Num. 14:35)" (Sanh 10:3; Neusner, 605).

grains described in the Torah—wheat, rye, oats, barley, and spelt), and the grains themselves. Just by sitting on the shelf they've become contaminated—just as Yeshua warns his followers not to become contaminated by the leaven of the Pharisees and of Herod.

Commentators debate what this "leaven" might be. Matthew (16:12) explains that it's the teaching of the Pharisees (and Sadducees); Luke (12:1) defines it as "hypocrisy." But Mark, in typical fashion, lets the narrative itself reveal the meaning of this leaven. The Pharisees and Herod (8:15) are two very different parties with very different agendas, but both agendas block their ability to recognize Yeshua and his work in their midst. The Pharisees, whom Yeshua has just confronted, are leavened with unbelief regarding his words and deeds and we can assume that Herod is too. Yeshua warns his disciples against allowing this leaven to permeate their hearts as well—as it seems to be doing when they focus on their bread supply instead of the wonders that they've been experiencing. He again encounters hardness of heart among his own inner circle (Mark 6:52, cf. 3:5). Yeshua's mention of the heart here also extends his recent teaching about the heart as the source of the "wicked things . . . that make a person unclean" Mark 7:21–23). Inability to recognize the presence of God's Kingdom is a warning about a spiritual heart condition. But here Yeshua raises the issue of a hardened heart as a question—"Have your hearts been made like stone?"— implying that there's still hope for the hard-hearted talmidim.

Yeshua has turned away from the Pharisees, but he brings his talmidim with him. And he will intensify his instructions to them after our episode, and Season One, conclude with another question: "And you still don't understand?"

Derash

- Yeshua seems to be responding to the Syro-Phoenician woman's request in a way that highlights the distinct place of the Jewish people within the Kingdom of God. In that case,

Mark's metaphor would have implications similar to those in Paul's famous metaphor of the olive tree:

> And if the root is holy, so are the branches. But if some of the branches were broken off, and you — a wild olive — were grafted in among them and have become equal sharers in the rich root of the olive tree, then don't boast as if you were better than the branches! However, if you do boast, remember that you are not supporting the root, the root is supporting you. (Romans 11:16b–18)

If we understand Yeshua's initial refusal to deliver the Syro-Phoenician woman's daughter as a test of faith, it may shed light on the whole messianic secret motif. Yeshua raises a barrier to his healing ministry that this Gentile woman can only breach by "great trust" as Yeshua puts it in Matthew's version (Matt. 15:28). The ethnic-religious barrier elicits this greater faith. In the same way, Yeshua's practice of secrecy may be designed to elicit greater faith than if he had come out in full public display. He reveals himself in acts of power and compassion to those with eyes to see, rather than through explicit statements. Mark repeatedly points out that those with eyes to see are often the outsiders and the unqualified—including even a Syro-Phoenician woman—rather than those closest to Yeshua. We might consider how this faith-evoking hiddenness is still at work today.

- In commenting on the feeding of the 4000, Elijah Zvi Soloveitchik cites a talmudic insight:

  > See the power of charity! By being denied a mouthful of bread, those who were close have been made distant; by being granted a mouthful of bread, those who were distant have been drawn near. Amon and Moab, our neighbors, refused us nourishment, and were rejected from entering the community of God (Deuteronomy 23:4, 5); Jethro, estranged from us by birth, was hospitable to Moses

(Exodus 2:20), and his descendants had the honor of sitting in the Sanhedrins (1 Chronicles 2:55).[12]

This saying is especially poignant if the crowd in Mark 7 is indeed made up of Gentiles, who are, like Jethro, "estranged from us by birth." The circumstances in Mark 7 are a reversal of those cited in the Talmudic dictum, where the Gentiles provide food rather than receive it. Nonetheless Yeshua draws them near through feeding them.

- Shortly after the initial miraculous supply of manna in Exodus, the Israelites came to a place with no water and complained bitterly against Moses, who then accused them of testing God (Exod. 17:1–7). In Mark, however, "Jesus himself is tested and thus assumes the role of God in the Exodus narrative."[13] If this is so, we might consider how Mark portrays the deity of Messiah through such subtle hints and narrative parallels rather than explicitly, and what this subtle portrayal in itself reveals about the character of Messiah Yeshua.

- The talmidim apparently absorb the leaven of spiritual hardness of the Pharisees and Herod, so that Yeshua must raise the question—"Have your hearts been made like stone?" As noted above, asking a question here implies that there's still hope for the hard-hearted talmidim. Further, Yeshua's reference to a heart of stone reflects the promise of Ezekiel 36: "I will give you a new heart and put a new spirit inside you; / I will take the stony heart out of your flesh and give you a heart of flesh" (v. 26). The promise of future redemption includes replacing the heart made like stone with a heart of flesh. In the presence of Messiah this redemption is already unfolding, and Yeshua seems taken aback that it hasn't yet transformed his closest followers. His question to them also draws us into the story, because we also must

---

12. Soloveitchik, 329, citing b.Sanhedrin 103b.
13. Marcus, *Mark 1–8*, 504.

provide an answer. The custom of cleansing the leaven for Passover reminds us that our lives can become corrupted by the surrounding atmosphere, hardened to the evidence of God at work in our midst. We too might need to respond to the final question, "And you still don't understand?"

SEASON 2

ON THE WAY TO JERUSALEM

8:22–10:52

The second season of our biopic treatment of the life of Yeshua opens in Galilee, in the town of Beit-Tzaidah on the northern shore of Lake Kinneret, and it concludes in Jericho, on the way to Jerusalem. Thus, Season 2 provides the transition from Yeshua's popular, if misunderstood, Galilean ministry, to his final week in Jerusalem culminating in betrayal, crucifixion, and resurrection. This transitional season is in itself a journey, both geographical and spiritual, as the talmidim learn more deeply (although still not fully) what it means to follow Yeshua. Accordingly, the Greek word *hodos* or "way" appears seven times in this season (8:27; 9:33, 34; 10:17, 32, 46, 52). This sequence includes an introductory appearance in 8:27 "on the way" to the towns of Caesarea Philippi, and a final appearance in the last verse, 10:52, as a blind man receives his sight and follows Yeshua "on the way" (literal translation).

This geographical progression is framed by two accounts of healing a blind man, the first in Beit-Tzaidah, our opening scene (8:22–26), and the second in Jericho, our final scene (10:46–52). Within this framework, Mark portrays another healing, or at least a lessening, of the blindness of Yeshua's talmidim. One of them, Peter, correctly declares Yeshua's true identity as Messiah. Peter soon afterwards joins two other talmidim in being granted a vision of Yeshua in his glory and hearing a voice from heaven declare, "This is my Son, whom I love. Listen to him!" (9:7). But as with the blind man of Beit-Tzaidah, the healing of the blindness of the talmidim is gradual. After Peter recognizes Yeshua as Messiah, Yeshua details three times what that title entails and what awaits him in Jerusalem—betrayal, arrest, and crucifixion followed by resurrection (8:31; 9:31; 10:33–34). The talmidim struggle to grasp the meaning and implications of this revelation and Season 2 includes Yeshua's efforts to prepare them for what lies ahead. This thread is interrupted by a halakhic discussion between Yeshua and some Pharisees about divorce. Even here, though, the emphasis on teaching the disciples continues, as Yeshua privately expands on his divorce-remarriage halakha with them (10:1–12).

Along with Yeshua's three-fold description of his coming ordeal (and the talmidim's three-fold failure to understand), Season 2 describes three miracles. Between the two healings of blindness is a third miracle, a boy's deliverance from demonic oppression following Yeshua's revelation in glory on the "high mountain" (9:2; 14–29). Like Season 2 itself, the account of the boy's deliverance is transitional, the final direct encounter with the demonic realm in Mark's Besorah. This season's whole framework of three miracles of restoration—two by touch—might remind us of a saying from Tolkien's *The Return of the King* (ch. 8), "The hands of the king are the hands of a healer."

This miracle-working king, however, is on his way to a horrific death, as Yeshua reminds his talmidim repeatedly. But he also makes it clear that this death will lead to resurrection; this death is ultimately not a defeat, but a divine reversal, overturning the powers of this world to reveal the power of the World to Come. In Season 3, the forces opposing Yeshua will work through the collusion of Jewish religious gatekeepers and Roman secular authorities to condemn him. Before that time comes, Yeshua provides intensive instructions to his insider core group on what it means to follow him, even to Jerusalem.

Season 2, Episode 1 (10)

Turning-point— The First Warning

8:22–9:1

Overview

Season 2 opens in Beit-Tzaidah on the northern shore of Lake Kinneret, an area with a Jewish majority. There, as in Gentile territory not long before (7:31–37), Yeshua performs a healing that Mark recounts in great detail, unlike his more usual terse accounts. After this healing, the restoration of sight to a blind man, Yeshua departs from Beit-Tzaidah and continues on his northward journey, leading his talmidim to the region of Caesarea Philippi near the headwaters of the Jordan.

On the way, he asks his talmidim who they think he is, raising the question that has been underlying Mark's account all along. Peter steps forward with the right response—"You are the Messiah." Yeshua responds in turn by detailing the suffering, rejection, and death that he faces as the Messiah, as well as the promise that he will rise again. Peter tries to rebuke him for saying that these terrible things will happen to him, but instead Yeshua rebukes Peter in the hearing of all the talmidim and goes on to recount the cost of following him, a cost that reflects his own journey of sacrifice and suffering. Finally, Yeshua speaks of the other side of his messianic identity; yes, he is the suffering servant, but he's also the Son of Man who will come in glory. He declares that some of those present with him will see the Kingdom of God in its power.

Peshat

8:22–26

> [22] They came to Beit-Tzaidah. Some people brought him a blind man and begged Yeshua to touch him. [23] Taking the blind man's hand, he led him outside the town. He spit in his eyes, put his hands on him and asked him, "Do you see anything?" [24] He looked up and said, "I see people, but they look like walking trees." [25] Then he put his hands on the blind man's eyes again. He peered intently, and his eyesight was restored, so that he could see everything distinctly. [26] Yeshua sent him home with the words, "Don't go into town."

Yeshua and his band stop at Beit-Tzaidah for a second time after a first visit mentioned in Mark 6:45. The town's name means "House of Fish," perhaps describing the main occupation of its inhabitants. As so often in Mark, Yeshua's reputation precedes him there and the townsfolk bring him a blind man for healing. They beg Yeshua to touch him, which is appropriate enough, since Yeshua has often healed by touching the afflicted (1:31, 41; 5:23; 6:5; 7:33), or being touched by them (3:10; 5:27–28; 6:56). But what follows is not the usual. Yeshua touches the blind man by taking him by the hand and leading him out of town. There he spits in his eyes (or perhaps applies saliva to his eyes), an unusual procedure that resembles Yeshua's healing of the deaf man in 7:31–37, where, in similar fashion, Yeshua led the man out of town to be healed. Now, after applying saliva to the blind man's eyes, Yeshua puts his hands on him, which results in another unusual feature—the healing is only partial. The man can see, but only dimly, and Yeshua must touch his eyelids again to bring about full recovery.

The similarities to the healing of the deaf man link these two accounts and suggest that they hint at something beyond themselves, perhaps the Age to come, as foreseen by the prophet:

> Then the eyes of the blind will be opened,
> and the ears of the deaf will be unstopped;
> then the lame man will leap like a deer,
> and the mute person's tongue will sing. (Isa. 35:5–6a)

These two healings also reverse the blindness and deafness that Isaiah foretold in another prophecy, the one Yeshua had cited as describing the response of outsiders to his parables: "They may be always looking but never seeing; / always listening but never understanding" (Mark 4:12 // Isa. 6:9–10). Perhaps the time has come for those around Yeshua, and especially the Twelve, to begin hearing and seeing on a deeper level. Mark describes the extended healing process in 8:22–25 with a profusion of words, nine in all, about sight and seeing—"see," "look," "eyes," "eyesight," "peered"—in our version. These words echo Yeshua's saying to his talmidim at the end of Season 1: "Don't you see or understand yet? Have your hearts been made like stone? You have eyes — don't you see? You have ears — don't you hear?" (8:17–18).

> We are immediately struck by Mark's emphasis on sight in the present miracle as opposed to the emphasis on blindness and lack of comprehension in the previous story (8:14–21). The juxtaposition of the two stories is a clue that the lingering blindness of the disciples may also be relieved, as is the blindness of the man at Bethsaida, by the continued touch of Jesus. . . . The two-stage cure in the present miracle thus suggests a *process* of revelation—as much for the disciples, we suspect, as for the blind man at Bethsaida.[1]

This process of revelation, often rather plodding, will prevail throughout Season 2. And throughout, we have to recognize that in Mark's account the talmidim never seem to reach the point of seeing everything clearly, as the blind man finally does. [2] This ironic

---

1. Edwards, 241, 244.
2. Schnabel, 193; France 322–23; Joel Marcus, *Mark 8–16: A New Translation with Introduction and Commentary*, vol. 27A, Anchor Yale Bible. New Haven; London: Yale University Press, 2009.

contrast with the fully restored sight of the blind man will be especially evident in our next scene.

8:27–33

> [27] Yeshua and his talmidim went on to the towns of Caesarea Philippi. On the way, he asked his talmidim, "Who are people saying I am?" [28] "Some say you are Yochanan the Immerser," they told him, "others say Eliyahu, and still others, one of the prophets." [29] "But you," he asked, "who do you say I am?" Kefa answered, "You are the *Mashiach*." [30] Then Yeshua warned them not to tell anyone about him. [31] He began teaching them that the Son of Man had to endure much suffering and be rejected by the elders, the head *cohanim* and the Torah-teachers; and that he had to be put to death; but that after three days, he had to rise again. [32] He spoke very plainly about it. Kefa took him aside and began rebuking him. [33] But, turning around and looking at his talmidim, he rebuked Kefa. "Get behind me, Satan!" he said, "For your thinking is from a human perspective, not from God's perspective!"

The crossing to Beit-Tzaidah was the final journey by water of Yeshua and his band. From now on, they will proceed on land, and the words "way" or "on the way" will reappear numerous times, as noted earlier. This slower, step-by-step journey involves, among many other things, healing the deafness and blindness of the Twelve, a process that isn't fully completed within Mark's account.

The region of Caesarea Philippi at the northern frontier of the biblical land of Israel is the geographical turning-point in this journey. The transcendent vision coming in 9:2–8 most likely takes place on the "high mountain" (9:2) of Hermon, which is the northernmost outpost of this whole region. From there, Yeshua will turn his steps toward Jerusalem. The interlude in the region of Caesarea Philippi is also the dramatic turning-point. Before this scene, Yeshua has been announced on a supernatural level as the Son of God, but the ordinary folks of the Galil and its surroundings, as well as his own followers, continue to wonder who he is and what kind of power he is wielding (1:27; 2:12; 4:41; 7:37). When Yeshua raises the question of his identity with the talmidim, they report some of the mistaken ideas that the people have come up with (8:28; cf. 6:14–15). But Yeshua presses on to the real issue: who do *they*, his closest followers, believe him to be? One of them, Kefa or Peter, finally provides the right answer: "You are the *Mashiach*, the Messiah" (8:29).

This answer is so momentous, so transformative, that we might forget that this is the first time the title "Messiah" appears in Mark's Besorah since its opening line. Now that someone finally pronounces the title, it will appear five more times before Mark concludes his narrative (9:41; 12:35; 13:21; 14:61; 15:32), for a momentous total of seven appearances in this Besorah.[3] It's striking that Yeshua speaks of himself as Son of Man immediately after Peter identifies him as Messiah (8:31). He will employ this title twelve more times in Mark's account, as we shall see.

The Jewish scholar Daniel Boyarin notes,

> The equation of the Son of Man and his suffering with the Christ is made absolutely clear in [8:29–31] as well [as in 9:12]. This all makes the most sense if we assume that Jesus is alluding to the Son of Man figure from Daniel and his fate, which is to be crushed for a time, two times, and half a time before rising triumphant.[4]

The "crushing" Boyarin refers to is a reference to Daniel 7:25–27, in which the role of the Son of Man has been taken up by "the holy ones of the Most High," who are handed over to the anti-God forces "for a time, times and half a time," before finally receiving "the greatness of the kingdoms under the whole heaven" (Dan. 7:18, 25–27). Boyarin goes on to show how this picture of a suffering and then triumphant Son of Man/Messiah rests upon

---

[3]. The term makes another appearance in 13:22, referring to "false Messiahs," or "false Christs," but this phrase is actually one word in Greek, *pseudochristos*.
[4]. Boyarin, 136–37, referencing Daniel 7:25–27. For a discussion of these verses as applying to the Son of Man, see Boyarin, 35–52.

Isaiah 53, *as understood within the Jewish world of Yeshua's day.* Therefore, he writes,

> There is no essentially Christian (drawn from the cross) versus Jewish (triumphalist) notion of the Messiah, but only one complex and contested messianic idea, shared by Mark and Jesus with the full community of the Jews.[5]

As part of this complex messianic idea, the term "Messiah" would normally make one think of a kingly figure, as in one of its most dramatic appearances in the Tanakh:

> Why are the nations in an uproar,
> the peoples grumbling in vain?
> The earth's kings are taking positions,
> leaders conspiring together,
> against ADONAI
> and his anointed. (Psa. 2:1–2)

"His anointed" is literally "his Messiah" in the Hebrew, the one who will vanquish God's enemies, the "nations" and "peoples" taking positions against ADONAI. In Yeshua's time these opposing forces would include the earthly power of Rome and the false deities and unclean spirits arrayed against God's kingdom. With the hope of such deliverance in the background, it's not hard to see why Peter/Kefa rejects Yeshua's prediction of his own suffering and death, and why Yeshua so roundly overrides Peter's objections: "at the beginning Peter, as the representative of the disciples, displays a wisdom transcending that of other humans (8:27–30), but at the end he is ranged on the side of demonized humanity against the revelation of God (8:33)."[6] The wording in this citation is precise: Peter is not ranged on the side of Jewish expectations of a military, triumphant Messiah against Yeshua's prediction of suffering—rather Peter is on

---

5. Boyarin, 155. Note that the suffering servant passage in Isaiah actually begins at 52:13 and continues through the whole of chapter 53. For simplicity, we'll sometimes refer to Isaiah 53, which is actually Isaiah 52:13–53:12.
6. Marcus, *Mark 8–16*, 610.

the side of "demonized humanity," the inherent human resistance against God's redemptive ways, especially as they entail suffering.

As with the blind man who is only healed incrementally, the enlightenment of the talmidim, let alone the crowds, will take time. Yeshua begins the process by telling the talmidim about his suffering and death "plainly" (vs. 32)—a word used only here in Mark and in contrast with Yeshua's usual use of paradox and secrecy. Nevertheless, Peter rejects suffering and death, thus meriting the rebuke: "Get behind me, Satan! For your thinking is from a human perspective, not from God's perspective!" (8:33).

This rebuke includes the final mention of Satan by name in Mark's account, and encounters with demonic spirits will also cease after the following chapter. How do we explain this absence of demonic opposition as Mark reaches its climax? Perhaps, as Yeshua nears Jerusalem, Satan's strategy shifts from demonic harassment to direct assault culminating in crucifixion. This outcome seems increasingly inevitable as Yeshua and his band approach the holy city, a center of both ecclesial and secular power, where those powers collude in his execution. Satan and his demonic minions leave the stage in the second half of Mark and let the human powers complete their task of opposing Yeshua and his redemptive mission. But if Satan is behind the events leading to the crucifixion, that's never stated explicitly, and in our current passage Satan is represented by someone trying to convince Yeshua to *avoid* his coming crucifixion. There's another, perhaps more plausible, explanation for the withdrawal of Satan after Season 2 of Mark.

Yeshua's rebuke of Peter reflects Zechariah 3:2—"ADONAI said to *ha-satan* [Hebrew for "the Accuser"], "May ADONAI rebuke you, Accuser/*Satan*! Indeed, may ADONAI, who has made Jerusalem his choice, rebuke you!" In this scene, "in the presence of the High Priest Joshua—Jesus in Greek!—God rebukes Satan with similar language. Peter cannot imagine a messiah who suffers and dies, and Jesus' sharp response defines this passage as a central, defining moment in the Gospel."[7] In this interpretation, as we've noted, Yeshua's rebuke of Peter is the turning-point, sealed by his three-fold announcement that he will indeed suffer and die in Jerusalem. The extended confrontation with the demonic realm of Season 1 reaches its climax with Yeshua's decisive renunciation of Satan and his anti-God value system here at the beginning of Season 2. Satan's absence in the final chapters of Mark, then, may reflect Yeshua's utter rejection of the satanic suggestion to avoid the cross. From this perspective, Satan is not inspiring the events leading up to the crucifixion, as in the first explanation of his absence after this scene, but has already withdrawn in defeat when it becomes apparent that the crucifixion (and resulting resurrection) will indeed take place.

From either perspective, the crucifixion, which might appear to be a triumphal outcome for Satan, will turn out to be his decisive defeat and triumph for the kingdom that Yeshua inaugurates, for "after three days he will rise," as he declares three times on the way to Jerusalem (8:31; 9:31; 10:34). And the disciples, despite not understanding this three-fold declaration, continue to follow Yeshua to Jerusalem and, despite abandoning him in his suffering (14:41, 50, 66–72), will be summoned to rejoin him in Galilee after his resurrection. If Yeshua's closest followers can be restored after being deceived by the adversary, we can hope for restoration for all who have been led astray.

8:34 – 9:1

> [34] Then Yeshua called the crowd and his *talmidim* to him and told them, "If anyone wants to come after me, let him say 'No' to himself, take up his execution-stake, and keep following me. [35] For whoever wants to save his own life will destroy it, but whoever destroys his life for my sake and for the sake of the Good News will save it. [36] Indeed, what will it benefit a person if he gains the whole world but forfeits his life? [37] What could a person give in

---

7. Wills, "Mark," JANT, 87.

exchange for his life? [38] For if someone is ashamed of me and of what I say in this adulterous and sinful generation, the Son of Man also will be ashamed of him when he comes in his Father's glory with the holy angels.

9 Yes!" he went on, "I tell you that there are some people standing here who will not experience death until they see the Kingdom of God come in a powerful way!"

As noted, we have arrived at a turning-point in our narrative, but it's not clear that this is also a turning-point for the talmidim, or for the crowd following Yeshua. Peter recognizes who Yeshua really is, but then rebukes him for describing what he must go through because of who he really is. When Yeshua rebukes Peter in turn, he has his eye on all the talmidim (8:33), and now he begins to tell the talmidim as well as "the crowd" what it really means to follow him. The term "talmidim" or "disciples" has already appeared throughout Mark, but this is the first time that the requirements for being a talmid, beyond the simple "follow me," are laid out in full. From the outset, following Yeshua is demanding, as Shim'on and Andrew, Yaakov and Yochanan leave their livelihood and families (1:17–20), and Levi Ben-Halfai leaves his tax-collection booth (2:14) in response to Yeshua's summons. But now the talmidim learn that this summons is far more radical: it means following Yeshua in taking up the execution-stake and being prepared to relinquish one's life upon it.[8]

Following Yeshua may require giving up one's own life, or "soul" as in some translations, and it's best to understand this in literal terms before seeking other meanings. We've already seen indications of what a faithful testimony of the Kingdom of God might require, most strikingly in the fate of Yochanan the Immerser (6:16ff), but also in the plotting of the P'rushim and Herodians (3:6),

---

8. CJB uses "execution-stake" instead of the more usual "cross" to translate the Greek *stavros*, which simply means a stake, without reference to its particular shape (*New International Dictionary of New Testament Theology*, Vol. 1, ed. Colin Brown [Grand Rapids: Zondervan, 1982], 391). The word "cross" has connotations to a Jewish audience that might be misleading.

and the mounting opposition to Yeshua throughout his time in the Galil. Now Yeshua makes it clear that this price is not incidental, but inherent to discipleship. It is also notable that Yeshua demands loyalty not only to himself, but also to his message, the "Good News" (8:35) or Besorah—loyalty both to himself and to "what I say" (8:38). This message is the iconic one proclaimed from the beginning:

> The time has come,
> God's Kingdom is near!
> Turn to God from your sins
> and believe the Good News! (1:15)

The use of the term "Good News" in Mark 8:35 is its first appearance since the prologue, even though Mark's entire account had been introduced as the Good News, or the beginning of the Good News (1:1). Moreover, this Good News or Besorah is inextricably linked to Yeshua himself, so that it will be mentioned again in an identical context in 10:29, and then only two more (very significant) times in the final scenes of Yeshua's earthly ministry: 13:10 and 14:9, as we shall see.

Now Yeshua challenges his followers, or would-be followers, with the cost of proclaiming this Besorah. And he warns them against shrinking back, "For if someone is *ashamed* of me and of what I say in this adulterous and sinful generation, the Son of Man also will be *ashamed* of him when he comes in his Father's glory with the holy angels" (8:38, emphasis added). Boyarin highlights "ashamed" here as a key to understanding Peter's rebuke of Yeshua back in 8:32. Peter is not repudiating the picture of a suffering Messiah in favor of a typically Jewish concept of a conquering hero, as is often claimed; rather, he is *ashamed* of Yeshua's very Jewish picture of a Messiah who is "despised and . . . a man of pains, well acquainted with illness. / Like someone from whom people turn their faces . . ." (Isa. 53:4). "But if any are ashamed of Jesus in his humiliation and crucifixion, the exalted Son of Man (Jesus vindicated) will be ashamed of them in the final moment, when he comes in glory with his angels (Daniel 7)."[9] As commentator Joel Marcus notes,

> it would be a mistake to reduce Davidic messianism to religious militancy; the Davidic king of Isa. 11:1–10 is not only a successful warrior but also a righteous judge on whom the spirit of wisdom rests, and the "Christ" of *Psalms of Solomon* 17 not only crushes hostile Gentile armies but also has mercy on the nations and shepherds his own people in holiness.[10]

This nuanced understanding helps counter the stereotype of first-century Judaism as expecting only military-political deliverance, a stereotype that has distorted the image of Jews and Judaism in the Christian world for centuries.

Two other aspects of Mark 8:38 are worthy of note.

First, this saying is the first time Yeshua speaks about his coming in glory, the Second Coming, when he returns to the earth after his death and resurrection. To do so, he reshapes the drama of Daniel 7:13–14. There, the Son of Man comes with the clouds of heaven, approaches the Ancient One, is led into his heavenly throne room, and receives authority. Here, in Mark 8, the Son of Man "comes in his Father's glory with the holy angels," echoing the language of Daniel 7, but implying that he's come back to earth to actually exercise the authority given to him in Daniel's heavenly court scene. Yeshua uses similar "Son of Man" language in 13:26, which also seems to be about the Second Coming, and in 14:62, which might not be, as we'll see. Regardless, Yeshua's message is clear: those who are loyal to him in these times of trial and persecution will be rewarded; those trying to avoid the cost of fierce loyalty to Yeshua will have a price to pay in the end.

---

9. Boyarin, 140–141.
10. Marcus, *Mark 8–16*, 1105.

Second, Yeshua's use of "generation" in 8:38 reflects the Torah's account of the "crooked and perverted generation" that came out of Egypt (Deut. 32:5, 20). Paradoxically, Yeshua's language here both reproves those of his day who are ashamed of him, and ties their story—including their rejection of God's deliverer—into the whole narrative of the people of Israel.

This brings us to the meaning of our final verse, 9:1. We are in the Peshat, or "plain sense" section of our commentary, and the plain sense of 9:1 seems at first glance to be that Yeshua is still looking beyond his death and resurrection to the time of his return, the time when they "see the Kingdom of God come in a powerful way," which is another way of saying "when he comes in his Father's glory," as in 8:38. In this interpretation, he's promising that some of those hearing him at that time would see the Second Coming . . . but he'd be mistaken, because this glorious event still hasn't taken place. But if Yeshua is mistaken on such a vital point, we have some real problems. So, is this sort of interpretation really the clearest "plain sense" of this verse?

The wording itself suggests other possibilities. Seeing the Kingdom "come in a powerful way," as our translation has it, or "after it has come with power" in the ESV, sounds different from seeing the Son of Man coming in his Father's glory. These translations are trying to reflect the grammar of the Greek original, which indicates that

> They are not to see the "coming" of the [Kingdom of God], but rather to witness the fact that it *has* come. The prediction thus focuses not on its arrival, but on the point at which its presence, already a reality, is (a) visible and (b) displayed [in power].[11]

Jewish New Testament scholar AJ Levine points out that reading Mark 9:1 as a prediction of the Second Coming isn't only a problem for us, but would also be a problem for Mark's original audience.

---

11. France, 344. Bracketed words are translations of words in Greek in the commentary itself.

Mark's readers knew that Jesus had not returned. Matthew and Luke wrote later than Mark, and they both (Matthew 16:28; Luke 9:27) include the comment that some of the disciples would not die before they saw the Kingdom manifest. Neither Gospel is expecting the return of Jesus a week from Tuesday.[12]

Levine goes on to note that the *power* of the Kingdom, referred to in 9:1 "can be experienced by those who take up Jesus's message of the Kingdom: of repentance, of care, of support." She continues,

> The message is therefore one of hope. Since it follows Jesus's prediction that *it is necessary that the Son of Humanity . . . be killed and after three days rise* (Mark 8:31; also 9:31; 10:33–34), we can conclude that the Kingdom is experienced in both the cross (Jesus's willingness to die as a ransom for many) and the Resurrection (God's fidelity to Jesus).[13]

In this reading, 9:1 is not a restatement of 8:38, but a contrast, an unexpected shift, which would be typical of the Markan Yeshua. Yeshua will return in his Father's glory to bring reward and punishment to humankind at some future point, but there are also some standing here right now who are going to see the Kingdom appearing in power. This reading also ties 9:1 into the following scene, when some of those who are standing there are going to see Yeshua in glorified form.

Regardless, the sense of expectancy in 9:1 reminds us of a similar sense in the iconic Jewish prayer, the Kaddish:

> May He establish His kingdom
> in your lifetime and in your days,
> and in the lifetime of all the house of Israel,
> swiftly and soon – and say: Amen. (*Koren Siddur*)

---

12. Levine, Mark, 56–57.
13. Levine, 57.

Derash

- In a midrash, Rabbi Benjamin ben Levi and Rabbi Jonathan ben Amram say that "all may be presumed to be blind, until the Holy One, blessed be He, enlightens their eyes" (*Genesis Rabbah* 53.14). From that perspective, the spiritual blindness portrayed in Mark is not exceptional, but typical of human nature, including our own, apart from God's enlightening touch—or rather, as Mark makes abundantly clear, apart from God's rigorous process of enlightenment.

    Yeshua will warn his talmidim three times about what awaits him—and them—in Jerusalem (8:31; 9:31; 10:33–34), and he'll include an announcement of his resurrection each time. The talmidim react to his prophecy of suffering and death, but seem to miss the promise of his resurrection. They're quick enough to reject the notion of a suffering Messiah, but slow indeed to imagine, let alone believe in, a resurrected Messiah. What does this tell us about human nature? About our own response to suffering?

- Each of Yeshua's three declarations of what awaits him is followed by a description of what it means to follow him, perhaps most forcefully in the first description, which appears in this episode: "If anyone wants to come after me, let him [1] say 'No' to himself, [2] take up his execution-stake, and [3] keep following me" (8:34). This threefold call to follow Yeshua even unto death echoes the threefold command of the Shema to love the LORD your God, "with all your heart, and with all your soul, and with all your might" (Deut. 6:5). This commandment follows the declaration, "Hear, Israel! ADONAI our God, ADONAI is One" (Deut. 6:4).

    A talmudic commentary tells of Rabbi Akiva's execution by the Roman authorities after the Bar Kokhba revolt (ca. 135 CE). As he is being executed, Akiva tells his followers, "'All my days I have been troubled by the verse: With all your soul, meaning: Even if God takes your soul. I said to myself: When will the opportunity be afforded me to fulfill this verse? Now that it has been afforded me, shall I not fulfill it?' He prolonged his uttering of the word [from the Shema]: One, until his soul left his body as he uttered his final word: One" (Berakhot 61b, Sefaria.org).

We might consider how Akiva's response to the Shema sheds light on Yeshua's teaching, and vice versa: "Whoever wants to save his own soul will lose it, but whoever loses his soul for my sake and for the sake of the Besorah will save it" (Mark 8:35, literal translation).

- Another midrash rooted in the same period of Roman persecution in the second century CE compares the binding of Isaac in Genesis 22:6–8 to execution upon the stake, an all-too-familiar scene to the Jews of that trying time: "'And Avraham took the wood of the burnt-offering,' like one who carries his stake on his shoulder. . . . 'And they went both of them together,' one to bind and the other to be bound, one to slaughter and the other to be slaughtered" (Genesis Rabbah 56:3).

  The full text in Genesis says, "And Avraham took the wood of the burnt-offering, and *laid it on Isaac his son*." In the midrash, Isaac willingly bears the wood, "like one who carries his [execution] stake on his shoulder," a stunning reflection of Yeshua's final journey to the place of execution, and of his demand, "If anyone wants to come after me, let him say 'No' to himself, take up his execution-stake, and keep following me." As radical as this call is, it is not foreign to the Jewish context and ethos of Yeshua's time, nor to the centuries that followed, even up to our own.

- Yeshua's call to take up his execution-stake and follow him is so radical that it often gets sidelined in real life. We might imagine that we'll be willing to undergo persecution and even death for his sake, but it remains theoretical, and meanwhile we find ourselves complaining about the lesser deprivations we actually do face, like a boring job, a demanding marriage partner, or achy joints. How do we translate Yeshua's radical demands into real-life applications in the 21st century world? Yeshua's warning against being ashamed of him may be especially relevant for Jewish Yeshua-followers, who are often stigmatized and socially rejected—sometimes even by family—for identifying with him. We'd do well to remember Yeshua's words to his original followers, words of challenge and promise that also apply to us:

> Yes! I tell you that there is no one who has left house, brothers, sisters, mother, father, children or fields, for my sake and for the sake of the Good News, who will not receive a hundred times over, now, in this age, homes, brothers, sisters, mothers, children and lands — with persecutions! — and in the age to come, eternal life. (Mark 10:29–30 CJB modified)

Season 2, Episode 2 (11)

A Mountain-top and a Crowd

9:2–29

Overview

We are still in the territory around Caesarea Philippi in the north, and Yeshua has finally clarified to his followers that as the Son of Man he will suffer and die in Jerusalem—and be raised from the dead. He has told them of the rewards and judgment that await when the Son of Man appears in glory, and added that some of them would not die before they "see the Kingdom of God come in a powerful way" (9:1). Now, "six days later," Yeshua takes three of his talmidim away with him to a high mountain, where he appears to them in a glorified form, with Elijah and Moses at his side. The three talmidim are terrified and then they hear a voice from out of a cloud declaring, "This is my Son, whom I love. Listen to him!" Afterward, Yeshua instructs the talmidim to tell no one what they've seen, and goes on to speak again about his coming resurrection, with the talmidim still not understanding.

When they return to the rest of the talmidim, they encounter a large and agitated crowd. Yeshua's followers have tried and failed to drive an evil spirit out of a boy, and his father begs Yeshua to help, "if you can." Yeshua responds, "What do you mean, 'if you can'? Everything is possible to the one who believes!" The man responds with the poignant line (as in most translations), "I believe; help my unbelief." The boy is dramatically delivered in what turns out to be the final direct encounter with evil spirits in Mark.

From there, Yeshua and his band continue on their way through the Galil, and Yeshua tells them for the second time that he will be betrayed and crucified and will rise from the dead after three days. Again the talmidim don't understand what this means and instead direct their energies to arguing over who among them is the greatest. Yeshua tells them that true greatness means humility and service. He places a child in front of them, puts his arms around him, and says that whoever welcomes such a child in his name welcomes him and also the One who sent him. Yeshua goes on to portray the life of faithfulness and radical loyalty to him that is the pathway to eternal life in the coming Kingdom. As in our last episode, Yeshua states the demands of a life of faithfulness in the starkest terms: "If your eye makes you sin, pluck it out! Better that you should be one-eyed but enter the Kingdom of God, rather than keep both eyes and be thrown into Gei-Hinnom." As Yeshua continues to lead his talmidim toward the encounter in Jerusalem, he makes it clear that the stakes in this journey are the highest possible.

Peshat

9:2–13

[2] Six days later, Yeshua took Kefa, Ya'akov and Yochanan and led them up a high mountain privately. As they watched, he began to change form, [3] and his clothes became dazzlingly white, whiter than anyone in the world could possibly bleach them. [4] Then they saw Eliyahu and Moshe speaking with Yeshua. [5] Kefa said to Yeshua, "It's good that we're here, Rabbi! Let's put up three shelters — one for you, one for Moshe and one for Eliyahu." [6] (He didn't know what to say, they were so frightened.) [7] Then a cloud enveloped them; and a voice came out of the cloud, "This is my Son, whom I love. Listen to him!" [8] Suddenly, when they looked around, they no longer saw anyone with them except Yeshua.

[9] As they came down the mountain, he warned them not to tell anyone what they had seen until after the Son of Man had risen from the dead. [10] So they kept the matter to themselves; but they continued asking each other, "What is this 'rising from the dead'?"

¹¹ They also asked him, "Why do the *Torah*-teachers say that Eliyahu has to come first?" ¹² "Eliyahu will indeed come first," he answered, "and he will restore everything. Nevertheless, why is it written in the *Tanakh* that the Son of Man must suffer much and be rejected? ¹³ There's more to it: I tell you that Eliyahu has come, and they did whatever they pleased to him, just as the *Tanakh* says about him."

Mark's precise timeline here—"Six days later"—links the following scene to the verse just before it, suggesting that seeing the glorified Yeshua, as they are about to, somehow equates with seeing "the Kingdom of God come in a powerful way." Further, "six days later" means that the vision about to be described happens on day seven, the number of completion and perfection in biblical chronology. The timing also reflects the account of Moshe ascending Sinai, waiting for six days, and then receiving the Torah on the seventh day (Exod. 24:15–16). The high mountain in Mark 9 is most likely Mount Hermon, which is the highest peak in the region (a ski destination for modern Israelis) and the peak closest to Caesarea Philippi. It's also the northernmost of the three peaks often mentioned as possible sites of this epiphany—the others being Mount Tabor, the traditional site, a good distance to the southwest; and Mount Meron, in the same general direction as Mount Tabor but somewhat closer to Caesarea Philippi.

On the mountain, the talmidim see Yeshua transformed—the term in the original is a form of "metamorphosis," not "transfiguration," which appears only in Luke. He is clothed in supernaturally white garments, with Eliyahu and Moshe standing beside him, apparently still alive. And indeed, Eliyahu's death is never recorded in Scripture; rather, he is taken up into the heavens in the sight of his successor Elisha (2 Kings 2:11). Moshe's death is recorded in the Torah, but "to this day no one knows where his grave is" (Deut. 34:6), leaving room for "later Jewish traditions [saying] that Moses was translated directly to heaven.'"[1] It's perhaps more relevant to this scene that both figures have a role in the end-time expectations of those days: Eliyahu will appear "before the coming

---

1. Schnabel, 210.

of the great / and terrible Day of ADONAI' (Mal. 3:23 [4:5]), and the prophet "like Moshe" (Deut. 18:15ff.) was expected before the end as well.[2] Indeed, before Malachi announces the coming of Eliyahu, he exhorts his listeners, speaking in the voice of ADONAI:

> Remember the Torah of Moshe my servant,
> which I enjoined on him at Horev,
> laws and rulings for all Israel. (Mal. 3:22 [4:4])

Finally, as this citation from Malachi reminds us, both figures are also associated with a "high mountain," in this case, Mount Horev or Sinai. On this mountain Moshe received the Torah, and to this mountain centuries later Eliyahu fled to escape the wrath of Jezebel (1 Kings 19:8).

Kefa/Peter is flabbergasted at the vision and proposes setting up three shelters for the three figures, because he doesn't know what to say. In apparent response, a cloud covers them and a voice speaks from the cloud—another reflection of Mount Sinai (Exod. 24:15–16). This is the second *bat qol* or "voice from heaven" that we hear in Mark and, like the first (1:11), it declares that Yeshua is "my Son, whom I love." Here, however, it speaks not to Yeshua directly, but to the three men around him, adding an admonition, "Listen to him!" This voice is more like the *bat qol* of rabbinic literature, speaking to a group rather than an individual, and providing direction from on high.[3] The voice confirms Peter's confession in 8:29 and expands upon it: Yeshua is the Messiah and also the uniquely beloved and authoritative Son of God, who is to be heard and obeyed. "Listen to him" may also point to Yeshua as the Prophet like Moses, "to whom you shall listen" (Deut. 18:15, 19).

All of this adds up to another example of the deep integration of Yeshua's story into the broader narrative of all Israel. Commentators

---

2. This is the implication of the question put to Yochanan the Immerser in John 1:21, after he declares that he's not the Messiah: "Are you 'the prophet'?" Note that this question comes after they ask whether he is Eliyahu. CJB adds the clarification: "Are you 'the prophet,' the one we're expecting?"

3. Perhaps the earliest reference to a *bat qol* appears in Avot 6:2, which is a later addition to the Mishnah (Dovi Seldowitz, "Bat Kol: The Voice of Heaven in Rabbinic Literature" [https://www.sefaria.org/sheets/372842.74?lang=en&with=all&lang2=en]).

have sometimes seen Eliyahu and Moshe appearing in this scene in order to be superseded by Yeshua. After all, Kefa's proposal to put up three shelters to somehow protect or enshrine all three figures is brushed aside. The voice from heaven speaks only of Yeshua, and instructs us to "Listen to him," without mention of the other two. And, when the vision fades, the talmidim see only Yeshua. But it's more likely that Eliyahu and Moshe show up, not to receive their walking papers, but to validate Yeshua and his ministry. When they are "speaking with Yeshua" (9:4), it's probably not to discuss their retirement plans, but to discuss and affirm the prophetic drama about to unfold as Yeshua and his talmidim return on their way toward Jerusalem, the scene of his betrayal, crucifixion, and resurrection.

In my comments on 1:1 I claimed that "applying the title 'Son of God' to a specific man would not necessarily sound outrageous to second-temple Jewish ears." The phrase is used in some contexts to denote the chosen, Davidic king, as in 2 Samuel 7:14—"I will be a father for him, and he will be a son for me"—and Psalm 2:7.

> I will proclaim the decree:
> ADONAI said to me,
> "You are my son;
> today I became your father."

The whole context of our scene on the mountain, however, suggests a more profound meaning of "Son of God." Yeshua's appearance is transformed and a voice out of the cloud, reminiscent of the glory-cloud of Exodus, announces his Sonship. It's not a stretch to see Mark hinting, with his usual subtlety, at the divine nature of Messiah Yeshua in this scene.

On the way down the mountain, Yeshua instructs the disciples not to speak of this event until after he rises from the dead, and they continue to ponder among themselves the meaning of rising from the dead. Mention of the resurrection triggers a question about Eliyahu (whom they just saw). They most likely share the widespread Jewish hope in a resurrection to come, which will occur at or right after the Day of the LORD. Yeshua, however, seems to be announcing that it's coming soon, right after his death, which is one reason they have such trouble putting it all together. Is the Day of the LORD that near at hand? Doesn't Eliyahu come first, "before the coming of the great / and terrible Day of ADONAI"? They ask Yeshua about this and he says that Eliyahu must indeed come first to restore everything, as the prophet foretold,[4] but the Tanakh also says that the Son of Man must suffer and be rejected, by implication *before* Eliyahu can make his appearance.

This whole sequence of events may be hard for the talmidim to grasp, but the "idea of the suffering of the Son of Man is anything but an alien import into Judaism; in fact, it is its very vocation," according to Daniel Boyarin.[5] By saying that this idea is Judaism's "very vocation," Boyarin seems to mean that it's the calling of "the Jewish mode of biblical interpretation, midrash," to discover and expound upon this revolutionary idea of a suffering Messiah, an idea that "would not have been at all foreign to Jewish sensibilities, which derived their very messianic hopes and expectations from such methods of close reading of Scripture [i.e. midrash], just as Jesus did."[6] Why then are the talmidim so slow to comprehend this whole idea? We'll explore this question in our Derash section shortly. For now, we'll heed Yeshua's midrashic note that "Eliyahu has come" in the person of Yochanan the Immerser, "and they did whatever they pleased to him, just as the Tanakh says about him" (9:13). Of course, the Tanakh does not say explicitly that Eliyahu himself will suffer to prepare for the Day of the LORD, but it does make it clear that faithfulness to God's calling, especially faithfulness as a prophet, will entail suffering, and that suffering in turn opens the way to redemption.

---

4. This notion reflects the final verse of Malachi's prophecy:
    He will turn the hearts of the fathers to the children
    and the hearts of the children to their fathers;
    otherwise I will come and strike the land
    with complete destruction. (3:24 [4:6])
5. Boyarin, 148.
6. Boyarin, 148, 149.

9:14–29

¹⁴ When they got back to the talmidim, they saw a large crowd around them and some Torah-teachers arguing with them. ¹⁵ As soon as the crowd saw him, they were surprised and ran out to greet him. ¹⁶ He asked them, "What's the discussion about?" ¹⁷ One of the crowd gave him the answer: "Rabbi, I brought my son to you because he has an evil spirit in him that makes him unable to talk. ¹⁸ Whenever it seizes him, it throws him to the ground — he foams at the mouth, grinds his teeth and becomes stiff all over. I asked your talmidim to drive the spirit out, but they couldn't do it." ¹⁹ "People without any trust!" he responded. "How long will I be with you? How long must I put up with you? Bring him to me!" ²⁰ They brought the boy to him; and as soon as the spirit saw him, it threw the boy into a convulsion. ²¹ Yeshua asked the boy's father, "How long has this been happening to him?" "Ever since childhood," he said; ²² "and it often tries to kill him by throwing him into the fire or into the water. But if you can do anything, have pity on us and help us!" ²³ Yeshua said to him, "What do you mean, 'if you can'? Everything is possible to someone who has trust!" ²⁴ Instantly the father of the child exclaimed, "I do trust — help my lack of trust!" ²⁵ When Yeshua saw that the crowd was closing in on them, he rebuked the unclean spirit, saying to it, "You deaf and dumb spirit! I command you: come out of him, and never go back into him again!" ²⁶ Shrieking and throwing the boy into a violent fit, it came out. The boy lay there like a corpse, so that most of the people said he was dead. ²⁷ But Yeshua took him by the hand and raised him to his feet, and he stood up.

²⁸ After Yeshua had gone indoors, his talmidim asked him privately, "Why couldn't we drive it out?" ²⁹ He said to them "This is the kind of spirit that can be driven out only by prayer."

Yeshua's descent from the mountain-top continues. First, he had to deal with the lack of understanding among his closest talmidim, their continued stumbling over his coming death and resurrection. Now he encounters a lack of trust among the wider circle of his talmidim, who have tried and failed to drive an evil spirit out of a boy. It's not hard to understand Yeshua's exasperation, which Mark portrays with characteristic candor, as he records Yeshua's chastisement of the crowd as well as of the feckless talmidim: "People without any trust! How long will I be with you? How long must I put up with you?" (9:19). The original Greek and most translations have the word "generation" (*genea* in Greek) here, translating "People without any trust" as "faithless generation," which echoes a description of the Israelites in the Torah, and Yeshua's words in Mark 8:38, as we saw in our last episode. Apparently, victory over demonic spirits is Discipleship 101, and Yeshua is longing to move on to deeper lessons for those who would follow him.

He tells the bystanders to bring the demonized boy to him and when they do, the unclean spirit throws the boy into a convulsion . . . and Yeshua engages his father in conversation, "How long has this been happening to him?" This turn might recall Yeshua's delay on the way to heal the daughter of Ya'ir, when he pauses for a moment to talk with the woman with the issue of blood, and Ya'ir's daughter dies (5:23–35). Yeshua's timing might seem callous, but he is calm in the face of all opposition, even death itself, because he is about to overcome it.

The father of the demonized boy describes how the spirit has been tormenting the boy since childhood and then begs Yeshua to help, "if you can do anything." The very human Yeshua of this scene responds with apparent indignation, "What do you mean, 'if you can'? Everything is possible to someone who has trust!" What starts out sounding like a word of rebuke turns into an exhortation to trust and the father responds with one of the most memorable lines in Scripture: "I believe; help my unbelief." In the presence of the trusting/not-trusting father, Yeshua commands the spirit to depart and never return. The spirit comes out, after shrieking, throwing the boy into a violent fit, and leaving him as if dead. Yeshua takes the corpse-like boy by the hand and stands him up on his feet—a reminder of Yeshua's raising of the dead daughter of Yair, another father, back in Episode 6.

This encounter will be the final deliverance session in Mark's Besorah, coming shortly after the final explicit mention of Satan in our last episode. The evil spirits, and even their chief, Satan himself, seem to go offstage for the rest of the drama. Spiritual warfare advances largely through tactical victories over demonic forces in Season One. It gives way to a broader strategic confrontation with evil embodied in human authorities in Seasons Two and Three.

In this instance, after the crowds depart and the talmidim have Yeshua to themselves, they ask him why they were unable to drive out this particular evil spirit. After all, he'd sent them out not long before with "authority over the unclean spirits," and they had "expelled many demons, and they anointed many sick people with oil and healed them" (6:7, 13). Their question seems reasonable enough, but Yeshua's answer is typically enigmatic—"This kind cannot be driven out by anything but prayer" (literal translation). It's enigmatic enough that many early manuscripts add "and fasting" after "prayer," to help explain what was missing in the talmidim's efforts. "This kind" has also been taken by some commentators as part of the explanation, implying that an unclean spirit causing muteness and convulsions is uniquely difficult to expel. But nowhere else in Mark is such grading of difficulty implied, and it's hard to imagine that the unclean spirit here is a tougher customer than the demonic legion in the Gerasene graveyard (5:1–13).

The unembellished wording here may suggest that the talmidim were still relying on the authority Yeshua granted them back in chapter 6 and were trying to drive out the demon with a simple command, but without grounding it in prayer.

> Jesus' point is this: while his personal authority allows him to drive out a demon, even a legion of demons, with a simple word of command, the disciples' authority is delegated authority, which means that in their encounters with demons they always need to acknowledge their dependence upon God by praying that God will help them drive out the demons.[7]

Yeshua's answer is a reminder as our episode closes that the Kingdom of God does not advance through magic formulas or foolproof methods, but through deep prayerful connection with the

---

7. Schnabel, 219.

King. Yeshua is inherently and always connected with the Kingdom but his talmidim must work continually to keep that connection alive and active.

Derash

- AJ Levine supports the idea that the "Metamorphosis" of Mark 9:2–8 would have "been seeing the kingdom of God come in power," as in Mark 9:1. She continues,

    > Whereas the disciples have difficulty believing that Jesus will die and so they cannot take the next step to accept his prediction of his being raised from the dead, they can now experience, before his Passion, part of his true nature. They see him in his full power and glory. That vision, fleeting as it is, may be enough to sustain them, and all disciples subsequently, as they wait for the Parousia.[8]

    Levine's final sentence is challenging: can we draw upon Mark's testimony of the glorified Messiah to sustain us as we await the Parousia—Messiah's return—which can sometimes seem long overdue?

    Knowing Mark's skill as a storyteller, we realize it's no accident that Yeshua's encounter with his followers' failure and unbelief—and his resulting irritation—is pictured right after the glorious revelation on the mountain top. Before we explore the implications of this both-and portrayal, we can also recognize the midrashic element in Mark's storytelling. The high mountain is like Sinai, the place of glorious vision, and when Yeshua descends, as Moshe descended after the glorious theophany in which he received the Torah, he, like Moshe, encounters a divided and unsettled crowd, "people without any trust" (9:19 cf. Exod. 32:15–20). This crowd, with its unbelief and discord, doesn't come close to the apostasy of the golden calf, but it does provide another link between Yeshua and Moshe, a link that helps explain Yeshua's visceral reaction in this scene.

---

8. Levine, *Mark*, 58.

- This juxtaposition of a glorious epiphany of Yeshua with a very human picture of his exasperation shortly afterwards provides an essential reminder. In some way beyond our full understanding, Messiah Yeshua is both human and divine, both transcendent and earthbound. But this linkage can sound abstract and theoretical. It's perhaps more to the point to realize that the God described in Scripture as the Creator and Sustainer of all things, the God who promises and fulfills, is actually right there with us in all that we experience as humans—including suffering. And, moreover, it's not only that God is there suffering along with us, which is, of course, a huge deal on its own, but that God experiences this suffering himself, and it gets to him. "In all their affliction he was afflicted . . . / he lifted them up and carried them all the days of old" (Isa. 63:9a ESV). And this whole picture is the face, the knowable aspect, of the one true and living God. We can't really know who God is without recognizing this quality in him.

  I'm writing these words during the dark days of Israel's war against Hamas, just a few days after learning that three of our hostages, finally able to escape from captivity, were mistakenly fired upon and killed by IDF troops. This disaster came after weeks of prayer by thousands of people for protection over the hostages, and for their speedy release. And on the cusp of these prayers being answered at least for these three, they are mistakenly killed. Couldn't God have prevented this tragic error, simply by opening the eyes of the IDF soldiers to see that these three men were trying to surrender? There's not likely to be an answer to this question, beyond the one revealed repeatedly in Mark's Besorah. The God who answers prayers, who promises and fulfills, endures himself the pain of prayers not answered and of disappointment as unspeakable as that borne by the families of these three young men.

  The one revealed in transcendent glory in the Metamorphosis and later through the resurrection does not shield us from the disorder and disappointment of human life. Rather, he somehow endures this broken world, and accompanies us as we journey through it.

- Yeshua tells the father of the demonized boy, "All things are possible for one who believes," eliciting the unforgettable response: "I do believe—help my unbelief!" (9:24, my translation). Perhaps this agonized father senses that God does not wait for our faith to be fully formed and perfect before he acts on it, and so he cries out, "Help me!"

> Unbelief is not a sign of rejection or disloyalty; unbelief is the place where one asks for help. I don't have the emotional capacity to continue another day: help me. I don't have the psychological stamina to face another moment: help me. I don't believe I can finish this paper or pass this exam: help me. The call for help shows that there remains a modicum of belief, if not in the self then in someone else who can help bear or relieve the burden.[9]

In Yeshua's world, that "someone else" is God. As Yeshua demonstrates repeatedly, God takes whatever belief, whatever trust, we can offer up from amidst our unbelief, and leverages that toward his merciful purposes.

In a similar vein, the great twentieth-century Jewish thinker Abraham Joshua Heschel discovered through his own spiritual practice "something which is far greater than my desire to pray. Namely, God's desire that I pray. There is something which is far greater than my will to believe. Namely, God's will that I believe."[10]

---

9. Levine, *Mark*, 77.
10. Abraham Joshua Heschel, "Toward an Understanding of Halacha," in *Abraham Joshua Heschel, Moral Grandeur and Spiritual Audacity: Essays edited by Susannah Heschel* (New York: Farrar, Straus and Giroux, 1996), 131.

Season 2, Episode 3 (12)

A Second Warning is Misunderstood

9:30–50

Overview

Yeshua's band departs from the region of Caesarea Philippi to continue on their way through the Galil and on to Jerusalem. For a second time, Yeshua warns his talmidim about his coming betrayal, death, and resurrection, and for a second time, the talmidim fail to understand. Instead of asking him to explain, they start arguing with each other about who is the greatest among them. Yeshua takes this as an opportunity to teach them about true greatness, drawing a child close to himself and telling his followers that whoever welcomes a child in his name, welcomes both him and the One who sent him.

Possibly hoping to change the subject, one of the talmidim, Yochanan, reports that he told someone who was expelling demons in Yeshua's name to stop, "because he wasn't one of us." Again, Yeshua turns a misguided statement into a teachable moment, telling his talmidim that his Kingdom doesn't need to be sealed off and protected, but is expansive, and "whoever is not against us is for us." He goes on to warn these inner-circle talmidim against offending even his humblest followers, and against allowing their own evil inclinations to destroy their share in eternal life. Yeshua describes the alternative to eternal life, the fire of Gei-Hinnom, in the starkest terms. He goes on to urge his talmidim to do whatever it takes to avoid it, even figuratively cutting off their own offending hand or foot, or plucking out an eye that leads to sin.

Yeshua concludes on a more positive note, urging them to be like an offering that is salted before being presented to ADONAI, and to be at peace with each other. The demands of discipleship are great and the dangers of falling short are dire, but through faithfulness to Yeshua and to each other, their lives will be fit to present as an offering to the LORD.

Peshat

9:30–37

> [30] After leaving that place, they went on through the Galil. Yeshua didn't want anyone to know, [31] because he was teaching his talmidim. He told them, "The Son of Man will be betrayed into the hands of men who will put him to death; but after he has been killed, three days later he will rise." [32] But they didn't understand what he meant, and they were afraid to ask him.
>
> [33] They arrived at K'far-Nachum. When Yeshua was inside the house, he asked them, "What were you discussing as we were traveling?" [34] But they kept quiet; because on the way, they had been arguing with each other about who was the greatest. [35] He sat down, summoned the Twelve and said to them, "If anyone wants to be first, he must make himself last of all and servant of all." [36] He took a child and stood him among them. Then he put his arms around him and said to them, [37] "Whoever welcomes one such child in my name welcomes me, and whoever welcomes me welcomes not me but the One who sent me."

As Yeshua leads his band through the Galil on the way to Jerusalem, he desires to keep a low profile so that he can focus on instructing them. His demonstration of the kingdom through healing the deaf, blind, and afflicted and driving out unclean spirits has now given way to direct instruction. And what is the content of this teaching? His impending betrayal, death, and resurrection. This is the second time Yeshua has told his followers what awaits him in the days ahead, but it's the first time he mentions betrayal specifically, echoing Isaiah's description of the suffering servant, who "after forcible arrest and sentencing . . . was taken away, and none of his generation protested" (Isa. 53:8). Marcus comments that the Greek word for betrayal or "handing over" appears in the Septuagint translation (LXX) of Isaiah 53:6, 12, "where [it] is used to speak of God's delivery of his Suffering Servant to death," and goes on to note,

> But the verb also appears in Dan. 7:25–27 LXX, in which "the holy ones of the Most High," who are linked with the "one like a son of man," are "turned over to the hands" of their enemy until the moment of eschatological vindication, which elsewhere in Daniel is associated with resurrection (Dan. 12:1–3).[1]

By adding betrayal to his forecast of what awaits in Jerusalem, Yeshua both links it even more firmly to Jewish prophecy, and intensifies the warning to the disciples: they are facing betrayal along with everything else. Like the first warning, however, this second one seems incomprehensible to the talmidim. Apparently they just can't take Yeshua's words in their simple, literal sense, but they're afraid to ask him what he really means, perhaps—the reader might suspect—because they don't want to know.

Instead of seeking to understand, then, the talmidim begin to argue with each other about who among them is the greatest, perhaps reacting to Yeshua's favoring of the three disciples that he took with him to the high mountain of his epiphany in our last episode. Apparently, Yeshua either hears their argument, or senses what it's about, and asks the talmidim what they were discussing on the way, shaming them into silence. But he is gentle with them, as he responds with a second description (after 8:34–38) of what it means to follow him. Mark has noted that they are in "the house" in K'far-Nachum (9:33), which we've already described as a sort of home base for Yeshua's Galilean ministry (see commentary on 1:21–28). Here he sits down in the customary

---

1. Marcus, *Mark 8–16*, 667.

posture of a teacher to impart instructions that both bring closure to his ministry in the Galil and prepare the talmidim for what lies ahead. But it's not the sort of teaching they might expect: "If anyone wants to be first, he must make himself last of all and servant of all" (9:35).

This teaching is another reflection of Isaiah's servant, who "will be raised up, exalted, highly honored," but also "so disfigured that he didn't even seem human and simply no longer looked like a man" (Isa. 52:13–14). So, who is a "great" follower? One who drops the whole comparison game and acknowledges that he is *last* and least great. One who devotes his energies not to competing with the other followers, but to serving them. Indeed, this "great" follower is the servant of *all*, not just of other kingdom insiders. Yeshua's description of discipleship dismantles the whole religious framework that his followers—and religious followers in general—seem to assume.

Since we're back to the basics, Yeshua makes his instructions particularly clear and concrete—acting them out as well as speaking them. They're in a friendly house and there are some children around, so Yeshua takes one, stands him right in the middle of this group of big men, and welcomes him into this place of honor by embracing him.[2] Yeshua is demonstrating a divine reversal in which he reverses the ways of this world to reveal the ways of the World to Come. "The kingdom belonging to children seems to be an idea distinctive to Jesus, yet in keeping with his radical approach to the Jewish idea of end-time inversion."[3] Yeshua is enacting this reversal to inspire his talmidim to use whatever position they might gain in the household of Messiah to welcome and affirm the low-status and vulnerable around them.

---

2. France, 374; Schnabel, 222–223.
3. Keener, 293.

9:38–50

³⁸ Yochanan said to him, "Rabbi, we saw a man expelling demons in your name; and because he wasn't one of us, we told him to stop." ³⁹ But Yeshua said, "Don't stop him, because no one who works a miracle in my name will soon after be able to say something bad about me. ⁴⁰ For whoever is not against us is for us. ⁴¹ Indeed, whoever gives you even a cup of water to drink because you come in the name of the Messiah — yes! I tell you that he will certainly not lose his reward.

⁴² "Whoever ensnares one of these little ones who trust me — it would be better for him to have a millstone hung around his neck and be thrown in the sea. ⁴³ If your hand makes you sin, cut it off! Better that you should be maimed but obtain eternal life, rather than keep both hands and go to Gei-Hinnom, to unquenchable fire! ⁴⁵ And if your foot makes you sin, cut it off! Better that you should be lame but obtain eternal life, rather than keep both feet and be thrown into Gei-Hinnom! ⁴⁷ And if your eye makes you sin, pluck it out! Better that you should be one-eyed but enter the Kingdom of God, rather than keep both eyes and be thrown into Gei-Hinnom,

⁴⁸ where their worm does not die,
and the fire is not quenched.

⁴⁹ Indeed, everyone is going to be salted with fire. ⁵⁰ Salt is excellent, but if it loses its saltiness, how will you season it? So have salt in yourselves — that is, be at peace with each other."

Yochanan raises a question, perhaps to change the subject. He reports that he saw someone casting out demons in Yeshua's name, and he stopped him, "because he wasn't one of us." Perhaps Yochanan is wondering whether the welcome Yeshua is promoting extends even to an outsider and his unauthorized use of their spiritual resources. His words reflect another common misconception among religious movements, the idea that it's a "brand," to use current terminology, that needs to be protected and guarded against interlopers. Yeshua makes it clear that his brand doesn't need to be protected against outsiders; rather, those who do deeds of power in Yeshua's name from whatever motive will not be able to speak ill of him, "For whoever is not against us is for us" (9:40). In a different context, confronting those who defame his ministry of deliverance from evil spirits, Yeshua says, "Those who are not with me are against me" (Matt. 12:30 // Luke 11:23). Is Yeshua contradicting himself here? Or are the different Besorah writers not paying attention to each other? Craig Keener notes, "Modern interpreters often find [Yeshua's] sayings hopelessly contradictory and incoherent when we fail to familiarize ourselves with catchy figures of Jewish speech, expecting instead developed doctrinal pronouncements."[4] This note will be especially helpful as we consider Yeshua's words through the rest of this episode. In the current context, it's clear that when someone is advancing Yeshua's ministry of deliverance, even "unofficially," he welcomes it. On the level of supernatural conflict, which has been such a pervasive theme in Mark's account up to this point, there are just two sides, and those who drive out unclean spirits are on Yeshua's side. Indeed, one who simply gives the talmidim a cup of water because they bear Yeshua's name will be rewarded.

With that clarification, Yeshua turns the attention of his talmidim back to the "little ones," like the child he had just placed in their midst. Those who fail to welcome them and instead trip them up in some way risk divine judgment. This warning leads into Yeshua's famous, and troubling, words about cutting off your hand or foot or plucking out your eye if it leads you to sin. It seems obvious that these words aren't meant literally, but are a powerful statement of the gravity of sin and judgment, and the need for radical self-denial in response. But less obvious to most readers is the whole context here, where the "sin" to avoid would seem to be that of causing a little one—a fellow believer in Yeshua (9:42)—to stumble. This

---

4. Keener, 267.

transgression can be done directly, by tempting them to sin, or indirectly, by living in a way that discredits the name of Yeshua and undermines their ability to trust God. This second way of tripping up a "little one" seems to be far more common than the first.

The offending hand, foot, and eye might be instruments of the rivalry and domination that Yeshua warns against as he's sitting with his followers in the house in K'far Nahum. And, of course, the message applies more broadly, as a warning not only against causing someone else to stumble, but against stumbling oneself. It's a warning against sin in general, and an exhortation to do whatever it takes to renounce sinful behavior. Repentance isn't a matter of pious words, but of a complete realignment of life's priorities, of how one handles, walks in, and looks upon the world. The hand-foot-eye sequence also traces the act of sin back to its source in the mind and imagination:

"If your *hand* offends you …": Don't *commit* sins! (9:43)

"If your *foot* offends you …": Don't *go anywhere* where you may commit sins! (9:45)

"If your *eye* offends you …": Don't even *think* about committing sins! (9:47)[5]

Equally serious—and troubling—is Yeshua's description of the destination of the unrepentant sinner. Whatever its exact nature, it would be better to have a millstone tied around your neck and be thrown into the sea than to be cast into *Gei-Hinnom* (9:43, 45, 47). This destination is called "hell" in most translations, which loses the specific reference to the Valley of Hinnom in the Hebrew (or *Gehenna* in the Greek). This is a ravine just to the south of ancient Jerusalem, which became a refuse dump, with perpetual fires consuming what had been discarded there. And it's a garbage dump with a history, where centuries before, Israelite idol-worshipers would cause a son or daughter "to pass through fire [as a sacrifice] to

---

5. Marcus, *Mark 8–16*, 697.

Molekh" a false god (2 Kings 23:10; see also Jer. 7:30–34). The fires of Gei-Hinnom became a symbol of judgment, of what later would be called hell.

This passage is often used to shape speculation about the nature of this hell that it's warning us against. Yeshua says of those cast into it that "their worm does not die, / and the fire is not quenched" (9:48). Does this mean that those who are condemned remain eternally conscious of their torment in hell? This is the picture brilliantly portrayed in Dante's *Inferno*, as well as in countless sermons, with less literary flourish. But is this picture the only, or best way, to understand Yeshua's words here? I'll devote some time to this question in our Derash section below, because, ironically enough, the idea of the eternal conscious torment of the damned often becomes a cause of offense for "little ones" who might be struggling to put their faith in Yeshua. It's hard for them to trust a God who would maintain anyone in a state of relentless suffering for all time. For now, it's enough to note that Yeshua's description of Gei-Hinnom comes from the closing words of the book of Isaiah:

> For as the new heavens and the new earth
> > that I make
> shall remain before me, says the LORD,
> > so shall your offspring and your name remain.
> From new moon to new moon,
> > and from Sabbath to Sabbath,
> all flesh shall come to worship before me,
> declares the LORD.
>
> And they shall go out and look on the dead bodies of the men who have rebelled against me. For their worm shall not die, their fire shall not be quenched, and they shall be an abhorrence to all flesh. (Isa. 66:22–24 ESV)

Those who dwell in the new heavens and the new earth remain in God's presence; those on the outside, who have rebelled against God, are "dead bodies," to be consumed by undying worms and unquenchable fire.[6] There's no sense in Isaiah that they are conscious during this after-death process. The contrast here is between those who *live* in the redeemed creation and those who are *dead*. Yeshua may be making the same contrast when he speaks of "eternal life" (9:43, 45) or entering the Kingdom of God (9:47) versus being cast into the fires of Gei-Hinnom. The fire is eternal in the sense of being unchangeable and affecting the realm beyond time, but those cast into it do not necessarily remain eternally conscious. As one prominent Evangelical commentator states,

> It remains a matter of doctrinal debate whether the unquenchable fire (an echo of Is. 66:24) refers to the unending conscious torment of those committed to it or to a fire which destroys but which never goes out because new fuel is continually added. The wording of this pericope does not in itself settle the question either way, quite apart from the danger of using vivid traditional imagery to establish formal doctrine.[7]

Whatever the exact nature of eternal judgment, then, this is a solemn warning indeed, but Yeshua follows it up with a more positive, if also puzzling, note. He picks up the fire imagery of the previous verses to tell his followers that they, indeed everyone, will be "salted with fire." This may be a reference to Leviticus 2:13, which decrees that every (grain) offering is to be "salted with salt" (literal translation), and refers to the "salt of the covenant of your God." Since the offering is dedicated to the LORD through a portion burned with fire (Lev. 2:2, 9), it's not a big stretch to speak of it being salted with fire. With this practice in the background, Yeshua recasts the fire of eternal judgment as a fire of purification that makes the offering fit to be presented to the LORD. Therefore "salt is excellent" (9:50). Then Yeshua recasts the salt, as he did the fire, to represent

---

6. Some early manuscripts of Mark repeat the reference to the worm and fire as verses 44 and 46. CJB follows a common practice of leaving these verses out, in accord with the best manuscripts, which explains the absence of these verse numbers in CJB.
7. France, 382. "Pericope" refers to a distinct unit within a larger narrative, generally a smaller unit than our episodes. The pericope in this case is Mark 9:42–50

the peace—shalom—that is to prevail among Yeshua's followers. The admonition to "have salt in yourselves" addresses both the argument of 9:34 about who is the greatest, and the divisiveness reflected in 9:38 and 42.

All of this imagery highlights the notion that following Yeshua is like presenting one's life as an offering to ADONAI, enduring suffering and even death to present oneself in complete dedication to him. When Yeshua-followers fall into the competitiveness and elitism of the dominant culture, they lose their saltiness, their fitness as an offering. But living with each other in true shalom sustains their saltiness, our saltiness, and renders our lives an acceptable offering to the LORD.

Derash

- The hidden Messiah theme is highlighted at the beginning of this episode when Yeshua "didn't want anyone to know" as he led his talmidim through the Galil. And, as we've seen, it runs throughout Mark as even these close talmidim don't really grasp who Yeshua is. *Midrash Tehillim*, "Midrash on the Psalms" (21:1), will later comment concerning the heir of David: "This is the Messiah, the Son of David, who is hidden until the time of the end."[8]

  In the wider Jewish world, Messiah, in the person of Yeshua, remains hidden to this day, only to be revealed at "the time of the end." What are the implications for Jewish followers of this hidden Messiah? How might Yeshua's teachings about true discipleship as recorded in Mark be especially helpful in this context?

- In the same vein, if the idea of a suffering Messiah was part of the Jewish thinking of Yeshua's time, as noted above, why are his talmidim so slow to comprehend this idea? We won't answer this question by contrasting the supposedly triumphalist messianic expectations of Judaism with the new revelation of a

---

8. Cited in Marcus, *Mark 8–16*, 669.

Messiah who must suffer to redeem humankind, as is often attempted. The idea of a suffering Messiah was already a Jewish theme, along with the vision of a victorious Messiah.[9] Instead, we might suspect that accepting a suffering and crucified Messiah is contrary to human nature, not just to Jewish sensibilities; it's something we don't understand because, consciously or not, we find it threatening. We might ask ourselves how embracing this essential element of Yeshua's message might change things for us.

- A friend of mine rejects the traditional idea of hell because it is unjust: "Infinite punishment for finite crimes." But, ironically, he believes the Bible clearly describes hell as a place where the condemned remain conscious and in torment throughout all eternity, and therefore he rejects the Bible itself, along with faith in Yeshua. In response, it's fair to ask whether the notion of hell that my friend rejects is the only, or best, way to understand the biblical data.

First, we should remember that the language of the whole section of Mark 9:42–50 is highly metaphorical, as noted in the commentary cited above (fn. 5). We're not ready to literally apply the admonition to cut off our hand or foot, but can still pay heed to the underlying message. In the same way, we don't need to believe in a worm that literally never dies or a fire that's literally never quenched to hear Yeshua's warning of divine judgment with the utmost gravity

Second, the term "hell" or "gehenna" is completely absent from the sermons of Peter, Stephen, and Paul recorded in the Book of Acts, as well as from the writings of Paul. We don't give Paul priority over the Gospels, but his more detailed theological approach helps us understand how the first generation of Yeshua's followers understood and applied the Master's teachings. Apparently they didn't see hell or the fear of hellfire (as opposed to fear of divine

---

9. See our discussion of 8:27–33, drawing on the work of Daniel Boyarin, which shows how the "picture of a suffering and then triumphant Son of Man/Messiah rests upon Isaiah 53, *as understood within the Jewish world of Yeshua's day.*

judgment in general) as central to Yeshua's messages, or as a great motivator to belief. They did speak of divine judgment, but not in the sort of terrifying terminology that developed in later centuries. For example, in 1 Thessalonians, probably Paul's earliest letter, he speaks of "the impending fury of God's judgment" (1:10; cf. 2:16), but there's no specific mention of an afterlife, let alone of eternal consciousness in hell. Likewise, in Paul's later and more theologically developed letter to the Romans, he speaks of divine judgment without reference to hell:

> To those who seek glory, honor and immortality by perseverance in doing good, he will pay back eternal life. But to those who are self-seeking, who disobey the truth and obey evil, he will pay back wrath and anger.
>
> Yes, he will pay back misery and anguish to every human being who does evil, to the Jew first, then to the Gentile; but glory and honor and shalom to everyone who keeps doing what is good, to the Jew first, then to the Gentile. (Rom. 2:7–10)

Finally, the notion of the immortality of the soul, and hence its continuing consciousness after death, may be derived more from Greek philosophy, especially Plato and the neo-Platonism that was thriving in Second Temple times, than on the Hebrew Bible. In the Hebrew Bible, the human soul or spirit is inherently mortal, as God tells Adam after his sin, "you are dust, and you will return to dust" (3:19). Adam and Eve would need to continually eat from the Tree of Life in order to live forever, and they are driven away from it (Gen. 3:22). Accordingly, the Jewish hope of an afterlife is based on belief in the resurrection, not on the inherent immortality of the soul.[10] Paul's discussion of resurrection in

---

10. Martha Himmelfarb, "Afterlife and Resurrection" in JANT, 691–95. Himmelfarb mentions Daniel 12:2–3, which does speak of "many" who awaken from the sleep of death to "shame and everlasting contempt," and raises some objections to seeing this as a picture of universal damnation of the wicked. Furthermore, as with the imagery in Isaiah 66, it may be the shame and contempt themselves that are everlasting, not the consciousness of the doomed.

1 Corinthians 15 reflects this same hope in the resurrection—in this case centered on the resurrection of Messiah Yeshua—not on any supposed immortality of the soul.

Bottom line: Yeshua's warning of judgment to come in Mark 9 is to be taken most seriously, but its impact doesn't depend on taking all its details literally. It's not given as dogma about the nature of eternal judgment, but as a wake-up call about the reality of that judgment.

- Salt is an essential part of reciting *Hamotzi*, the blessing over the challah, as the family gathers around the table for Erev Shabbat. The foundational sixteenth-century guide to Jewish law and custom, *Shulchan Aruch*, provides this instruction:

> It is required to have salt set on the table before breaking bread, and to dip the piece of bread over which *Hamotzi* is said into the salt—because the table represents the altar and the food symbolizes the offerings. As it is said (Leviticus 2:13): "With all thine offerings thou shalt offer salt." (*Shulchan Aruch*, 41:6)

After citing this rule, the traditionally-oriented guide *Jewish Spiritual Practices* provides further commentary based on Leviticus 2:13b, "Nor shall you suffer the salt of the covenant of your God to be lacking [from your offering]."

> The salt, then, symbolizes the abiding covenant between the Jewish people and God. We can call to mind our covenant and our relation with God, and this supports us if our divine service is poor—for if we are unworthy now, we have faith that God still wants His children at His table.[11]

Yes, God wants his children, his little ones, as Yeshua calls us, at his table. And he wants us living in covenant with him and with each other, living in *B'rit Shalom* (Isa. 54:10; Ezek. 37:26), the covenant of peace, as a preview of the Shalom of the Age to Come.

---

11. Yitzhak Buxbaum, *Jewish Spiritual Practices* (Northvale, NJ; London: Jason Aronson, 1990), 240–41.

Season 2, Episode 4 (13)

Further Instructions Along the Way

10:1–31

Overview

Yeshua finally departs from the Galil for Y'hudah and the region beyond the Yarden. In these new areas, as in the old, crowds gather around him, and so do Pharisees, who test him with a question: is it permissible for a man to divorce his wife? Yeshua directs them back to the Torah itself, and they respond correctly that the Torah does permit divorce. But Yeshua leads them more deeply into the Torah to shed light, not just on the divorce issue, but on the very nature of marriage as God intended it from "the beginning of creation." Sitting with his talmidim in a private house, Yeshua goes on to tell them that divorce, or at least remarriage after divorce, is forbidden.

While they're in the house, people start bringing children to Yeshua for him to touch them, and the talmidim try to stop them. But Yeshua rebukes them and again speaks of children as exemplars of the kingdom, embracing them and blessing them with the laying on of his hands.

As Yeshua continues on his journey, a man runs up to him, kneels before him, and asks what he must do to inherit eternal life. As he did with the Pharisees, Yeshua directs the man back to the Torah itself, in this case listing several of the Ten Commandments, which lead to life. The man says that he has kept all of them since his youth. Yeshua looks at him with love and, again as with the Pharisees, leads him more deeply into the Torah, telling him to sell all he has, to give the proceeds to the poor, and to follow him. The man departs in sadness because he has many possessions, and Yeshua turns to his talmidim, saying, "How hard it is going to be for people with wealth to enter the Kingdom of God!" The talmidim are amazed at this statement and ask how anyone can be saved. Yeshua replies that it may be impossible for human beings, but with God everything is possible. Peter then reminds Yeshua that he and the other talmidim, unlike the wealthy man, have indeed left everything to follow him. Yeshua responds by describing their rewards in this age, along with persecution, as well as in the age to come, where they will receive eternal life. He concludes with an iconic saying: "The first will be last, and the last will be first!"

Peshat

10:1–12

> Then Yeshua left that place and went into the regions of Y'hudah and the territory beyond the Yarden. Again crowds gathered around him; and again, as usual, he taught them. [2] Some *P'rushim* came up and tried to trap him by asking him, "Does the Torah permit a man to divorce his wife?" [3] He replied, "What did Moshe command you?" [4] They said, "Moshe allowed a man to **hand his wife a *get*** and divorce her." [5] But Yeshua said to them, "He wrote this commandment for you because of your hardheartedness. [6] However, at the beginning of creation, God **made them male and female.** [7] **For this reason, a man should leave his father and mother and be united with his wife,** [8] **and the two are to become one flesh**. Thus they are no longer two, but one. [9] So then, no one should break apart what God has joined together." [10] When they were indoors once more, the *talmidim* asked him about this. [11] He said to them, "Whoever divorces his wife and marries another woman commits adultery against his wife; [12] and if a wife divorces her husband and marries another man, she too commits adultery."

As we've noted, Mark structures his account geographically, and he lets us know here that we're no longer in the Galil, but in Judea, the territory surrounding our final destination, Jerusalem. He creates a bit of confusion, however, by mentioning "the territory beyond the Yarden," which is not part of Judea, but on the other side of the Jordan River. Apparently, as in his earlier time in the Galil, Yeshua is not limiting his ministry to the land of Israel, but venturing at times beyond it. Also, as in his days in the Galil, he is confronted by Pharisees who raise a question to test or entrap him, which Mark describes with the Greek word *peirazo*, meaning to "test," or "tempt," or "try" (as in a legal contest). The same verb in the original Greek is linked to the Pharisees in 8:11, where they "test" Yeshua by demanding a sign from heaven, and 12:15 where Yeshua charges them, along with some members of Herod's party, of trying to trap him with a trick question (which he deals with handily, as we'll see). Tellingly, the same Greek word has already made one other appearance, back in our Prologue, when Satan *tests* Yeshua in the wilderness for forty days (1:13). Apparently, Yeshua's critics have gone beyond legitimate question-and-response dialogue into a level of opposition that plays right into the purposes of the arch-accuser, the Adversary himself.

As often happens, the Pharisees' intended trap seems to be a simple enough question: "Does the Torah permit a man to divorce his wife?" Yeshua in turn responds, in good Jewish fashion, with a simple question of his own, "What did Moshe command you?" Jewish law today is relatively permissive concerning divorce, but the Talmud (Gittin. 90a) records a debate between the School of Hillel, which permitted divorce for nearly any cause, and the School of Shammai, which was much more restrictive. It may be that this sort of debate underlies the trick question of the Pharisees; which school will Yeshua align with? He'd probably draw flak either way.[1] Yeshua avoids their trap by going to the heart of the issue. Yes, Moshe does permit divorce, and he provides a safeguard, a *get* or document of divorce that allows the wife to remarry (Deut. 24:1–4). As stated in the Mishnah (Gittin. 9:3) the *get* means "You are free to marry anyone you want." A state of divorce with ineligibility to remarry is simply not in view in the Jewish world of that, or any,

---

1. The debate in the Talmud is recorded centuries after Yeshua's time, but Hillel and Shammai actually lived and taught a generation before Yeshua.

time. But for Yeshua this provision is a concession for hardness of heart, and he takes his interlocutors back to the very origin of marriage in the creation account to address their question fully.

Yeshua builds his case against divorce on the phrase from Genesis 2:24, "and the two are to become one flesh." In the plainest reading, this phrase alludes to the sexual union of man and woman, but in the wider context of Genesis 2:18–25 it also describes the intimate relational union of marriage, which not only creates physical fruitfulness, but also solves the dilemma of human loneliness, and, as we'll explore further in our Derash section, entails a covenant relationship with God. Ethicist David Gushee notes that "one flesh" may also apply to the children who come forth from the physical intimacy of man and woman. The child is "a literal embodiment of her parents' oneness," and her well-being is normally dependent on the parents remaining together, especially within the original setting of Mark's account.[2] Therefore, Yeshua concludes, "What . . . God has joined together, let not man separate" (Mark 10:9 ESV).

In typical fashion, after this bold and unsettling teaching, Yeshua explains its ramifications to his talmidim in private. Since each marriage reflects the creative work of God himself, humans don't have the authority to terminate it. If they divorce and remarry, they're actually in a state of adultery. This teaching is clear enough, but is it livable in the world that we inhabit today, which is still in need of redemption? Accordingly Matthew provides a fuller and more flexible citation of Yeshua's teaching: "Now what I say to you is that whoever divorces his wife, except on the ground of sexual immorality, and marries another woman commits adultery!" (Matt. 19:9). Paul adds that if an unbeliever abandons their marriage with a believer, "the [believing] brother or sister is not enslaved — God has called you to a life of peace" (1 Cor. 7:15). In the first century context this "life of peace" implies freedom to remarry. .

Gushee assumes "a Jewish audience for Jesus' original teaching," notes Yeshua's alignment with Shammai's strict position

---

2. David P. Gushee, *The Moral Teachings of Jesus: Radical Instruction in the Will of God* (Eugene, OR: Cascade, 2024), 36. Gushee notes that Yeshua's teaching on divorce is preceded and followed by two affirmations of the value of children (Mark 9:33–37; 10:13–16).

on divorce and "his profound concern for women's and children's well-being," and goes on to raise the question:

> Is it too much to imagine Jesus saying to his male audience: how dare you misread both the letter and spirit of God's law to abandon your wives and throw your children into misery? That is just adultery, it violates the seventh commandment, and it certainly violates God's intent for marriage.
>
> What that says about our divorce situations today—many of which are about interpersonal misery, not mere preference for someone new—is not an easy question.[3]

Beyond the complex questions of how this teaching is to be applied today, Yeshua's halakhic strategy here is striking. He goes back to the creation account and the ideal state of human life before the expulsion from Eden to establish a standard for his followers. Specific rulings and guidelines are important, but we will understand and apply them best within the big framework of God's purposes in creating all things. The world we live in now is still broken, and human life is still shaped by lust, greed, and hardness of heart, but Yeshua summons his followers to live in alignment with the original goodness of creation, which will be restored and consummated in the end. Through his presence among us now, the restoration of creation is already set in motion, even amidst the prevailing hardness of heart, and his followers can live accordingly.

10:13–16

> [13] People were bringing children to him so that he might touch them, but the *talmidim* rebuked those people. [14] However, when Yeshua saw it, he became indignant and said to them, "Let the children come to me, don't stop them, for the Kingdom of God belongs to such as these. [15] Yes! I tell you, whoever does not receive the Kingdom of God like a child will not enter it!" [16] And he took them in his arms, laid his hands on them, and made a *b'rakhah* over them.

---

3. Gushee, 36.

Children are another reminder of the original male-female union, which God blesses with the words "be fruitful and multiply" (Gen. 1:28). It seems obvious why parents would want their children to be touched by the master teacher who has imparted wisdom and healing (often by touch) to so many. What's not so obvious is why his talmidim would rebuke them. Perhaps they see their master's ministry as serious, adults-only business, or perhaps they're aware of his packed schedule and trying to protect it from what they consider to be a distraction. Yeshua's response is another example of Mark's faithful portrayal of Messiah's humanness: "he became indignant." He'll rebuke the talmidim and then go beyond the requested touch to take the children in his arms, lay hands on them, and say a blessing, a *b'rakhah*.

Yeshua may be especially indignant over his followers' attempted ban on children because he had not long before placed a child among them as an example of the humility that's required in God's kingdom, telling them, "Whoever welcomes one such child in my name welcomes me, and whoever welcomes me welcomes not me but the One who sent me" (9:37). The talmidim again (as in 6:41–52 or 8:4, 14–17) fail to connect the dots, so Yeshua makes the connection unavoidably clear: "The Kingdom of God belongs to such as these" and whoever doesn't receive it "like a child will not enter it!" (10:14–15). And because he's not just using these children as props or sermon illustrations, he touches them, taking them into his arms and blessing them.

10:17–31

[17] As he was starting on his way, a man ran up, kneeled down in front of him and asked, "Good rabbi, what should I do to obtain eternal life?" [18] Yeshua said to him, "Why are you calling me good? No one is good except God! [19] You know the *mitzvot* — **'Don't murder, don't commit adultery, don't steal, don't give false testimony**, don't defraud, **honor your father and mother**, . . .'" [20] "Rabbi," he said, "I have kept all these since I was a boy." [21] Yeshua, looking at him, felt love for him and said to him, "You're missing one thing. Go, sell whatever you own, give to the

poor, and you will have riches in heaven. Then come, follow me!" ²² Shocked by this word, he went away sad; because he was a wealthy man.

²³ Yeshua looked around and said to his *talmidim*, "How hard it is going to be for people with wealth to enter the Kingdom of God!" ²⁴ The *talmidim* were astounded at these words; but Yeshua said to them again, "My friends, how hard it is to enter the Kingdom of God! ²⁵ It's easier for a camel to pass through a needle's eye than for a rich man to enter the Kingdom of God." ²⁶ They were utterly amazed and said to him, "Then who can be saved?" ²⁷ Yeshua looked at them and said, "Humanly, it is impossible, but not with God; with God, everything is possible." ²⁸ Kefa began saying to him, "Look, we have left everything and followed you." ²⁹ Yeshua said, "Yes! I tell you that there is no one who has left house, brothers, sisters, mother, father, children or fields, for my sake and for the sake of the Good News, ³⁰ who will not receive a hundred times over, now, in the *'olam hazeh*, homes, brothers, sisters, mothers, children and lands — with persecutions! — and in the *'olam haba*, eternal life. ³¹ But many who are first will be last, and many who are last will be first!"

Yeshua asks the man who calls him "Good rabbi," "Why do you call me good?" It's a paradoxical question, because it doesn't seem inappropriate for someone to address an honored figure as "Good rabbi" or "Good doctor" or "Good teacher." Indeed, Yeshua might seem overly modest in rejecting the phrase, as too humble in the way former Israeli Prime Minister Golda Meir famously warned about: "Don't be so humble; you're not that great."[4]

If we take Yeshua's paradoxical response literally, it seems like there are two opposing ways of understanding it. The most obvious sense is that Yeshua is denying any claim to deity. Amidst all the indications that he is no mere human, and all the questioning of who he really is, he wants to make it clear that—whoever he is—he is not

---

4. https://quoteinvestigator.com/2019/10/25/humble/

the one true God, who alone is good. But there's been so much evidence in Mark that Yeshua's power and authority are far beyond the merely human level that we might do better to read these words differently: "Why are *you* calling me good? Do you know who I really am?" This response challenges the rich man to realize more fully who he's talking to, whom he has neatly labeled without much thought "Good rabbi." If I'm truly good, Yeshua may be implying, and if God alone is truly good, what is this saying about me in relation to God? If I display the goodness that belongs only to God in what I say and do, perhaps "Good rabbi" means more than you think. And if that's so, I have the right to call you to abandon everything and to follow me . . . and to reward this devotion with the eternal life that you're asking me about.

We've seen enough of Mark's skill as a storyteller to suspect he's not being careless or simplistic when he records Yeshua's words here. Rather, he may be deliberately highlighting Yeshua's use of paradox, as he's done before (for example, 7:24–30; 8:14–21) to make a deeper point. Yeshua is both an ordinary mortal who, like all of us, doesn't merit the title "good," and the one human who uniquely bears God's goodness in himself . . . and is qualified to answer the deepest of questions, "What should I do to obtain eternal life?"

In response to the question, Yeshua says, "You know the *mitzvot*," the commandments given by God on Mount Sinai, which every serious Jew would know and take to heart. Connecting these commandments with eternal life reflects the words of Moses himself: "You are to follow the entire way which ADONAI your God has ordered you; so that you will live" (Deut. 5:30 [33]). This exhortation may also help explain why Yeshua adds the fifth commandment, to honor father and mother, to his list of commandments six through ten.[5] This commandment is the first one with a promise, as Paul notes in Ephesians 6:2: "Honor your father and mother, as ADONAI your God ordered you to do, so that you will live long and have things go well with you in the land ADONAI your

---

5. In Jewish writings the Ten Commandments are more commonly called the Ten Words, reflecting the Hebrew term *Aseret Dibrot* or *Devarim* (Exod. 34:28; Deut 4:13, 10:4) and the fact that the Ten open with "I am ADONAI," which is not in itself a commandment.

God is giving you" (Deut. 5:16). Of course, "life" in this context is referring to life in this world, as the full citation of Deuteronomy 5:30 reveals: "You are to follow the entire way which ADONAI your God has ordered you; so that you will live, things will go well with you, and you will live long in the land you are about to possess."

The Torah speaks of long life in the promised land, but after centuries of exile, conflict, and foreign occupation in the land, Jewish readers began to apply this promise to the life to come, to the resurrection foreseen by Isaiah (26:19; 60:19–21) and Daniel (12:2–3).[6] We've already heard Yeshua speak of "eternal life" in contrast with the fires of Gei-Hinnom (Mark 9:43), and now he addresses the rich man's question of how this life is to be gained. "The man believes in a future resurrection of the body and in life after death, but he knows that participation in the eternal life cannot be taken for granted."[7]

The Torah—literally "Instruction"—teaches the way to life for the obedient. The man knows this and claims to have followed these instructions, "since I was a boy." At these words, "Yeshua, looking at him, felt love for him and said to him, 'You're missing one thing' . . ." (10:21). He goes on to summon the man to sell all he has, give the proceeds to the poor, and follow him. We might think of love for humankind as a major quality of Yeshua's whole ministry, and love is indeed a major theme in John's account of the Yeshua's life. But in Mark this is the only person Yeshua is explicitly said to love, and the only other appearance of the word "love"—the familiar *agape* in the Greek—is in Yeshua's discussion of the Shema in 12:29–31. Perhaps Yeshua feels love for this man because he sees into his longing soul, which desires more from God despite all that he already has, both in material wealth and in the treasure of obedience to Torah. But the man proves unable to respond to Yeshua's summons, and goes away sad, exemplifying Yeshua's warning about the seed sown among thorns, which is choked out by "the worries of the world, the deceitful glamor of wealth and all the other kinds of desires" (Mark 4:18–19).

---

6. Marcus, *Mark 8–16*, 720.
7. Schnabel, 239.

Yeshua turns to his talmidim and tells them how hard it's going to be for the rich to enter the Kingdom of God. The talmidim are shocked to hear this, but Yeshua intensifies the picture: it's easier to get a camel through the eye of a needle than to get a rich man into the Kingdom . . . but with God everything is possible.[8] At this, the ever-helpful Kefa notes that he and his fellow talmidim have left everything behind to follow Yeshua. Yeshua assures them all that they will "receive a hundredfold now in this time," for all they have given up to follow him, and then adds—in line with his two recent warnings about what awaits them in Jerusalem—"with persecutions." And then Yeshua adds one new element to the reward: "and in the age to come eternal life" (10:30).

Messiah's mention of eternal life here provides a bookend to this whole extended scene, which began with the question, "What must I do to inherit *eternal life?*" (10:17, emphasis added). And it makes plain once again what's at stake in this matter of following Yeshua. He's not just a charismatic sage or wonder-worker attracting followers, like other Galilean teachers of his time,[9] but he's the one who holds the keys to life in the Age to Come. And the reality of that Age will be unsettling to the values and priorities of this age, for "many who are first will be last, and the last first" (10:31). This echo of the divine reversal theme introduced in Season 1 (see Prologue, 1:1–13) sets the stage for the final episode on our way to Jerusalem, where its full implications will finally be made evident.

Derash

- Some midrashic writings explore the notion that the first union of male and female is accomplished only after a third party, the LORD himself, brings the woman to the man. "And the LORD God fashioned the rib He had taken from the man into a woman; and He brought her to the man" (2:22 JPS).

---

8. Forget about the idea of a narrow door for pedestrians within the large double gate in the wall of Jerusalem called the "needle's eye," which a camel might get through if it were unloaded and coaxed to crouch down. No such gate has ever been identified (France, 405).
9. Keener, 255–76.

Nahum Sarna comments, "As noted in a midrash, the image may well be that of God playing the role of the attendant who leads the bride to the groom. Without doubt, the verse conveys the idea that the institution of marriage is established by God Himself."[10] And so we have here not only the origin story of human sexuality, but of marriage itself, which is given by God to protect and sanctify that sexuality. Furthermore, as Sarna implies, God's involvement as attendant in the primal wedding suggests the role of community, here represented by the one attendant, in subsequent weddings.

Genesis Rabbah, a collection of early midrashic writings, also pictures God as a participant in the original wedding

> R. Abbahu said: The Holy One, blessed be He, took a cup of blessing and blessed them. . . . R. Simlai said: We find that the Holy One, blessed be He, blesses bridegrooms, adorns brides, visits the sick, buries the dead, and recites the blessing for mourners. He blesses the bridegrooms, as it is written, And God blessed them; He adorns brides, as it is written, *And the Lord God built the rib . . . into a woman* (Gen. 2:22).[11]

This portrayal establishes the ideal triangular shape of marriage as a covenant between a man, a woman, and the Almighty. It's an imaginative portrayal that has had tremendous positive impact on the real-world experience of countless marriages. We might ask how it can continue to have such impact in a 21st-century world that is radically redefining the meaning of male and female and of human sexuality itself.

---

10. *The JPS Torah Commentary: Genesis*, commentary by Nahum M. Sarna (Philadelphia: Jewish Publication Society, 1989) 23, citing Yal. Gen. 24 and Gen. R. 18:4.
11. Genesis R. 8:13 on Genesis 1:28.

- The poet Mary Oliver poignantly reminds us of the realities of being a child, realities that shed light on the story of Yeshua blessing the children.

  > Adults can change their circumstances; children cannot. Children are powerless, and in difficult situations they are the victims of every sorrow and mischance and rage around them, for children feel all of these things but without any of the ability that adults have to change them. Whatever can take a child beyond such circumstances, therefore, is an alleviation and a blessing.[12]

Furthermore, the story of Yeshua blessing the children reminds us of the Jewish blessing upon our children at the onset of Shabbat. Over our sons we echo Jacob's words of blessing in Genesis 48:20: "May God make you like Ephraim and Manasseh." And over our daughters we invoke the names of the Matriarchs of Genesis: "May God make you like Sarah, Rebekah, Rachel, and Leah." And then we recite the Aaronic Benediction, Numbers 6:24–26, over them all. Yeshua has used children as a symbol of innocence, dependency, and vulnerability (9:36–37, 42; 10:14–15), and this story also reminds us of how highly children were, and are to this day, valued in the Jewish household.

Yeshua's blessing on the children also highlights the importance of touch in his ministry, which in turns hints at the significance of the Ruler of the Universe drawing near in the person of Messiah to touch us one-by-one. In current jargon, people talk about being "seen," as in feeling that someone else really recognizes and understands who they are. But being touched is even more intimate. Being seen still allows some distance, and its current popularity as a term might reflect the conditions of social media, where you post stuff to be seen, and to track how many views you get, even

---

12. Mary Oliver, "Staying Alive," *Upstream: Selected Essays* (New York: Penguin, 2016), 14.

while keeping some distance, and even possibly fabricating, or at least touching up, what your viewers actually get to look at. But touch overcomes the distance, which is why we're so sensitive to intrusive or inappropriate touch, and so appreciative of the authentic hug, or of touch during prayer.

- In Yeshua's dialogue with the rich man, he looks at him and feels love for him. The rich man might feel like Yeshua "sees" him, to use the contemporary phrase we've just discussed. Yeshua's love sees beyond the man's riches, and even beyond his hesitancy, to recognize his yearning heart—even though in the end the yearning isn't strong enough. This "seeing" lifts Yeshua's love beyond the usual polarization of rich and poor, privileged and disadvantaged. It's clear throughout the Besorah that Yeshua is for the poor and disadvantaged, which is a radical position for this lofty and divine figure to take. But Yeshua's stance becomes even more radical as he reveals he's not *against* the rich and privileged. He understands them too, and calls them along with the others to follow him. The love of Messiah lifts us above the polarized climate of today.

- Nevertheless, Yeshua's call inevitably raises the question of whether this summons to the rich man applies to all who would follow Yeshua or just to this questioning individual. Is a vow of poverty required of all who would follow Yeshua? In the style of Jewish teachers of the time, Yeshua doesn't intend to present a systematic treatment of every issue he talks about, but is concrete and personal in a way that modern, Western readers don't always understand. As Keener notes,

    > Unfortunately for some of his interpreters, Jesus employed this same evocative, engaging teaching style [as his Jewish contemporaries], regularly seeking to evoke specific responses rather than to provide direct proof-texts for subsequent theological systems.[13]

---

13. Keener, 267.

What does seem universal here is the call to make Yeshua—not the theoretical Yeshua, but the Yeshua we can follow with our two feet—the overriding priority of our lives. Nevertheless, if we are too quick to dismiss Yeshua's critique of wealth or to limit it to only this special case, we might have the same skewed relationship with material things as the man who "went away sad."

- Yeshua sums up his portrayal of the rewards of following him with his saying, "many who are first will be last, and many who are last will be first!" (10:31). This saying is repeated in slightly different forms in Matthew and Luke, mostly simply as, "Thus the last ones will be first and the first last" (Matt. 20:16; compare Luke 13:30). It suggests that the story of the rich man, along with its implications for discipleship, is about divine reversal, or "the 'upside down' values of God's kingdom."[14] Our next episode will open with Yeshua on the road going up to Jerusalem, where the upside-down values of the Kingdom will collide with the standard values of power and domination. Before we head up to Jerusalem, it might be a good moment for us to consider our own values regarding material resources and worldly power—how evident is Divine Reversal in the way we conduct our lives and guard our souls?

---

14. France, 399.

Season 2, Episode 5 (14)

The Third Warning

10:32–52

Overview

As Yeshua and his followers start out on the final leg of their journey up to Jerusalem, Yeshua reminds the Twelve what awaits him—and by implication, them—in the Holy City. This is his third warning and it is more detailed than the first two, but it includes the same main points of rejection, execution, and resurrection after three days. As with the first two warnings, Yeshua's closest followers just don't get it. Two of them, Ya'akov and Yochanan, request a favor of Yeshua—that he would seat them on his right and on his left when he is in his glory. Yeshua tells them they don't know what they are asking or what is required of them as his followers.

When the other ten talmidim hear of the request of Ya'akov and Yochanan, they are outraged at them, and Yeshua turns this whole drama of religious competition and jockeying for position into a radical teaching on servanthood—with himself as the prime exemplar: "For the Son of Man did not come to be served, but to serve—and to give his life as a ransom for many." This verse is one of the most cited and discussed in Mark's whole Besorah, but its core message is simple enough: the highest "status" in the kingdom that Yeshua is announcing is service to and on behalf of others, even to the point of self-sacrifice. It's a message of particular urgency as Yeshua and his band pass through Yericho, the final station on the way to Jerusalem.

On the way out of Yericho, Yeshua is approached by a blind beggar, Bar-Timai, who had been sitting by the side of the road. He called out to Yeshua as Son of David and pleaded for his pity. Yeshua asks what he wants from him, and the beggar says, "Rabbi, let me be able to see again." In contrast with the healing of a blind man that opened Season 2, this healing is instantaneous and, also in contrast, it culminates in the healed man following Yeshua on the road ahead as Season 2 draws to a close.

Peshat

10:32–40

> [32] They were on the road going up to Yerushalayim. Yeshua was walking ahead of them, and they were amazed — and those following were afraid. So again taking the Twelve along with him, he began telling them what was about to happen to him. [33] "We are now going up to Yerushalayim, where the Son of Man will be handed over to the head *cohanim* and the Torah-teachers. They will sentence him to death and turn him over to the *Goyim*, [34] who will **jeer at him, spit on him, beat him** and kill him; but **after three days, he will rise.**"
>
> [35] Ya'akov and Yochanan, the sons of Zavdai, came up to him and said, "Rabbi, we would like you to do us a favor." [36] He said to them, "What do you want me to do for you?" [37] They replied, "When you are in your glory, let us sit with you, one on your right and the other on your left." [38] But Yeshua answered, "You don't know what you're asking! Can you drink the cup that I am drinking? or be immersed with the immersion that I must undergo?"
>
> [39] They said to him, "We can." Yeshua replied, "The cup that I am drinking, you will drink; and the immersion I am being immersed with, you will undergo. [40] But to sit on my right and on my left is not mine to give. Rather, it is for those for whom it has been prepared."

The road we're on literally goes "up" as it passes by Jericho, which sits at 800 feet below sea level, and climbs up to Jerusalem at 2600 feet above sea level. It also goes "up" to the holiness and exalted status of the City of David. Mark tells us that those following

Yeshua along the way are "amazed," probably because Yeshua is so openly and publicly going to the home base of his most intense enemies, including those who had already begun conspiring to destroy him (3:6). Some of them are not only amazed, but also afraid—for Yeshua and perhaps for themselves. Yeshua doesn't do much to assuage their fears as he takes the Twelve aside to paint a more detailed picture of what awaits them.

This third foretelling adds important details to the first two (8:31, 9:31). In all three, Yeshua pointedly calls himself "Son of Man," but only now adds that the Son of Man will be betrayed or "handed over" to the Jewish authorities, implying that he is to be betrayed by one of his own. He also adds the details that the Jewish authorities will in turn hand him over to the Gentiles to carry out the death sentence, and that the Gentiles will mock and abuse him on the way to his execution.

As with the first two warnings, Yeshua's closest followers seem to miss the point. Ya'akov and Yochanan ask for special treatment after Yeshua goes through this ordeal and comes into his glory. They seem to ignore or minimize the suffering he's just described in detail. Yeshua tells them that they don't know what they're talking about, and employs imagery to make it clearer: his suffering is a bitter cup that he must drink, a total immersion he must endure, rather than a mere unpleasant interlude.

> The cup is a metaphor for one's portion in life, what one has been given to "drink," whether of good or ill. It can sometimes symbolize a happy fate, for example, the overflowing cup of Ps 23:5 and the "cup of salvation" in Ps 116:13; in the OT and related literature, however, the cup is usually the . . . chalice of the Lord's wrath, the affliction that he pours out upon those who richly deserve divine punishment.[1]

Yeshua, of course, doesn't deserve divine punishment, and that is precisely the point, as we'll see in the following verses. He is

---

1. Marcus, *Mark 8–16*, 747.

drinking the cup on behalf of others, and asking Ya'akov and Yochanan if they are able to do the same. Likewise with the "immersion" Yeshua speaks of. It refers to a deep experience of suffering, which will be undeserved, but for the benefit of "many" (10:45).

Mark doesn't reveal how much of all this even Yeshua's closest followers really grasp. But if we compare all three accounts of Yeshua foretelling his suffering, we can discern a progression in the talmidim's understanding. They're like the blind man of Beit-Tzaidah at the beginning of our season, who gradually regains his sight, stage by stage (8:22–26). Likewise, after Yeshua's first announcement, Kefa takes him aside and rebukes him (8:32)—rejecting the plan altogether. After the second announcement, the talmidim don't reject it, but they don't understand it either, and they don't ask Yeshua to explain. Instead, they change the subject and get into an argument about who's the greatest among them (9:32–34). Finally, with the third announcement, at least a couple of the followers get that it's describing the path to glory for Yeshua . . . and ask for a special share of that glory. They are still sidestepping the issue of suffering and death, but at least they have a sense of where things are headed. And they continue to follow Yeshua.

Yeshua's response to the request of Ya'akov and Yochanan—"it is not mine to give" (10:40)—can be understood as another statement of Yeshua's limitations, like his inability to do miracles when he visited his hometown (6:5), or his words to the rich man in our last episode, "Why are you calling me good? No one is good except God!" (10:18). He is the heir of David, the anointed king of the Davidic dynasty, who will come in glory to sit on David's throne—but God is the ultimate authority and Yeshua can't simply hand out favors. The mystery of Yeshua's divine-human status confronts us again, and the question "Who is this?" remains intact. But there's another implication of "it's not mine to give." In this kingdom, positions of status are not handed out along the usual lines of who you know, how much you can contribute, or what family you belong to. Perhaps Yeshua is not contrasting himself and God so much as contrasting his kingdom with all other kingdoms. Status in this kingdom isn't gained by the usual means of power and influence, but is reserved for those "for whom it has been prepared"—a mysterious phrase that propels us into the next scene.

10:41–45

> [41] When the other ten heard about this, they became outraged at Ya'akov and Yochanan. [42] But Yeshua called them to him and said to them, "You know that among the *Goyim*, those who are supposed to rule them become tyrants, and their superiors become dictators. [43] But among you, it must not be like that! On the contrary, whoever among you wants to be a leader must be your servant; [44] and whoever wants to be first among you must become everyone's slave! [45] For the Son of Man did not come to be served, but to serve — and to give his life as a ransom for many."

The other ten key talmidim are "outraged" at the request of Ya'akov and Yochanan, not because it reveals how immature these two are, but because the ten see this request as coming at their expense. If Ya'akov and Yochanan get the best seats in the house, they don't. They are thinking of Yeshua's kingdom as a system of status and competition like most human institutions. There's only so much status or favor or power to go around, and if you get more, I get less. But Yeshua goes on to contrast his kingdom with merely human institutions, employing "a concise description of the Roman political system" in 10:42–45 to drive home his point.[2] Yeshua's kingdom embodies a divine reversal of the power and prestige that fuel human affairs. Here the path to advancement is through service, and to attain the highest rank means being a slave to all.

The underlying terminology of 10:43–44 makes it clear that Yeshua is talking about slavery, not just servanthood in a more benign sense. The underlying Greek word in 10:43 is *diakonos*,

---

2. Wills, "Mark," JANT, 92.

"servant," and it contrasts with *doulos*, "slave," in 10:44. Yeshua's first-century Jewish audience knew first-hand the meaning of *doulos*, and of the ransom that Yeshua speaks of in the following verse.

> Today these ideas of slavery and ransom sound like metaphors only; in antiquity they were all too real. People were taken into captivity and sold in slave markets; their families and friends would, if possible, ransom them back.[3]

The idea of voluntarily lowering oneself to the status of a slave would sound absurd, perhaps scandalous, especially to Jews, who were accustomed to invoking their defining saga of redemption from slavery in Egypt, not only at Passover, but also throughout the prayers and customs of the entire year. A.J. Levine highlights the radical nature of Yeshua's teaching, along with others we've heard in Mark's Besorah:

> People would be horrified at being told to hate their parents, they would be horrified at being told to sell all they had and give to the poor, and they would be horrified to think of giving up their freedom. And now he has our attention.[4]

In this context Yeshua utters what is arguably the climactic verse in Mark's Besorah so far: "The Son of Man did not come to be served, but to serve—and to give his life as a ransom for many" (10:45). Ransom, as we've noted, is connected with slavery, and there's a great deal to explore in this connection. Scholars discuss the meaning of ransom and the nature of Yeshua's entire earthly mission in this saying, and we'll join in this discussion shortly. But first we should note that in context, the verse is primarily a call to service, Yeshua calls his followers to be "everyone's slave," just as he will soon be when he offers up his own life on behalf of many.

---

3. AJ Levine, *The Difficult Words of Jesus: A Beginner's Guide to His Most Perplexing Teachings* (Nashville: Abingdon, 2021), 58–59. Levine notes, "probably over half of the population of the Roman Empire was enslaved or descended from slaves. . . (56).
4. Levine, *Difficult Words*, 60.

We might expect Yeshua to say "on behalf of *all*" here, rather than "many." This unexpected "many" echoes another "many" we heard at the end of our last episode: "many who are last will be first!" (10:31). Here again we might have expected Yeshua to say *all* those who are last will be first, or at least to speak more generally, as he does on another occasion: "Thus the last ones will be first and the first last" (Matt. 20:16). And there's another unexpected "many" later in our account, when Yeshua lifts the cup at his last Passover and says "This is my blood, shed on behalf of many" (14:24). Again, we might expect Yeshua to include "all" here: "This is my blood, shed on behalf of all." By saying "many" in these three contexts, Yeshua may simply be recognizing that not all will respond to his ransoming work, and not all will partake of the cup of his covenant, but many will. It's a little harder to see why he would limit "the last will be first" to many rather than all, but perhaps Yeshua recognizes that even among the "last" are those who will not respond in a way that would make them "first."

But another explanation of the wording here seems more likely. The unexpected "many" in Mark echoes the "many" in Isaiah's description of the suffering servant:

> After this ordeal, he will see satisfaction.
> "By his knowing [pain and sacrifice],
> my righteous servant makes *many* righteous;
> it is for their sins that he suffers.
> Therefore I will assign him a share with the *many* [lit. translation],
> he will divide the spoil with the mighty,
> for having exposed himself to death
> and being counted among the sinners,
> while actually bearing the sin of *many*
> and interceding for the offenders." (Isa. 53:11–12, emphasis added)

As in Mark, we might expect Isaiah to say that the servant bears the sins of "all"; "many" is a bit unexpected, and it had also shown up in Isaiah 52:14–15, for a total of five appearances in this single passage. Yeshua may be echoing this usage in his threefold use of "many" in 10:31, 10:45, and 14:24. One commentator notes that Mark 10:45

> ... echoes the spirit, if not the exact wording, of Isaiah's Servant of the Lord, whose "life [is] a guilt offering" (Isa. 53:10) and who "will justify many, and ... bear their iniquities" (53:11). Although the reference to ransoming "many" may suggest either preferential or partial treatment, this is scarcely its meaning. In Semitic grammar, "the many" normally stands for totality, all. "The many" is not a select and worthy few; rather, in its five uses in Isaiah 53 the expression refers to the very "transgressors" and "sinful" for whom the Servant pours out his life.[5]

This linkage to Isaiah 53 helps us understand what Yeshua means by "ransom" in 10:45. Ransom, in English as well as the underlying Greek term, *lytron*, normally entails paying a price, as in the ransom of captives, or the ransom of one sentenced to death or other punishment. Exodus 13 pictures ransom in this sense in its instructions about the ransom of the firstborn male, a practice still followed today in Jewish life under the name *Pidyon HaBen*, ransom of the son. The Septuagint, the widely used ancient Greek translation of the Tanakh, employs *lytron* terminology in Exodus 13:13—"You are to ransom every firstborn son"—and again in 13:15, as Moses goes on to instruct the Israelites:

> When, at some future time, your son asks you, "What is this?" then say to him, "With a strong hand ADONAI brought us out of Egypt, out of the abode of slavery. When Pharaoh was unwilling to let us go, ADONAI killed all the firstborn males in the land of Egypt, both the firstborn of humans and the firstborn of animals. This is why I sacrifice to ADONAI any male that is first from the womb of an animal, but all the firstborn of my sons I ransom." (Exod. 13:14–15 CJB modified)

Yeshua's "ransom" terminology in Mark 10:45 might well remind his original audience of this passage and the familiar ritual of *Pidyon*

---

5. Edwards, 327.

HaBen, which it establishes. This ritual served to reenact each year the last of the ten plagues, the slaying of the firstborn, the redemption of Israel's firstborn, and ultimately the ransom or redemption of Israel, God's firstborn, from bondage in Egypt to serve ADONAI (Exod. 4:22–23). This same dynamic is in play in the ransom that Yeshua brings. Those in bondage to "Egypt," the powers of this age, are freed to serve God.

> This ransom saying . . . is of central importance in Mark's narrative because it is the clearest Markan reflection on the saving purpose of Jesus' death (cf. 14:24). That death is to be a "ransom," a payment of the price that the "many" are unable to pay themselves. . . . [T]his ransom is conceived as a slave price: Jesus sells himself into slavery in order to liberate his brothers and sisters from bondage.[6]

And what is the source of this bondage? Why are we enslaved? We can return to Isaiah 53 for a clue: "my righteous servant makes many righteous; it is for their sins that he suffers" (Isa. 53:11). Yeshua is the suffering servant, whom Isaiah describes in words that evoke another ritual, not of Passover, but of Yom Kippur, the Day of Atonement. On that day, the "scapegoat" bears "all the transgressions, crimes and sins of the people" out into the desert and away from the dwellings of the Israelites (Lev. 16:21–22). Likewise, Isaiah's servant bears "our diseases," and our guilt.

> We all, like sheep, went astray;
> we turned, each one, to his own way;
> yet ADONAI laid on him
> the guilt of all of us. (Isa. 53:4–6; see also 11)

Yeshua's simple language of ransom in Mark 10:45 stirs up the profound realities of atonement and deliverance from sin that underlie the annual holy days of Passover and Yom Kippur to this day.

---

6. Marcus, *Mark 8–16*, 757.

Reflecting the language of Isaiah 53 in Mark 10:45 brings us full circle back to Mark's opening reference to Isaiah 40: "The voice of one crying in the wilderness" (Mark 1:3). It emphasizes that the prophecy of Isaiah, especially the second section of Isaiah beginning with "Comfort, comfort my people" (Isa. 40:1), undergirds Mark's entire narrative. And the ransom language also points forward to our next season, in which Yeshua will in actuality offer himself as a ransom for many.

We need to remember, though, that the point of this saying in its original context isn't to explore the meaning of Yeshua's ransom, but to emphasize Yeshua's example as a servant, following his instructions to the talmidim about true greatness: "Whoever among you wants to be a leader must be your servant; and whoever wants to be first among you must become everyone's slave!" (10:43–44). Yeshua, the Son of Man, who will be "given rulership, glory and a kingdom, so that all peoples, nations and languages should serve him" (Dan. 7:14), doesn't rest on this privilege, but instead sells himself into slavery to ransom his fellow sons and daughters of man from slavery. Yeshua's summation of this whole feat can stand as the theme verse of the entire Besorah of Mark: "For the Son of Man did not come to be served, but to serve — and to give his life as a ransom for many."

From this verse, Joel Marcus provides a beautiful segue into the final scene in this episode:

> Within the larger framework of Isaiah, the servant's sacrifice becomes the means by which the divine warrior wins his amazing victory over death and its allies—a triumph that includes miraculous events such as valleys being elevated, the desert blooming, and the blind joyfully receiving their sight (see Isa. 29:18; 35:1–7; 40:1–11; 42:1–17). It is not surprising, then, that our passage about the slave-like death of the Son of Man is immediately followed by one in which the Son of David miraculously opens the eyes of the blind.[7]

---

7. Marcus, *Mark 8–16*, 757.

10:46–52

⁴⁶ They came to Yericho; and as Yeshua was leaving Yericho with his *talmidim* and a great crowd, a blind beggar, Bar-Timai (son of Timai), was sitting by the side of the road. ⁴⁷ When he heard that it was Yeshua from Natzeret, he started shouting, "Yeshua! Son of David! Have pity on me!" ⁴⁸ Many people scolded him and told him to be quiet, but he shouted all the louder, "Son of David! Have pity on me!" ⁴⁹ Yeshua stopped and said, "Call him over!" They called to the blind man, "Courage! Get up! He's calling for you!" ⁵⁰ Throwing down his blanket, he jumped up and came over to Yeshua. ⁵¹ "What do you want me to do for you?" asked Yeshua. The blind man said to him, "Rabbi, let me be able to see again." ⁵² Yeshua said to him, "Go! Your trust has healed you." Instantly he received his sight and followed him on the road.

Yericho, or Jericho, is the last big town on the way to Jerusalem and, as noted above, it's the beginning of a long ascent from 800 feet below sea level to Jerusalem sitting at 2600 feet above sea level. As Yeshua and his band are leaving Yericho to begin this ascent, they encounter a blind beggar, just as they had encountered a blind man at the beginning of this season, shortly before their departure from Galil (8:22–26). Thus, the two healings of the blind form bookends for our entire Season 2, the journey from the Galil to Jerusalem. The first healing, as we've discussed, was gradual, and foreshadows the gradual process by which the talmidim began to grasp who it was that they were following. This second healing is instantaneous. After the first healing, Yeshua sends the now-seeing man home; after this healing, the healed beggar follows Yeshua on the road that will take them to Jerusalem. If the first healing provides a metaphor for the gradual enlightenment of the talmidim, this healing may foreshadow the conclusion of the discipling process: trust that brings healing, restored sight, and following Yeshua.

Other details in this account stand out. First, the beggar calls out to Yeshua as "Son of David." On the one hand, this title may seem inadequate after we've heard Kefa telling Yeshua, "You are the *Mashiach*" (8:29), and Yeshua speaking of himself as the exalted

Son of Man, invoking Daniel's vision (Dan. 7:13–14; Mark 8:31, 38; 9:9, 31). On the other hand, "Son of David" is virtually synonymous with Mashiach (Messiah), David's most illustrious heir, and it's a particularly appropriate title to invoke as we begin the ascent to Jerusalem, the City of David.

This blind man, in contrast with the earlier blind man, seems to understand a great deal from the start. Or does he? Mark notes that he also calls Yeshua "Rabbi," which is clearly a lesser title than Son of David, let alone Messiah. Granted, the blind man uses an exalted form, *Rabbouni*, but the CJB accurately conveys the sense that this still means "Rabbi" in this context. In its other appearances in Mark, "Rabbi" doesn't do so well. Its first usage is from the mouth of Peter, when he suggests that they build three shelters for the three figures of Moses, Elijah, and Yeshua, because he doesn't know what to say (9:5–6).[8] Then, in our next episode, Peter will say, "Rabbi! Look! The fig tree that you cursed has dried up!" (11:21), but doesn't seem to understand the import of this sign. Finally, Y'hudah (Judas) calls Yeshua "Rabbi" when he kisses him as a sign for those coming to arrest him (14:45). So, the term "Rabbi" has a troubling connotation, but, as is so often in Mark, there's much nuance in the story. When Bar-Timai says "Rabbi," it implies trust and nearness: Yeshua had already called him to come near, and Bar-Timai had already cast aside his protective outer garment to appear in his vulnerability and entreat him in a human,follower-to- rabbi sort of encounter. For Bar-Timai, whose trusting response gains his healing, Yeshua really is the supreme teacher, Rabbouni.

Yeshua responds to the blind man's approach with simple words, "What do you want me to do for you?" (10:51)—the same words he spoke to Ya'akov and Yochanan earlier when they asked for a favor (10:36). Yeshua's words are the same, but the requests are radically different. The two sons of Zavdai are seeking privileged treatment, hoping to be elevated above their fellow talmidim; a request Yeshua cannot grant. The blind man simply wants to be made whole, to be able to live a normal life and, we imagine, be free of the need to beg.

---

8. Regarding this verse, Levine notes, "ironically, the earliest literary reference to someone as 'rabbi' comes from the New Testament" (Levine, *Mark*, 64).

His request is granted in full, and he becomes a model talmid, not seeking self-advantage but simply trusting the Son of David, and making that trust evident in following him on the road that leads to Jerusalem and all that awaits us there.

Derash

- Yeshua contrasts the dynamics of his kingdom with the dynamics of the human institutions of his day—and ours—institutions that revolve around power and those who wield it. People might not love such figures but, Yeshua implies, they might love to be like them. One parallel to such people in our time are the celebrities, the superstars of the various media, who increasingly influence (and even compete in) the political realm as well. We can also sometimes observe the fascination, and near-worship, around celebrities in the religious world, even among those who profess to follow Yeshua. How has this admiration of celebrity corrupted the message that Yeshua originally handed on to his followers? How can it be counteracted in the world today?

  One counteracting force is the theme of Divine Reversal, summarized in Yeshua's words in 10:31 (as well as numerous other places in Mark): "But many who are first will be last, and many who are last will be first!" Scholar Craig Keener writes about the similar idea of "eschatological inversion," the "widespread Jewish expectation" that God will raise up the lowly and humble the proud, in the Age to Come if not this age. Keener continues:

  > It is Jesus' particular application of this expectation in his ministry that is frequently distinctive. For example, Jesus declares that the kingdom belongs to children (Mk. 9:37; 10:14–15)—to those lowly in status and dependent on the heavenly Father.[9]

---

9. Keener, 293.

If Yeshua's kingdom belongs to children, to the low-status and those who serve, how should that shape the religious culture of our times? What would it look like if the notion of voluntarily becoming "everyone's slave" (10:44) really took hold?

- We've noted the connection between Mark's portrayal of Yeshua and the suffering servant of Isaiah 52:13–53:12, which is present throughout this Besorah, but never explicit. Mark's climactic verse, 10:45, may be the clearest linkage to Isaiah 53. It portrays one who comes not to be served but to serve and give his life as a ransom—"by his knowledge shall . . . my *servant* make many to be accounted righteous, and he shall bear their iniquities" (Isa. 52:11 ESV, emphasis added). This servant is hidden and waiting to be revealed, as in a famous midrash:

    > Rabbi Joshua ben Levi once asked Elijah the prophet: "When will the Messiah come?"
    >
    > Elijah replied: "Go and ask him himself."
    >
    > "And by what sign may I recognize him?"
    >
    > "He is sitting among the poor, who are afflicted with disease [Isa. 53:4]; all of them untie and retie the bandages of their wounds all at once, whereas he unties and rebandages each wound separately, thinking, perhaps I shall be wanted to appear as Messiah and I must not be delayed."
    >
    > Joshua thereupon went to the Messiah and greeted him: "Peace unto thee, master and teacher!"
    >
    > To this he replied, "'Peace unto thee, son of Levi."
    >
    > "When will you come, master?"
    >
    > "Today."
    >
    > He returned to Elijah . . . and said: "He spoke falsely to me. For he said he would come today and he has not come."
    >
    > Elijah rejoined: "This is what he said! [Ps. 95:7]: Today – if you would but hearken to His voice." (Babylonian Talmud, Sanh 98a)

This midrash on Isaiah 53 sees the Messiah as afflicted and hidden among the poor who are also afflicted, awaiting the day of his return. Yeshua says no one knows the timing of his return, even himself, but only the Father, and calls us to remain alert. How are we doing on that account? How can Messiah's example of watchful waiting, pictured in this midrash, guide us as we await his return?

- Yeshua tells Bar-Timai, "Your trust has healed you," and one commentator notes:

> The word for "healed" (Gk. *sōzō*) also means "saved," combining both physical and spiritual dimensions. In Bartimaeus's case the word is doubly appropriate, for "he received his sight" and "followed Jesus along the road." The latter description designates the model disciple for Mark. Jesus has transformed Bartimaeus from a beggar beside the road (v. 46) to a disciple on the road (v. 52). Faith that does not lead to discipleship is not saving faith. Whoever asks of Jesus must be willing to follow Jesus ... even on the uphill road to the cross.[10]

Accordingly, this commentator adds: "the healing of Bartimaeus is surely the sum and center of all that Mark desires to convey about faith and discipleship." That's a bold claim. If it's true, we might consider what insights into faith and discipleship we can gain from this account. How does the example of Bartimaeus/Bar-Timai help prepare us to respond to the rejection, betrayal, and death that lie ahead for Yeshua?

---

10. Edwards, 331.

SEASON 3

JERUSALEM: WELCOME, REJECTION, AND RESURRECTION

11:1–16:8

In Season 3, we reach Jerusalem, which has been our destination all along, where we'll remain through the conclusion of this Besorah. We arrive just a few days before Passover, and the Besorah will end during the festival itself.

Passover is one of the three Pilgrim Festivals, on which the Torah commands every man "to appear in the presence of ADONAI your God in the place which he will choose" (Deut. 16:16). Yeshua distinguishes himself among the pilgrims by entering the holy city mounted on a donkey, instead of simply on foot. He is greeted by a friendly crowd before he pays a brief visit to the Temple, but tension builds the next day as Yeshua returns to the Temple courts and drives out the merchants and money-changers doing business there. On the following day—on the way to his third visit to the Temple—Yeshua gives a profound lesson on faith and forgiveness. When he arrives in the Temple courts he is challenged by the religious gatekeepers who demand to know who gave him the authority to shake up the status quo in the Temple system. Yeshua confronts their insincerity and refuses to answer.

Yeshua then turns things around by challenging his adversaries with a parable that they realize is about them. They back down from direct confrontation, aware of the level of support Yeshua enjoys among the crowds, but others step forward to challenge him. Pharisees, Herodians, and Sadducees continue to question him, hoping to trip him up or expose him to rejection or worse, until one Torah-teacher asks a sincere question that results in fruitful dialogue. Finally, Yeshua raises a question of his own: why do the teachers call Messiah the Son of David, when David himself (in Psalm 110) calls him "lord"? This question reflects the mystery underlying so much of Mark's account: Just who is this wonder-working Galilean rabbi?

As Yeshua and his band leave the Temple compound that day, he predicts that all the magnificent buildings they see will be torn down. He goes on to provide a detailed description of coming events that looks beyond the destruction of the Temple to the apocalyptic signs leading up to his return. Yeshua doesn't provide a specific time frame, but instead exhorts his hearers to remain vigilant, for challenging times must be endured before his final coming.

Meanwhile, the authorities continue seeking a way to arrest Yeshua without provoking the crowds. When Yeshua is dining at a home just outside Jerusalem, a woman comes up and pours costly ointment over his head, which he commends as a sign of great devotion, an anointing for his coming burial. Y'hudah (Judas), one of the Twelve, apparently provoked by this scene, leaves and goes to the religious authorities to strike a deal to turn Yeshua over to them at the right time.

When Passover finally arrives, Yeshua and the Twelve regather in the holy city. Before the Passover meal, Yeshua tells them that one of them will betray him. During the meal, he takes *matzah*, the traditional unleavened bread, and the traditional cup of wine, pronounces the blessings, and passes them to his talmidim, describing these elements as his body and his blood of the covenant, "shed on behalf of many people."

After the meal, the whole group goes out to the Mount of Olives, where Yeshua adds to his announcement of betrayal a warning that they will all disown him that very night. And he reminds them that he will be raised up, and will regather them back in the Galil, thus bringing the geographical setting of our biopic full circle. Yeshua and his followers continue on to a place called Gat Sh'manim, "Oil

Press," where Yeshua prays in preparation for the ordeal ahead. His prayer ends as his follower Y'hudah arrives with a band of armed men who arrest Yeshua and bring him to the cohen hagadol, the high priest, to stand trial. Numerous witnesses come forward with false accusations, but they contradict each other, so that finally the cohen hagadol asks Yeshua point-blank whether he is the Messiah. Yeshua responds that he is, and describes "Messiah" in the exalted language of Psalm 110 and Daniel. At this, the religious authorities declare Yeshua guilty of blasphemy and worthy of death. They decide to hand him over to the Roman governor, Pilate, who has the power to impose capital punishment. Yeshua's thrice-repeated prediction from our last season is coming fully to pass: "the Son of Man will be handed over to the head *cohanim* and the Torah-teachers. They will sentence him to death and turn him over to the Goyim, who will jeer at him, spit on him, beat him and kill him; but after three days, he will rise" (Mark 10:33–34, cf 8:31, 9:31).

Yeshua is led off to Gulgolta, "Place of the Skull," and nailed to a Roman execution stake with a notice of the charge against him posted above his head: THE KING OF THE JEWS. Soldiers, bystanders—including priests and Torah-teachers—and even two criminals crucified on either side of Yeshua continue to mock him. When he lets out a loud cry and then breathes his last, the Roman officer overseeing the execution declares, "This man really was a son of God!" in a final response to the unspoken question underlying Mark's whole Besorah, "Who is Yeshua?"

Although Yeshua has been deserted and abused, some of his women followers remain close enough to witness his death. Yosef of Ramatayim is also present, and he goes to Pilate to ask for Yeshua's body. Pilate grants the request and Yosef provides the first stages of a proper burial before Shabbat. Two of the women witnesses see the tomb where Yeshua is placed and return after Shabbat with spices to complete his burial. When they arrive at the tomb, they see that the heavy stone sealing its entrance has been rolled away. They go inside and encounter a young man in a white robe, who tells them that Yeshua isn't there, but has been raised from the dead. He instructs them to tell his talmidim that he is going ahead of them to the Galil. But they are so awestruck that they flee the tomb and don't tell anyone, because they are afraid. This famously unresolved scene concludes our season, and leaves Mark's entire account of the ultimate Jewish life with us.

Season 3, Episode 1 (15)

Yeshua Enters Jerusalem

11:1–33

Overview

Yeshua's long-anticipated arrival at Jerusalem has finally come, and Yeshua chooses to enter the Holy City in a distinctive way, not like the other pilgrims arriving for the upcoming Passover celebration. Rather, he enters riding a young donkey. He is greeted by a crowd of pilgrims who spread their garments, along with green branches, on the road before him and welcome. They greet him with phrases from Psalm 118, customarily recited at this time. Entering the city, Yeshua goes straight to the Temple courts, takes a good look, and then departs for the nearby village of Beit-Anyah to spend the night with the Twelve.

The next day, on the way back to Jerusalem, Yeshua spots a fig tree in leaf, but with no fruit. He curses it in the hearing of the Twelve, saying, "May no one ever eat fruit from you again!" and continues on to the Temple courts. There, he drives out all who are buying and selling, citing the words of Isaiah and Jeremiah—the Temple was to be a house of prayer for all humankind, but instead it had become a "den of robbers." This flagrant challenge of the status quo leads the chief priests and their scribes to search for a way to do away with Yeshua, but without stirring up the big crowd, mostly of pilgrims visiting for Passover, which supports him.

The following day, as Yeshua and the talmidim approach the holy city, they pass the fig tree and see that it has withered to the roots. When Kefa points this out in amazement, Yeshua exhorts him and the rest of the talmidim to have "the kind of trust that comes from God." With this sort of faith fueling their prayers, everything would be possible. He also instructs them to practice forgiveness toward others as they pray.

Yeshua and his band continue on to Jerusalem and enter the Temple courts for the third time. There they're confronted by the chief priests, along with scribes and elders, who challenge Yeshua to reveal by what authority he had acted the day before. Yeshua counters with a challenge of his own: Was the immersion of Yochanan from Heaven or from a merely human source? The religious authorities refuse to respond because either answer will create problems for them: if they validate Yochanan's immersion, it calls into question why they don't validate Yeshua like Yochanan did; if they discredit it, they risk stirring up the crowds against them. They refuse to answer and Yeshua therefore refuses to reveal by what authority he has cleansed the Temple.

Peshat

11:1–11

> [1] As they were approaching Yerushalayim, near Beit-Pagei and Beit-Anyah, by the Mount of Olives, Yeshua sent two of his *talmidim* [2] with these instructions: "Go into the village ahead of you; and as soon as you enter it, you will find a colt tied there that has never been ridden. Untie it, and bring it here. [3] If anyone asks you, 'Why are you doing this?' tell him, 'The Lord needs it,' and he will send it here right away."
>
> [4] They went off and found a colt in the street tied in a doorway, and they untied it. [5] The bystanders said to them, "What are you doing, untying that colt?" [6] They gave the answer Yeshua had told them to give, and they let them continue. [7] They brought the colt to Yeshua and threw their robes on it, and he sat on it.

⁸ Many people carpeted the road with their clothing, while others spread out green branches which they had cut in the fields. ⁹ Those who were ahead and those behind shouted,

"Please! Deliver us!"

"Blessed is he who comes in the name of ADONAI!"

¹⁰ "Blessed is the coming Kingdom of our father David!"

and,

"You in the highest heaven! **Please! Deliver us!**"

¹¹ Yeshua entered Yerushalayim, went into the Temple courts and took a good look at everything; but since it was now late, he went out with the Twelve to Beit-Anyah.

The details of Yeshua's long-awaited entry into Jerusalem appear to be prearranged. The talmidim can go into the nearby village, find a colt conveniently tied up, and simply untie it and lead it back to Yeshua. Mark mentions two towns, Beit-Pagei and Beit-Anyah. The first is "otherwise unknown,"[1] but the second, Beit-Anyah, is where Yeshua and his band will spend their initial nights during the visit to Jerusalem (Mark 11:11). It makes a second appearance shortly afterwards when an unnamed woman anoints Yeshua there in the house of Shimon (Mark 14:3), which may well be the same house they were staying in. It's likely that this is the village that the talmidim enter to find the tied-up donkey. They are to untie the donkey, and if anyone asks them what they're doing—which is likely enough in a small town where an apparent act of theft would not be overlooked—they're to simply say, "The Lord needs it." In the event, it all turns out exactly as Yeshua had described. It's not clear whether these advance arrangements had all been made through ordinary human communication or by divine providence, but the significance of the as-yet-unridden donkey colt isn't hard to see. The prophet Zechariah had proclaimed centuries before:

---

1. Amy-Jill Levine, *The Gospel According to Luke*, JANT, 155.

> Rejoice with all your heart, daughter of Tziyon!
> Shout out loud, daughter of Yerushalayim!
> Look! Your king is coming to you.
> He is righteous, and he is victorious.
> Yet he is humble — he's riding on a donkey,
> yes, on a lowly donkey's colt. (Zech. 9:9)

Long before Zechariah prophesied, Jacob had spoken of Judah "tying his donkey to the vine," after declaring that Judah would wield the ruler's staff (Gen. 49:10–11). The connection between this prophecy and Yeshua's entry isn't as clear as the connection with Zechariah 9, but Yeshua does emphasize that the chosen donkey colt will be found tied up, if not to a vine, perhaps hinting at the words of Jacob.

The two talmidim untie the donkey, bring it to Yeshua, and throw their robes on it as a sort of saddle. When Yeshua mounts the donkey, people in the crowd take off their robes as well and spread them on the road leading to the city. Others cut green branches in the fields and spread them on the road, both cushioning the ride and demonstrating their devotion to Yeshua.[2] The crowd greets Yeshua with words from Psalm 118, including the words of welcome, "Blessed is he who comes in the name of ADONAI!" Psalms 113 through 118 are the *Hallel* or "Praise" psalms of Jewish tradition, and are recited to this day at the three pilgrimage festivals of Passover, Shavuot, and Sukkot, as well as during Hanukkah, to commemorate the days when worshipers would recite them on their way to the Temple. "Blessed is he who comes," or *Baruch ha-ba*, can be used simply as "Welcome" in Modern Hebrew, and the crowd, probably made up of pilgrims in Jerusalem for Passover, welcomes Yeshua in exalted terms here, as he proceeds toward the Temple courts.

---

2. It's likely that most or all of these branches would be from palm trees, because they would lie flat on the ground, while other branches might create a messier pathway that could even trip the donkey. John (12:13) reports that the crowd of pilgrims took branches of palm trees and went out to meet Yeshua as he approached Jerusalem.

Mark notes that all this takes place on the Mount of Olives, which rises to the east of Jerusalem, slightly higher than the Temple Mount. It's from the Mount of Olives that travelers today gain the famous view of the old city of Jerusalem, with the golden Dome of the Rock in the foreground where the holy Temple once stood. And according to Zechariah, it's on the Mount of Olives that ADONAI will stand when he returns to defend Jerusalem in its final battle at the end of days (Zech. 14:3–4). Just as Yeshua deliberately rides a "lowly donkey's colt" into Jerusalem to echo Zechariah's prophecy, then, so does he deliberately approach Jerusalem "by the Mount of Olives," foreshadowing a more decisive visit to come. In the Besorah accounts, the mount has eschatological implications, and the Jewish historian Josephus also "associates the location with a messianic figure: 'There came out of Egypt about this time to Jerusalem, one that said he was a prophet, and advised the multitude of the common people to go along with him to the Mount of Olives."[3]

In light of all this prophetic expectancy, Yeshua's first moments when he finally arrives in Jerusalem seem anti-climactic. He enters the city, goes straight to the Temple courts, takes a good look around . . . and then departs. Students of the Gospels often speak of Yeshua's "triumphal entry," but in Mark's portrayal, the triumph is so low-key as to go unnoticed. This entry might be better understood as a foretaste, a hint, of the triumphal entry to come, foretold by Zechariah, rather than its fulfillment.

11:12–25

> [12] The next day, as they came back from Beit-Anyah, he felt hungry. [13] Spotting in the distance a fig tree in leaf, he went to see if he could find anything on it. When he came up to it, he found nothing but leaves; for it wasn't fig season. [14] He said to it, "May no one ever eat fruit from you again!" And his *talmidim* heard what he said.

---

3. Levine, "Luke," JANT, 155, citing Antiquities of the Jews, 20.169.

¹⁵ On reaching Yerushalayim, he entered the Temple courts and began driving out those who were carrying on business there, both the merchants and their customers. He also knocked over the desks of the money-changers, upset the benches of the pigeon-dealers, ¹⁶ and refused to let anyone carry merchandise through the Temple courts. ¹⁷ Then, as he taught them, he said, "Isn't it written in the Tanakh, **My house will be called a house of prayer for all the *Goyim*.** But you have made it into a **den of robbers!**" ¹⁸ The head *cohanim* and the Torah-teachers heard what he said and tried to find a way to do away with him; they were afraid of him, because the crowds were utterly taken by his teaching. ¹⁹ When evening came, they left the city.

²⁰ In the morning, as the *talmidim* passed by, they saw the fig tree withered all the way to its roots. ²¹ Kefa remembered and said to Yeshua, "Rabbi! Look! The fig tree that you cursed has dried up!" ²² He responded, "Have the kind of trust that comes from God! ²³ Yes! I tell you that whoever does not doubt in his heart but trusts that what he says will happen can say to this mountain, 'Go and throw yourself into the sea!' and it will be done for him. ²⁴ Therefore, I tell you, whatever you ask for in prayer, trust that you are receiving it, and it will be yours. ²⁵ And when you stand praying, if you have anything against anyone, forgive him; so that your Father in heaven may also forgive your offenses." ²⁶

This scene is another example of Mark's "sandwich" technique. Yeshua curses the fig tree and the next day we see the results of that curse, but in between these two events, Mark tells the story of Yeshua cleansing the Temple. This technique adds drama to the narrative and it also provides a hint to its meaning.

> Given the sandwiching (intercalation) of the Temple incident between the cursing and the withering of the tree, we can read the scene as a parable of judgment on the Temple. The tree/Temple, in this configuration, operate according to their nature. Jesus had hoped that, with his presence in Jerusalem, the Temple would change its nature, from sin to sanctity, corruption to compassion.

But the Temple Herod remodeled remained true to its original nature; it did not bear fruit when Jesus appeared. Therefore, both Temple and tree are rotten, cursed, and both will be destroyed.[4]

Teachers and preachers sometimes speak of the fig tree as a symbol of Israel, and one commentator, William Lane, speaks of its cursing here as "a prophetic sign warning of God's judicial action against the nation,"[5] probably thinking of the judgment to come in the year 70, when the Romans crushed the Jewish revolt and destroyed the Temple. Levine's interpretation cited above, on the other hand, avoids the supersessionist implications of treating the fig tree as a symbol of the people Israel. And Lane, after referring to "judicial action against the nation," goes on to narrow the scope of that judicial action even more than does Levine. He astutely notes that the mention of Yeshua's "popularity with the people" in this context (11:18) "has the effect of showing that it was not the Jewish people that are rejected, but the Temple authorities and their scribal supporters (cf. Ch. 3:6)."[6] The fig tree isn't expressly employed in the Tanakh as a symbol of Israel or of the Temple. But Jeremiah employs figs as a symbol of the fruit that God expects, and does not find, among the Israelites (Jer. 8:13). The prophet later compares the leaders of Judah and Jerusalem to bad figs, figs so bad as to be inedible (24:1–10, 29:17; cf Hos. 9:10, Mic. 7:1).

Mark's note that Yeshua felt hungry when he spotted the fig tree serves as a reminder of his humanity; indeed, judging from what immediately follows, we might wonder whether he is "hangry"— driven to anger by his hunger. But this detail may also suggest that Yeshua is hungering for Jerusalem's repentance and for the sort of

---

4. Levine, *Mark*, 91–92. Ironically, despite Levine's stellar record of combatting supersessionism, her description of the Temple as "rotten, cursed", and worthy to be "destroyed," although she ascribes that viewpoint to Mark, not Yeshua or herself, could serve to fuel it.
5. Lane, 402.
6. Lane, 408.

welcome from her leaders and influencers that he received from the crowd when he first entered the city (11:8–10).

The fig tree isn't a symbol of Israel per se, but it does appear a few times linked with the grape vine as a symbol of peace and order for the people of Israel, especially in Micah 4:4 (cf. 1 Kings 5:5; 2 Kings 18:31 // Isa. 36:16), as the prophet describes the conditions of the age to come:

> Each person will sit under his vine
> and fig tree, with no one to upset him,
> for the mouth of *ADONAI-Tzva'ot*
> has spoken.

Yeshua's cursing of the fig tree, then, might symbolize the overthrow of the false security offered by the Temple authorities in collusion with the Roman occupiers, to make way for the true security coming with the Kingdom of God. This coming kingdom doesn't displace Israel, because its sovereign is the heir of David, the King of Israel. Moreover, it seems unlikely that Yeshua is cursing the Temple itself, when he has just invoked its prophetic significance as a house of prayer and taken bold action to cleanse it. The pigeon-dealers and money-changers that he confronts are doing business within the very Temple courts, likely in the court of the Gentiles, which might have a lesser value to the religious establishment, but is essential to the Temple's prophetic role as a house of prayer for all nations.[7]

The idea that the symbolic curse is directed against the false fig tree of the religious establishment, not Israel as a whole, or even the Temple, is supported by a parable coming in our next episode, the story of the wicked tenants (12:1–12). The "the head *cohanim*, the Torah-teachers and the elders" (11:27) realize that this tale is directed against *them* (12:12). Furthermore, these opponents feared

---

7. Turner and Bock, 500; France, 437–38. France concludes, however, with describing the cleansing as "a symbolic declaration of eschatological judgment," implying that it points to judgment on the Temple, and perhaps on Israel itself.

Yeshua "because the crowds were utterly taken by his teaching" (11:18), as was evident when they welcomed him into the holy city by spreading their garments on his path and lauding him with words of the Hallel psalms (11:8–10). Yeshua's critics also feared the crowd because they regarded Yochanan, who had so publicly endorsed Yeshua, as a genuine prophet (11:32). In sum, Mark takes pains to emphasize that whoever or whatever the curse might be aimed at, it is not the people of Israel as a whole.

Yeshua approaches the fig tree knowing that it's not time for it to bear fruit, as he approaches Jerusalem knowing it's not time for the city as a whole, and especially for the power structures within the city, to bear the fruit of repentance and recognize him as King Messiah. As he has said three times, he must endure rejection and death. But he has also said that after three days he will rise—and there will be a time when he will be recognized as King (Mark 13:24ff; 14:61–62).

With his usual irony, standing by the fig tree, Yeshua turns this scene of barrenness and curse into a glorious lesson on prayer. Apart from questions about the meaning of the withered fig tree is the question of how Yeshua made it wither up at all. The Master replies simply, "Have the kind of trust that comes from God!" (11:22). The CJB here provides a helpful expansion of the original Greek, usually translated as "Have faith in God," which "could also be interpreted as 'hold onto the faithfulness of God.'"[8] Yeshua is not exalting faith as some kind of supernatural force that humans can wield on their own; rather, he is declaring that *God's* faithfulness makes all things possible, as he had recently reminded the father of the demonized boy (9:23), as well as his talmidim wondering how anyone could be saved (10:27). He's exhorting his followers to put their trust in the faithfulness of God.

This trust in God, however, requires active human engagement; it's not passive, and prayer is a human act. Yeshua has already

---

8. Marcus, *Mark 8–16*, 794.

mentioned prayer in this episode with reference to the Temple as a house of prayer. He has just cleansed the Temple, but it remains under the corrupt authority of the religious- political establishment. Now Yeshua turns his attention to the communal prayer of his followers, which requires unswerving faith in God and, as we'll see, a posture of forgiveness. Yeshua again employs hyperbole to make his point, as he had done recently with the image of a camel going through the eye of a needle (10:25), or the demand that a leader in his kingdom must become the slave of all (10:44).[9] So, here, he is not speaking of literally casting mountains into the sea, and speculation on what mountain he may be referring to (with the mount sometimes thought to be the Temple Mount) seems beside the point.

The more relevant issue is the claim that we get whatever we want in prayer if we don't doubt and have enough faith (11:23–24). If we take this saying without nuance, it seems to turn prayer into a human accomplishment rather than a gift. Even worse, it could be turned on those whose prayers don't appear to be answered, as if it's their own fault. But perhaps we're still in hyperbolic territory, and the point is to encourage unwavering trust in God when we pray, not to elevate faith as a metaphysical power we can drum up on our own. Faith, deep and abiding trust in God, is itself a gift from God. Yeshua links this kind of trust with forgiveness, which he tells his followers to practice whenever they pray, so that God will forgive their offenses.

Approaching God requires a pure heart and clean hands (Psa. 24:3–5) and holding a grievance against another is defiling to oneself—and evidence of a lack of trust in God as the supreme judge, the very trust we need to engage in prayer.

---

9. I call this hyperbole because Yeshua uses the specific term for "slave," not for "servant," here. A slave answers to one master, however, not to everyone as Yeshua directs. Slavery is involuntary, but Yeshua calls men and women to follow him willingly. It's a hyperbolic use of the term.

The theme of forgiveness was introduced early in Mark, beginning with the Prologue, which portrays Yochanan's "immersion involving turning to God from sin in order to be forgiven" (1:4). Yeshua's first conflict with religious authorities was over his claim to have "authority on earth to forgive sins" (2:10). Not long after, he taught about God's willingness to forgive all sins and even blasphemies, except for blasphemy against Ruach Hakodesh (3:28–29). Now, for the first time, Yeshua teaches on human forgiveness, instructing his talmidim to forgive each other "so that your Father also who is in heaven may forgive you your trespasses" (11:25).[10]

Yeshua's teaching on prayer is demanding, with its call to unwavering faith and unconditional forgiveness, but it is also filled with promise. Yeshua's opening words on effective prayer, as we've seen, get to the heart of the issue: "Have the kind of trust that comes from God!" (11:22).

11:27–33

> [27] They went back into Yerushalayim; and as he was walking in the Temple courts, there came to him the head *cohanim*, the Torah-teachers and the elders; [28] and they said to him, "By what authority do you do these things? Or who gave you the authority to do them?" [29] Yeshua said to them, "I will ask you just one question: answer me, and I will tell you by what authority I do these things. [30] The immersion of Yochanan — was it from Heaven or from a human source? Answer me." [31] They discussed it among themselves: "If we say, 'From Heaven,' he will say, 'Then why didn't you believe him?' [32] But if we say, 'From a human source, . . .'" — they were afraid of the people, for they all regarded Yochanan as a genuine prophet. [33] So they answered Yeshua, "We don't know." "Then," he replied, "I won't tell you by what authority I do these things."

---

10. Mark 11:26—"But if you do not forgive, neither will your Father who is in heaven forgive your trespasses"—does not appear in the best manuscripts of Mark, and is relegated to the margin in CJB.

Yeshua returns to the scene of the "crime"—the same Temple courts he'd cleansed the day before—and is immediately challenged by the Temple gatekeepers. I've simplified the CJB translation of this passage, in line with the Greek original, for the sake of clarity, and also because the term it uses for ordination or authorization, *s'mikhah*, is probably anachronistic in this context. But the gatekeepers' challenge is clear enough: who gave Yeshua the authority to rearrange the furniture in the Temple that they manage and maintain?

Even as he's being questioned by the authorities, Yeshua takes charge of the situation. He'll answer their question only if they answer his question about the source of Yochanan's authority first, as he emphasizes with his demand, "Answer me" (11:30). But Yeshua's question already hints at the answer to their question. The source of his authority, he implies, is the same as the source that validates Yochanan's ministry—Heaven. This is a familiar circumlocution for God, a respectful way to refer to the supreme authority without overusing or misusing his actual title. (Matthew uses this circumlocution repeatedly as he usually refers to the Kingdom of Heaven instead of the Kingdom of God as in the other Besorot.) If they want to reject Yeshua's claim to authority they'll have to reject Yochanan's claim to authority, which is accepted by substantial numbers of those gathered in Jerusalem—some of whom are perhaps even listening in on this debate. Yochanan's public endorsement of Yeshua led to "a general belief that John had acknowledged Jesus as his successor."[11] So the gatekeepers know they can't recognize Yochanan without recognizing Yeshua in the process. But they also know it's unsafe to publicly repudiate Yochanan, so they respond, "We don't know" (11:33). It's a safe but telling answer, like the "No comment" response we hear so often in the news stream. In this case, it's "a damning admission: the highest religious authorities in the land claim not to know whether John,

---

11. Marcus, *Mark 8–16*, 797. See also France, 455; Turner and Bock, 503.

whose reputation for piety had been sealed by his martyrdom, had been sent by God."[12]

In one move, Yeshua deftly escapes the gatekeepers' trap and calls into question their own claim to authority. He also implies that he does indeed have authority over the Temple and the way it's being managed, which is the highest sort of authority, since the Temple is the site of God's own presence in the midst of his people. When ADONAI gave Moses the instructions for the Tabernacle, the predecessor of this Temple, he said, "They are to make me a sanctuary, so that I may live among them" (Exod. 24:8). In the prophecy that Yeshua cites as he cleanses the Temple (Isa. 56:7), ADONAI calls it "my house." And the prophet Malachi has foretold not only the role of Yochanan—casting the authorities' "no comment" in the worst possible light—but also Yeshua's entry into the Temple:

> Look! I am sending my messenger to clear the way before me; and the Lord, whom you seek, will suddenly come to his temple. Yes, the messenger of the covenant, in whom you take such delight — look! Here he comes," says *ADONAI-Tzva'ot*. (Mal. 3:1)

By coming to his temple and taking charge of it, Yeshua is claiming authority at the very highest level. Critics who say that Yeshua never claimed to be the Messiah, at least in Mark, are stopped short here. Yet, in line with his ongoing role as the Messiah-not-yet-recognized (Isa. 53:1–3), Yeshua leaves his identity and source of authority unstated, but evident to those with eyes to see, as our episode closes.

Derash

- When Yeshua rides into Jerusalem on a donkey foal, he is reflecting Zechariah 9:9, as we noted above. A midrash links Zechariah 9:9 with Daniel 7:13–14, which we've considered at a couple of points in this commentary:

---

12. Marcus, *Mark 8–16*, 800.

> **It is written: "There came with the clouds of heaven, one like unto a son of man . . ."** (Dan. 7:13–14). **And it is written: ". . . lowly and riding upon a donkey** and upon a colt, the foal of a donkey" (Zech. 9:9). Rabbi Alexandri explains: **If** the Jewish people **merit** redemption, the Messiah will come . . . **with the clouds of heaven. If they do not merit** redemption, the Messiah will come **lowly and riding upon a donkey.**[13]

Mark portrays just one Messiah, of course, who is both lowly and glorious. This midrash suggests that how we'll see Messiah depends on us. I'll change its wording a bit: if we receive the king who is "lowly and riding upon a donkey" in a worthy manner, then we will be worthy to see him come "with the clouds of heaven."

- In a similar way, the Mount of Olives has a two-fold meaning. It's the promised site of ADONAI's embodied return to his people (Zech. 14:3–4), and thus a site of messianic expectancy, but it's also on the route out of the holy city. It's first mentioned in the Tanakh in the account of David's flight from Jerusalem ahead of his rebellious son Absalom: "David continued up the road to the Mount of Olives, weeping as he went up, head covered and barefoot; and all the people with him had their heads covered and wept as they went up" (2 Sam. 15:30). Centuries later, the prophet Ezekiel sees the glory of ADONAI, which has already departed from the "house" (Ezek. 10:18–19), rise "from within the city and [stand] over the mountain which is on the east side of the city" (Ezek. 11:23). East is the direction of exile, and Ezekiel's vision immediately takes him in the Spirit "to the exiles in the land of the Kasdim" or Chaldeans (Ezek. 11:24). This aspect of the Mount of Olives hints at the rejection Yeshua will face after his "triumphal" entry, and it also hints

---

13. Talmud, Sanhedrin 98a, www.Sefaria.org. Sefaria places the actual wording of the Talmudic passage in bold, with explanatory text in regular font. The Talmud's minimalistic style often requires some interpretive wording to make sense to a typical reader.

at the restoration to come, just as David returned to reign in Jerusalem after Absalom's defeat, and as ADONAI promised to return the exiles to their land. "Then they will be my people, and I will be their God" (Ezek. 11:20). In the rejection, death, and resurrection that he has repeatedly foretold, Yeshua enacts the defeat, exile, and coming restoration of his people Israel.

- In his exhortation to pray with unswerving trust, Yeshua instructs us to forgive others, and he reminds us of our need to be forgiven ourselves. Perhaps the boldness of faith needs to be tempered with awareness of our human fallibility. We can command the mountain to be thrown into the sea, and whatever we ask for in prayer, Yeshua says, "trust that you are receiving it, and it will be yours" (11:24). That sort of power might go to our heads, so we're also reminded of our need to forgive and to be forgiven. Commenting on similar verses in Matthew, Rabbi Soloveitchik cites the Talmud (*Rosh Hashanah* 17a):

    > He who passes over his right to exact legal punishment is forgiven of all his iniquities, as it is said: *Pardoning iniquity and forgiving transgression* (Micah 7:18). Whose iniquity does God pardon? He who forgives transgression.[14]

    Soloveitchik is expounding on Yeshua's model prayer, which includes the request, "Forgive us what we have done wrong, / as we too have forgiven those who have wronged us" (Matt. 6:12). Yeshua continues:

    > For if you forgive others their offenses, your heavenly Father will also forgive you; but if you do not forgive others their offenses, your heavenly Father will not forgive yours. (Matt. 6:14–15)

    We can understand how forgiving others is essential to good human relations, and to our own mental and emotional

---

14. Soloveitchik, 119.

health. Now we're reminded that forgiveness is a reflection of the character of God, who revealed himself to Moses, as "merciful and compassionate, slow to anger, rich in grace and truth; showing grace to the thousandth generation, forgiving offenses, crimes and sins" (Exod. 34:6–7). Practicing forgiveness merits being forgiven, and it brings us into alignment with the God who forgives, thereby empowering our prayers.

Season 3, Episode 2 (16)

Inquest in Jerusalem

12:1–44

Overview

Soon after he arrives in Jerusalem, Yeshua is confronted with a series of questions designed to trip him up and expose him to rejection or worse. Our last episode ended with the first in this series of direct challenges in Jerusalem. Now, Episode 2 of Season 3 opens with a challenge that Yeshua directs to the religious authorities who are questioning him: the story of a vineyard with wicked tenants, which the questioners realize is aimed at them. They back down from direct confrontation, aware of the level of support Yeshua enjoys among the crowds gathered in Jerusalem, but others step forward to challenge Yeshua.

In a second encounter, some Pharisees along with some members of Herod's party pose a tough question: is it in accord with Torah to pay taxes to Caesar, the Roman Emperor, or not? Yeshua asks for a denarius, a standard Roman coin of trade and taxation, holds it up, and asks whose image and inscription are on it. When the questioners say the image and inscription belong to the Emperor, Yeshua replies, "Give the Emperor what belongs to the Emperor. And give to God what belongs to God!"—or in the classic language of the King James Version: "Render to Caesar the things that are Caesar's, and to God the things that are God's." Mark tells us "they were amazed at him," and the confrontation ends.

The third encounter comes as some *Tz'dukim*, or Sadducees, approach Yeshua. The Sadducees don't believe in the resurrection, because they don't see it being taught in the Torah. They put before

Yeshua what they might have thought would be a "gotcha" question. After some flattering remarks, they raise a hypothetical case of a woman who married six brothers in succession after her first husband, their brother, died childless, to fulfill a requirement of the Torah that they are to produce children for their brother. The brothers all die one by one without producing any offspring. And then the Sadducees spring the question—in the resurrection, whose wife will this woman be? Yeshua shows how his foes with their question fail to understand the nature of the resurrection as foreshadowed in the Torah and steps out of their trap.

A fourth encounter has a more positive tone. One of the Torah-teachers recognizes that Yeshua is answering well, and asks him which is the greatest of the mitzvot. Yeshua responds with the Shema, the mitzvah of loving ADONAI your God "with all your heart, with all your soul, with all your understanding and with all your strength," and adds the commandment "to love your neighbor as yourself." The Torah-teacher agrees with him and goes on to expand on his teaching. Yeshua commends the man, "You are not far from the Kingdom of God," and the series of questions comes to an end.

Then Yeshua raises a question of his own. Why do the Torah-teachers say the Messiah is the Son of David, when David himself (in Psalm 110) calls him "lord"? Yeshua's question captures the crowd's attention and he goes on to expand his critique of Torah-teachers who put on a self-serving show of religiosity, but fall far short of the two great commandments to love God and love your neighbor. Finally, he points to a poor widow who gives an offering at the Temple that looks meager but represents the whole-hearted love for God commanded in the Shema, because out of her poverty, she "has given everything she had to live on."

Peshat

12:1–12

> ¹ Yeshua began speaking to them in parables. "A man planted a vineyard. He put a wall around it, dug a pit for the wine press and built a tower; then he rented it to tenant-farmers and left. ² When harvest-time came, he sent a servant to the tenants to collect his share of the crop from the vineyard. ³ But they took him, beat him up and sent him away empty-handed. ⁴ So he sent another servant; this one they punched in the head and insulted. ⁵ He sent another one, and him they killed; and so with many others — some they beat up, others they killed. ⁶ He had still one person left, a son whom he loved; in the end, he sent him to them, saying, 'My son they will respect.' ⁷ But the tenants said to each other, 'This is the heir. Come, let's kill him, and the inheritance will be ours!' ⁸ So they seized him, killed him and threw him out of the vineyard. ⁹ What will the owner of the vineyard do? He will come, destroy those tenants and give the vineyard to others! ¹⁰ Haven't you read the passage in the *Tanakh* that says,
>
> 'The very rock which the builders rejected
> has become the cornerstone!
> ¹¹ This has come from *ADONAI*,
> and in our eyes it is amazing'?"
>
> ¹² They set about to arrest him, for they recognized that he had told the parable with reference to themselves. But they were afraid of the crowd, so they left him and went away.

In reading Mark, it's always a good practice to identify the personal pronouns, like "them" in our opening verse. This is most likely the same group Yeshua is responding to in the previous paragraph, "the head *cohanim*, the Torah-teachers and the elders" (11:27). Yeshua has rebuffed their demand that he declare the source of his authority, and now he tells them a mysterious story, a parable about a man and his vineyard.

Like the fig tree in our previous episode, the vineyard is often taken to be a symbol of Israel, but in this case there's clear evidence for that connection.

> The choice of a vineyard as the setting for the parable signals that Jesus is telling the story of God's dealings with Israel: the vine or vineyard is a well-known symbol for Israel (Judah) regarding the nation's relationship to [the LORD] (Ps. 80:8–18; Isa. 1:8; 5:1–7; 27:2–6; Jer. 2:21; 12:10; Ezek. 19:10–14; Hos. 10:1).[1]

The clearest of the references listed here is Isaiah's "song about my loved one and his vineyard" (Isa. 5:1). This vineyard is carefully planted and tended, but it fails to produce good fruit, so that finally the "loved one," its owner, abandons it to the elements. The prophet declares,

> Now the vineyard of *ADONAI-Tzva'ot*
> is the house of Israel,
> and the men of Y'hudah
> are the plant he delighted in.
>
> So he expected justice,
> but look — bloodshed! —
> and righteousness, but listen —
> cries of distress! (Isa. 5:7)

Yeshua pictures a similar vineyard, with an owner who lovingly plants and tends it, but there are crucial differences between his story and Isaiah's. Yeshua's owner rents out the vineyard to tenant farmers—a common practice in the Galilee of Yeshua's day—and, again in contrast with Isaiah's story, the vineyard isn't the problem, the tenants are. If we read the vineyard as a symbol of Israel, it's clear that the tenants are those "managing" Israel, that is, the same religious authorities trying to give Yeshua a hard time. And, indeed, at the end of the parable, "they (the head *cohanim*, the Torah-

---

1. Schnabel, 282.

teachers and the elders) recognized that he had told the parable with reference to themselves" (12:12).

Within this framework, the parable seems clear enough, although the behavior of the different characters seems odd in some regards. The owner keeps sending servants to collect what is due him, even after they are repeatedly beaten, abused, and finally killed. The tenants aren't just greedy, but wildly abusive, inviting revenge. But the owner doesn't give up on the tenants or—in contrast with Isaiah's story—abandon the vineyard. Instead, he intensifies his efforts and sends his son, thinking the tenants will surely respect him. The tenants, however, recognize the son and, perhaps irrationally, see his visit as an opportunity to usurp his inheritance. They kill him and cast him out of the vineyard, bringing upon themselves judgment, as the owner destroys them and gives the vineyard to others. In a real-life account one wouldn't expect the owner to extend so much mercy—sending messenger after messenger—before finally dealing with the tenants, and one would certainly not expect him to expose his beloved son to these murderous tenants. Why would the landowner expect anything different from them?

All this points to God's boundless, even irrational, compassion for his people and, more specifically, for their leaders. He continually reaches out through his prophets to bring the authorities to repentance, so that they will tend his vineyard properly. Finally, in an act of mercy that seems so risky as to be foolhardy, he sends his son, which in the end only serves to confirm the irredeemable hardness of the tenants. They, not the vineyard, must be replaced. I use the word "replaced" deliberately to counter supersessionist or "replacement" readings of this parable. William Lane, for example, correctly notes that the vineyard itself isn't at fault here, as it is in Isaiah 5, but that Yeshua "directed his words specifically to the leaders of the people, and not to the people themselves." But then he concludes, "The sacred trust of the chosen people will be transferred to the new Israel of God."² This wording seems to pivot back to faulting the vineyard and looking for a new one to replace it, and it employs a concept that doesn't appear at all in Mark (or, arguably, the rest of the NT), "the new Israel of God." Instead, the drama of this entire episode (and much of Season 3) is one of conflict between Yeshua and the authorities in the midst of the "vineyard" of Israel. But the multitude within Israel supports Yeshua so that the authorities are afraid to push back too hard against him (Mark 12:12; 11:18, 32).

Yeshua ends the parable itself with a citation of Psalm 118.

> The very rock which the builders rejected
> has become the cornerstone!

In the context of the parable, "the builders" would be the tenants, who in turn represent the religious authorities, as the authorities themselves recognized. Their rejection of Yeshua is foreseen in Scripture, as is his essential role as the cornerstone of God's purposes for Israel and the world.

12:13–17

> ¹³ Next they sent some *P'rushim* and some members of Herod's party to him in order to trap him with a *sh'eilah* [question]. ¹⁴ They came and said to him, "Rabbi, we know that you tell the truth and are not concerned with what people think about you, since you pay no attention to a person's status but really teach what God's way is. Does Torah say that taxes are to be paid to the Roman Emperor, or not?"
>
> ¹⁵ But he, knowing their hypocrisy, said to them, "Why are you trying to trap me? Bring me a denarius so I can look at it." ¹⁶ They brought one; and he asked them, "Whose name and picture are these?" "The Emperor's," they replied. ¹⁷ Yeshua said, "Give the Emperor what belongs to the Emperor. And give to God what belongs to God!" And they were amazed at him.

---

2. Lane, 419.

Here's another scene that opens with an undefined "they," and the most likely subject is again "the head *cohanim*, the Torah-teachers and the elders." They got bested by Yeshua in the previous encounter and now they send surrogates to have another go at it. It can be objected that the religious authorities aren't really in a position to give orders to the *P'rushim* or Pharisees, and especially not to Herod's party.[3] But the Pharisees and Herodians had long since been colluding on how to do away with Yeshua (Mark 3:6), and it's not hard to imagine that the Temple authorities got in on the conversation and "suggested" the encounter that we're discussing here.

These questioners opt for a different approach from that of the authorities back in 11:28. Instead of confrontation, they opt for flattery, calling Yeshua "Rabbi" ("Teacher" or *didaskalos* in Greek), which may sound flattering but in Mark often hints at a limited understanding of Yeshua and his role (for example, 4:38; 5:35; 10:17, 35). After heaping insincere praise upon Yeshua, they pose a *sh'eilah*, a question, regarding halakha, Jewish law as derived from the Torah. The Pharisees may be hoping that Yeshua will weaken his uncompromising approach to Torah—and damage his reputation—by allowing payment of taxes to the pagan authorities who occupy the Holy Land. Herod's party, on the other hand, joins in to entice Yeshua into upholding Torah in a way that defies Rome in the most sensitive of areas, taxation. He loses either way.

Yeshua's response is to ask for a denarius, "the required coinage for tax payment" to the Roman authorities.[4] Tellingly, Yeshua doesn't have a denarius and has to request one from his flattering opponents. This may be a trap of his own, revealing that at least some of his opponents have made an accommodation with Rome. Whatever their position on paying taxes to the Emperor, they're

---

3. We don't have enough information to fully define "Herod's party," but it's evident that they're connected in some way with the Herodian dynasty, which was ruling Galilee at the time. Wills, "Mark," JANT (76) describes them as "supporters of Herod Antipas, Rome's client-ruler of Galilee," and references the account of Herod's execution of John in Mark 6:17–29.

4. France, 465.

using his currency in everyday life. When they hand the denarius to Yeshua he looks at it, shows it to them, and asks whose name and picture it bears. It is Caesar, of course, indicating that the coin belongs to him, and can go back to him. "But give to God what belongs to God." Yeshua slips the trap and raises a profound truth—one that amazes his hearers. One can maintain loyalty to God, and render him his due, even under Roman occupation. Furthermore, no matter how oppressive that occupation might seem, there is still a kingdom that belongs to God, and they can remain loyal to that.

12:18–27

> [18] Then some *Tz'dukim* came to him. They are the ones who say there is no such thing as resurrection, so they put to him a *sh'eilah*: [19] "Rabbi, Moshe wrote for us that **if a man's brother dies and leaves a wife but no child, his brother must take the wife and have children to preserve the man's family line.** [20] There were seven brothers. The first one took a wife, and when he died, he left no children. [21] Then the second one took her and died without leaving children, and the third likewise, [22] and none of the seven left children. Last of all, the woman also died. [23] In the Resurrection, whose wife will she be? For all seven had her as wife."
>
> [24] Yeshua said to them, "Isn't this the reason that you go astray? because you are ignorant both of the Tanakh and of the power of God? [25] For when people rise from the dead, neither men nor women marry — they are like angels in heaven. [26] And as for the dead being raised, haven't you read in the book of Moshe, in the passage about the bush, how God said to him, '**I am the God of Avraham, the God of Yitz'chak and the God of Ya'akov**'? [27] He is God not of the dead, but of the living! You are going far astray!"

The third encounter in Yeshua's ongoing inquest in Jerusalem concerns the resurrection to come. The *Tz'dukim*, or Sadducees, don't believe in the resurrection, probably because they don't find evidence for it in the Torah. They forego the flattery of the previous party, except for the title "Rabbi," which, as noted, is often linked to a misunderstanding of Yeshua and his mission. Instead, they cut to the chase with what they must have thought would be a devastating question. The Torah requires the brother of a married man who dies without offspring to marry his widow and the "first child she bears will succeed to the name of his dead brother, so that his name will not be eliminated from Israel" (Deut. 25:6). So what about the (doubtless imaginary) case of a deceased man who had six brothers, who each in turn marry the widow and die, leaving no offspring? The woman ends up marrying seven men—so whose wife will she be in the Resurrection to come? Gotcha!

Yeshua responds first by noting that when people rise from the dead they neither marry nor are given in marriage, but are like angels in heaven (12:25) who do not marry, according to a widespread belief within second-Temple Judaism.[5] Then he cites an unexpected proof-text from Torah, the very sort of evidence that the Sadducees have missed in their study of Torah. ADONAI identifies himself repeatedly in Torah as the God of Abraham, Isaac, and Jacob, and he is not the God of the dead, but of the living. Resurrection isn't just hinted at in Torah, but is essential to its picture of God, a point that Yeshua's opponents entirely miss as they go astray in their doctrine. It's worth noting that "Resurrection" in this debate is not so much the question of individual life after death. Rather, it is seen as a future event that will affect all Israel (or perhaps all humankind), which is why our translation capitalizes it: the Resurrection to come. In the event, the *Tz'dukim* have no rebuttal to make against Yeshua's argument nor his claim that they have gone astray.

12:28–34

> [28] One of the Torah-teachers came up and heard them engaged in this discussion. Seeing that Yeshua answered them well, he asked him, "Which is the most important *mitzvah* of them all?" [29] Yeshua answered, "The most important is,

---

5. Wills, "Mark," JANT, 96; France 472–74.

'*Sh'ma Yisra'el, ADONAI Eloheinu, ADONAI echad* [Hear, O Isra'el, the Lord our God, the Lord is one], [30] and you are to love ADONAI your God with all your heart, with all your soul, with all your understanding and with all your strength.'

[31] The second is this:

'You are to love your neighbor as yourself.'

There is no other *mitzvah* greater than these." [32] The Torah-teacher said to him, "Well said, Rabbi; you speak the truth when you say that he is one, and that there is no other besides him; [33] and that loving him with all one's heart, understanding and strength, and loving one's neighbor as oneself, mean more than all the burnt offerings and sacrifices." [34] When Yeshua saw that he responded sensibly, he said to him, "You are not far from the Kingdom of God." And after that, no one dared put to him another *sh'eilah*.

This fourth encounter in the series differs from the others, as the questioner appears to be sincere, to have a genuine interest in hearing Yeshua's answer to a worthwhile question. "Jesus, then, is being invited by his friendly interlocutor to enter into an ongoing Jewish discussion."[6] Matthew records the same interchange, but interprets it differently. There, the Torah-teacher asks Yeshua the question to "trap him" (Matt. 22:35), and his response to Yeshua's question isn't recorded at all. Also, uniquely in Mark, and reflecting a more in-house and friendly discussion, Yeshua begins his citation of the greatest commandment with its opening words "*Sh'ma Yisrael*, Hear O Israel," which would have been familiar words to a Jewish audience of Yeshua's day, as they are to most Jewish people today. Matthew, writing years later, begins with the next line and the command to love ADONAI with all your heart, soul, and strength (Matt. 22:37). Bible students don't usually think of Mark as being a more Jewish gospel than Matthew, but in this instance it is. In Mark, Yeshua expands on the Hebrew text, which has a three-fold

---

6. Marcus, *Mark 8–16*, 842.

command—to love ADONAI with all one's heart, soul, and strength—by adding a fourth, "with all your understanding." This expansion may reflect the richness of the three original components of the commandment, which is explored in rabbinic discussions over the centuries. Soloveitchik notes that the words *with all your understanding*, "are not in the text of the Torah; however, they are absolutely implied. Yeshua adds them by his own initiative, by way of commentary, and entirely in the same spirit as our sages."[7]

The Torah-teacher accepts Yeshua's words and expands upon them with a brief teaching of his own, drawing on Hosea 6:6, "For what I desire is mercy, not sacrifices, / knowledge of God more than burnt offerings." In typical fashion, this teacher cites a passage from the Prophets to reflect on the teachings of Torah. Yeshua commends the Torah-teacher scribe and pronounces a favorable verdict upon him. Still, this teacher, like the recognized followers of Yeshua, and even the Twelve, is still in process, not far from the Kingdom, but not there yet.

In Mark's account, then, Yeshua seems to deeply engage with the Jewish teaching and practice of his day, and in this case to affirm it. All of this is consistent with Mark's portrayal of the Jewish community as including a large pro-Yeshua element, and of Yeshua's teachings as resonating with the community, although not, of course, with most of its leaders. Nonetheless, even among the leaders there is this one Torah-teacher who is starting to recognize what Yeshua is about. Perhaps Mark portrays him in so much detail in the hope that he'll be an example of more such Torah-teachers.

As for the substance of Yeshua's teaching here, citing the Sh'ma as the greatest commandment would not be controversial in the Jewish world of his day, nor would joining it with "Love your neighbor as yourself" (Lev. 19:18), although Yeshua is the first (but by no means the only) Jewish teacher on record to do so.[8] Love of

---

7. Soloveitchik, 365.
8. France, 477–78; Edwards 372; Marcus, *Mark 8–16*, 843.

God is incomplete if it is not joined with active, engaging love for the people around us. Yeshua demonstrates both aspects of this love throughout his earthly journey, and especially in the climactic days to come, when he will give his life as a ransom for many (10:45), and yield to the father's will above his own (14:36).

12:35–44

> [35] As Yeshua was teaching in the Temple, he asked, "How is it that the *Torah*-teachers say the Messiah is the Son of David? [36] David himself, inspired by the *Ruach HaKodesh*, said,
>
> '*ADONAI* said to my Lord,
> "Sit here at my right hand
> until I put your enemies under your feet." '
>
> [37] David himself calls him 'Lord'; so how is he his son?"
>
> The great crowd listened eagerly to him. [38] As he taught them, he said, "Watch out for the kind of *Torah*-teachers who like to walk around in robes and be greeted deferentially in the marketplaces, [39] who like to have the best seats in the synagogues and take the places of honor at banquets, [40] who like to swallow up widows' houses while making a show of *davvening* at great length. Their punishment will be all the worse!"
>
> [41] Then Yeshua sat down opposite the Temple treasury and watched the crowd as they put money into the offering-boxes. Many rich people put in large sums, [42] but a poor widow came and put in two small coins. [43] He called his *talmidim* to him and said to them, "Yes! I tell you, this poor widow has put more in the offering-box than all the others making donations. [44] For all of them, out of their wealth, have contributed money they can easily spare; but she, out of her poverty, has given everything she had to live on."

Yeshua turns from the Torah-teacher who is not far from the Kingdom to challenge Torah-teachers of another sort, who seem to be abundant in Mark. He poses an intriguing question based on the word "Lord/lord," which has just appeared in his citation of the Shema, a question challenging the Torah-teachers who speak of Mashiach ben David, Messiah Son of David. Since David calls the Messiah "lord," how is he David's son? Yeshua, in typical fashion, leaves the question unanswered, for the hearers to consider. His point is probably not to deny the Messiah's descent from David (he recently responded favorably to an appeal to him as Son of David in 10:47–49), but to hint at an even loftier identity, not fully disclosed. Perhaps the concept of Mashiach ben David is ready for expansion, and the "great crowd" seems ready as well. They listen eagerly to Yeshua, or "hear him gladly," as in the ESV and other translations—providing more evidence of the wide support for Yeshua on the Jerusalem street (along with 11:18, 32, and 12:12, as we've seen).

Yeshua takes advantage of this teachable moment with the crowd to warn them of the "the kind of Torah-teachers who like to walk around in robes and be greeted deferentially in the marketplaces" (12:38). The CJB captures the sense of this verse better than most translations, which place a comma (which doesn't exist in the Greek original) after "Torah-teachers," or more commonly "scribes," as in the ESV: "Beware of the scribes, who like to walk around in long robes and like greetings in the marketplaces." This punctuation creates the sense that all scribes like to walk around in long robes and we should beware of them as a class. But without punctuation it can be read as a warning against the particular scribes, or "the kind of Torah-teachers" who like to walk around in long robes, as in the CJB.[9] This translation aligns better with Yeshua's recent positive interaction with a scribe/Torah-teacher, and with Mark's frequent reminders of those Jews who seem to get what Yeshua is talking about.

---

9. Accordingly, Marcus translates 12:38 as, "Watch out for those scribes who like to go around in long robes, and like greetings in the marketplaces," and concludes: "the example of the good scribe a few verses earlier (12:28–34) shows that the evangelist does not think that all scribes are of the vainglorious sort he is depicting here" (*Mark 8–16*, 852).

Yeshua ends his discourse by pointing out just such a Jew, an elderly widow who embodies obedience to the great commandment to "love ADONAI your God with all your heart, with all your soul, with all your understanding and with all your strength," by casting "everything she had to live on" into the Temple offering-box. Yeshua extols her offering right after warning the crowd about the sort of Torah-teachers "who like to swallow up widows' houses while making a show of praying at great length" (12:40, modified). The contrast could not be clearer, nor could the picture of the love of God be more challenging. True Torah piety entails sacrifice, self-sacrifice that draws upon the very substance of one's life to serve God.

Derash

- In the parable of the vineyard, the wicked tenants see the son coming to collect what is due his father and say, "This is the heir. Come, let's kill him, and the inheritance will be ours!" (12:7–8). This scene reminds us of the story of another son, Joseph son of Jacob. When his brothers see him coming, representing his father—who is, of course, their father as well—they say, "Look, this dreamer is coming! So come now, let's kill him and throw him into one of these water cisterns here. Then we'll say some wild animal devoured him. We'll see then what becomes of his dreams!" (Gen. 37:19–20). Joseph had dreamt of his brothers bowing before him as the "heir," the uniquely chosen one of the father, and they hoped to counteract that choice by doing away with him.

  With typical subtlety, Yeshua uses a parable to tie his story as the rejected deliverer to the story of Joseph, the rejected son who brings deliverance to his entire family, and to the surrounding nations as well. The figure of Mashiach ben Yosef, Messiah son of Joseph, appears in rabbinic literature as far back as the Talmud itself:

> What is the cause of the mourning [mentioned in Zechariah 12:12]?—Rabbi Dosa and the Rabbis differ on the point. R. Dosa explained, *The cause is the slaying of Messiah the son of Joseph . . .* since that well agrees with the Scriptural verse, *And they shall look upon me because they have thrust him through, and they shall mourn for him as one mourneth for his only son.* (Sukkah 52a)[10]

The parable ends with the son rejected, killed, and thrown out of the vineyard. Joseph is likewise rejected, fake-killed, and thrown out of his family and their dwelling place. But he is raised up in the end. How does the notion of Messiah the son of Joseph enrich our understanding of Yeshua's mission, especially as recounted in Mark? What implications does this figure have for the Jewish people's relationship with Yeshua as Messiah down the centuries, and today as well?

- Yeshua's instruction to "Render to Caesar" can be applied to political involvement within today's polarizing and contentious climate. The entire culture in both the USA and Israel seems permeated with partisanship and the demand to choose sides in an ongoing cultural-political warfare. Party operatives seek to redirect religious loyalties and values into political affiliation. On the one hand, Yeshua's words do affirm a certain responsibility to the secular authorities, also evident in Jeremiah's words to the Babylonian exiles: "Seek the welfare of the city to which I have caused you to go in exile, and pray to ADONAI on its behalf; for your welfare is bound up in its welfare" (Jer. 29:7). On the other hand, Yeshua's saying marks the limits of the state, for no matter what it might demand, we still render to God what belongs to God, and we remain free to serve him. The Kingdom that Yeshua is inaugurating doesn't require the overthrow of Roman occupation in the here-and-now, although it will

---

10. As cited in my book *A Life of Favor: A Family Therapist Examines the Story of Joseph and His Brothers* (Clarksville, MD: Lederer, 2017), 59; see the discussion of Messiah ben Joseph, 59–63 and 98–101.

surely prevail over it in the end. We might consider how well we are keeping the two realms—what belongs to the Emperor and what belongs to God—distinct, how well we are keeping the demands of Caesar from encroaching on God's dominion.

- In Mark, Yeshua says the "greatest commandment" begins with the first line of the Shema, "Hear O Israel . . ." This contrasts with Matthew, which begins with "Love the Lord your God with all your heart . . ." As we saw above, this difference may be part of Mark's picture of Yeshua deeply connected with everyday Jewish life, where the Shema is recited daily in the Temple. It also may reflect the simple fact that "Sh'ma" in Hebrew is an imperative verb. Yes, the first line of the Shema is a prologue to the commandment to love God, but it's also a commandment in its own right, an imperative, as noted by Rabbi Lord Jonathan Sacks of blessed memory.

> In the Shema, God, through the Torah, speaks to us. The word Shema itself means "listen," and the recital of the shema is a supreme act of faith-as-listening: to the voice that brought the universe into being, created us in love and guides us through our lives.[11]

In a sense, then, the greatest commandment is "Listen!" It's not more important than *V'ahavta*, "And you shall love," but part of it. By listening, hearing, and receiving from God, we are empowered to love him wholeheartedly. Yeshua's citation of "Listen, Israel" here hints at a motif he will develop a few days later in his teaching on the end times, which concludes, "And what I say to you, I say to everyone: stay alert!" (Mark 13:37). Spiritual vigilance is essential to following Yeshua.

---

11. *Koren Siddur,* 198.

- A popular interpretation of "You are to love your neighbor as yourself" is that it requires us to love ourselves so that we can love others, or even that it's telling us we can't really love others unless we love ourselves. But such interpretations may be more rooted in modern psychology and values than in the original context of the Torah. There, self-love is not a matter of healthy self-esteem but rather the simple reality that we normally watch out for ourselves, take care of ourselves, and seek to get our needs met. In like manner, the Torah teaches—and Yeshua emphasizes—that we are to watch out for others and seek to meet their needs just as we do our own. Of course, the wholeness that God mercifully provides for us does enable us to do such things for others, and loving ourselves empowers us to fully love others, but the actual *command* here is to love our neighbor.

In his commentary on this passage, Elijah Zvi Soloveitchik cites a story about the two famous, and often competing, sages Shammai and Hillel (Babylonian Talmud, Shabbat 31a):

> One day, a pagan came to Shammai and said to him, "I will convert to your religion if you can teach it to me in its entirety in the length of time that I can stand on one leg." Shammai became angry and told him to leave. Our man went to Hillel, made him the same proposition, and Hillel convinced him with this response: *"That which you would not have others do to you, do not do to them.* This is the Torah; the rest is commentary. Go and study it!"[12]

Hillel, unlike Yeshua, doesn't cite "the most important mitzvah," the Shema, but he does effectively paraphrase the second mitzvah, "love your neighbor as yourself." It is Yeshua's particular genius to link the two commandments, to suggest that love of God is somehow made complete by love of our neighbor. In another setting, a

---

12. Soloveitchik, 366–67.

Torah expert responds to these linked commandments with a not-unreasonable question: "And who is my 'neighbor'?" (Luke 10:29). In response, Yeshua tells his famous story of a victimized Jew lying on the roadside and a Samaritan passerby who turns aside to give him the kind of help he'd undoubtedly want to receive if he were in that situation himself. Apparently my "neighbor" in the second great mitzvah is anyone who needs me to be a neighbor. As we learn to absorb and act on this insight, we may become, like Mark's Torah-teacher, "not far from the Kingdom."

Season 3, Episode 3 (17)

A View of Things to Come

13:1-37

Overview

Yeshua has spent some days in the Temple courts being questioned and challenged by various religious authorities, and challenging them in turn. Now, along with his band of followers, he makes what turns out to be his final departure from the Temple. As they are leaving, one of these followers notes the splendid stones and buildings of the Temple compound, and Yeshua tells him that all these structures will be torn down and "not a single stone will be left standing!" (13:2).

When they arrive on the Mount of Olives, opposite the Temple Mount, four of the talmidim ask Yeshua privately *when* these things will happen, and *what* will be the warning signs. Yeshua's response takes up the rest of our episode and provides a view of events after his departure, until the time of his eventual return. As he responds to the two-fold question, Yeshua is more concerned with equipping his followers to withstand the days to come, than with giving them a template for interpreting an "end-times" scenario. He warns the men gathered around him that the coming events will be unsettling and dangerous, for them as well as for all who will live through them. Wars, earthquakes, and famines will be just the beginning of "birth pains" (13:8), trials of increasing intensity that will finally culminate in the return of Messiah. The details of the timing and the warning signs—the information sought by the four talmidim—are complex and not always orderly, but Yeshua's message to his talmidim here is clear enough: Remain alert; be on guard against false prophets and false Messiahs. At the same time, he pictures them proclaiming the Good News before religious and secular authorities, and eventually to all the nations.

Yeshua goes on to zero in on a series of events foreshadowed or predicted in the Book of Daniel, apparently centered on Jerusalem and the Temple. In 13:24–27, Yeshua appears to shift his focus from the historical period leading up to and including the destruction of the Temple in 70 CE, to "those days, after that trouble." At that time, unmistakable warning signs will precede his appearing as the Son of Man, coming in the clouds to gather his elect from the "four winds, from the ends of the earth to the ends of heaven" (13:27).

Yeshua concludes his portrayal of the time to come with the analogy of a fig tree beginning to sprout and put forth its leaves—a sure sign that summer is near. In the same way, unparalleled signs will precede both the destruction of the Temple and the eventual coming of the Son of Man. Yeshua has responded to the two-fold question raised by the four talmidim, but says that no one knows the day or hour when all this will take place. Accordingly, he ends his account of things to come with another warning for all who hear him to remain alert until the end.

Peshat

13:1–4

> [1] As Yeshua came out of the Temple, one of the *talmidim* said to him, "Look, Rabbi! What huge stones! What magnificent buildings!" [2] "You see all these great buildings?" Yeshua said to him, "They will be totally destroyed — not a single stone will be left standing!"
>
> [3] As he was sitting on the Mount of Olives opposite the Temple, Kefa, Ya'akov, Yochanan and Andrew asked him privately, [4] "Tell us, when will these things happen? And what sign will show when all these things are about to be accomplished?"

Yeshua's words to his band as they make what turns out to be their final departure from the Temple courts must have been shocking indeed. The Temple built by Herod was considered one of the wonders of the ancient world, as described by the Jewish historian Josephus:

> The exterior of the building wanted nothing that could astound either mind or eye. For, being covered on all sides with massive plates of gold, the sun was no sooner up than it radiated so fiery a flash that persons straining to look at it were compelled to avert their eyes, as from the solar rays. To approaching strangers it appeared from a distance like a snow-clad mountain; for all that was not overlaid with gold was of the purest white.[1]

It's no wonder that Yeshua's followers were dazzled by the sight of this Temple. They express their amazement with the words, "Look, Rabbi!"—using the title for Yeshua that in Mark generally indicates limited or skewed understanding. Accordingly, Yeshua takes their awe and amazement as another teachable moment, as he had leveraged his dispute with the Pharisees about purity laws (7:14–23), or the talmidim's mistaken attempt to keep someone outside their circle from invoking his name (9:38–41), to convey some vital lessons. In other teachable moments, Yeshua's response might have been more than his hearers expected, but here it's totally unexpected. It's not hard to imagine the talmidim's shock when Yeshua announces the coming total destruction of all that they're gazing upon.

As often in Mark, Yeshua reveals the full meaning of his unsettling words first to those closest to him, in this case, the same three men who accompanied him to see his transfiguration or metamorphosis on the mountain—Kefa, and the brothers Ya'akov and Yochanan (9:2)—now joined by Kefa's brother Andrew. These men ask a question in two parts: When will this catastrophe happen, and what will be its warning signs? This suggests that they expect it to be coming in their days and so they need to know when and how to prepare. As Yeshua paints the picture, he seems to shift his

---

1. Josephus, *The Jewish Wars*, 5.222–23, as cited in Schnabel, 315.

attention from the two pairs of brothers to all his followers, and in his concluding words he will address "everyone" (13:37).

Yeshua addresses his followers seated on the Mount of Olives opposite the Temple.

> Jesus' symbolic exit from the Temple and his prophecy of its destruction are followed by a third threatening action: he takes a seat on the Mount of Olives, opposite the Temple Mount, and looks back toward the doomed structure (13:3a). The sitting posture is often associated in biblical texts both with teaching and judgment.[2]

Yeshua's "judgment seat" has become a spot well-known to travelers to Jerusalem down to this day, an ideal site to gaze upon the Temple Mount from the east. As noted back in chapter 11, the Mount of Olives appears by name twice in the Tanakh. It is identified as the site of ADONAI's promised return to his city and his people in Zechariah 14:3–4, and is therefore a place of prophetic expectancy. But it's also on the route out of the holy city, first mentioned by name in the account of David's flight from Jerusalem ahead of his rebellious son Absalom: "David continued up the road to the Mount of Olives, weeping as he went up, head covered and barefoot; and all the people with him had their heads covered and wept as they went up" (2 Sam. 15:30). Now, David's Son departs via the Mount of Olives, not weeping, but speaking words of mournful impact. David fled the city to save his life, and also to spare it from the sword of Absalom (2 Sam. 15:14), entrusting his eventual return to the LORD (2 Sam. 15:25).[3] Yeshua's departure will not spare the city, as he will make clear in the following words, but his eventual return is assured, as he will also make clear. Yeshua will return temporarily to the city for his final Passover and all that ensues, but his departure from the Temple itself is final.

---

2. Marcus, *Mark 8–16*, 873.
3. The Mount of Olives also plays a key role as the route of departure and return in the prophetic vision of Ezekiel 10 and 11, as noted in Season 2, Episode 4, but it is not explicitly named there.

13:5–13

⁵Yeshua began speaking to them: "Watch out! Don't let anyone fool you! ⁶Many will come in my name, saying, 'I am he!' and they will fool many people. ⁷When you hear the noise of wars nearby and the news of wars far off, don't become frightened. Such things must happen, but the end is yet to come. ⁸For peoples will fight each other, and nations will fight each other, there will be earthquakes in various places, there will be famines; this is but the beginning of the 'birth pains.'

⁹"But you, watch yourselves! They will hand you over to the local *Sanhedrin*s, you will be beaten up in synagogues, and on my account you will stand before governors and kings as witnesses to them. ¹⁰Indeed, the Good News has to be proclaimed first to all the *Goyim*. ¹¹Now when they arrest you and bring you to trial, don't worry beforehand about what to say. Rather, say whatever is given you when the time comes; for it will not be just you speaking, but the *Ruach HaKodesh*. ¹²Brother will betray brother to death, and a father his child; children will turn against their parents and have them put to death; ¹³and everyone will hate you because of me. But whoever holds out till the end will be delivered.

The term "eschatology," the study of the final days or end times, can sound far-out and theoretical, but Yeshua's words here are far from theoretical. He's speaking to his followers in concrete terms about life-and-death matters that will require their constant vigilance. He will repeat his admonition in 13:5, "Watch out!" or *blepo* in the Greek, three more times (13:9, 23, 33). Toward the end of these instructions on the Mount of Olives, he'll mobilize another verb, "stay alert"—*gregoreuo* in Greek—three times to drive home his message: "What I say to you, I say to everyone: stay alert!" (13:27; also 13:24, 25). Unlike Kefa, Ya'akov, Yochanan, and Andrew—and many readers today—Yeshua's attention isn't so much on the timing and the signs of the end times, but on admonishing his followers to be alert and watchful, no matter what and when.

Yeshua's initial response to the talmidim's twofold question is to tell them that wars, earthquakes, and famines are *not* signs of the end, but conditions of life throughout the time to come. "For Jesus, the salient question is not the 'when' of the end-time, but the 'how' of living with this expectation."[4] The catastrophic events to come are only the beginning of "birth pains" (13:8), the pains that precede childbirth with increasing intensity as the moment of delivery approaches. The term here suggests both the intensity of suffering and the longing for the joy of the child's birth. It also carries a sense of inevitability, suggesting that the pain is necessary to bring about the desired end. The prophets of the Tanakh sometimes employ such imagery to picture suffering that comes suddenly and inescapably in a context of judgment (Isa. 13:8; 27:17–18; Jer. 6:24; 22:23; Hos. 13:13). Micah employs the imagery in a similar fashion, but ends with a note of hope:

> Be in pain! Work to give birth
> like a woman in labor, daughter of Tziyon!
> For now you will go out of the city
> and live in the wilds till you reach Bavel.
> There you will be rescued;
> there ADONAI will redeem you
> from the power of your enemies. (Mic. 4:10)

The "birth pains" that are just beginning in Yeshua's description of the end times are also necessary, inevitable, and the prelude to rescue and redemption. They entail suffering for the sake of the Good News, as Yeshua's followers will be brought before both Jewish and Gentile authorities, including "the local *Sanhedrins*" (13:9). "Sanhedrins" here is a literal translation, or really transliteration, of the Greek original, but it's perhaps unfortunate, first because it implies a formal or official religious council, THE Sanhedrin, when it often appears in a more common sense as an assembly or council. This reality is reflected in the CJB use of the

---

4. Levine, *Mark*, 114.

plural—"Sanhedrins"—here, suggesting "local Jewish courts of law in Judea and beyond, including Jewish diaspora communities."[5] Also, the word "Sanhedrin" often appears in anti-Jewish or supersessionist interpretations and texts in support of negative stereotypes; a more mundane, but still accurate, translation like "council" might be better here.

Joel Marcus notes two significant aspects of the Greek word translated "They will hand you over" in 13:9.

> The first is its background in Isaiah 52–53 LXX, where the Lord's Suffering Servant is "turned over" to an ignominious death but ends up being exalted and glorified (Isa. 52:13; 53:12); the verb thus already hints at the salvation that Jesus prophesies at the end of our passage.... The second important aspect of [the word] is its use elsewhere in the Gospel, where it is applied to the arrest of John the Baptist (1:14) but more often to Jesus' own betrayal and death (3:19; 9:31; 10:33; 14:10–11, 18, 21, 41–42, 44; 15:1, 10, 15). The word itself, then, implies what Jesus says explicitly at the end of the verse: the disciples' delivery into the hands of their enemies will be "for my sake" [or "on my account," 13:9 CJB].[6]

In this perilous context, our passage also includes one of the rare direct references to the Holy Spirit or *Ruach HaKodesh* in Mark. The Spirit plays a major role in the Prologue, beginning with Yochanan's promise that the one coming after him "will immerse you in the *Ruach HaKodesh*" (1:8). In the next scene, the Ruach descends upon Yeshua as he emerges from the waters of the Yarden, and then drives him into the wilderness where he is tempted by the Adversary for forty days (1:10–12). Afterward, the Ruach is mentioned only once, in Yeshua's warning against blaspheming the Holy Spirit (3:29), until we come to the episode preceding the current one. There, Yeshua cites Psalm 110, in which "David himself, inspired by the *Ruach HaKodesh*, said, **'ADONAI said to my Lord...**" (12:36).

---

5. Schnabel, 320.
6. Marcus, *Mark 8–16*, 885.

The promise of immersion in the Ruach has not been forgotten, however, and now for the first time, in 13:11, Mark speaks of ordinary followers being empowered by the Spirit. Two points stand out here: First, the Spirit empowers believers in the midst of service and persecution, enabling them to remain faithful; second, this empowerment comes in the form of utterance. Just as David *spoke* words "inspired by the *Ruach HaKodesh*," so ordinary Yeshua-followers will *speak* words of testimony empowered by the Ruach HaKodesh before those sitting in judgment against them.

As Marcus noted above, the trials of the talmidim in the time to come reflect the trials of Messiah Yeshua himself. He has repeatedly foretold his coming betrayal and crucifixion, as well as his resurrection after three days. Now he tells his followers in detail about the share in his sufferings that will fall upon them, including betrayal by their own family members, just as Yeshua will be betrayed by one of the Twelve. But the resurrection—the final victory—is also in sight, as "whoever holds out till the end will be delivered" (13:13).

13:14–27

> [14] "Now when you see **the abomination that causes devastation** standing where it ought not to be" (let the reader understand the allusion), "that will be the time for those in Y'hudah to escape to the hills. [15] If someone is on the roof, he must not go down and enter his house to take any of his belongings; [16] if someone is in the field, he must not turn back to get his coat. [17] What a terrible time it will be for pregnant women and nursing mothers! [18] Pray that it may not happen in winter. [19] For there will be **worse trouble** at that time **than there has ever been from the very beginning**, when God created the universe, **until now; and there will be nothing like it again.** [20] Indeed, if God had not limited the duration of the trouble, no one would survive; but for the sake of the elect, those whom he has chosen, he has limited it.

²¹ "At that time, if anyone says to you, 'Look! Here's the Messiah!' or, 'See, there he is!' — don't believe him! ²² There will appear false Messiahs and false prophets performing signs and wonders for the purpose, if possible, of misleading the chosen. ²³ But you, watch out! I have told you everything in advance!

²⁴ In those days, after that trouble,

the sun will grow dark,
the moon will stop shining,
²⁵ the stars will fall from the sky,
and the powers in heaven will be shaken.

²⁶ Then they will see **the Son of Man coming in clouds** with tremendous power and glory. ²⁷ He will send out his angels and gather together his chosen people from the four winds, from the ends of the earth to the ends of heaven.

The focus shifts with verse 14, from the broad view of birth pains characterized by wars "nearby and far off," and "earthquakes in various places," to a specific event in a specific place, the region of Y'hudah (or Judaea). Indeed, Yeshua's focus here is so specific that critical scholars sometimes claim that Mark recorded this prediction after the fact; in other words, they claim that Mark's Besorah was written after the Roman destruction of the Temple in 70 CE, and portrays Yeshua as predicting this disaster to help make sense of it and also to bolster his credibility. But if this were the case, it's odd that there's no mention of the Temple being burned when it was destroyed, when Josephus records a colossal fire as one of the main icons of destruction.[7] And Yeshua's words here make perfect sense as an advance warning to those he is addressing, in the mode of the Hebrew prophets.

Likewise, the "abomination that causes desolation" (13:14) is something that would make sense to Mark's original audience, as is

---

7. *Jewish Wars* VI. iv. 17, cited by Lane, 453.

evident in his note, "let the reader understand the allusion."[8] If Yeshua is describing the destruction of the Temple here, however, his language in 13:19 might seem problematic. The suffering of the Jewish people during and after the first rebellion against Rome was vast and nearly unimaginable, but not unparalleled in human history, and it tragically isn't the case that "there will be nothing like it again." Yeshua may be employing hyperbole here, as is often the case with prophetic speech, and moreover he is directly quoting Joel 2:2 and Daniel 12:1. It's also worth noting that the events Yeshua foretells in 13:14–23 do not mark the end of history. Yeshua warns his followers to flee for safety and says the events will be cut short for the sake of the elect. He says "there will be nothing like it again" (Joel 2:2), and even if this must be understood as hyperbole, it implies that there will be a period of time following these events.

In 13:24, Yeshua goes on to describe what happens "after that trouble," perhaps moving from the talmidim's first question about when the Temple will be destroyed to their additional question, "And what sign will show when all these things are about to be accomplished?" (13:4b). "All these things" may comprise more events, and later events, than "these things" concerning the Temple itself. If so, can we identify a likely event for "the abomination that causes desolation" in the period before the Temple's destruction? The writings of Josephus may provide an answer.

> At the beginning of the war [against Rome], in the winter of AD 67/68, Jewish militants (the Zealots) occupied the Temple Mount and usurped the high priesthood (Josephus, *War* 4.147–157). Ananus, the oldest of the chief priests, is reported as saying, "How wonderful it would have been if I had died before seeing the house of God full of countless abominations and its unapproachable, sacred precincts crowded with those whose hands are red with blood!" (*War* 4.163).[9]

---

8. The reference to a "reader" rather than a "hearer" suggests that this is a comment by Mark the writer rather than part of Yeshua's original oral discourse. Mark's account includes a number of asides like this, e.g. 2:10b; 3:30; 7:3–4, 11b, 19b; 16:4b.
9. Schnabel, 325. In this section Schnabel also cites Josephus in detail to document the incomparable sufferings of the Jewish people in their first revolt against Rome.

Accordingly, this commentator goes on to claim,

> The confusion about Jesus' "eschatological discourse" in Mark 13 stems largely from the fact that so-called end-time "specialists" do not interpret the text in its historical context but "mine" these verses for predictions that are seen to be fulfilled in the most recent past, in the present and/or in the imminent future, often in an attempt to pinpoint the time of Jesus' second coming.[10]

And, of course, pinpointing the time of the second coming is exactly what Yeshua ends up telling his followers he's *not* going to do (13:32). Instead, his point is that they are to remain alert and watchful until the end (13:5, 9, 13, 23, 33, 37).

Before we hear Yeshua's final exhortation, however, we get a glimpse of what lies ahead after the unparalleled troubles of 13:14–20 and the outbreak of false messiahs and false prophets in 13:21–22. The birth pains endured within the natural course of events will give way to supernatural signs in the heavens, as foretold by the prophets (Isa. 13:10; 34:4; Ezek. 32:7; Joel 2:10; 3:4 [2:31]; 4:15 [3:15]; Hag. 2:6, 21). These signs portend the unmistakable appearing of the true Messiah, "the Son of Man coming in clouds with tremendous power and glory" (13:26). As we've seen, Yeshua introduced the title "Son of Man" for himself back in the early days of his ministry, in a little house in K'far-Nachum, when he pronounced forgiveness on a man as he was healing him: "the Son of Man has authority on earth to forgive sins" (2:10). "Son of Man" becomes the title Yeshua uses for himself most frequently in Mark (2:10, 28; 8:31, 38; 9:9, 12, 31; 10:33, 45; 13:26; 14:21 [twice], 41, 62), and here in 13:26 he explicitly links the title to Daniel's description of the coming of the Son of Man. If there has been any doubt about the meaning of this title, it is now dispelled. Amidst his description of persecution and catastrophes to come, Yeshua provides assurance to his followers—he is the Son of Man who will bring history as we know it to its consummation in undeniable fashion.

---

10. Schnabel, 329.

The gathering of the elect or "his chosen people" in 13:27 is, of course, a major theme in the Tanakh, founded in the words of Moses himself, such as Leviticus 26:44–45 and Deuteronomy 30:1–10, and pictured in compelling fashion by Ezekiel many centuries later, after the Babylonian conquest (Ezek. 36–37; see also Isa. 43:5–7; Zech. 2:6). The question here is whether Yeshua is referring to the same "elect" or "chosen people" as Moses and the Prophets. He has already said that for the sake of the elect the horrific days following the destruction of the Temple will be cut short (13:20). Given the setting of these events in the Jewish heartland of Y'hudah or Judaea, the elect here likely has the same meaning as in the Tanakh, namely the people Israel. Moreover, the promise that this chosen group will be regathered "from the four winds" would apply to the Jewish people scattered at that time throughout the Mediterranean world and beyond, with a large remnant still in Mesopotamia. The promise echoes the many promises of Israel's regathering in Moses and the Prophets. Another mention of the elect, though, might suggest a more limited group: False prophets and false signs will abound "for the purpose, if possible, of misleading the chosen" (13:22). This wording implies that Yeshua is referring to a select group within Israel, his own followers, who would be special targets of the efforts to deceive, but also specially protected—a chosen people within the chosen people.[11]

Perhaps the most important implication of 13:27 is that Yeshua speaks of "*his* chosen people," a people chosen by the Son of Man. Moses and the Prophets speak of Israel as chosen by ADONAI, to be protected and ultimately regathered by him. The Son of Man takes on this divine prerogative, sharing in the glory of the Ancient of Days, as pictured in Daniel 7. When Yeshua chose the Twelve to be with him and to be sent out with power (3:13–14), they did not replace the Twelve Tribes, but served as their representatives.

---

11. I'm tempted to apply this description, "a chosen people within the chosen people," to today's Messianic Jewish community, of which I am a member.

Likewise, the chosen ones here include Yeshua's followers and all Israel, apart from those who explicitly oppose Yeshua (or blaspheme the Holy Spirit as in 3:28–29). By calling them "*his* chosen people," Yeshua hints at his own divine status.

13:28–37

> [28] "Now let the fig tree teach you its lesson: when its branches begin to sprout and leaves appear, you know that summer is approaching. [29] In the same way, when you see all these things happening, you are to know that the time is near, right at the door. [30] Yes! I tell you that this people will certainly not pass away before all these things happen. [31] Heaven and earth will pass away, but my words will certainly not pass away. [32] However, when that day and hour will come, no one knows — not the angels in heaven, not the Son, just the Father. [33] Stay alert! Be on your guard! For you do not know when the time will come.
>
> [34] "It's like a man who travels away from home, puts his servants in charge, each with his own task, and tells the doorkeeper to stay alert. [35] So stay alert! for you don't know when the owner of the house will come, [36] whether it will be evening, midnight, cockcrow or morning — you don't want him to come suddenly and find you sleeping! [37] And what I say to you, I say to everyone: stay alert!"

Yeshua concludes his compelling picture of the end times with two metaphors. The first is a fig tree beginning to sprout: just as this is a sure sign that summer is near, so all the things that he has described are a sure sign that his return is at hand. "All these things" could be taken to mean the entire picture of Mark 13, but Yeshua had clearly said that some of the conditions he described were not signs of the end, but only the beginning of birth pains (13:8). He had repeatedly emphasized the need for endurance, and the possibility of escape, and had warned against being misled by false messiahs and false signs. It's only in "those days, after that trouble" (13:24) that the unmistakable signs appear. No one knows when that will be, not even the Son, but only the Father (13:32), implying that these final signs will appear suddenly and unexpectedly, and so the faithful must stay alert at all times.

Our second metaphor portrays Yeshua-followers as servants in a household, with the owner away on a journey. Actually, they are like the doorkeeper in this household, who needs to be especially watchful for the owner's return, which can happen at any time. None of the servants want to be caught sleeping, and so Yeshua wraps up by repeating his admonition: Stay alert!

Both metaphors point to a sudden and extraordinary future event or series of events, rather than to the longer string of events described earlier in Mark 13, which call for endurance. The final events, in contrast, call for vigilance. Such a reading may shed light on a verse here that many readers have found puzzling, usually translated as something like, "this generation will not pass away until all these things take place" (13:30 ESV; see also KJV, NASB, NIV, NRSV). In our reading, this saying would refer not to the generation that sees the beginning of birth pains or the destruction of the Temple, but to the one that sees the signs in the heavens. CJB resolves this issue by translating "this generation" as "this people." This is a plausible, but questionable, rendering of the underlying Greek word, *genea*, which generally means "generation" in the ordinary, time-related sense. The generation that sees the heavenly signs "in those days, after that trouble," will surely see the Son of Man coming in the clouds with great power and glory.[12] But difficult—and puzzling—times will come first, and so Yeshua ends by repeating his admonition three times (13:33, 35, 37), not just to the talmidim of his day, but to all: "Stay alert!"

---

12. France 494–546 provides a coherent interpretation of Mark 13 that doesn't see it as speaking of the *parousia*, or return of Messiah, at all. In this reading, "this generation" is literally the generation that Yeshua addresses at the time, which will see the destruction of the Temple and the reign of the Son of Man in the historic events that follow. He acknowledges that this is a "minority view" among commentators on Mark (France, 500).

Derash

- The Talmud, in Sanhedrin 97–98, records extensive discussions about the timing and conditions of the coming of Messiah, often picturing a period of conflict and decline (not unlike Mark 13:6–8) leading up to it. Accordingly, some of the rabbis in these discussions express a wish *not* to see the Messiah's coming because of all that precedes it.

    And so too **Rabbi Yoḥanan said: Let** the Messiah **come, but** after my death, so that **I will not see him. Reish Lakish said to him: What is the reason** that you are concerned? [Reish Lakish goes on to suggest some possible reasons, and Rabbi Yoḥanan responds:] **Rather,** the reason I am concerned is **that it is written** with regard to the day of God: **"Ask now, and see whether a man gives birth. Why, then, do I see every man with his hands on his loins, as a woman in labor, and all faces turned green?"** (Jeremiah 30:6).[13]

    This language, of course, echoes the "birth pains" phraseology of Mark 13, and the idea that Messiah's coming (or return) will inevitably be preceded by a time of great trial. Another Talmudic passage, Shabbat 118a, mentions the "pangs of Messiah" that precede his arrival. This imagery may help us understand the times we live in today, but the discussion in tractate Sanhedrin discourages speculation about the timing:

    Rabbi Yonatan says: May those who calculate the end of days be cursed, as they would say once the end of days that they calculated **arrived and** the Messiah **did not come,** that **he will no longer come** at all. **Rather,** the proper behavior is to continue to **wait for his** coming, **as it is**

---

13. *Sanhedrin* 98b. Both citations from the Talmud in this section are from Sefaria.com: *The William Davidson Talmud* (Koren - Steinsaltz). Wording in bold is the translation itself, with the regular font indicating explanatory words added.

> stated: **"Though it tarry, wait for it."** Lest you say we are expectantly **awaiting** the end of days **and** the Holy One, Blessed be He, **is not awaiting** the end of days and does not want to redeem His people, **the verse states: "And therefore will the Lord wait, to be gracious to you; and therefore will He be exalted, to have mercy upon you;** for the Lord is a God of judgment; happy are all they who wait for Him" (Isaiah 30:18).[14]

Again, the resonance with Yeshua's instructions is striking—"Stay alert! Be on your guard! For you do not know when the time will come" (Mark 13:33). We might consider how these texts help us avoid the sort of end-times speculation that is rampant in some parts of today's religious scene, and how they can help us understand—and remain faithful through—the times we live in.

- Joel Marcus comments on the unusual phrase in Mark 13:27, "from the ends of the earth to the ends of heaven," noting that it's possible that . . .

  > Mark would interpret it as implying a distinction between the elect gathered "from the end of the earth" = those still alive at the parousia and the elect gathered "from the end of heaven" = those already dead when Jesus returns. Cf. *1 En.* 39:3–7, where the abode of the sainted dead, "the righteous and elect," is "at the ends of heaven" (cf. 70:1–4). Mark 13:27, then, may picture something like 1 Thess. 4:15–17: Christ descends from heaven, both living and deceased believers rise to meet him, and subsequently both groups are forever "with the Lord" in the air.[15]

After describing this apocalyptic scene to his Thessalonian brothers and sisters, Paul exhorts them to "encourage each other with these words" (1 Thess. 4:18). He's writing at

---

14. Sanhedrin 97b.
15. Marcus, *Mark 8–16*, 905.

about the same time as Mark, but there seems to be a different bottom line here: encourage each other vs stay alert! But perhaps these two admonitions aren't so different. Maintaining a lively hope in Messiah's return, even if lengthy and difficult times intervene, may be essential to keeping watch for his return. Perhaps hope and vigilance reinforce each other. And both provide direction for Yeshua-followers of the 21st century, who have been waiting long enough that we might grow discouraged (lacking hope) or complacent (not staying alert). Instead, we can practice hopeful vigilance, confident that Messiah will come in the timing that the Father determines.

Season 3, Episode 4 (18)

The Last Passover

14:1–42

Overview

Our episode opens two days before Passover, with the religious authorities seeking a way to arrest Yeshua ahead of the festival to avoid provoking a riot among the crowds.[1] Before Mark reveals the outcome of that plot, though, he shifts the focus to a home in Beit-Anyah, just outside Jerusalem, where Yeshua is dining. A woman approaches him with an alabaster jar of costly ointment, breaks the jar, and pours the ointment over Yeshua's head. Some of those gathered there scold the woman for her extravagance, which they see as wasteful, but Yeshua praises her for her devotion to him, saying she has anointed his body for burial, and her deed will be retold wherever the Good News is proclaimed. Then Y'hudah (Judas) departs and strikes a deal with the head priests to turn Yeshua over to them at the right time.

To prepare for Passover, Yeshua sends two of his followers back into Jerusalem and tells them they will be met by a man carrying a water-jar who will lead them to a large, upstairs room furnished and ready, where they can prepare the Passover meal. Later, after Yeshua arrives there with the Twelve, he tells them that one of them will betray him. They are shocked, and Yeshua says the Son of Man must die as the Tanakh foretells, but woe to the one who betrays him. As

---

[1]. In the Jewish world of Yeshua's day, like today, "Passover" referred to the two holidays of Leviticus 23:5, 6–8 that were "combined into one festival with sacrifice of the paschal [Passover] lamb and the eating of Unleavened Bread during the seven days following" (Wills, "Mark," JANT, 98). This commentary follows the same usage.

they are eating, he takes the matzah, the unleavened bread of Passover, recites the blessing over it, breaks it, and gives it to those with him, saying, "Take it! This is my body." In the same way, he takes the traditional cup of wine, pronounces the blessing, and gives it to his talmidim to share, telling them it is his blood of the covenant, "shed on behalf of many people." Afterwards, the whole group sings from the Hallel (Psalms 113–119), as was (and still is) customary for Passover.

After the meal, they go out again to the Mount of Olives, where Yeshua adds to his announcement of betrayal a notice that they will all desert him when he is struck down. But, he tells them, he will be raised up, and will go ahead of them back to the Galil. Kefa (Peter) insists that he will never desert him, even if all the others do, and that he is ready even to die with him. But Yeshua forewarns him that before the cock crows twice to welcome a new day, Kefa will deny him three times.

The band continues on to a nearby place called Gat Sh'manim, "Oil Press," where Yeshua takes Kefa, Yochanan, and Yaakov a little further with him and asks them to watch with him as he prays. He goes off to pray in great distress and anguish, asking the Father to take the cup of suffering and death from him, if it is possible, but also accepting whatever must come. Yeshua returns three times to the three talmidim and finds them sleeping instead of keeping watch, and finally says, "Enough!" The time of his betrayal has arrived, and the betrayer is approaching.

Peshat

14:1–11

> [1] It was now two days before *Pesach* (that is, the festival of *Matzah*), and the head *cohanim* and the *Torah*-teachers were trying to find some way to arrest Yeshua surreptitiously and have him put to death; [2] for they said, "Not during the festival, or the people will riot."

³ While he was in Beit-Anyah in the home of Shim'on (a man who had had *tzara'at*), and as he was eating, a woman came with an alabaster jar of perfume, pure oil of nard, very costly. She broke the jar and poured the perfume over Yeshua's head. ⁴ But some there angrily said to themselves, "Why this waste of perfume? ⁵ It could have been sold for a year's wages and given to the poor!" And they scolded her. ⁶ But he said, "Let her be. Why are you bothering her? She has done a beautiful thing for me. ⁷ For you will always have the poor with you; and whenever you want to, you can help them. But you will not always have me. ⁸ What she could do, she did do — in advance she poured perfume on my body to prepare it for burial. ⁹ Yes! I tell you that wherever in the whole world this Good News is proclaimed, what she has done will be told in her memory."

¹⁰ Then Y'hudah from K'riot, who was one of the Twelve, went to the head *cohanim* in order to betray Yeshua to them. ¹¹ They were pleased to hear this and promised to give him money. And he began looking for a good opportunity to betray Yeshua.

Yeshua has repeatedly told his followers what is awaiting him in Jerusalem, including betrayal (8:31; 9:31; 10:33). Now, in a striking use of the intercalation or sandwich technique, Mark sets the stage for that betrayal. Our episode opens two days before Passover, with the authorities looking for a way to arrest Yeshua in secret and have him put to death before the holy day, to avoid inciting a riot among the crowds, which, as we're reminded again, are largely favorable to Yeshua. This is the first layer of the sandwich. Then the focus shifts to the home of Shim'on (a man who had had *tzara'at*, or so-called "leprosy") in Beit-Anyah just outside the holy city. As Yeshua is dining there, an unnamed woman approaches him with a flask of ointment, "pure oil of nard, very costly," which she pours out on Yeshua's head. Some of those dining with Yeshua criticize the woman and her "waste" of this valuable resource, but Yeshua defends her, saying that she has anointed him for burial, and that her act of devotion will be remembered wherever the Good News is proclaimed. That's the second level of the sandwich, and the third level tells of Y'hudah going to the priests with his offer to betray Yeshua when the time is right.

As always, the sandwich technique adds depth to the story. It suggests a contrast between the laudable devotion of the woman—who, like another unnamed woman gave extravagantly, "everything she had to live on," in devotion to God (12:44)—and Y'hudah, who accepted an offer of money in exchange for betraying Yeshua.

The sandwich here also provides insight into Y'hudah's motivation. The woman pours oil on Yeshua's head as a token of her devotion to him, but this anointing also points to Yeshua's status as the Anointed One (the meaning of "Messiah" in Hebrew). A few days earlier, on his way up to Jerusalem, Yeshua had already responded to an appeal to him as "Son of David" (Mark 10:47–52), a messianic title. Shortly afterwards, he underscored his status as Messiah when he rode into Jerusalem on a donkey, fulfilling the prophecy of Zechariah 9:9, and accepted the adulation of the crowds as they called out, "Blessed is he who comes in the name of ADONAI" (Mark 11:9–10; Psa. 118:25–26)—a greeting fit for a king. And then he entered the Temple courts and drove out those doing business there, implying the sort of authority one would expect of the Messiah (Mark 11:15–17, 27–33; see this commentary on those verses).

The notion of Yeshua as Messiah is in the air, but, like David's anointing as king in 1 Samuel 16, this anointing in Beit-Anyah is outside the public eye, in a private home with just a small group present. Like his ancestor David, who is publicly recognized as king only after a number of years (2 Sam. 2:4), Yeshua must be for a time a king in secret. So, instead of simply accepting this symbolic anointing and affirming that he's the Messiah—who is expected to show up at Passover—Yeshua defines this anointing as part of his preparation for burial. The custom at the time was to cleanse the body after death, anoint it with fragrant oil and spices to preserve its dignity (by ensuring that it didn't smell) through the process of burial, and wrap it in a shroud. So, does the anointing in the house of Shim'on signify Messiahship or impending burial? "Mark's principle of irony would suggest both."[2] Instead of taking charge at this critical moment as Messiah, the Anointed One, Yeshua reaffirms that he must die first.

After this, Mark shifts the focus onto Y'hudah, who goes to the chief priests to betray Yeshua. It may be that hearing Yeshua talk again about his death at this critical moment is the last straw for him. He wants Yeshua to bring immediate liberation from Rome and restore the kingdom of David—and instead he's going to allow himself to be crucified!

In the middle section of this sandwich, Yeshua doesn't just defend the woman who anoints him, but he says "wherever in the whole world this Good News is proclaimed, what she has done will be told in her memory" (14:9). This saying is striking for two reasons. First, it reveals that "this Good News," introduced within the local setting of the Galil (Mark 1:1, 14–15), will be told throughout the whole world, far beyond the Jewish setting of Mark's account. Second, it leaves the woman nameless, which is odd since what she has done will be declared everywhere. Elijah Zvi Soloveitchik heightens the paradox when he interprets "in her memory," or "as a memorial to her," to mean, "Everywhere that my name is mentioned with honor . . . the name of this woman will also be cited for praise."[3] But we don't know her name! Irony is again at play here—the named and well-known twelve talmidim still don't grasp what Yeshua is all about, but this anonymous woman does. In addition, Mark may be employing "protective anonymity," leaving her unnamed because she was still alive at the time of his writing and would have been in danger of arrest for sedition if he revealed her identity.[4]

---

2. Wills, "Mark," JANT, 99.
3. Soloveitchik, 375.
4. Bauckham 190–94. Bauckham cites Gerd Theissen as the source of the category of "protective anonymity."

Shim'on the homeowner, in contrast, is identified by name. Shim'on is a very common name among Jewish men of the time, which explains why he needs the nickname, "the Leper," as in most translations. The CJB treats this not as a nickname, but as a parenthetical remark "(a man who had had *tzara'at*)." Either way, Mark's first readers might think, "Oh, *that* Shim'on." Apparently, he was a figure known to Mark's original audience, and hosting a meal where something subversive happened is not as culpable as actually performing the subversive deed—namely, anointing Yeshua just before Passover—so he is named to identify the specific setting. Once again the eyewitness nature and the early dating of Mark's account shine through, as does the drama of the moment:

> We should surely understand that Judas reports the incident of the anointing to the chief priests, for whom it must constitute significant evidence that Jesus and his disciples are planning an imminent messianic uprising. Perhaps we should also suspect that it was this incident—with its unavoidable confirmation by Jesus that he will undertake the messianic role only on his own terms as a vocation to die—that led Judas to defect. Thus the anointing provides both added cause for the chief priests to take swift action against Jesus and also the means to do so in the shape of Judas's offer.[5]

As Passover arrives, the stage is set for the culminating scenes of Mark's account, the betrayal, arrest, crucifixion, and resurrection that Yeshua has repeatedly foretold, and which must come to pass according to the prophetic plan.

14:12–31

> [12] On the first day for matzah, when they slaughtered the lamb for Pesach, Yeshua's *talmidim* asked him, "Where do you want us to go and prepare your Seder?" [13] He sent two of his *talmidim* with these instructions: "Go into the city, and a man carrying a jar of water will meet you. Follow him; [14] and whichever house he enters,

---

5. Bauckham 192–93.

tell him that the Rabbi says, 'Where is the guest room for me, where I am to eat the Pesach meal with my *talmidim*?' [15] He will show you a large room upstairs, furnished and ready. Make the preparations there." [16] The *talmidim* went off, came to the city and found things just as he had told them they would be; and they prepared the Seder.

[17] When evening came, Yeshua arrived with the Twelve. [18] As they were reclining and eating, Yeshua said, "Yes! I tell you that one of you is going to betray me." [19] They became upset and began asking him, one after the other, "You don't mean me, do you?" [20] "It's one of the Twelve," he said to them, "someone dipping matzah in the dish with me. [21] For the Son of Man will die, just as the Tanakh says he will; but woe to that man by whom the Son of Man is betrayed! It would have been better for him had he never been born!"

[22] While they were eating, Yeshua took a piece of matzah, made the *b'rakhah*, broke it, gave it to them and said, "Take it! This is my body." [23] Also he took a cup of wine, made the *b'rakhah*, and gave it to them; and they all drank. [24] He said to them, "This is my blood, which ratifies the New Covenant, my blood shed on behalf of many people. [25] Yes! I tell you, I will not drink this 'fruit of the vine' again until the day I drink new wine in the Kingdom of God."

[26] After singing the *Hallel*, they went out to the Mount of Olives. [27] Yeshua said to them, "You will all lose faith in me, for the Tanakh says,

'I will strike the shepherd dead,
and the sheep will be scattered.'

[28] But after I have been raised, I will go ahead of you into the Galil." [29] Kefa said to him, "Even if everyone else loses faith in you, I won't." [30] Yeshua replied, "Yes! I tell you that this very night, before the rooster crows twice, you will disown me three times!" [31] But Kefa kept insisting, "Even if I must die with you, I will never disown you!" And they all said the same thing.

Before we consider the details of this scene, we encounter the question of its timing. Broadly speaking, we are in the season of Passover, which includes the days of preparation leading up to the festival itself. "On the first day for matzah" here is not day one of the festival of matzah (and the word for "festival" doesn't appear at all in the Greek text); rather, it is the day on which *chametz*, leaven or the opposite of matzah, is removed from the home. Mark's language parallels Exodus 12:15a: "For seven days you are to eat matzah—on the first day remove the leaven from your houses." If one is to eat matzah for seven days, all leaven must be removed the day *before*, and so Rashi comments on the "first day" in this verse, **"It is called 'the first' because it precedes the seven** days of the festival itself." He goes on to cite a similar use of "first" in Job 15:7, and an additional basis for his interpretation in Exodus 34:25: **"do not slaughter over** *chametz*, **etc."**; which means – **"Do not slaughter the [Passover offering] while** *chametz* **still exists in your possession."** As this edition of Rashi notes:

> This verse clearly states that your *chametz* should no longer be in existence at the time of the slaughtering of the sacrifice after the noon of the fourteenth of Nissan which is on the eve of the festival. Therefore, there is no *chametz* left to eliminate by the first day of the festival – the next day, the fifteenth of Nissan.[6]

All of this supports Mark's wording in 14:12, "the first day for matzah, when they slaughtered the lamb for Pesach," which points to the fourteenth day of Nissan. The festival of Passover itself begins after sundown, that is, at the beginning of the fifteenth day of Nissan. Therefore, apparently, Yeshua will be arrested during the festival, not beforehand, as the authorities had hoped at the beginning of our episode. This chronology has fueled a vast discussion among commentators, especially those seeking to

---

6. *Rashi: The Saperstein Edition, Exodus*, ed. Rabbi Yisrael Isser Zvi Herczeg (Brooklyn: Mesorah, 1997), 118. Text in bold indicates Rashi's actual wording, with explanatory phrases in regular font.

reconcile the account of Mark (as well as Matthew and Luke) with John's Besorah, which places the betrayal and crucifixion on the day before Passover, that is, at the same time as the Passover lambs are being offered, not on Passover itself (John 18:28; 9:14, 31). Resolving this issue is beyond the scope of this commentary with its focus on Mark itself. Following France and Brown, however, we'll consider the possibility that Yeshua held this final Passover meal a day early, on the evening that began Nissan 14, because he knew that he would be crucified later that day, that is, the following morning, and wanted to have this final, prophetic meal with his followers before that took place.[7] This view has some advantages, including:

- It syncs with the authorities' intention to arrest Yeshua "not during the festival" (Mark 14:2).

- It helps resolve the question of the Jewish authorities convening and holding a trial, and supporting a public execution at the hands of Rome, on the first day of Passover (Mark 14:53ff.).

- It helps resolve the discrepancy with the account in John, which appears to have Yeshua dying on the same day as the Passover lamb.

- It aligns with a tradition recorded in the Babylonian Talmud, *Sanhedrin* 43a, that Yeshua was killed on the eve of Passover, that is, on the day before Passover began. The Talmud, of course, was put into writing much later than the events in Mark (fifth-sixth centuries CE), but contains much older oral material, and this particular item is presented as something that has been taught or handed down.

---

7. France, 559–564; Raymond E. Brown, *The Death of the Messiah* (New York: Anchor, 1993), 1361–73, offers a detailed overview of different views on this issue and concludes, "Thus there are solid reasons for judging as historical that Jesus died on Thn/Fd [Thursday night-Friday], the 14th of Nisan, the day on which paschal lambs were sacrificed, and the eve of the 15th of Nisan on which the paschal meal would be eaten."

Nonetheless, we can't be dogmatic on this issue and it is clear that Yeshua's final supper is a Passover meal, with deep Passover imagery, whether it was held on the usual date or a day early. The meaning of Passover in those days is also clear. Passover is held in the first month, the month of Aviv, or springtime (Exod. 12:2–3, 23:15; Deut. 16:1), making it the first of the pilgrimage festivals, when all the men of Israel, representing all their households, went up to Jerusalem to worship ADONAI (Exod. 23:17; Deut. 16:16–17). Going up to Jerusalem was a privilege and blessing, and the atmosphere in the city during Passover was one of great joy. By Yeshua's time, Passover had also become a festival of expectation. At some point it became known as *Zeman Cherutenu*, the Season of Our Freedom or Deliverance—a time to not only remember redemption past but also to look forward to redemption to come: "In that season we were redeemed and in that season we shall be redeemed."[8] This expectancy is bolstered by the description of Passover as a night of vigil, or keeping watch (Exod. 12:42).[9]

Returning to Mark's narrative, it was in the midst of just such an atmosphere of joy and expectancy that Yeshua sent two of his talmidim back to Jerusalem (since they'd been spending their nights outside the holy city) to prepare for the feast itself. When they enter the city, they'll be met by a man carrying a water jar who will lead them to a place "furnished and ready," where they can prepare for the feast. This scene is a strikingly similar to the one a few days earlier, when Yeshua sent two talmidim into a village where they spent their nights, probably the same Beit-Anyah where he was anointed, (Mark 11:11; Matt. 21:17), to procure a donkey colt for his

---

8. Mekhilta, a midrashic commentary on the halakhic aspects of Exodus possibly as early as the third century CE.

9. CJB has Exod. 12:42 as "a night when ADONAI kept vigil," which "continues to be a night when *ADONAI* keeps vigil," supporting the past and future implications of the verse—keeping vigil for redemption to come. ESV exemplifies a more typical translation: "It was a night of watching by the LORD, to bring them out of the land of Egypt; so this same night is a night of watching kept to the LORD by all the people of Israel throughout their generations." Most modern translations are similar to this.

ride into Jerusalem. Both events are either pre-arranged or foreseen in great detail, and both involve key moments in the unfolding revelation of who Yeshua is and what he has come to do. In Mark 11, Yeshua presents himself as the king riding on a donkey, foretold in Zechariah 9:9. Now, Yeshua continues to reveal his identity in even greater depth.

As the meal begins, Yeshua tells the Twelve "that one of you is going to betray me" (14:18). The reader is prepared for this announcement, and has even learned the identity of the betrayer, but the Twelve are shocked and openly question who it could possibly be. But the betrayer won't be revealed to them until later, when Yeshua announces his approach in the garden of Gat Sh'manim (14:32). For now, the meal continues, and after some preliminaries—perhaps the blessing and eating of the *karpas,* or green herb, dipped in salt water as in the traditional Seder—Yeshua takes up the matzah, which, along with the Passover lamb and bitter herbs, is an iconic food of Passover, a symbol of the entire Festival. Yeshua recites the blessing over the matzah, breaks it, and passes it among his disciples, with words that likely shocked them again—"This is my body" (14:22). Yeshua embodies in himself the story of redemption and, by offering up his body, as he is now enacting in advance, will bring that redemption to pass.

The Passover Seder (or whatever elements of it are already in place in Yeshua's time) is a response to the command to "remember" the deliverance from Egypt (Exod. 12:13, 13:3; Deut. 16:3). And remembrance in Scripture is not just a function of the individual mind, but of the whole community, reliving past events in the present day, as the Haggadah declares:

> In every generation one must see oneself as though having personally come forth from Egypt, as it is written: "And you shall tell your child on that day, 'This is done because of what the Lord did for me when I came forth from Egypt'" [Exod. 13:8]. It was not our ancestors alone whom the Holy One, blessed be He, redeemed; He redeemed us too, with them, as it is written: "He

brought us out from there that He might lead us to, and give us, the land which He promised to our ancestors" [Deut. 6:23].[10]

Yeshua brings this remembrance to life by stepping into the midst of it and offering himself, bodily, as God's means of deliverance. From there, Yeshua simply moves on to recite the blessing over the wine and distribute it to his followers. We are so familiar with the account of what's become known as the Last Supper that we might forget that wine is not part of the instructions for the Passover meal given in Exodus. Rather, it is an element added by custom, which became codified in the Mishnah (ca. 200 CE), by which time four cups of wine were mandatory.

> **And** the distributors of charity should **not give** a poor person **less than four cups of wine** for the Festival meal of Passover night. **And** this *halakha* applies **even** if the poor person is one of the poorest members of society and receives his food **from the charity plate.**[11]

Wine is often a symbol of joy in the Tanakh, and the joy of Passover, time of our redemption, is so great that it merits—or rather, requires—four cups. The fact that this requirement was so firmly established by 200 CE, suggests that it may well have been in place as early as Yeshua's time. In any event, Yeshua takes the cup (Mark doesn't tell us which of the four it is), recites the traditional blessing, and gives it to his talmidim to drink. And then he adds—doubtless shocking them again—"This is my blood, which ratifies the New Covenant, my blood shed on behalf of many people" (14:24). The original Greek here is much simpler, as in ESV: "This is my blood of the covenant, which is poured out for many." (The word "new" is inserted before "covenant" in some manuscripts.) The reference to "many" here links this verse to Mark 10:45, and from there back to

---

10. *Passover Haggadah Revised Edition,* Trans. Rabbi Nathan Goldberg (Hoboken, NJ: Ktav, 1993). This element of the Haggadah is based on Mishnah Pesachim 10:5,
11. M. Pesachim 10:1, Koren-Steinsaltz edition
(https://www.sefaria.org/Mishnah_Pesachim.10?lang=en).

Isaiah 53:10–12, as we discussed back in Season 2, Episode 5 (pp. 218-220). The shed blood, like the broken matzah/body of the preceding verse, hints at death and sacrifice. Before the talmidim have time to ponder these words and their ominous implications, however, Yeshua adds a note of hope: "Yes! I tell you, I will not drink this 'fruit of the vine' again until the day I drink new wine in the Kingdom of God" (14:25). Passover celebrates both redemption past and redemption to come, when the Kingdom of God will be present in its fullness, when *ADONAI-Tzva'ot*

> will make for all peoples
> a feast of rich food and superb wines,
> delicious, rich food and superb, elegant wines. (Isa. 25:6)[12]

Yeshua and his friends conclude the Passover meal by singing "a hymn," as in most translations, or singing the *Hallel*, according to the CJB. *Hallel* means "Praise," and refers to Psalms 113–118, with their theme of praise, which are traditionally chanted during the three pilgrimage festivals, as well as other joyous holidays. As with other details of Yeshua's Passover meal, we don't know whether this tradition dates all the way back to that time, but it's not at all unlikely. Reciting the Hallel is mentioned in Mishnah Pesachim 10.6 as a traditional practice at the Seder. From there, Yeshua and his band go out to the Mount of Olives, a normal way of departure from Jerusalem, but also, as we saw in our last episode, a place of prophetic significance, and the route of David's departure from Jerusalem when he was temporarily deposed by Absalom. There Yeshua warns his talmidim that he is about to be struck dead, and they will all lose faith and be scattered. Kefa responds, "Even if everyone else loses faith in you, I won't" (14:29), but Yeshua tells him that on that very night, before the rooster crows twice, he will

---

12. France, 572, notes that the wine here is literally "well aged and mature," but "the frequent references to 'new wine' . . . in the OT show that it was understood to be a sign of prosperity and good living," and one of the Dead Sea Scrolls "specifically mentions the drinking of [new wine] in the presence of the Messiah."

"disown" him three times. Disowning or denying Yeshua is perhaps not as dire as betraying him, but only one talmid betrays Yeshua, whereas they all are about to desert him.

14:32–42

> ³² They went to a place called Gat Sh'manim; and Yeshua said to his *talmidim*, "Sit here while I pray." ³³ He took with him Kefa, Ya'akov and Yochanan. Great distress and anguish came over him; ³⁴ and he said to them, "My heart is so filled with sadness that I could die! Remain here and stay awake." ³⁵ Going on a little farther, he fell on the ground and prayed that if possible, the hour might pass from him: ³⁶ "*Abba!*" (that is, "Dear Father!") "All things are possible for you. Take this cup away from me! Still, not what I want, but what you want." ³⁷ He came and found them sleeping; and he said to Kefa, "Shim'on, are you asleep? Couldn't you stay awake one hour? ³⁸ Stay awake, and pray that you will not be put to the test — the spirit indeed is eager, but human nature is weak."
>
> ³⁹ Again he went away and prayed, saying the same words; ⁴⁰ and again he came and found them sleeping, their eyes were so very heavy; and they didn't know what to answer him.
>
> ⁴¹ The third time, he came and said to them, "For now, go on sleeping, take your rest. . . .There, that's enough! The time has come! Look! The Son of Man is being betrayed into the hands of sinners! ⁴² Get up! Let's go! Here comes my betrayer!"

For Yeshua and his talmidim, the traditional night of watching for redemption has become a night of watching for the great distress that must come before redemption. Yeshua's humanity is most evident here in Gat Sh'manim—the "Oil Press" on the Mount of Olives—as he enlists his three closest followers to keep watch with him, saying, "My heart is so filled with sadness that I could die!" (14:34). Yeshua's prayer itself also arises from his humanity and vulnerability, as he first pleads with his Father—"Abba" in the original—to spare him the cup of suffering he is about to drink, and then submits to the Father's will over his own. Addressing God as Father is not unique to Yeshua; it echoes language in Torah and the Prophets, like Deuteronomy 32:6, Isaiah 63:16 and 64:7, Jeremiah 31:8 [9]; and Malachi 1:6. In the Psalms, the anointed heir of David is portrayed as crying out to God, "You are my father [*avi*], my God, the Rock of my salvation" (89:27 [26]). Still, the appearance here of the Aramaic "Abba" is striking, and there's no evidence of its use as a personal, individual address for God in other Jewish sources of the period.[13] It's a distinctive quality of Yeshua's prayer, reflecting his near relationship with the Father, which Paul echoes in Galatians 4:6 and Romans 8:15.

Yeshua asked his closest talmidim to "stay awake" nearby during this time of intensive prayer, employing the same word that he used at the end of his description of the end times, translated "stay alert" in CJB, where it appears three times in 13:34–37. Likewise the same original Greek word is repeated three times in 14:34–38, where the talmidim, most notably Kefa, fail to stay awake. Yeshua returns three times to find them sleeping and the reader might wonder, if the talmidim cannot keep watch with their master for one night of prayer, how will they manage to keep watch during the trying times that lie ahead at the end of the age? The language of these two scenes also provides a contrast. In Mark 13 Yeshua exhorts his followers, "Stay alert! Be on your guard! For you do not know when the time will come" (13:33). They are to watch *for him* and his coming. Now he calls his closest followers to watch *with him* as he seeks God in prayer.

Yeshua concludes his prayers and his admonitions of Kefa, Ya'akov and Yochanan with the announcement that the time has come. "Get up! Let's go! Here comes my betrayer!" (14:42). The theme of betrayal serves to bookend our entire episode, from Y'hudah's offer just before Passover (14:10) to his completion of the deal now after Yeshua's final supper. The theme of betrayal

---

13. Brown, 172–73.

intensifies the portrayal of Yeshua's trial. He is about to undergo suffering so great that he begs the father to take it from him, and he is handed over to this suffering by one of his closest followers. The betrayal theme also serves as a link between David, the anointed king, and Yeshua the Son of David. David endured betrayal multiple times, including Saul's turning against him (2 Sam. 18:8–11; 19:1), and the rebellion of Absalom his favored son (2 Sam. 15:7–10), in which David's counselor Ahithophel colluded (2 Sam. 15:12, 31). David captured such experiences in several Psalms, perhaps most notably 41:10 [9]. "Even my close friend, on whom I relied, / who shared my table, has turned against me." (See also Psa. 35:11–16). If Yeshua is anointed as Son of David, and receives public accolades as the Son of David, he also experiences betrayal as David did, at the hands of those he loved. This betrayal opens the way for Yeshua's arrest, his trials before the Jewish council and the Roman governor, and the death sentence that follows, as we approach our final two episodes.

Derash

- In the Torah (Exod. 12:3, 46) Moses instructs Israel that each household is to sacrifice a lamb on Passover and consume it together. This teaching leads to the traditional observance of the Passover meal house by house, with the father officiating as head of the household. Jewish tradition adds another teaching, that the household is to be especially open to guests and visitors on Passover. According to Jewish custom, at the beginning of the Seder, those who are about to celebrate the Passover story recite together, "All who are hungry—let them come and eat! All who are needy—let them come and celebrate the Passover with us!"

    Yeshua institutes a new household within Israel, made up of those who follow him, and held together by the power of his shared life. His final Passover meal reflects the traditional sense of invitation, as he passes the matzah to his followers after the blessing and says, "Take it! This is my body"

(14:22). Likewise with the cup, which he takes and gives to his followers so that all can drink of it (14:23–24). As usual, Mark is sparing of words. There is only an implicit invitation with the cup, which is expanded in the other Gospels: "All of you, drink from it! For this is my blood, which ratifies the New Covenant, my blood shed on behalf of many, so that they may have their sins forgiven" (Matt. 26:27–28).

In the traditional Seder, we tell the story of Passover over the matzah and the cup, then we say the blessings and partake of each, thereby partaking of the whole story along with the blessing itself. Building on this venerable tradition, Yeshua invites those who follow him to partake of him, not as a replacement of Passover, but as the heart of the Passover story. Because he is risen, his followers form a new household within Israel, displaying his life and inviting all Israel, as well as a remnant from the nations, to partake as well.

- Readers of various perspectives have been fascinated with the figure of Judas. And some have sought to soften the picture of Judas by imagining that he was somehow cooperating with Yeshua who, after all, needed to die to accomplish his mission. But Dante places Judas in the ninth and lowest circle of his Inferno, the place of eternal punishment for betrayal. In the Gospel narratives, Y'hudah/Judas emerges as a real person, not just a symbol of evil. Reading Mark's account, we can imagine Judas as a disillusioned follower. He started out as one of the Twelve, one of those whom Yeshua wanted, who came to him, and who were sent out to preach and have authority over demonic forces (3:13–15). But from there, whether gradually or all at once, Judas goes over to the dark side. Luke, writing some years later, reveals that Satan entered into Judas just before he went to the authorities, apparently empowering him to do his evil deed. And John, another 10–20 years after that (but still in the first century), adds that Judas kept the moneybag for Yeshua's band of followers and was a thief, motivated at least in part by the reward offered for betraying Yeshua (and probably upset about the "waste" of a valuable commodity by the woman who anointed Yeshua).

If discipleship is one of the key themes of Mark, we might consider what lessons in discipleship we can gain from the tragic tale of Y'hudah.

- Yeshua's Seder ends with "singing the *Hallel*," Psalms, 113–118, as is the custom to this day, mentioned, as we've noted above, in the Mishnah, Pesachim 10.6. Joel Marcus comments:

  > These psalms are peculiarly appropriate in the present context, since they speak of the righteous person feeling the tug of the underworld, falling into distress and sorrow, and calling on God to save his life (116:3–4; cf. Mark 14:32–42). Yet they also promise that the death of the Lord's faithful ones is precious in his sight, that the living rather than the dead will praise him (115:17–18), and that God will raise the lowly from the dust (113:7) and free them from death (116:8). Near its conclusion, the final Hallel psalm proclaims: "I shall not die but live, and declare the works of the Lord," because "the Lord . . . has not delivered me to death," and "the stone that the builders rejected has become the cornerstone" (118:17–18, 22–23; my trans.)—the last being words that the Markan Jesus quoted two chapters earlier in reference to his resurrection (Mark 12:10–11). The concluding psalms of the Passover seder, then, prefigure the story of suffering and triumph that is about to unfold.[14]

Suffering lies ahead for Yeshua, as even the Psalms of Praise recognize, but it's suffering that blazes the path to life and redemption. This pathway is the route of discipleship as expounded throughout Mark, and the example of the original disciples urges us to keep steadfastly to that pathway on our own journey to life with God.

---

14. Marcus, *Mark 8–16*, 971.

Season 3, Episode 5 (19)

Betrayal, Desertion, Arrest, and Trial

14:43–15:20

Overview

After Yeshua's agonized prayer in Gat Sh'manim, the events he has long foretold unfold in relentless progression. Y'hudah appears with a heavily armed cohort and identifies Yeshua with a kiss. As the men lay hands on Yeshua to lead him away, one of the talmidim tries to resist, striking the high priest's servant with his sword. But Yeshua doesn't offer any resistance and says that the Tanakh must be fulfilled. At that, all the talmidim desert him and run off, along with a mysterious young man who sheds his nightshirt to escape capture and runs away naked.

The armed crowd leads Yeshua to the cohen hagadol and a whole assembly of priests, Torah-teachers, and elders, who seek to find sufficient evidence for a death sentence. Various witnesses come forward to provide false testimony, including the accusation that Yeshua threatened to destroy the Temple and replace it with another one built without hands. The false testimonies do not agree, and when the cohen hagadol asks Yeshua to respond, he says nothing. Finally, the cohen hagadol asks Yeshua point-blank whether he is *Mashiach, Ben-HaM'vorakh*, Messiah the Son of the Blessed One. Yeshua responds that he is, and adds words from Daniel 7 and Psalm 110, "Moreover, you will see **the Son of Man sitting at the right hand of** *HaG'vurah* **and coming on the clouds of heaven**" (Mark 14:62). At this, the religious authorities declare Yeshua guilty of blasphemy and worthy of death, spitting at him and beating and mocking him.

While all this is going on, Kefa is in the courtyard outside, sitting with the guards and warming himself by a fire. One of the chief priest's serving girls sees Kefa and identifies him as one of Yeshua's followers, which he immediately denies. He goes out to the entryway and the girl accuses him again, so that he repeats his denial. Finally, some bystanders, alerted by Kefa's Galilean accent, accuse him of being "one of them," and he denies even knowing Yeshua at all. Immediately he hears a rooster crow for the second time, and remembers Yeshua's prediction of his denial. He throws himself to the ground and bursts into tears.

With the approach of morning, the cohen hagadol and his party decide to hand Yeshua over to Pilate, the Roman authority in Jerusalem, who had the power to sentence him to crucifixion. Pilate immediately asks Yeshua the question most relevant to Rome: "Are you the King of the Jews?" Yeshua acknowledges the charge and makes no further defense, even amidst multiple accusations by the head priests. Pilate had a custom of releasing one prisoner during the festival, and when the crowd reminded him of this practice, he offered to release Yeshua, whom he was convinced was innocent. Instead, the crowd asked for Bar-Abba, who had committed murder during a recent insurrection. When Pilate asked what they wanted done to Yeshua, the crowd cried out, "Crucify him—Put him to death on the stake!" Pilate complied, handing Yeshua over to his soldiers, who mocked him by dressing him in purple, weaving a crown of thorns for his head, and saluting him as King of the Jews. Then they hit him on the head with a stick, spat on him and kneeled in mock worship of him. Then they stripped him of the purple robe and led him away to the execution site.

Peshat

14:43-52

⁴³ While Yeshua was still speaking, Y'hudah (one of the Twelve!) came, and with him a crowd carrying swords and clubs, from the head *cohanim*, the *Torah*-teachers and the elders. ⁴⁴ The betrayer had arranged to give them a signal: "The man I kiss is the one you want. Grab him, and take him away under guard." ⁴⁵ As he arrived, he went right up to Yeshua, said, "Rabbi!" and kissed him. ⁴⁶ Then they laid hold of Yeshua and arrested him; ⁴⁷ but one of the people standing nearby drew his sword and struck at the servant of the *cohen hagadol*, cutting off his ear.

⁴⁸ Yeshua addressed them: "So you came out to take me with swords and clubs, the way you would the leader of a rebellion? ⁴⁹ Every day I was with you in the Temple court, teaching, and you didn't seize me then! But let the *Tanakh* be fulfilled." ⁵⁰ And they all deserted him and ran away. ⁵¹ There was one young man who did try to follow him; but he was wearing only a nightshirt; and when they tried to seize him, ⁵² he slipped out of the nightshirt and ran away naked.

Throughout the entire drama of arrest and desertion, Yeshua exudes a sense of calm and control. The drama begins when Y'hudah and his armed band break into Yeshua's final moments with his followers. The authorities had desired to arrest Yeshua in secret to avoid stirring up the festival multitudes in Jerusalem. This strategy required an insider, one who could lead their guards to where Yeshua would be at night, out of the eyes of the public, and in Y'hudah they found an ultimate insider—one of the Twelve! as in CJB. He identifies the Master with an intimate sign, the declaration "Rabbi!" and a kiss of greeting. Yeshua rebukes those coming to arrest him, making it clear that he is not trying to lead a rebellion, but that doesn't sway them. All is unfolding as he had already predicted, and as it must unfold so that the Scriptures may be fulfilled.

Yeshua's calm sense that this all must come to pass, however, doesn't get through to his followers. First, one of them takes up a sword and attacks the servant of the high priest. He is described as *the* servant, not just "a servant," and may have been leading the arresting party. The sword thrust is wild and cuts off his ear. Like the betrayer, this attacker is an insider, but unlike Y'hudah, he remains unnamed in Mark's account, which may be another indication of how close to the events it describes Mark's Besorah is. It was created early enough that its characters are still alive, and their behavior is still a current concern of the authorities, both Jewish and Roman, or it's at least early enough that it draws on the oral sources that reflect that crucial period. It's notable that when John tells the story decades later, he names both the servant, Malchus, and the attacker, none other than Kefa or Simon Peter (John 18:10). By John's time anonymity is no longer required, and Peter's misguided effort might explain why he is so fearful in the following scene as he sits in the courtyard of the same high priest whose servant (or slave) he attacked in Gat-Sh'manim.[1]

Before we get to that scene, however, we see all the talmidim running off when they realize that Yeshua is actually submitting to the arrest. Here Mark pictures another anonymous character, unique to his account, a young man wearing only a *sindon*, a linen cloth or "nightshirt" as in CJB. However we translate this Greek word, it is uncommon, and appears in only one other scene in Mark, when Yosef of Ramatayim, Joseph of Arimathea, purchases a "linen" sheet and wraps Yeshua's body in it for burial. Matthew and Luke mention the burial cloth but not the linen nightshirt abandoned by the young man.[2] It's another indication of the early, eyewitness nature of Mark's Besorah, and the young man who eluded arrest remains anonymous for his own protection. We'll explore the meaning of this cloth further in our next episode, but

---

1. Bauckham, 193–95.
2. Matthew 27:59 and Luke 23:53 both allude to the linen burial cloth and are the only other appearances of *sindon* in the entire NT.

for now it serves as an ominous hint of things to come. Just as Yeshua foretold, this arrest and the ensuing trial will result in his death and burial, symbolized by that same linen cloth. For now, whoever the young man might have been—and speculation abounds—he embodies the desertion of all Yeshua's followers, a shameful desertion that leaves them naked and vulnerable.

14:53–52

⁵³ They led Yeshua to the *cohen hagadol*, with whom all the head *cohanim*, elders and *Torah*-teachers were assembling. ⁵⁴ Kefa followed him at a distance right into the courtyard of the *cohen hagadol*, where he sat down with the guards and warmed himself by the fire.

⁵⁵ The head *cohanim* and the whole *Sanhedrin* tried to find evidence against Yeshua, so that they might have him put to death, but they couldn't find any. ⁵⁶ For many people gave false evidence against him, but their testimonies didn't agree. ⁵⁷ Some stood up and gave this false testimony: ⁵⁸ "We heard him say, 'I will destroy this Temple made with hands; and in three days I will build another one, not made with hands.'" ⁵⁹ Even so, their testimonies didn't agree.

⁶⁰ The *cohen hagadol* stood up in the front and asked Yeshua, "Have you nothing to say to the accusations these men are making?" ⁶¹ But he remained silent and made no reply. Again the *cohen hagadol* questioned him: "Are you the *Mashiach*, *Ben-HaM'vorakh*?" ⁶² "I AM," answered Yeshua. "Moreover, you will see **the Son of Man sitting at the right hand of** *HaG'vurah* **and coming on the clouds of heaven.**" ⁶³ At this, the *cohen hagadol* tore his clothes and said, "Why do we still need witnesses? ⁶⁴ You heard him blaspheme! What is your decision?" And they all declared him guilty and subject to the death penalty.

⁶⁵ Then some began spitting at him; and after blindfolding him, they started pounding him with their fists and saying to him, "Let's see you prophesy!" And as the guards took him, they beat him too.

The arresting party brings Yeshua to the high priest and a gathering of other priests, elders, and Torah-teachers, the same authorities that had recently challenged him after he cleansed the Temple (11:27). It's significant, then, that the specific charges that Mark records here concern the Temple. Under the Romans, the Jewish authorities may have been allowed to impose the death penalty in cases involving violations against the Temple, but did not have the power of capital punishment in other matters.[3] Or they may have been able to impose the death penalty in accord with the stipulations of Torah, but had to turn to the Roman authorities to actually carry it out.[4] It's also significant that, even though the Sanhedrin was seeking the death sentence throughout its proceedings, it did not accept what was obviously false testimony. When the various witnesses failed, the cohen hagadol shifted to a different issue, Yeshua's claim to Messiahship, and questioned him directly about that.

Before we consider Yeshua's response and its implications, the term "Sanhedrin" in this account deserves some consideration. The term has a distinctly Jewish—and often anti-Jewish—flavor but it can also carry a more neutral sense of an assembly of any sort. So it's not clear how formalized the "Sanhedrin" that heard the case against Yeshua was. Commentator Craig Evans notes that "the entire council," or the "whole Sanhedrin" as in CJB (Mark 14:55) doesn't necessarily mean a formal sitting of the Sanhedrin.

> What is probably meant is that several members of the Sanhedrin have convened at the home of Caiaphas and that most, perhaps all, of them were interested in seeking testimony against Jesus. The use of ὅλον, "entire," which is hyperbolic, may have been intended to underscore how fully Jesus' passion predictions had been

---

3. Schnabel, *Mark*, 373, citing Philo and Josephus.
4. Lane, *Mark*, 529–30, along with various other commentaries. In John 18:31 the high priest's party delivers Yeshua to Pilate, saying they don't have the power to put anyone to death, hoping that Pilate will order his execution. On the other hand, "Acts 7.58 – 60; 23.20; 25.9–11, 22, 30 imply that the Jews, and/or the Sanhedrin, did have the power to carry out a capital sentence, though these verses can be explained in other ways" (Adele Reinhartz, *The Gospel According to John*, JANT, 213fn.).

fulfilled.... If this gathering of priests and elders is recognized for what it is—an informal hearing designed to gain a consensus among Jewish authorities that Jesus should be handed over to the Romans with a capital recommendation—then objections that have been raised against its historicity on the grounds that the rules of capital trials have been violated (as laid down two centuries later in *m. Sanh.* 4–7) are quite beside the point.[5]

The text Evans cites, m. *Sanh.* 4–7, is Tractate Sanhedrin of the Mishnah, which covers laws for trying capital cases, a good number of which would have been violated in the trial of Yeshua. But Jewish life and practice of the Mishnaic period had changed in many ways since the time of Yeshua. We were able to gain some insights into Yeshua's last Passover based on tractate Pesachim in the Mishnah (see the discussion of Mark 14:12–31), but applying practices described in the Mishnah to invalidate details of Mark's Besorah written 150 years earlier is going too far. The sort of gathering Evans describes fits well with Mark's account and with what we know of the history of that time. This was not necessarily a kangaroo court. The authorities are seeking a death penalty for Yeshua, but they're not accepting false testimony, which is why the high priest finally asks Yeshua directly whether he is Messiah, knowing that the "wrong" answer could be construed as blasphemy. As it turns out, Yeshua, who has been sparing of words since his arrest, responds simply, "I am,"[6] but goes on to provide an expanded answer to this question, the "wrong" answer that seals his fate.

Yeshua says that he is the Messiah, son of the Blessed One, as the *cohen hagadol* puts it, and adds phrases that make clear what he means by this title. He will soon be revealed ("you will see...") as the Son of Man, the exalted figure from Daniel 7, seated at the right hand of the Mighty One, as described in Psalm 110:1, and coming on

---

5. Craig A. Evans, *Mark 8:27–16:20*, vol. 34B, Word Biblical Commentary (Dallas: Word, 2001), 444.
6. CJB puts this answer in caps, "I AM," to reflect its similarity to ADONAI's "I AM" in Exodus 3:13–14, but Yeshua's response may simply be a normal, although rather terse, way of answering the question, as in most translations. At any rate, a claim to be "I AM," as in Exodus is not added to the charge of blasphemy.

the clouds of heaven (Dan. 7:13). In this context "coming on the clouds" doesn't seem to refer to the Second Coming, Yeshua's return to the earth at the end of the age, but to his post-resurrection ascension to the heavenly throne. But, how is it that he can tell the high priest that he will *see* this? He may be referring to the evidence of his ascension through the outpouring of the Ruach, hinted at in 13:11 and described more fully in Acts 1:5 and 2:32–36. On the other hand, in Mark 13:26 Yeshua employs the same language from Daniel 7 to speak of his return at the end of the age: "Then they will see **the Son of Man coming in clouds** with tremendous power and glory." Standing before the high priest, he may again be referring to the coming day of judgment from heaven, when he comes "on the clouds." This day may not arrive in the lifetime of those now standing in judgment of Yeshua, but it will entail a revelation to all humankind of Yeshua as the supreme and enthroned judge, as a fulfilment of Isaiah 40:5, where "all flesh" will see the glory of ADONAI (see also Isa. 49:26, 66:23; Luke 3:6). In either case, within the earthy, eyewitness framework of Mark, Yeshua doesn't provide much detail about the heavenly realm or the culmination of this age, but what he does provide is clear: Yeshua claims the supreme authority of the Son of Man, who is given dominion over all "peoples, nations and languages," and "an eternal rulership that will not pass away" (Dan. 7:14).

This scene also reflects Mark's distinctive use of irony. Throughout his Besorah, Yeshua has not directly taken on the title of Messiah, and in fact has elicited it from his followers just once, with his probing question, "Who are people saying I am?" When Kefa answers correctly, "You are the *Mashiach*," Yeshua warns them not to tell anyone about him (Mark 8:27–30). Now, the Messiah title finally takes center stage and Yeshua fully owns it, but it has come on stage as evidence for the prosecution that will lead to Yeshua's death at the hands of Rome. Yeshua's disclosure of this exalted nature as Messiah is blasphemy on the face of it to the authorities questioning him. Ironically, he has finally let himself be revealed in full only to seal his own fate.

14:66–72

⁶⁶ Meanwhile, Kefa was still in the courtyard below. One of the serving-girls of the *cohen hagadol* ⁶⁷ saw Kefa warming himself, took a look at him, and said, "You were with the man from Natzeret, Yeshua!" ⁶⁸ But he denied it, saying, "I haven't the faintest idea what you're talking about!" He went outside into the entryway, and a rooster crowed. ⁶⁹ The girl saw him there and started telling the bystanders, "This fellow is one of them." ⁷⁰ Again he denied it. A little later, the bystanders themselves said to Kefa, "You must be one of them, because you're from the Galil." ⁷¹ At this he began to invoke a curse on himself as he swore, "I do not know this man you are telling me about!" — ⁷² and immediately the rooster crowed a second time. Then Kefa remembered what Yeshua had said to him, "Before the rooster crows twice, you will disown me three times." And throwing himself down, he burst into tears.

Before we move on to Yeshua's trial before Pilate, the scene shifts from the court of the high priest to the courtyard outside. Kefa has followed Yeshua at a distance to arrive in the courtyard, where he takes a seat and warms himself by the fire. A serving girl of the chief priest sees Kefa and identifies him as one of Yeshua's followers, which he immediately denies. He goes out from the courtyard and the girl accuses him again, so that he must repeat his denial. Finally, some other bystanders accuse him of being "one of them," and he denies even knowing Yeshua at all. Immediately the rooster crows for a second time. Kefa remembers Yeshua's prediction of his denial, throws himself to the ground, and begins to weep. He won't be mentioned again until after the resurrection, when the angel tells the women who have discovered the empty grave, "But go and tell his *talmidim*, especially Kefa, that he is going to the Galil ahead of you" (16:7). Kefa's collapse seems complete, and it typifies a failure to follow Yeshua that all other talmidim are to avoid. Yet Kefa will be forgiven and granted a place, even a pre-eminent place, among those who gather around the risen Messiah.

15:1–20

As soon as it was morning, the head *cohanim* held a council meeting with the elders, the *Torah*-teachers and the whole *Sanhedrin*. Then they put Yeshua in chains, led him away and handed him over to Pilate. ² Pilate put this question to him: "Are you the King of the Jews?" He answered him, "The words are yours." ³ The head *cohanim* too made accusations against him, ⁴ and Pilate again inquired of him, "Aren't you going to answer? Look how many charges they are making against you!" ⁵ But Yeshua made no further response, to Pilate's amazement.

⁶ Now during a festival, Pilate used to set free one prisoner, whomever the crowd requested. ⁷ There was in prison among the rebels who had committed murder during the insurrection a man called Bar-Abba. ⁸ When the crowd came up and began asking Pilate to do for them what he usually did, ⁹ he asked them, "Do you want me to set free for you the 'King of the Jews'?" ¹⁰ For it was evident to him that it was out of jealousy that the head *cohanim* had handed him over. ¹¹ But the head *cohanim* stirred up the crowd to have him release Bar-Abba for them instead. ¹² Pilate again said to them, "Then what should I do with the man you call the King of the Jews?" ¹³ They shouted back, "Put him to death on the stake!" ¹⁴ He asked, "Why? What crime has he committed?" But they only shouted louder, "Put him to death on the stake!" ¹⁵ So Pilate, wishing to satisfy the mob, set Bar-Abba free for them; but he had Yeshua whipped and then handed him over to be executed on the stake.

¹⁶ The soldiers led him away inside the palace (that is, the headquarters building) and called together the whole battalion. ¹⁷ They dressed him in purple and wove thorn branches into a crown, which they put on him. ¹⁸ Then they began to salute him, "Hail to the King of the Jews!" ¹⁹ They hit him on the head with a stick, spat on him and kneeled in mock worship of him. ²⁰ When they had finished ridiculing him, they took off the purple robe, put his own clothes back on him and led him away to be nailed to the execution-stake.

With the approach of morning, the Jewish authorities—the same three groups mentioned in 8:31, 11:27, and 14:43, 53, along with the "whole Sanhedrin"—hold a final consultation and decide to hand Yeshua over to Pilate, the Roman governor. The "head *cohanim*" will continue to take the lead in accusing Yeshua from this point on, as in 15:3, 10, and 11. With the decision to turn to Pilate, the narrative becomes even more ominous. Rome not only holds the ultimate governing authority, but also practices the cruel and dehumanizing punishment of crucifixion. As we've seen, Yeshua seals his destiny by accepting the designation "Mashiach/Messiah" for himself and then describing Messiah in terms that reflect the Scripture but can be labeled as blasphemous by his accusers. Messiah, or "Anointed One," entails kingship, the status of the anointed heir of David, and taking on that title makes Yeshua liable to Roman punishment as well. Even if the Jewish authorities can impose capital punishment in some cases, they may realize they're on more solid footing if they hand Yeshua, "King of the Jews," over to Rome. They also might feel the Romans will owe them something if they help them suppress an emerging rebellion among their fellow Jews. And, finally, it may be that they not only want Yeshua put to death, but they also want his death to be by crucifixion, a degrading punishment that will be a decisive blow against any claim of royal status by Yeshua or his followers.[7] It's no accident that soon the assembled crowd, probably stirred up by the Jewish authorities (and probably not the same crowd that had greeted Yeshua with praise and adulation shortly before[8]), will demand crucifixion when Pilate asks them what he should do with Yeshua.

> Some suggest that while Jesus was popular among his fellow pilgrims from Galilee, he was rejected by the inhabitants of Jerusalem, many of whom were dependent on the temple for their

---

7. Crucifixion was normally reserved for the execution of slaves, but also applied to lower-class political rebels (like a Galilean peasant claiming to be king), so it was particularly degrading (France, *Mark*, 633).
8. Brown, 801.

livelihood and who had been provoked by Jesus' attitude to the temple (see 14:58). The Jewish aristocracy would have hated Barabbas, whose activities threatened their authority, but they feared Jesus because he was a greater threat on account of his popularity among the people.[9]

The claim to be Messiah and King of the Jews constitutes a threat to both Jewish and Roman authorities. Pilate's question, "Are you the King of the Jews?" (15:2) parallels the high priest's question, "Are you the *Mashiach*?" (14:61), and both constitute a veiled accusation. Just as the Sanhedrin has set up Yeshua for a charge of blasphemy, Pilate sets him up for a charge of sedition, because only Caesar and those authorized by him can claim kingship. Darrell Bock notes, "In Mark, 'King of the Jews' is a description attributed to Jesus exclusively by those who were responsible for his execution—namely, Pilate, the hostile crowd, the soldiers, the chief priests, and the scribes (15:2, 9, 12, 18, 26, 32)."[10] By answering Pilate's question, "Are you the King of the Jews," with "The words are yours," Yeshua allows this accusation to stand. He accepts the title, but makes it clear that like "Messiah," it's a title cited by his accuser, not by himself.

In Pilate's presence Yeshua says nothing further, and Pilate is amazed at his silence in the face of an accusation that can cost him his life. Yeshua had also met the earlier accusations before the Sanhedrin with silence (14:61), in both instances reflecting Isaiah's description of the servant:

> Though mistreated, he was submissive —
> he did not open his mouth.
> Like a lamb led to be slaughtered,
> like a sheep silent before its shearers,
> he did not open his mouth. (Isa. 53:7)

---

9. Schnabel, 402.
10. Turner and Bock, 543.

Pilate had a practice of releasing one prisoner during a festival, or perhaps specifically during Passover, and the crowd has apparently come together to demand this release. Pilate offers them Yeshua, recognizing that he's not a real threat to the Roman order, but the crowd rejects Yeshua in favor of Bar-Abba, a rebel who had committed murder during a recent insurrection. Bar-Abba, or Barabbas, means literally "son of a/the father," which presents us with another great irony. Bar-Abba is an ordinary man, an ordinary son of a father, although apparently extraordinary in his resistance to Rome. Yeshua is extraordinary, uniquely Son of the Father, and is no real threat to Rome. Pilate seems to realize this, leading him to offer Yeshua's release, while he'd doubtless be pleased to get rid of Bar-Abba. But the crowd seeks release for Bar-Abba, not for Yeshua, so that Yeshua becomes the substitute for Bar-Abba, thus foreshadowing the atoning death that he's about to undergo to "give his life as a ransom for many" (Mark 10:45).

Readers of Mark and the other Besorot sometimes interpret the actions of Pilate or Rome as relatively innocent here, with "the Jews" as uniquely guilty of Messiah's death. *The Jewish Annotated New Testament* captures this sort of interpretation in simple terms: "Mark places the blame on the Jews."[11] But in reality, Pilate's guilt here is obvious: he realizes that Yeshua is innocent of a capital offence and nevertheless, "wishing to satisfy the mob," hands him over to be flogged and "executed on the stake" (15:15). The Jews who call out for Yeshua's death, for all their evildoing, are at least motivated by religious zeal, however misguided; Pilate carries out the death sentence knowing it is unjust but willing to sacrifice an innocent life to maintain a superficial calm during the festival.

In the account of Yeshua's Roman trial, "handed over" in 15:15 is the third appearance of the phrase in the Greek original. The trial began when the head *cohanim* "put Yeshua in chains, led him away and *handed him over* to Pilate" (15:1). Soon enough Pilate realizes

---

11. Wills, "Mark," JANT, 103: cf. Marcus, Mark 8–16, 1027.

that "it was out of jealousy that the head *cohanim* had *handed him over*" (15:10), but cynically *hands over* Yeshua to the executioners. The same Greek word is used for the whole betrayal theme in the second half of Mark—9:31, 10:33; 14:10, 11, 18, 21, 41, 42, 44—tracing a progression (or descent) of betrayal from one of the Twelve, to the Jewish authorities, to the Gentile authorities, and to death itself. This universal betrayal may be another echo, however subtle, of Isaiah 53: "People despised and avoided [or rejected] him. . . . Like someone from whom people turn their faces, / he was despised; we did not value him" (vv. 3–4). This downward spiral of rejection is all within God's purposes, however, and is reversed when Yeshua rises as he foretold on the third day.

But first he must undergo another stage in his rejection and suffering, being "whipped" or scourged in the Roman fashion with a whip that contained embedded metal or bone scraps to tear off the flesh. The Roman soldiers turn this into a spectacle and gather their whole battalion to join in, putting on him a garment of purple—a color signifying high status—along with a crown woven of thorns. They mock the very idea that this miserable looking Jew, by now probably flogged to within inches of his life, could claim to be King of the Jews, when their Caesar was the true king. Then they put Yeshua's own garments back on him before leading him to the hill of execution. He will go to his death not in the outward garments of status but in ordinary garb, identifying fully with those for whose sake he endures this torment.

Derash

- Episodes 18 and 19 convey a tragic tale of failed discipleship, which delineates three ways of falling short, embodied by three iconic figures. First is betrayal, specifically betrayal by a close follower, embodied by Y'hudah. Yeshua warns his talmidim of this betrayal at the very beginning of the Passover meal. After the meal he warns of another level of failure, desertion, paraphrasing Zechariah 13:7:

> **'I will strike the shepherd dead,
> and the sheep will be scattered.'**

This desertion—or "loss of faith" as in CJB—plays out in Gat Sh'manim, when the talmidim fail to stay awake with Yeshua during his time of tortured prayer, and then flee when he is arrested. The desertion theme is embodied in the mysterious young man who follows "wearing only a nightshirt; and when they tried to seize him, he slipped out of the nightshirt and ran away naked" (14:51–52)—a complete and shameful failure of faithfulness to Yeshua. Finally, Kefa embodies the third way of failed discipleship: denial. When Yeshua warns of the coming desertion, Kefa protests that even if everyone else loses faith, he never will. Yeshua tells him that before the rooster crows twice Kefa will deny or "disown" him three times, and his denial unfolds here in Episode 19, so that Kefa/Peter is the iconic figure of denial.

Mark's portrayal of the full range of discipleship that falls short serves as a lesson for all who are called to follow Yeshua. It's clear that this is no easy calling and if we imagine that it is, we're setting ourselves up for failure. The three icons of failed discipleship—Y'hudah (betrayal), Kefa (denial), and the naked young man (desertion)—alert us to the challenge of sustained loyalty to a Messiah who suffers rejection not just in his initial appearance but today as well, in our secular and materialistic age. It's not popular or trendy to profess faith in Yeshua, nor is it meant to be. Following Yeshua remains a trial, and victory awaits us only as we remember his promise, "after I have been raised, I will go ahead of you into the Galil" (14:28).

- In her poem "Gethsemane," Mary Oliver portrays the second failure sketched out above:

  > Jesus said, wait with me. And maybe the stars did, maybe the wind wound itself into a silver tree, and didn't move, maybe the lake far away, where once he walked as on a blue pavement, lay still and waited, wild awake.

  > Oh the dear bodies, slumped and eye-shut, that could not keep that vigil, how they must have wept, so utterly human, knowing this too must be a part of the story.[12]

- For centuries the Jewish people have been charged with "killing Christ"—the horrific crime of deicide—but the picture we see in Mark is one of Jewish-Roman collusion. And it's a collusion of the authorities, not representing either people as a whole. In a recent paper, "The Death of Messiah," drawing upon the accounts in Luke and Acts, I write:

  > The apostles hold both Jews and Romans accountable for Messiah's death, those Jews and Romans who actually "gathered together" [Psa. 2:2 cited in Acts 4:26–27] in collusion with Herod and Pilate. Their verdict, however, bears a broader implication: Rome, the great Gentile power, and Israel, the chosen nation among the nations, together represent all humankind, which shares responsibility for the death of Messiah. With an eye on Luke's historical perspective, we might say that the great forces of human history—Israel and the nations—unite to resist God's incursion onto the stage of history through his Messiah.[13]

  Mark's account reflects a similar perspective on Messiah's death, including in his portrayal of the two parallel trials, before the Jewish council and before the Roman governor,

---

12. Oliver, *Devotions*, 129.
13. Russ Resnik, "The Death of Messiah: Human Agency and Divine Necessity," *Kesher: A Journal of Messianic Judaism*, Issue 39, Summer/Fall 2021: 43.

who agree in condemning Yeshua to death. Beyond these historical human forces, however, is the purpose of God, as Yeshua makes clear at the very moment of his betrayal, when we might expect him to resist: "But let the *Tanakh* be fulfilled" (14:28). A reader of Mark already knows that this fulfillment entails not only the sacrificial death of Messiah but even more the resurrection to come.

Human powers and authorities resist God and his anointed one because it is in their nature to do so. Likewise, the Messiah must suffer in full identification with humankind because it is in his nature to do so. The focus on human agency in Messiah's death must yield to a more profound drama: through Messiah's death and resurrection, God identifies with us in our deepest sin and alienation and raises us up into life that overcomes all adversity. As it is written, "Was it not necessary that the Messiah should suffer these things and enter into his glory?"[14]

As always in the Hebrew Scriptures, the path to glory must traverse the terrain of suffering. The Besorah of Mark portrays Messiah as the suffering servant of Isaiah 53 to point the way to resurrection and life. Yeshua warns his followers not only that he will be stricken, but that they will all be scattered, "But after I have been raised, I will go ahead of you into the Galil" (14:28). If Messiah himself must pass through suffering on the way to resurrection, should his talmidim expect a straight and untroubled path as they seek to follow him?

---

14. Resnik, "Death of Messiah," 45.

Season 3, Episode 6 (20)

Death and Resurrection

15:21–16:8

Overview

We have followed Yeshua to his final episode. He has been abandoned by his followers and handed over—by one of them—to the Jewish authorities, who in turn hand him over to the Roman governor, who hands him over to the executioners. On the way to the execution site, the soldiers enlist a Jew named Shim'on to carry Yeshua's execution-stake until they reach the site, Gulgolta. There they nail Yeshua to the stake, dividing his garments among themselves and placing the notice of the charge against him over his head: THE KING OF THE JEWS.

The mockery and debasement of Yeshua continue without reprieve. Even the two men crucified alongside him, on his right and on his left, insult him, as do those passing by the scene. Priests and Torah-teachers show up and hurl insults, sarcastically challenging him to come down from the cross and save himself, as he'd claimed to save others. Around noon, Yeshua cries out, *"Elohi! Elohi! L'mah sh'vaktani?*—My God! My God! Why have you deserted me?" and soon after lets out a loud cry and breathes his last. At that, the Roman officer overseeing the execution says, "This man really was a son of God!"

Although Yeshua's talmidim have deserted him, a good number of the women who had followed him stay close enough to witness the execution and Yeshua's death. Another would-be follower, Yosef of Ramatayim, a member of the Sanhedrin, also observes Yeshua's death and goes to Pilate to ask for his body, so he can provide a proper burial. Pilate is surprised to hear that Yeshua has died so quickly, but after confirming with the attending officer that he indeed has, he grants Yosef's request. Yosef wraps the body in a linen shroud, places it in a tomb carved in stone, and closes up the entrance. Two women who had followed Yeshua remain close enough to see where he has been laid.

Right after Shabbat, one of the two women, Miryam from Magdala, along with two other women, buys spices to complete Yeshua's preparation for burial. Early the next morning, the women go to the tomb and discover that the heavy stone sealing the entrance has been rolled away. They enter and, instead of finding Yeshua's body, encounter a young man in a white robe, who tells them that Yeshua isn't there, but has been raised from the dead. He instructs them to go and tell his talmidim that he is going ahead of them to the Galil, where he will meet them. They are awestruck and flee from the tomb, not saying anything to anyone, because they are afraid. On this note of irresolution our account comes to a close.

Peshat

15:21–32

> [21] A certain man from Cyrene, Shim'on, the father of Alexander and Rufus, was passing by on his way in from the country; and they forced him to carry the stake. [22] They brought Yeshua to a place called Gulgolta (which means "place of a skull"), [23] and they gave him wine spiced with myrrh, but he didn't take it. [24] Then they nailed him to the execution-stake; and they divided his clothes among themselves, throwing dice to determine what each man should get. [25] It was nine in the morning when they nailed him to the stake. [26] Over his head, the written notice of the charge against him read,
>
> THE KING OF THE JEWS

²⁷ On execution-stakes with him they placed two robbers, one on his right and one on his left. ²⁸ ²⁹ People passing by hurled insults at him, shaking their heads and saying, "Aha! So you can destroy the Temple, can you, and rebuild it in three days? ³⁰ Save yourself and come down from the stake!" ³¹ Likewise, the head *cohanim* and the *Torah*-teachers made fun of him, saying to each other, "He saved others, but he can't save himself!" ³² and, "So he's the Messiah, is he? The King of Isra'el? Let him come down now from the stake! If we see that, then we'll believe him!" Even the men nailed up with him insulted him.

Yeshua's sentence has been sealed and now the authorities will carry it out. They enlist a man named Shim'on to carry the execution-stake for Yeshua, who is so weakened from the severe beating ordered by Pilate that he's unable to carry it himself. Mark takes pains to identify this particular Shim'on, because he bears the most popular name for Jewish males of the time.[1] He's the Shim'on who happens to be from Cyrene in North Africa, which might have been enough information to identify him, but Mark adds that he is the father of Alexander and Rufus, assuming that these two would be known to his readers. These brothers preserve the eyewitness testimony received from their father as a bridge between the testimony of the talmidim, including Kefa, who have abandoned their role, and the testimony of the women eyewitnesses, as will be noted shortly. In this context, Shim'on, through his well-known sons, provides a compelling first-hand detail to the account.[2]

The grim procession comes to Gulgolta, the "place of a skull," a site just outside the walls of Jerusalem, where executed criminals could be put on public display without defiling the holy city itself. It's named "Skull" perhaps from its physical appearance, or perhaps simply because of its function as the site of execution.[3] There, the

---

1. Bauckham, 85.
2. Bauckham, 52.
3. France, 642. France adds, "It has also often been suggested that the smaller rocky mound (some four metres high) of the traditional site of the Church of the Holy Sepulchre might have been called Golgotha because it resembled (the top of) a skull."

soldiers offer Yeshua wine mixed with myrrh to deaden the terror and pain, but he refuses it, opting instead, as often suggested, to drink the cup his father had decreed for him (14:36). Commentator Craig Evans, on the other hand, claims that myrrh doesn't have pain-relieving properties. Instead, it was added as a fragrant enhancement to the finest wines, so that offering Yeshua this elegant wine was another way of mocking him as King of the Jews. As he did by keeping silent through most of his interrogation, Yeshua denies them the satisfaction of mocking him further and refuses the wine.[4] Undeterred, the soldiers continue the crucifixion process, dividing Yeshua's garments among themselves, "throwing dice to determine what each man should get" (15:24). Garments are objects of value in the first-century world and the soldiers may be looking for some side income, unconsciously fulfilling David's lament in Psalm 22, "They divide my garments among themselves; / for my clothing they throw dice" (vs. 19[18]). Finally, at nine in the morning, they nail Yeshua to the stake, with the notice of the charge against him nailed over his head: THE KING OF THE JEWS—another act of mockery, which ironically declares who Yeshua really is in one of the clearest ways in Mark's entire account.

Yeshua's execution-stake is placed between two ordinary criminals in another unintentional fulfilment of prophecy: "He was counted with transgressors" (Isa. 53:12).[5] Furthermore, the reflection of Psalm 22 continues as bystanders mock Yeshua and sarcastically challenge him to save himself.

> All who see me jeer at me;
> they sneer and shake their heads:
> "He committed himself to ADONAI,
> so let him rescue him!
> Let him set him free
> if he takes such delight in him!" (Psa. 22:8–9 [7–8])

---

4. Evans, 501.
5. This reference to Isaiah 53 is made explicit as verse 28 in some manuscripts of Mark 15.

Even the two crucified thieves, in the midst of their own pain and degradation, join in mocking Yeshua, perhaps because his claims of divine authority and power must seem absurd amidst his dehumanizing treatment.

15:33–39

> [33] At noon, darkness covered the whole Land until three o'clock in the afternoon. [34] At three, he uttered a loud cry, **"*Elohi! Elohi! L'mah sh'vaktani?*"** (which means, **"My God! My God! Why have you deserted me?"**) [35] On hearing this, some of the bystanders said, "Look! He's calling for Eliyahu!" [36] One ran and soaked a sponge in **vinegar**, put it on a stick and **gave** it to him **to drink**. "Wait!" he said, "Let's see if Eliyahu will come and take him down." [37] But Yeshua let out a loud cry and gave up his spirit. [38] And the *parokhet* in the Temple was torn in two from top to bottom. [39] When the Roman officer who stood facing him saw the way he gave up his spirit, he said, "This man really was a son of God!"

At Yeshua's third hour on the cross, around noon, darkness comes over the whole land for another three hours. And then Yeshua calls out "My God! My God! Why have you deserted me?" These are the opening words of Psalm 22, which has been in the background throughout the crucifixion scene, and now by echoing its first line Yeshua is invoking the contents of the whole psalm. It is sometimes heard in religious discussions (or arguments) that Yeshua might have claimed to be the Messiah and Son of God, but at his crucifixion he realizes that he's failed, that instead of attaining the throne of David, he's about to die a miserable death at the hands of the Roman oppressors, and he cries out in despair. But such a criticism ignores Yeshua's own prediction of his death, which he describes as necessary, not as contradictory to his messianic claims. He may have genuinely felt God's desertion at that point, but he had already foretold it and, even more importantly, his choice of words here highlights the prophetic significance of all that he's going through.

The "Son of Man goes as it is written of him" (Mark 14:21; cf. 14:49). Moreover, Yeshua is citing "a psalm of *David*" (Psa. 22:1), framing his sufferings as part of his assignment as the son of David.[6]

The bystanders, however, are clueless to all this and instead zone in on Yeshua's Aramaic *Elohi, elohi* (My God! My God!), which sounds like "Eliyahu," the name of the prophet who is to prepare the way for the coming of the Messiah (Mal. 3:23–24 [4:5–6]). But Eliyahu doesn't show up, so the bystanders continue their mockery, offering Yeshua vinegar in the place of the myrrhed wine of a few hours before, and again unconsciously fulfilling a lament of David, "in my thirst, they gave me vinegar to drink" (Psa. 69:22 [21]). Yeshua's cry not only invokes the words of Psalm 22; it also provides a poignant contrast with his earlier appeal to God as "Abba" at Gat Sh'manim (14:36). There he was asking the compassionate Father to spare him the cup of suffering and abandonment; now in the midst of that abandonment, he uses the less intimate "My God" in his final prayer.

After Yeshua refuses the vinegar he lets out a loud cry and "gives up his spirit." CJB emphasizes the presence of "spirit" or "pneuma" in the Greek original for this phrase, *exepneusen*, which is also reflected in the older translation "gave up the ghost" (KJV, ASV). We shouldn't read too much into this word, however, since it is often used as a simple description of dying, as in other translations, such as ESV and NRSV: "he breathed his last." What may be more significant is that Yeshua lets out a loud cry just before he dies, just as he had called out to God, *Elohi*, with a loud cry shortly before. He has been mercilessly flogged and then nailed through his flesh to a rough wooden beam, but he still has the strength to call out loudly. Mark in his typically sparse approach doesn't tell us what Yeshua cried, but Luke records words of trust in God, and John adds the triumphant phrase "It is accomplished!" (Luke 23:46; John 19:30). This detail helps explain the response of

---

6. See our discussion of 12:35–37.

the Roman officer upon seeing the way Yeshua died—with evident trust in God at his final moment.[7]

Before we consider the officer's response in more depth, we turn to another telling detail at the moment of Yeshua's death: "the *parokhet* in the Temple was torn in two from top to bottom" (Mark 15:38). The significance of this sign has been thoroughly debated in the commentaries, including extensive discussion on which *parokhet*, "veil" or "curtain," was torn, since the Temple had both an outer veil between the courtyard and the Holy Place, and an inner veil between the Holy Place and the Holy of Holies (CJB: "Especially Holy Place"; see Exod. 26:31–34). Marcus summarizes arguments for both possibilities, notes the strength of arguments for this being the outer veil, and then continues,

> But the parallel with the baptismal scene [Mark 1:9–11] provides equally strong evidence for the other theory, since at the baptism the dividing of the heavens allows something to emerge from behind them in a revelatory act, and this may be similar to what happens in 15:38–39 if the torn curtain is the inner one. All in all, the vocabulary considerations and greater religious importance of the inner veil make it a more likely candidate for the reference here.[8]

As Marcus notes, in Mark's "baptismal scene" (1:9–11), we saw heaven "torn open," translating a Greek word based on the root *schizo*, a rare term that appears only once more in Mark, here in 15:38. The appearance of the word only twice, and in two crucial scenes, one near the beginning and one near the end, calls us to examine the parallels between these two scenes, which form an *inclusio* to Mark's entire Besorah. In chapter 1 the heavens are torn open to reveal God's presence and enable the descent of his Spirit upon Yeshua. In Mark 15, the veil of the Temple is likewise torn open to signify new access to God's presence, and a new level of

---

7. France, 655
8. Marcus, *Mark 8–16*, 1057.

revelation to come with Messiah's resurrection. The root *schizo* also appears in the Greek translation of a relevant verse in Isaiah:

> We wish you would *tear open* heaven and come down, so the mountains would shake at your presence! (Isa. 63:19 [64:1], emphasis added)

Just as Yeshua's immersion at the Yarden and the response from heaven inaugurate a new era for Israel and ultimately for humankind, so does his death on the Roman cross.

Noting that the *parokhet* was torn from "top to bottom" suggests that it was not done by human hands, but by the Father himself, in response to the horrific death of the Son. In the Tanakh, the rending of a garment is a sign of mourning, as in Ya'akov's response to the report of Yosef's death: "Ya'akov tore his clothes and, putting sackcloth around his waist, mourned his son for many days" (Gen. 37:34; see also 37:29, Job 1:20). This expression of grief survives among Jewish mourners to this day as the ritual of *keriah* in which the closest family members tear their garments before the funeral. Yeshua dies as it is foretold and as it must be, but the One who ordains his death mourns nevertheless.

The Roman officer overseeing the execution would not have seen the tearing of the parokhet, but he would have seen Yeshua's demeanor upon the execution stake and heard his final cry of triumph and trust in God. He becomes the first—and only—human character in Mark's account to describe Yeshua as "son of God," rather than to employ this term in an accusatory question as the *cohen hagadol* had done (14:60). Whether the officer's remark should be translated "a son of God" as in CJB or "the Son of God," as in KJV, ESV, and numerous other versions, has little bearing on Mark's purpose here. We don't need to imagine an ordinary Roman soldier making a theological statement about the deity of Messiah. Rather, Mark cites the officer's actual words to provide a bookend with his first verse: "The beginning of the Good News of Yeshua the Messiah, the Son of God," and with the declaration from heaven that follows shortly thereafter, "You are my Son, whom I love" (1:11). Here is Mark's culminating, and perhaps most poignant, use of irony: The title pronounced by God himself is ignored and rejected by Jewish figures ranging from Galilean fishermen to the highest authorities, to finally be pronounced by an officer of the Roman occupation, who probably doesn't even realize what he's saying. This irony challenges us, the readers, to recognize and acknowledge who Yeshua really is, despite the misunderstanding, misrepresentation, and neglect that surround him to this day.

15:40–47

> [40] There were women looking on from a distance; among them were Miryam from Magdala, Miryam the mother of the younger Ya'akov and of Yosi, and Shlomit. [41] These women had followed him and helped him when he was in the Galil. And many other women were there who had come up with him to Yerushalayim.
>
> [42] Since it was Preparation Day (that is, the day before a Shabbat), as evening approached, [43] Yosef of Ramatayim, a prominent member of the Sanhedrin who himself was also looking forward to the Kingdom of God, went boldly to Pilate and asked for Yeshua's body. [44] Pilate was surprised to hear that he was already dead, so he summoned the officer and asked him if he had been dead awhile. [45] After he had gotten confirmation from the officer that Yeshua was dead, he granted Yosef the corpse. [46] Yosef purchased a linen sheet; and after taking Yeshua down, he wrapped him in the linen sheet, laid him in a tomb which had been cut out of the rock, and rolled a stone against the entrance to the tomb. [47] Miryam of Magdala and Miryam the mother of Yosi saw where he had been laid.

The women looking on from a distance at what appeared to be Yeshua's final moments sustain the thread of eyewitness testimony that the talmidim bore until "they all deserted him and ran away" (14:50). Kefa soon after denied him and disappeared from the narrative (14:70). The thread of witness had been taken up briefly by

Shim'on of Cyrene (15:21). Now, at the climactic scene of crucifixion, three women bear witness and, in typical Markan fashion, they are named—two named Miryam and one Shlomit. Miryam of Magdala, a town on the western shore of the Kinneret, is the Mary Magdalene of Christian translations and Christian legend, who according to Luke 8:2 was set free from seven demons. John adds a poignant account of Miryam's encounter with the risen Messiah, as the first one to see him after the resurrection (John 20:11–18). Mark's mention of three, or two, witnesses here may reflect the Torah's requirement of two or three witnesses in a criminal case, particularly a capital offense (Deut. 17:6, 19:15; cf. 1 Tim. 5:19).

Clearly Miryam is a key witness to the resurrection, and a prominent follower of Yeshua. Mark hints at her status by naming her three times (15:40, 47; 16:1) in this final sequence, with threefold repetition bearing its characteristic significance. The other Miryam also appears in the same three verses, but with varying descriptions: she is Miryam "the mother of the younger Ya'akov and of Yosi" (15:40), the mother of Yosi (without mention of Ya'akov) in 15:47, and mother of Ya'akov (without mention of Yosi) in 16:1.[9] The reason for this variance in description isn't clear, and may simply reflect Mark's typical economy with words, but the bigger picture is clear: three women witness the death of Yeshua and two of them see where he is buried.

The role of Miryam and the other women, however, will soon shift from bearing witness to providing a proper burial for their beloved rabbi. In Jewish tradition, care for the deceased is considered a great mitzvah, performed on behalf of one who can never repay us. It reflects the idea of *k'vod hamet*, honoring the

---

9. France (664) discusses the possibility that this Miryam is actually the mother of Yeshua, who also had two sons with the very common names Ya'akov and Yosi (Mark 6:3), but argues convincingly that she is a different Miryam, bearing another very common name of that period. It does seem unlikely that, if this Miryam is Yeshua's mother, Mark wouldn't mention that fact here, and would portray her as in a lesser role than that of Miryam of Magdala.

dead, which guides burial and mourning customs within the Jewish community to this day.[10] The first person Mark pictures as seeking to fulfill this mitzvah, even before the three women, is Yosef, a member of the Sanhedrin who is "looking forward to the Kingdom." He parallels the Torah-teacher whom Yeshua declares to be "not far from the Kingdom of God" (12:34). Both are Jewish leaders who don't fit the simple binary of "believer-unbeliever," but begin to apprehend the Kingdom of God proclaimed by Yeshua without being described yet as talmidim. Yosef is responding to the broad mitzvah of k'vod hamet and also, perhaps, to the more specific command to not allow the body of an executed person to remain exposed overnight, "because a person who has been hanged [or impaled] has been cursed by God — so that you will not defile your land" (Deut. 21:22–23).

Yosef boldly approaches Pilate and requests the body of Yeshua. Pilate is surprised that he has died so quickly, perhaps related to the unusual severity of the beating Yeshua received at the hands of the mocking soldiers. When the officer—perhaps the same officer who had pronounced Yeshua a son of God at the moment of death— confirms that he is indeed dead, Pilate grants Yosef's request. It's clear that Yosef is motivated by more than a desire to prevent the defilement cited in Deuteronomy 21 because he goes beyond the requirements of an ordinary burial. He provides a burial shroud of "linen" or *sindon*, the only use of this term in Mark aside from the scene a little earlier when a young man wearing only a *sindon*, a linen cloth or "nightshirt" as in CJB, flees the scene of Yeshua's arrest and leaves the sheet behind (14:51–52). A common cloth could be used as a shroud, but the linen sheet expresses more honor toward the corpse. The young man's shed garment is a symbol of failed discipleship, of desertion of Yeshua at the critical moment; the

---

10. K'vod Hamet is considered to be an aspect of Gemilut Hasadim, acts of hesed or lovingkindness, modeled by God himself according to the Talmud, Sotah 14a. The Mishnah, Shabbat 23:4–5, provides details of honoring the corpse, some of which are suspended for Shabbat.

shroud of 15:46 is a symbol of devotion to Yeshua, of coming close at another critical moment, to prevent further humiliation of the body left exposed overnight, or subjected to a disgraceful and hasty burial. Likewise, Yosef places Yeshua not in an ordinary burial site, but in a tomb cut out of rock, with a stone sealing the entrance, a place of honorable burial.

Commentator Michael Pakaluk notes that the term "corpse" in 15:45 "seems quasi-legal in the context and presumably echoes Pilate's own language," and continues,

> For the rest of the chapter, Mark never refers to the "corpse" or the "body" but always to Jesus, referring to the body constantly as "him": "taking him down, he wrapped him in the linen cloth. He placed him in a tomb." This personalistic language presumably expresses Mark's conviction that Jesus, though dead, is still alive.[11]

In a footnote, Pakaluk ties this insight into Roman Catholic thinking on the death of Jesus, but Mark's language here in 15:46 may simply reflect traditional Jewish respect for the deceased, magnified in Yeshua's case because of who he is. "After taking *Yeshua* down, [Yosef] wrapped *him* in the linen sheet [and] laid *him* in a tomb which had been cut out of the rock." The scene closes with Miryam of Magdala and Miryam the mother of Yosi witnessing where *he*—not the "corpse" or the "body"—was laid. They are accompanying Yeshua to his burial as far as they are able, which reflects the custom within k'vod hamet of attending the corpse, watching over it at all times from death to burial. The body is not to be left unattended. The women are there, however, not just to watch, but also to take note of the spot for their return after Shabbat.

16:1–8

When Shabbat was over, Miryam of Magdala, Miryam the mother of Ya'akov, and Shlomit bought spices in order to go and anoint Yeshua. ² Very early the next day, just after sunrise, they went to

---

11. Pakaluk, 279.

the tomb. ³ They were asking each other, "Who will roll away the stone from the entrance to the tomb for us?" ⁴ Then they looked up and saw that the stone, even though it was huge, had been rolled back already. ⁵ On entering the tomb, they saw a young man dressed in a white robe sitting on the right; and they were dumbfounded. ⁶ But he said, "Don't be so surprised! You're looking for Yeshua from Natzeret, who was executed on the stake. He has risen, he's not here! Look at the place where they laid him. ⁷ But go and tell his *talmidim*, especially Kefa, that he is going to the Galil ahead of you. You will see him there, just as he told you." ⁸ Trembling but ecstatic they went out and fled from the tomb, and they said nothing to anyone, because they were afraid.

The three women mentioned here are the same three mentioned in v. 40, with two of them later observing where the body was laid (15:47). Mark doesn't tell us why Shlomit is missing at that point, but the fact that he does not mention her there again supports the eyewitness nature of his account. He is citing the three or two women not as a traditional formulation, but with great specificity and concreteness. Bauckham notes the frequent usage of verbs of seeing in all three appearances of the three women (Mark 15:40, 47; 16:4–6), and concludes, "The way they are described seems to me to leave hardly any possible doubt that Mark is naming them as eyewitnesses of the most critical events of his whole Gospel narrative, and indicating that they were the source, immediate or proximate, of his own accounts of these events."[12]

The phrase "When Shabbat was over" (16:1) refers to Saturday night, after sundown, when shops could reopen and ordinary activities could resume. This moment is referred to as Motzei Shabbat in current Hebrew usage and is a lively time in Israel today with cafes and shops filling up with visitors and locals alike on Saturday night. This reference also points to the traditional Friday-Saturday-Sunday sequence for the crucifixion and resurrection. It's

---

12. Bauckham, 521.

beyond dispute that Yeshua rose early in the morning on the first day of the week, that is, Sunday. But readers can be thrown off by Yeshua's reference to rising "after three days," which in current English usage would imply that he spent three full days in the tomb. France notes, "Mark's phrase reflects [second-Temple] Jewish usage whereby 'after three days' would mean 'the day after tomorrow', but in a broader cultural context this idiom might not be understood."[13] France goes on to explain how Matthew and Luke, written later and within "a broader cultural context" replace "after three days" with the less idiomatic "on the third day." A parallel usage appears in the Scroll of Esther, where she sends a message to Mordekhai:

> "Go, assemble all the Jews to be found in Shushan, and have them fast for me, neither eating nor drinking for three days, night and day; also I and the girls attending me will fast the same way. Then I will go in to the king, which is against the law; and if I perish, I perish." . . . On the third day, Ester put on her royal robes and stood in the inner courtyard of the king's palace, opposite the king's hall. (Ester 4:16, 5:1)

As in the accounts of Yeshua's resurrection, the three-day language is flexible. Esther says she'll go in to the king after three days of fasting night and day, but actually goes "on the third day," which would be before the completion of three full days. Understanding this Jewish idiomatic usage helps clear up confusion about the timing of Yeshua's resurrection. And once again we see the on-the-ground first-century Jewish perspective of Mark's account.

As the women approach the tomb to complete Yeshua's burial, they wonder how they're going to get inside. They had seen the heavy stone rolled into place to close the entrance, but when they arrive they lift up their eyes and see that it's been rolled away. They enter the tomb, probably with some trepidation, and encounter "a young man" dressed in a white robe. The young man's unexplained appearance in the empty tomb, his white garments, and his lofty

---

13. France, 336–37.

proclamation—"He has risen, he's not here!"—all suggest that he is actually an angel, as Matthew (28:2–5) and John (20:12) later make explicit.[14]

The wording of the young man's announcement is significant: "But go and tell his talmidim, especially Kefa, that he is going to the Galil ahead of you" (16:7). He is reiterating Yeshua's own words: "But after I have been raised, I will go ahead of you into the Galil" (14:28). The young man singles out Kefa/Peter here as the only one among the talmidim mentioned by name, just as Kefa is the first of the talmidim to be mentioned by name—Shim'on at that point—at the beginning of the Besorah (1:16), and the one most frequently appearing by name afterwards. This detail supports the notion of Mark as the "Memoirs of Peter" or at least the record of Peter's firsthand account.[15] But typically for Mark, this detail also has an ironic element. Perhaps Kefa/Peter is named here because his failure is the greatest among the talmidim. They all deserted Yeshua at the end, but only Kefa is recorded as denying him, denying he even knew him at all (14:71). The simple Greek *kai* or "and" is rendered "especially" in our translation, but could also be read as "even" Kefa.[16] The triumph of Yeshua's resurrection, which overcomes the powers of death and sin, extends even to one who declared of him, "I do not know this man you are telling me about!"

Benefitting from this triumph, however, is linked to teshuvah, return/repentance, and teshuvah provides a key to Mark's famously enigmatic conclusion. But before we consider this key, we must ask whether 16:8 is the true conclusion. Most Bibles include 16:9–20 as an alternative ending, often with a footnote saying that it's not found in the earliest and best manuscripts. A shorter alternative conclusion also appears at times, but is even less likely to be the original. Most

---

14. Angels often appear or are described as men in the Tanakh, most famously in the account of Abraham's encounter with three "men" in Genesis 18 who turn out to be ADONAI and two angels.
15. "Memoirs of Peter" reflects the language of Papias, cited in Eusebius, *Historia Ecclesiae*, as noted in our Introduction, p. xvii. Cf. Pakaluk, xviff.
16. Marcus, *Mark 8–16*, 1086; cf. Schnabel, 438; France, 681.

scholars agree that the two alternative conclusions contain scriptural truth, but are not part of Mark's original. So either the original conclusion is lost, or this is it: "Trembling but ecstatic they went out and fled from the tomb, and they said nothing to anyone, because they were afraid."

I agree with the large number of scholars who see this as Mark's abrupt, enigmatic, and authentic ending.[17] First, this is the text we possess, and if there is a lost ending—as some conjecture—it has not been preserved. We can trust in divine oversight to preserve the true ending even if it is hard to accept as-is. Further, the wording of 16:1–8 is typical of Mark: spare, action-oriented, and not given to flowery terminology, in contrast with the alternative endings, which depart from Mark's characteristic style to echo material from the other Gospels in language that is a far cry from Mark's style. Finally, 16:1–8 forms a coherent epilogue, corresponding to the prologue of 1:1–13. The resurrection account takes place in Y'hudah (Judea) and will culminate back in Galilee, just as the prologue opens in Y'hudah and sets up the return to Galilee. The prologue introduces the theme of teshuvah, return/repentance (1:3–4, cf. 1:15), and the epilogue raises it again. The talmidim have failed throughout Yeshua's final days in Jerusalem, despite his warnings and his preparatory mentoring. In the end, the male disciples have all disappeared, and only the women are left, and even they are left paralyzed by fear. Now, through the young man, Yeshua calls his followers to turn around, to go back to the Galil, which we can see as an outward enactment of teshuvah, turning around spiritually. Back in the Galil they will indeed meet the risen Messiah as he foretold in 14:28—and they must turn around to get there.

"The Gospel thus ends with one last irony: followers are now, at the resurrection, told to proclaim what they have heard, but out of

---

17. Schnabel, 18–23, for example, provides a detailed but concise overview of the alternative endings and concludes that 16:1–8 is the original. In support he cites Marcus, *Mark 8-16* 1095.

fear they remain silent."[18] As with many of Mark's ironic moments, this "one last irony" leaves us with a challenge: Are we prepared to go beyond our historical or religious considerations of the resurrection of Yeshua and turn our lives around to actually meet him as the Risen One? The abruptness of Mark's ending is purposeful. Not the irony, but the promise of Yeshua has the final say: "he is going to the Galil ahead of you." The promise of this encounter overshadows the failure of the women and dominates the scene as our final episode draws to a close.

Derash

- What it means to follow Yeshua is revealed in Mark by the execution-stake, by the cross. Shim'on of Cyrene, enlisted to carry the execution-stake for the battered and weak Yeshua, becomes the iconic follower as he walks alongside Yeshua and shares his burden when all others have deserted him. He is acting under duress, of course, but nevertheless portrays the essence of discipleship: not just believing in, or even just following Yeshua, but *accompanying* him. He provides a counter-balance to Barabbas, introduced earlier, an outlaw delivered from the execution-stake as Yeshua takes his place (15:21; 6–15). Barabbas benefits, at least for the moment, from Yeshua's sacrifice without any response to Yeshua himself at all. Shim'on, at least for the moment, accompanies Yeshua and shares in his burden. In these moments as we approach the cross we might ask ourselves which of these two men we want to emulate.

- The defining role of the cross or execution-stake remains evident as Shim'on of Cyrene and Yeshua arrive at Gulgolta. There the soldiers nail Yeshua to the stake between two robbers, "one on his right and one on his left" (15:27)—the same position Ya'akov and Yochanan had requested earlier

---

18. Wills, "Mark," JANT, 106.

of Yeshua as a special favor: "When you are in your glory, let us sit with you, one on your right and the other on your left" (10:37).[19] The two brothers imagine an exalted reward for their faithfulness, a position of privilege right next to Yeshua, but the privilege pictured here is that of suffering alongside Yeshua. We might consider how this picture of the reward of discipleship aligns with the expectations and assumptions of Yeshua-followers today, including our own.

- The "young man" encountered in the tomb is termed a *neaniskon* in the original Greek, a word that appears in Mark only here and in the story of the young man who flees naked in 14:51–52, thereby linking the two stories. As noted in Episode 19 and again at 15:46, the *sindon* or linen cloth worn by the young man who fled may foreshadow the linen cloth of Yeshua's burial provided by Yosef of Ramatayim. The young man slips off the linen cloth to escape arrest. He runs away naked and shamed, but he is free. In the same way, the resurrected Yeshua has slipped off the sindon of his burial, not naked and not ashamed but, like the young man, free. Yeshua is released, not from arrest but from death itself. He does not run off, but he goes before his followers as the Risen Messiah to meet them in the Galil, as the young man tells the three awe-struck women.

- Scholars have discussed and debated the abrupt ending of Mark for centuries, with a current majority view that 16:8 is the true conclusion, as noted above. One objection to this view is that there's no precedent for a scriptural text to conclude in such an unresolved fashion. But the conclusion of the book of Jonah is also unresolved, ending with an unanswered question from ADONAI. Jonah is angry because his preaching against Nineveh has stirred its inhabitants to repentance, and God has accordingly spared

---

19. The exact terminology of 10:37 and 15:27 is a bit different, but when Yeshua denies their request in 10:40 he uses the same terminology as in 15:27, terminology that is used only in these two places in Mark, clearly linking them.

them. God asks Jonah if it's right for him to be so angry, and continues, "Shouldn't I be concerned about the great city of Ninveh, in which there are more than 120,000 people who don't know their right hand from their left — not to mention all the animals?" (Jonah 4:11). And the book closes without an answer.

- Jonah is the traditional reading for the afternoon of Yom Kippur, chosen because it aligns with the themes of repentance and divine compassion that reverberate throughout the services for that holiest of days. ADONAI's unanswered question to Jonah probes the hearer on Yom Kippur: If you desire to live under God's compassion, are you ready to extend that same compassion to others—even to undesirable others? Are you ready to do teshuvah, to turn away from judgmentalism and enmity and turn to God's pathway of mercy?

  Likewise, the unresolved ending of Mark probes us and poses the question of teshuvah. Are we ready to turn toward the risen Messiah, to not just give assent to the fact of his resurrection, but to partake of the new way of life it provides? Further, can we respond to Yeshua's resurrection not only as a sign that he is indeed Messiah the Son of God, but as the beginning of the resurrection of all, the beginning of divine redemption of the world? Unlike Jonah, the unanswered final question in Mark is unspoken. But it should be clear enough if we've heard the story with an open heart: Will we turn our lives around to encounter the risen Messiah who has gone before us? Will we let that encounter shape our lives from this moment on?

BIBLIOGRAPHY

Agnon, S. Y. *Days of Awe*. New York: Schocken, 1948.

Bauckham, Richard. *Jesus and the Eyewitnesses: The Gospels as Eyewitness Testimony,* 2nd Edition. Grand Rapids: Eerdmans, 2017.

The Bible, the Talmud, and the New Testament: Elijah Zvi Soloveitchik's Commentary to the Gospels, Edited, with an introduction and commentary, by Shaul Magid. Philadelphia: University of Pennsylvania Press, 2019.

Boyarin, Daniel. *The Jewish Gospels: The Story of the Jewish Christ*. New York: The New Press, 2012.

Brown, Raymond E. *The Death of the Messiah*. New York: Anchor, 1993.

Buxbaum, Yitzhak. *Jewish Spiritual Practices*. Northvale, NJ; London: Jason Aronson, 1990.

The Complete Jewish Study Bible, ed. Barry A. Rubin. NP: Hendrickson/Messianic Jewish Publishers and Resources, 2016.

John DelHousaye "A Pardes Reading of Mark," www.academia.edu /7066021/A_Pardes_Reading_of_The_Gospel_According_to_Mark? email_work_card=title.

The Delitzsch Hebrew Gospels: A Hebrew/English Translation. Marshfield, MO: Vine of David, 2011.

Edwards, James R. *The Gospel according to Mark*, The Pillar New Testament Commentary. Grand Rapids; Leicester, England: Eerdmans; Apollos, 2002.

Evans, Craig A. *Mark 8:27–16:20*, vol. 34B, Word Biblical Commentary. Dallas: Word, 2001.

France, R. T. *The Gospel of Mark: A Commentary on the Greek Text*. Grand Rapids/Cambridge: Eerdmans, 2002.

The Greek New Testament, eds. Kurt Aland, Matthew Black, Carlo M. Martini, Bruce M. Metzger, and Allen Wikgren, third edition. New York: United Bible Societies, 1975.

Gushee, David P. *The Moral Teachings of Jesus: Radical Instruction in the Will of God.* Eugene, OR: Cascade, 2024.

Heschel, Abraham Joshua, "Toward an Understanding of Halacha," in *Abraham Joshua Heschel, Moral Grandeur and Spiritual Audacity: Essays edited by Susannah Heschel.* New York: Farrar, Straus and Giroux, 1996.

Iverson, Kelly R. *Reading Mark.* Cascade Companions. Eugene, OR: Cascade: 2023.

The Jewish Annotated New Testament, Second Edition, eds. Amy-Jill Levine and Marc Zvi Brettler. New York: Oxford University Press, 2017.

The Jewish Study Bible, eds. Adele Berlin, Marc Zvi Brettler, and Michael Fishbane. New York: Oxford University Press, 2004.

The JPS Torah Commentary: Genesis, commentary by Nahum M. Sarna. Philadelphia: Jewish Publication Society, 1989.

Keener, Craig S. *The Historical Jesus of the Gospels.* Grand Rapids: Eerdmans, 2009.

Kinzer, Mark. "Beginning with the End," in *Israel's Messiah and the People of God: A Vision for Messianic Jewish Covenant Fidelity*, ed. Jennifer M. Rosner. Eugene, OR: Cascade, 2011.

Kinzer, Mark S. and Russell L. Resnik. *Besorah: The Resurrection of Jerusalem and the Healing of a Fractured Gospel.* Eugene, OR: Cascade, 2021.

The Koren Siddur, Introduction, Translation, and Commentary by Rabbi Sir Jonathan Sacks. Jerusalem: Koren, 2009.

Lane, William L. *The Gospel according to Mark.* Grand Rapids: Eerdmans, 1974.

Levine, Amy-Jill. *The Difficult Words of Jesus: A Beginner's Guide to His Most Perplexing Teachings.* Nashville: Abingdon, 2021.

Levine, Amy-Jill. *The Gospel of Mark: A Beginner's Guide to the Good News.* Nashville: Abingdon, 2021.

Levine, Amy-Jill. *Short Stories by Jesus: The Enigmatic Parables of a Controversial Rabbi.* New York: HarperOne, 2015.

Mansfield, M. Robert. *Spirit and Gospel in Mark.* Peabody, MA: Hendrickson, 1987.

Marcus, Joel. *Mark 1–8: A New Translation with Introduction and Commentary,* vol. 27, Anchor Yale Bible. New Haven; London: Yale University Press, 2002.

Marcus, Joel. *Mark 8–16: A New Translation with Introduction and Commentary,* vol. 27A, Anchor Yale Bible. New Haven; London: Yale University Press, 2009.

Milgrom, Jacob. *Leviticus 1–16: A New Translation with Introduction and Commentary,* vol. 3, Anchor Yale Bible. New Haven; London: Yale University Press, 2008.

Neusner, Jacob. *The Mishnah: A New Translation.* New Haven; London: Yale University Press, 1988.

New International Dictionary of New Testament Theology, Vol. 1, ed. Colin Brown. Grand Rapids: Zondervan, 1982.

Oliver, Mary. *Devotions: The Selected Poems of Mary Oliver.* New York: Penguin, 2017.

Oliver, Mary. "Staying Alive," *Upstream: Selected Essays.* New York: Penguin, 2016.

Pakaluk, Michael. *The Memoirs of St. Peter: A New Translation of the Gospel According to Mark.* Washington, DC: Regnery Gateway, 2019.

Passover Haggadah Revised Edition, trans. Rabbi Nathan Goldberg. Hoboken, NJ: Ktav, 1993.

Peace, Richard V. *Conversion in the New Testament: Paul and the Twelve.* Grand Rapids: Eerdmans, 1999.

Rashi: The Saperstein Edition, Exodus, ed. Rabbi Yisrael Isser Zvi Herczeg. Brooklyn: Mesorah, 1997.

Resnik, Russell. "The Death of Messiah: Human Agency and Divine Necessity," *Kesher: A Journal of Messianic Judaism*, Issue 39, Summer/Fall 2021

Resnik, Russell. *A Life of Favor: A Family Therapist Examines the Story of Joseph and His Brothers* Clarksville, MD: Lederer, 2017.

Resnik, Russell. *Divine Reversal: The Transforming Ethics of Jesus.* Clarksville, MD: Lederer, 2010.

Schnabel, Eckhard J. *Mark: An Introduction and Commentary*, Tyndale New Testament Commentaries, vol. 2. London: Inter-Varsity, 2017.

Talmud: The William Davidson Talmud. Koren – Steinsaltz. Sefaria.com.

Tanakh: The Holy Scriptures. Philadelphia: Jewish Publication Society, 1985.

Thiessen, Matthew. *Jesus and the Forces of Death: The Gospels' Portrayal of Ritual Impurity within First-Century Judaism.* Grand Rapids: Baker, 2021.

Turner, David and Darrell L. Bock, *Cornerstone Biblical Commentary, Vol 11: Matthew and Mark.* Carol Stream, IL: Tyndale House, 2005.

GLOSSARY

Apocalyptic	Writings pertaining to the climactic events of the end of the age
Bar Kokhba	Leader of the Second Jewish Revolt, 2nd century CE; his name means "Son of the Star" (Aramaic)
Barukh haba	"Blessed is he who comes," from Psalm 118
Bat qol	"Daughter of a voice." In rabbinic literature, a voice from heaven that expresses God's will
Besorah	A report of good news, or a glad proclamation; the same meaning as the English term "gospel"
Birkat Hamazon	Grace after the meal, based on Deuteronomy 8:10
Challah	Sabbath loaf of bread
Chametz	Leaven, or grain products likely to contain leaven; forbidden food on Passover
Christology	Theological study of the nature and character of Christ, the Messiah.
Circumlocution	Talking around a subject, out of respect or denial
Cohanim	Priests, the sons of Aaron
Cohen Hagadol	The High Priest
Davvening	Yiddish for praying
Darash	An imaginative or exploratory interpretation in biblical study; like *midrash*, based on the Hebrew word for "inquire" or "seek out"
Derash	A sermon or teaching, related to *darash*
Eschatology	The study of the end of this age and the in-breaking of the age to come
Gei-Hinnom	Valley of Hinnom outside Jerusalem; Hell
Gemilut Hasadim	Acts of *hesed* or kindness, such as caring for the needy or burying the dead, modeled by God himself according to the Talmud, Sotah 14a

Goyim	Non-Jews, Gentiles
Haggadah	Passover booklet of liturgy and readings used during the Seder
Halakha	Rabbinic interpretive law
Hallel	"Praise" in Hebrew, can refer to Psalms 113–118
Hamotzi	The blessing over bread to begin a meal
Hanukkah	The Festival of Dedication, or of Lights, celebrating the rededication of the Temple in the second century BCE
Havdalah	Prayers to conclude the Shabbat on Saturday night
Herodian	A Jewish party alongside the Pharisees and Sadducees, which advocated loyalty to the ruling Herod family
Hesed	Hebrew term meaning lovingkindness or covenant loyalty
Inclusio	A literary technique of marking off a section with a phrase of similar wording at its beginning and conclusion
Korban	A word appearing frequently in Leviticus (starting at 1:2) and in Numbers to denote an offering or gift to God
Josephus	First-century Jewish historian, known especially for his account of the first-century Jewish revolt against Rome
Kaddish	An iconic Jewish prayer, recited in one form in honor of the dead
Kashrut	Dietary laws (see *Kosher* below)
Kefa	Shim'on or Peter
Kiddush	Sanctification; blessing over a cup of wine to "set apart" an event
Kosher	Fit for consumption, clean. Primarily used to describe food, it can be applied to situations that are "fit," or "clean," like "kosher behavior"
LXX (70) or Septuagint	The widely used Greek translation of the Tanakh, which Mark often draws upon
Mashiach	Hebrew for Messiah, or the Anointed One

GLOSSARY

Mashiach ben David	Messiah Son of David, King Messiah
Mashiach ben Yosef	Messiah Son of Joseph, the suffering Messiah
Matzah	The unleavened bread used for Passover
Mekhilta	Midrashic commentary on the halakhic aspects of Exodus, possibly as early as the 3rd century CE
Midrash	Imaginative rabbinical commentary on the Torah and other Scriptures, written from about 500 CE to the medieval period
Mikveh	Special pool constructed for ritual water immersion
Mishnah	Oral Law based on Torah (the Written Law) put into writing around 200 CE
Mitzvah (mitzvot)	Commandment(s), good deed(s)
Niddah	"Removed, separated" in Hebrew; the period when a woman is forbidden to have sexual contact with her husband
Olam haba	The age to come
Olam hazeh	The present age
P'rushim	Pharisees, one of the major Jewish sects of the Second Temple period
Parasha	The section of the Torah read in the synagogue each week. Combined with the name of the specific portion it becomes parashat, as in Parashat Vayera, etc.
Pericope	A distinct unit within a larger narrative, generally a smaller unit than our episodes
Pesach	Passover, the festival of deliverance from Egypt
Peshat	The plain sense of a text in biblical interpretation
Pikuach nefesh	Literally "watching over a life (or soul)"—the principle that the preservation of human life overrides all religious restrictions
Rabbi/rabboni	"My great one/master" in Hebrew; used as a title for a teacher, it did not imply ordination as in later times
Rashi	Acronym for Rabbi Shlomo Yitzaki (1040-1105 CE), an influential commentator

Rosh Hashanah	Jewish New Year, "Head of the Year"
Ruach HaKodesh	The Holy Spirit
Sanhedrin	Israel's religious supreme council until 70 CE, or any council assembled for deliberation
Second temple era	The period after the Babylonian captivity between the building of the second temple around 516 BCE and its destruction by Rome in 70 CE
Seder	"Order" in Hebrew, the name of the Passover meal
Septuagint or LXX (70)	The widely used Greek translation of the Tanakh, which Mark often draws upon.
Sh'eilah	A question regarding halakha or general practice directed to a rabbi or teacher, expecting a detailed reply or "responsa"
Shema	"Hear" or "listen" in Hebrew; the opening word of a reading beginning with Deuteronomy 6:4; a foundational prayer or statement of faith
Shabbat	Sabbath, the seventh day of rest beginning on Friday evening
Shalom	Peace, health, contentment; a common Jewish greeting
Shavuot	Pentecost, the Feast of Weeks
Siddur (siddurim)	Jewish prayer book(s)
Sukkot	The Feast of Tabernacles
Supersessionist/ism	The idea that the church, or Christian teaching, replaces or supersedes Israel and the Torah
Teshuvah	"Turning" or "return" in Hebrew; repentance
Talmid (talmidim)	Disciple(s) or student(s)
Talmidot	Discipleship; following Yeshua
Talmud	Codified body of rabbinic thought; Mishnah plus the later Gemara. Completed in 6th century CE
Tanakh	Acronym for the Hebrew Scriptures: Torah (Law), Neviim (Prophets), Ketuvim (Writings), used in the Jewish world instead of "Old Testament"

GLOSSARY

Targum	An early paraphrase or translation of the scriptures into another language
Tisha b'Av	The ninth day of the month Av, anniversary of the destruction of both the first and second temples
Torah	Law or Instruction; five books of Moses
Tractate	A book of the Talmud
Tz'dukim	Sadducees, or righteous ones; a Jewish sect of the second temple era
Tzaddik	Holy man, or righteous one
Tzedakah	Righteousness, charity
Tzitzit, tzitziyot	Fringes worn on a garment, based on Numbers 15:37–41
Yeshua HaMashiach	Jesus the Messiah
YHVH	Yud-Heh-Vav-Heh, the Hebrew letters for the ineffable Name of God
Yom Kippur	Day of Atonement

INDEX

A

Adonai, xxi, xxiii, xxx, 6, 8, 9, 10, 11, 13, 17, 18, 36, 49, 68, 76, 82, 92, 93, 96, 105, 109, 111, 114, 117, 120, 121, 132, 144, 147, 148, 160, 161, 168, 174, 175, 176, 184, 192, 204, 218, 219, 227, 233, 234, 235, 238, 243, 244, 248, 249, 250, 255, 256, 258, 260, 261, 268, 270, 271, 276, 286, 292, 295, 307, 308, 322, 333, 336, 337

Age to Come, *Olam Ha-ba*, 5, 26, 39, 49, 57, 120, 145, 196, 206, 223

Andrew, xxiv, 23, 27, 29, 30, 31, 38, 48, 62, 163, 266, 267, 269

B

Bat qol, 343

believe, believer, xiii, xiv, xv, xvi, 23, 25, 45, 70, 71, 73, 75, 111, 119, 159, 164, 168, 171, 178, 182, 188, 193, 200, 241, 247, 254, 273, 321, 329

Bereisheet, Genesis, 20

Besorah, Good News, i, ii, vii, xxi, xxix, xxx, 5, 7, 9, 13, 14, 16, 18, 19, 20, 21, 22, 23, 25, 26, 28, 30, 32, 33, 46, 79, 81, 83, 84, 90, 119, 132, 154, 159, 162, 164, 169, 170, 178, 181, 188, 203, 209, 211, 216, 220, 224, 227, 229, 235, 266, 269, 270, 273, 283, 285, 287, 291, 304, 307, 308, 317, 325, 326, 333, 340, 341, 343

C

Cohanim, 343
Cohen Hagadol, 343

cross, execution stake, 2, 85, 86, 160, 162, 163, 167, 225, 229, 319, 323, 326, 335

crucify/crucifixion, 49, 153, 154, 161, 162, 164, 175, 272, 288, 291, 302, 311, 322, 323, 328, 331

D

Dead Sea, 295

death, 3, 36, 37, 54, 55, 59, 67, 80, 98, 99, 100, 101, 102, 103, 105, 106, 110, 111, 119, 124, 144, 154, 155, 158, 160, 161, 163, 165, 166, 168, 169, 173, 175, 177, 178, 183, 184, 191, 192, 194, 195, 205, 212, 213, 214, 217, 218, 219, 220, 226, 229, 239, 245, 255, 269, 271, 279, 284, 285, 286, 287, 295, 298, 300, 301, 302, 305, 306, 307, 308, 310, 311, 313, 314, 316, 317, 319, 323, 325, 326, 328, 329, 330, 333, 336

demon(s), demonic, 1, 24, 30, 54, 55, 60, 66, 73, 77, 90, 91, 92, 94, 101, 105, 112, 154, 161, 162, 178, 179, 299

E

eschatology, eschatological, 269
Exodus, xix, 18, 52, 57, 62, 67, 68, 88, 109, 110, 117, 147, 151, 175, 218, 290, 292, 294, 307, 342, 345

G

Galil, Galilee, xxiv, xxv, xxvi, xxvii, 1, 3, 4, 10, 14, 16, 23, 24, 25, 27, 28, 29, 30, 31, 33, 34, 35, 36, 37, 41, 42, 48, 55, 59, 60, 62, 64, 66, 73, 81, 85, 86, 87, 90, 93, 94, 96, 98, 99, 102, 104, 105, 111, 113, 146, 153, 158, 162, 164, 172, 183, 184, 186, 192, 197, 198, 221, 228, 230, 250, 253, 284, 287, 289, 309, 311, 315, 317, 320, 327, 331, 333, 334, 335, 336

Gat Sh'manim, 228, 284, 293, 296, 301, 315, 324

Gei-Hinnom, 172, 183, 187, 189, 190, 191, 205, 343

Genesis, *Bereisheet*, xv, xix, xxi, 7, 11, 16, 19, 20, 143, 168, 169, 200, 207, 208, 333, 340

Good News, *Besorah*, i, ii, vii, xxi, xxix, xxx, 5, 7, 9, 13, 14, 16, 18, 19, 20, 21, 22, 23, 25, 26, 28, 30, 32, 33, 46, 79, 81, 83, 84, 90, 119, 132, 154, 159, 162, 164, 169, 170, 178, 181, 188, 203, 209, 211, 216, 220, 224, 227, 229, 235, 266, 269, 270, 273, 283, 285, 287, 291, 304, 307, 308, 317, 325, 326, 333, 340, 341, 343

Goyim, Gentiles, xii, xvi, xx, xxii, 85, 90, 91, 93, 125, 132, 134, 135, 138, 139, 140, 142, 143, 144, 151, 212, 213, 215, 229, 236, 238, 269, 343

H

Halakha, 344

heal, healing, 1, 2, 3, 4, 24, 27, 32, 34, 35, 36, 41, 42, 44, 45, 50, 52, 53, 54, 55, 59, 61, 66, 97, 98, 99, 100, 102, 104, 106, 108, 109, 110, 114, 118, 137, 139, 140, 142, 146, 150, 153, 155, 156, 157, 158, 178, 184, 202, 212, 221, 222, 225, 275

Herod, 3, 42, 51, 107, 110, 111, 145, 148, 149, 151, 199, 237, 247, 252, 253, 267, 316, 344

Herodian, 54, 253, 344

Hesed, 344

High Priest, *Cohen Hagadol*, 161, 343

I

impurity, 3, 24, 34, 97, 99, 100, 101, 123, 129, 133

Isaiah, Yeshayahu, xxiii, xxiv, xxx, 6, 9, 10, 11, 12, 13, 15, 17, 18, 21, 26, 49, 75, 76, 79, 83, 93, 120, 124, 127, 142, 143, 145, 146, 157, 160, 185, 186, 190, 191, 193, 195, 205, 217, 218, 219, 220, 224, 225, 231, 250, 251, 271, 280, 295, 297, 308, 312, 314, 317, 322, 326

J

Jerusalem, Yerushalayim, xiv, xviii, xx, xxiv, xxv, xxvii, xxx, 3, 9, 12, 13, 16, 21, 29, 34, 59, 60, 64, 65, 66, 71, 102, 104, 123, 124, 125, 126, 128, 131, 153, 154, 158, 161, 162, 168, 171, 172, 175, 183, 184, 185, 189, 198, 206, 210, 211, 212, 221, 222, 223, 227, 228, 231, 232, 233, 234, 235, 236, 237, 239, 241, 242, 243, 244, 247, 254, 259, 266, 268, 283, 285, 286, 292, 295, 302, 303, 311, 321, 327, 334, 340, 343

John the Immerser, Yochanan, iv, xvii, xx, xxiv, 3, 5, 6, 9, 10, 11, 13, 14, 16, 21, 23, 25, 27, 30, 33, 37, 47, 48, 49, 62, 63, 98, 101, 107, 110, 111, 113, 119, 146, 158, 163, 172, 174, 176, 183, 187, 211, 212, 213, 214, 215, 222, 232, 239, 241, 242, 243, 266, 267, 269, 271, 284, 296, 297, 335

Jonah, Yonah, 87, 94, 336, 337

Jordan River, Yarden, xxv, 5, 9, 10, 14, 26, 60, 197, 198, 199, 271, 326

Josephus, 49, 235, 267, 273, 274, 306, 344

Judaism, i, xxiv, 5, 24, 33, 83, 102, 126, 131, 141, 165, 176, 193, 255, 316, 342

judgment, xxiv, 75, 76, 81, 87, 148, 171, 188, 190, 191, 193, 194, 195, 236, 237, 238, 251, 268, 270, 272, 280, 308

K

K'far-Nachum, Capernaum, 28

Kashrut, 344

Kefa, 61, 98, 101, 158, 159, 160, 172, 174, 175, 203, 206, 214, 222, 231, 236, 266, 267, 269, 284, 289, 295, 296, 297, 302, 304, 305, 308, 309, 315, 321, 327, 331, 333, 344

King, Kingdom, i, ii, iv, xxvii, xxx, 1, 2, 3, 4, 5, 6, 12, 20, 23, 24, 25, 26, 30, 32, 33, 36, 37, 39, 50, 52, 57, 61, 68, 69, 73, 74, 76, 77, 78, 80, 81, 82, 83, 88, 89, 103, 104, 107, 110, 112, 115, 117, 119, 132, 145, 149, 154, 155, 163, 164, 166, 167, 171, 172, 173, 179, 183, 187, 191, 198, 201, 202, 203, 206, 210, 233, 238, 239, 242, 247, 248, 256, 257, 258, 261, 264, 289, 295, 302, 310, 311, 312, 314, 321, 322, 327, 329, 344

Kingdom of God, xxx, 1, 2, 4, 20, 23, 25, 37, 50, 52, 57, 68, 69, 73, 74, 76, 77, 80, 81, 88, 89, 103, 104, 110, 116, 149, 155, 163, 166, 171, 172, 173, 179, 187, 191, 198, 201, 202, 203, 206, 238, 242, 248, 256, 289, 295, 327, 329

Kinneret, xxv, 1, 2, 3, 23, 25, 27, 28, 47, 59, 62, 73, 76, 85, 86, 99, 105, 108, 117, 118, 137, 141, 146, 153, 155, 328

Kosher, 129, 344

M

Mashiach, Messiah, 8, 158, 159, 222, 259, 260, 301, 305, 308, 311, 312, 344, 345

Matzah, 284, 345

Midrash, 192, 345

Mikveh, 345

Miryam of Magdala, 327, 328, 330

Mishnah, xxiv, 82, 99, 103, 125, 127, 148, 174, 199, 294, 295, 300, 307, 329, 341, 345, 346

Mitzvah (mitzvot), 345

Mount of Olives, 228, 232, 235, 244, 265, 266, 268, 269, 284, 289, 295, 296

N

Natzeret, Nazareth, 6, 10, 14, 23, 28, 29, 54, 98, 104, 106, 221, 309, 331

O

Olam haba, 345

Olam hazeh, 345

P

P'rushim, Pharisees, xxiii, 4, 42, 48, 51, 54, 59, 123, 125, 126, 127, 128, 129, 134, 138, 146, 147, 148, 149, 151, 154, 197, 199, 227, 247, 253, 267, 344, 345

Peraea, 111

Pesach, Passover, x, xxvii, 109, 148, 152, 216, 217, 219, 220, 227, 228, 231, 234, 268, 283, 284, 285, 286, 288, 290, 291, 292, 293, 294, 295, 297, 298, 299, 300, 307, 313, 314, 341, 343, 344, 345, 346

Pilate, 229, 302, 306, 309, 310, 311, 312, 313, 316, 319, 321, 327, 329, 330

preach, preacher, 59, 61, 62, 64, 69, 106, 107, 109, 110, 125, 299

proclaim, 1, 2, 8, 24, 31, 33, 61, 69, 90, 175, 334

purity, ritual purity, 3, 35, 36, 101, 103, 128, 129, 133, 134, 135, 137, 138, 267

R

rabbi/*rabboni*, ii, 101, 102, 120, 202, 203, 204, 222, 228, 328, 345, 346

Rashi, 82, 290, 342, 345

resurrection, xi, 15, 31, 63, 153, 154, 162, 165, 166, 168, 171, 175, 177, 181, 183, 184, 185, 194, 205, 211, 245, 247, 254, 272, 288, 300, 308, 309, 317, 326, 328, 331, 332, 333, 334, 337

righteous, righteousness, 33, 47, 48, 56, 112, 165, 217, 219, 224, 234, 250, 280, 300, 347

Ruach HaKodesh, Holy Spirit, i, 1, 2, 6, 9, 11, 14, 15, 17, 38, 60, 65, 67, 68, 70, 134, 258, 269, 271, 272, 277, 346

S

Samaria, 23

Sanhedrin, 34, 151, 244, 270, 279, 280, 291, 305, 306, 307, 310, 311, 312, 319, 327, 329, 346

Satan, *ha-Satan*, 19, 20, 60, 65, 66, 67, 68, 69, 75, 76, 77, 78, 89, 147, 158, 161, 162, 178, 199, 299

Septuagint or LXX (70), 346

serve, servant, xii, xxi, xxiii, xxiv, 3, 6, 17, 33, 46, 51, 60, 80, 90, 95, 114, 134, 137, 143, 147, 155, 160, 174, 184, 185, 186, 211, 215, 216, 217, 219, 220, 224, 237, 240, 249, 251, 260, 261, 297, 301, 303, 304, 312, 315, 317

Shabbat, Sabbath, xi, xxiv, xxx, 1, 23, 24, 28, 29, 32, 42, 50, 51, 52, 53, 54, 57, 81, 89, 98, 103, 125, 133, 190, 195, 208, 229, 263, 279, 320, 327, 329, 330, 331, 343, 344, 346

Shalom, 57, 196, 346

Shavuot, Pentecost, 234, 346

Shema, xxi, 168, 169, 205, 248, 259, 262, 263, 346

Shim'on of Cyrene, 328, 335

Siddur (siddurim), 346

sin, xi, 13, 36, 44, 45, 55, 65, 67, 70, 71, 76, 100, 108, 110, 172, 183, 187, 188, 189, 194, 217, 219, 236, 241, 317, 333

Son of David, xxii, 51, 52, 192, 212, 221, 222, 223, 228, 248, 258, 259, 286, 298, 344

Son of God, xxii, xxiii, xxviii, 5, 6, 7, 8, 16, 17, 20, 60, 61, 85, 89, 90, 130, 158, 174, 175, 323, 326, 337

Son of Man, xxii, xxiv, 33, 43, 45, 46, 49, 50, 52, 53, 60, 66, 90, 155, 158, 159, 163, 164, 165, 166, 171, 172, 176, 184, 193, 211, 212, 213, 215, 216, 220, 222, 229, 266, 273, 275, 276, 278, 283, 289, 296, 301, 305, 307, 324

Spirit, Holy Spirit, i, xxi, xxii, 1, 2, 6, 10, 11, 14, 15, 16, 17, 18, 19, 38, 50, 60, 66, 67, 68, 70, 109, 114, 121, 134, 244, 271, 272, 277, 325, 341, 346

Supersessionist/ism, 132, 346

T

Talmid (talmidim), 346

Talmidot, 346

Talmud, 34, 52, 120, 125, 199, 225, 244, 245, 260, 263, 279, 291, 329, 339, 342, 343, 346, 347

Tanakh, xii, xv, xx, xxi, xxx, 5, 9, 11, 15, 25, 51, 79, 88, 105, 114, 115, 160, 173, 176, 218, 236, 237, 244, 249, 254, 268, 270, 276, 283, 289, 294, 301, 303, 317, 326, 333, 342, 344, 346

Targum, 346

Temple, i, xxiv, 14, 100, 102, 126, 194, 227, 228, 231, 232, 233, 234, 235, 236, 237, 238, 240, 241, 242, 243, 248, 253, 255, 258, 260, 262, 265, 266, 267, 268, 273, 274, 276, 278, 286, 301, 303, 305, 306, 321, 323, 325, 332, 344, 345

Ten Towns, 85, 92, 104, 137, 139, 141, 143

Teshuvah, 25, 55, 94, 346

Torah, iv, xi, xiii, xiv, xv, xx, xxii, xxiii, xxiv, xxix, xxx, 7, 11, 18, 24, 26, 28, 29, 35, 36, 39, 41, 42, 44, 45, 47, 48, 49, 51, 52, 55, 56, 62, 65, 68, 88, 101, 110, 114, 115, 118, 120, 121, 123, 124, 125, 126, 127, 128, 129, 130, 131, 132, 133, 134, 135, 139, 143, 147, 148, 149, 158, 165, 173, 174, 177, 178, 180, 197, 198, 199, 205, 207, 212, 227, 228, 229, 236, 238, 241, 247, 248, 249, 250, 252, 253, 254, 255, 256, 257, 258, 259, 260, 262, 263, 264, 284, 297, 298, 301, 303, 305, 306, 310, 319, 321, 328, 329, 340, 345, 346, 347

trust, xviii, 25, 38, 42, 43, 44, 55, 81, 86, 97, 99, 100, 104, 106, 118, 130, 150, 177, 178, 180, 182, 187, 189, 190, 221, 222, 223, 225, 231, 236, 239, 240, 241, 245, 251, 324, 326, 334

Twelve, the, xxv, xxvii, 3, 18, 59, 60, 62, 63, 64, 65, 69, 70, 74, 79, 107, 108, 109, 110, 111, 112, 113, 118, 119, 146, 157, 158, 184, 211, 212, 213, 228, 231, 233, 257, 272, 276, 283, 285, 289, 293, 299, 303, 314, 342

Tzara'at, 34

Tzedakah, 347

Tzitzit, tzitziyot, 347

U

unclean, 3, 23, 24, 28, 29, 30, 32, 34, 35, 36, 54, 59, 60, 61, 65, 67, 76, 77, 78, 88, 89, 91, 92, 94, 99, 101, 105, 107, 108, 123, 124, 126, 128, 129, 130, 133, 134, 135, 138, 140, 149, 160, 177, 178, 179, 184, 188

Y

Y'hudim, Jews, i, xi, xii, xvii, xx, xxii, 6, 26, 45, 102, 125, 126, 131, 132, 133, 134, 140, 143, 160, 165, 169, 216, 235, 259, 302, 306, 310, 311, 312, 313, 314, 316, 322, 332, 343

Yarden, Jordan River, xxv, 5, 9, 10, 14, 26, 60, 197, 198, 199, 271, 326

Yerushalayim, Jerusalem, xiv, xviii, xx, xxiv, xxv, xxvii, xxx, 3, 9, 12, 13, 16, 21, 29, 34, 59, 60, 64, 65, 66, 71, 102, 104, 123, 124, 125, 126, 128, 131, 153, 154, 158, 161, 162, 168, 171, 172, 175, 183, 184, 185, 189, 198, 206, 210, 211, 212, 221, 222, 223, 227, 228, 231, 232, 233, 234, 235, 236, 237, 239, 241, 242, 243, 244, 247, 254, 259, 266, 268, 283, 285, 286, 292, 295, 302, 303, 311, 321, 327, 334, 340, 343

Yeshayahu, Isaiah, xxiii, xxiv, xxx, 6, 9, 10, 11, 12, 13, 15, 17, 18, 21, 26, 49, 75, 76, 79, 83, 93, 120, 124, 127, 142, 143, 145, 146, 157, 160, 185, 186, 190, 191, 193, 195, 205, 217, 218, 219, 220, 224, 225, 231, 250, 251, 271, 280, 295, 297, 308, 312, 314, 317, 322, 326

Yochanan, John the Immerser, iv, xvii, xx, xxiv, 3, 5, 6, 9, 10, 11, 13, 14, 16, 21, 23, 25, 27, 30, 33, 37, 47, 48, 49, 62, 63, 98, 101, 107, 110, 111, 113, 119, 146, 158, 163, 172, 174, 176, 183, 187, 211, 212, 213, 214, 215, 222, 232, 239, 241, 242, 243, 266, 267, 269, 271, 284, 296, 297, 335

Yom Kippur, 49, 94, 219, 220, 337, 347

Yonah, Jonah, 87, 94, 336, 337

Z

Zechariah, 13, 161, 233, 234, 235, 243, 261, 268, 286, 293, 315

Messianic Jewish
Publishers & Resources

We are a three-fold ministry, reaching Jewish people with the message of Messiah, teaching our non-Jewish spiritual family about their Jewish roots, and strengthening congregations with excellent resources.

Over 100 Messianic Jewish Books, Bibles & Commentaries available at your favorite Bookstore.

Endorsed by Christian Leaders and Theologians:

Dr. Jack Hayford
Dr. Walter C. Kaiser, Jr.
Dr. Marvin Wilson
Ken Taylor
Stephen Strang
Dr. R.C. Sproul
Coach Bill McCartney
and more!

800-410-7367
www.MessianicJewish.net